THE
CARICATURE of *LOVE*

A Discussion of Social, Psychiatric, and
Literary Manifestations of
Pathologic Sexuality

HERVEY CLECKLEY, M.D.

CLINICAL PROFESSOR OF PSYCHIATRY AND NEUROLOGY
MEDICAL COLLEGE OF GEORGIA
CHIEF OF SERVICE, PSYCHIATRY AND NEUROLOGY
UNIVERSITY HOSPITAL, AUGUSTA

D1719173

RED PILL PRESS

First published by The Ronald Press Company in 1957.

This 2011 edition is published by Red Pill Press, an imprint of
Quantum Future Group, 295 Scratch Branch Rd., Otto, NC, 28763.
3rd printing, August 2022.

ISBN: 978-1-897244-57-9

For
LOUISE

Entreat me not to leave thee, or to return from
following after thee; for whither thou goest, I will
go. . . . Where thou diest will I die, and there will
I be buried; The Lord do so to me, and more also,
if aught but death part thee and me.

PREFACE

This book has two chief themes: sexual disorder and its influences, and a critical examination of some concepts of sexuality which are prominent today in psychiatry and psychology. Many psychiatrists, psychologists, and sociologists have, in recent years, taken the position that society should exhibit a more liberal attitude toward sexual deviation. It has been repeatedly maintained that the public and the law are unduly influenced by prejudice and archaic tradition, that aberrant sexual practices are too harshly condemned by our culture. Some of the more enthusiastic advocates of change present homosexuality and other sexual practices generally regarded as abnormal in such a light that the reader is led to believe they should not be regarded as perversions of normal aim and impulse but as benign, or relatively benign, variations on a standard supported merely by convention. Prominent figures in literature, art, and history are cited as examples proving that erotic orientations generally regarded as undesirable and abnormal are consistent with the highest possible development and expression of the human spirit. Homosexuality, in particular, is often represented as a more or less normal equivalent of heterosexual love, and by some influential writers is even acclaimed as a superior way of life.

As a physician, I am well acquainted with the frustration and unhappiness that result from sexual disorder, and I have no wish to urge personal condemnation of its victims. It seems to me, nevertheless, both illogical and deeply regrettable to misidentify illness with health in unrealistic attempts to gain sympathy for those who are ill.

As everyone knows, the greatest works of literature often portray criminals, cynics, petty rascals, wastrels, hypocrites, whores, traitors, cranks, misers, and the psychotic, along with happy and appealing characters that range from the merely amiable to the heroic. It would be as foolish to condemn as morbid the creative artist who presents morbid characters as it would be to assume that the medical pathologist is enlisted in the cause of disease and death. Is it not true, however, that not only the philosopher, the essayist, and the critic, but also the novelist, poet, and dramatist often conveys in his work a good deal of his own taste, his own orientation, and his own evaluations of experience?

I have for many years been deeply impressed by pathologic reactions expressed or reflected in novels, plays, poetry, and other media of literary expression. Homosexuality, algolagnia, cynical futility, misogyny, impotence, profound ennui, and a basic disgust of life are often so presented that the reader is led to feel that such reactions are accepted as the mark of special and highly refined esthetic sensibilities. These reactions are pervasive in many of the literary productions currently praised by critics. This literature, which often achieves the triumph of formal awards and prizes, tends in every generation to attract cults of devotees. Though relatively few in number and exclusive in taste, such groups frequently attain considerable influence in determining esthetic standards.

It is my belief that a serious confusion of psychiatric disorder with mental health is promoted by these tastes and judgments. My extensive experience as a psychiatrist has revealed nothing to me that could support this esthetic creed, and has left me with the strong conviction that pathologic sexual behavior in my patients is a genuine psychiatric illness. It is a disability that seriously distorts their reaction to some of the axioms of human life. The essential emptiness or perversion of erotic experience in the case histories presented in this volume is compared and correlated with many similar examples drawn from literature which convey the inner life and the emotional products of sexual disorder.

Alleged psychiatric and psychological discoveries have played an important part in the statements and implications of some who argue that homosexuality and other deviations are relatively or approximately normal reactions. Some of the popular theoretical concepts widely regarded as valid psychiatric discoveries are so unrealistic that those who support them find it necessary to alter the meaning of commonplace words in order to define and discuss them with straight faces. Such concepts are, nevertheless, so fashionable today, so identified in many minds with the idea of progress and scientific achievement, that it is scarcely an exaggeration to say that he who dares to question them is often made to feel guilty of impiety.

I have devoted a considerable portion of this book to a critical examination of several of these concepts: bisexuality, castration fear, the normal homoerotic component of the libido, instincts-in-hibited-in-their-aims, and the alleged universal stage of homosexuality. Although these concepts were not devised by psychiatrists and psychologists for such a purpose, several of them have been used by lay writers to support the contention that the impulses of sexual disorder are natural, and its practices an acceptable equivalent of heterosexual love. Most of these concepts are so ambiguously formulated that they lend themselves readily to use by those who would enlighten us with claims that science has made absurd certain values and orientations generally regarded as basic to health and civilization. It is widely believed that the concepts I discuss are scientific discoveries, soundly supported by genuine evidence. For this reason I examine the methods by which they have been devised.

The two chief themes of this book, therefore, are closely related and interdependent. In order to deal satisfactorily with them and with their interrelations, it has been necessary to turn from one to another, to take up again a theme which was developed and then set aside until its connections were established with other themes.

I am hopeful that my treatment of homosexuality in works so often regarded as good modern literature will stimulate spirited discussion among teachers of literature. I am sure that what I have to say concerning the concepts of sexuality which are prominent today in psychology and psychiatry should be of interest to my fellow psychiatrists, to clinical psychologists, to doctors of medicine, social workers, probation officers, and perhaps also to lawyers and judges.

The argument of this book would have been weakened had I not been able to support my contentions with quotations from dozens of sources. Appreciation is expressed to the publishers, authors, and editors who have generously permitted my use of such quotations, which are individually acknowledged in the "Sources" at the end of each chapter.

It is a pleasure to express my appreciation to a number of medical colleagues and other friends who assisted me in the preparation of this work. Among those who read the manuscript and made valuable suggestions are Dr. W. P. Robison, Dr. B. F. Moss, Jr., Dr. F. B. Thigpen, Dr. Lester Bowles, Dr. Allen Turner, Dr. Julius Johnson, Mr. P. F. Robinson, Jr., Mr. James F. Fulghum, Miss Melville Doughty, and my sister, Mrs. Connor C. Goodrich.

The difficult task of indexing this book was completed by Miss Hella Freud Bernays, who also contributed important editorial assistance. It is a privilege to record my appreciation to her and also to Dr. J. McV. Hunt, whose critical comments have played a substantial part in the formulation of this material. Miss Louise Fant of the University of Georgia Library graciously assisted me in obtaining necessary information about obscure copyrights.

I also wish to thank Mrs. Cornelia C. Fulghum, Miss Anne Jamison, and Mrs. Jacqueline S. Williford, who generously and effectively aided in reading proof, checking references, and in many other ways.

Dr. Corbett H. Thigpen, my medical associate of many years, has afforded me constant stimulus and encouragement during innumerable hours of discussion as this work progressed. His observation and thought almost as directly as my own have gone into this presentation. His limitless generosity in relieving me of other duties enabled me to complete it.

My indebtedness is great, indeed, to my daughter, Mary Cleckley Dolan, who obtained permissions that enabled me to use the many quotations. It is a true pleasure to express to her my deep appreciation for this and for her other important contributions.

Most of all I am grateful to my wife, Louise M. Cleckley, who spent hundreds of hours working with me on the manuscript. Her judgment and taste have afforded me guidance I could not have found elsewhere. Without her inspiration and genuine collaboration this book could not have been written.

Hervey Cleckley

Augusta, Georgia
  April, 1957

CONTENTS

THE
CARICATURE OF LOVE

Chapter 1
A SEXUAL RENAISSANCE?

For several decades our printing presses have been worked overtime in the production of books about sex. Who can count the volumes, technical and fictional, that have appeared since young Scott Fitzgerald captivated a generation with portraits of the flapper and accounts of her technique in necking and petting under the catalytic influence of bathtub gin? Soon afterward judge Ben Lindsey dismayed conservatives when he proposed companionate marriage (1) and announced the revolt of modern youth. (2) Victorian proprieties, everyone seemed to discover, were hypocritical devices to thwart honest love-making.

The subject has been discussed with such vigor and prolixity that a hypothetical visitor from some other planet might conclude that these exciting things between male and female had just been discovered by mankind. We have been told repeatedly that the last three decades, in contrast particularly to the 1890's, should be considered a period of emancipation from unrealistic and priggish evasions. Though some moralists have denounced as evil, or dangerous, the greater freedom of behavior and discussion between male and female, most responsible observers would probably agree that the acceptance of carnal sexuality as a real and honorable aspect of human relations promotes happiness in marriage without jeopardizing basic social and religious values.

Such values were flatly rejected by some who attracted much attention. The more extreme emancipators insisted that monogamous love relations were stultifying, that true and beautiful sexual passion could not blossom without a free change of partners. V. F.

Calverton, in *The Bankruptcy of Marriage*, enthusiastically pro-claims:

Many ideas that have been entertained in the past as demonstrated and definite are now seen to have been founded upon nothing other than prej-udice and rationalization. In the fanatical defense of chastity as the basis of feminine virtue, and of post-nuptial fidelity as the test of womanly honor we discern nothing particularly lofty or spiritual. Upon analysis it becomes simply a convention associated with a property concept. . . . Love, as we of the modern age understand it, was disdained as vulgar by the Greeks. Monogamous love, of all loves, is most curiously recent. Love when it was so idealized by poets was seldom thought of as a part of mar-riage. Marriage was an economic transaction. Love was more often adul-terous. Romantic love and monogamous marriage were contradictions until our modern age. Romantic love in the days of chivalry was particu-larly pagan and heroic.

. . . the present direction of sex attitudes is the only one that holds forth hope as a rich incentive. The escape from the old ethics can only be viewed as an advance. (3)

Whether for better or for worse, young people at the beginning of this era repeatedly voiced their delight over the discovery that women's legs need no longer be called limbs. For a while, consid-erable amusement was derived from talk about the dull old days, now fortunately past, when a wife addressed her husband as Mr. So-and-So even in accepting a proposal to perform her "marital duties." Smatterings of psychoanalytic theory captivated "intellec-tuals" and Bohemians during the 1920's and, in fact, passed read-ily on to college sophomores who tried to persuade girls in parked cars that "repression of their sexual drives" was no longer fashion-able and indeed might bring disaster to them.

The Petty girl and the bikini bathing suit each in turn served to keep the public aware that advancement continued. If the vaunted tide of liberation seemed to slow at times, new and often explosive impetus always recurred. The first Kinsey report perhaps stirred up more talk and writing about sex than any other dozen events during the entire period. The second report also evoked a good deal of excitement.

No doubt, good has come from some of this. Let us assume that ordinary men and women have benefited by the less evasive atti-tude toward sexual matters, by the more general, open acceptance of what is physically sensuous in love relations. But has the al-leged emancipation brought us the sexual utopia predicted by so many of the early leaders? Aside from any question of ethics, has a new erotic joy come into being? Has a fresh, lusty, and voluptuous satisfaction prevailed? Throughout these three decades, allegedly spent in rediscovering the natural and long-neglected beauties of the flesh, some features have been seen to emerge that are not at all compatible with the claims of its spokesmen.

Let us turn back for a moment to the modest beginnings of this era. Even the relatively innocent "petting parties" of *This Side of Paradise* were thought by many young readers to indicate a defiance of prudery and hypocrisy, a triumph of healthy attitudes and natural passions. Fitzgerald's hero in this story, Amory Blaine, a boy in his early teens, shows considerable sophistication in obtaining his first kiss. This is his reaction to the achievement:

Sudden revulsion seized Amory, disgust, loathing for the whole incident, he desired frantically to be away, never to see Myra again, never to kiss anyone; he became conscious of his face and hers, of their clinging hands, he wanted to creep out of his body and hide somewhere safe out of sight, up in the corner of his mind. (4)

Why this revulsion from what even the most staid of his parents' generation usually found delightful?

Hemingway, in *The Sun Also Rises*, portrays Lady Brett as busily exercising all the new sexual freedom. (5) She seems, however, to use it chiefly for petty spite and is able to derive little more than ennui from her exploits. The reader is not shocked by a demonstration of hot lust driving men and women to deplorable conduct. Instead, he is chilled by the absence of any discernible passion in this callous and devitalized caricature of the human female. Of those who in this period called for revolt against prudery and moralistic restraint, few were more articulate and influential than H. L. Mencken. This messiah of the new generation, who in the 1920's cried out against inhibition and called for wine, women, and song, offers this incitement to young men:

The most effective lure that a woman can hold out to a man is the lure of what he fatuously conceives to be her beauty. This so-called beauty, of course, is almost always a pure illusion. The female body, even at its best, is very defective in form; it has harsh curves and very clumsily distributed masses; compared to it the average milk-jug, or even cuspidor, is a thing of intelligent and gratifying design—in brief, an objet d'art . . .

A man, save he be fat, i.e., of womanish contours, usually looks better in uniform than in mufti; the tight lines set off his figure. But a woman is at once given away; she looks like a dumb-bell run over by an express train. Below the neck by the bow and below the waist astern there are two masses that simply refuse to fit into a balanced composition. Viewed from the side, she presents an exaggerated S bisected by an imperfect straight line, and so she inevitably suggests a drunken dollar-mark. Her ordinary clothing cunningly conceals this fundamental imperfection. It swathes those impossible masses in draperies soothingly uncertain of outline. But putting her into uniform is like stripping her. Instantly all her alleged beauty vanishes. (6)

Perhaps the Sage of Baltimore was not serious. He may have wanted merely to annoy the ladies a little. But who will say his observations do not, at least faintly, echo Odo de Cluny and the other ascetics who so vigorously rejected woman in the flesh?

Could it be that, freed from so many taboos, the new generation does not know what to do with its so newly won emancipation? As time passes, the characters presented by Noel Coward on the stage in *Private Lives* and *Design for Living* (7) and by Evelyn Waugh in his novels (8) seem to be having even less fun with their sexual freedom. Unhampered by the old restraints such as honor or fidelity, they show little heart for it when they force themselves languidly into sin through anemic efforts at adultery. The feelings of a circumspect Victorian couple, who took no greater liberty in "spooning" than to hold hands, seem gloriously lusty and abandoned in comparison with these pseudopassions devoid of warmth, these snickerings, and eunuch-like gesticulations.

It has been said that the Victorian moralists tried, in the name of decency, to take sex out of love. Conversely, have we now developed zealots who are ashamed and shocked and bewildered by love; who, in another sort of prudery, insist that sex be "uncontaminated" by personal passions and enduring commitments? So feeble and perverse are the erotic reactions prominently displayed in current belles-lettres that an ordinary reader might deserve forgiveness should he wonder if our era is, perhaps, being interpreted chiefly by spiritless geldings. A finical disdain for the normal and natural warmth of life seems deeply characteristic of many who have become the high priests of culture in this paradoxical epoch. The naive still believe that it is natural for poets to sing of love-making. Yet T. S. Eliot, proclaimed by high authorities the foremost bard of our century, seldom brings up anything at all pertaining directly to this subject. His characters in *The Cocktail Party* (9) seem to recognize no choices except that between a marriage of meaningless boredom and adultery that is both sordid and tepid, until martyrdom is revealed to them as a third possibility. In "Lune de Miel" (10) he is for once less remote and offers a brief comment on a honeymoon. Of this, Bobbins, one of the few critics dissenting from an almost uniform adulation of Eliot, has dared to say:

There is no recognition of beauty but an absorption in dirt and filth. Eliot is so fearful of the generative process that he can see only ugliness in sex . . . there is no response to the decent joy and freshness of young married love; all that the disgusted Eliot can see are sweaty legs covered with flea-bites. (11)

The unhappy Franz Kafka, whose pathologic despairs still captivate the most sophisticated critics, seems to have restricted his artistic reactions to sexual love to the statement that "coitus is a punishment inflicted upon two who find too much happiness in being with each other." (12)

Perhaps no other influence has been so important as that of Freud in changing popular attitudes toward sex. Though he is distinctly apart from those who vociferously condemned conventional morality, his theories of sex, often in gross distortion, are generally cited in support of the revolution. Concepts of a dynamic unconscious were embraced by lay writers long before they attracted much attention in medical circles. Hoffman, in his *Freudianism and the Literary Mind*, gives an interesting picture of socially rebellious young novelists, intellectuals, artists, Bohemians, and poseurs announcing enthusiastically to each other the discovery in themselves, through analysis, of latent homosexuality, the need for incest, and other unusual aspirations. (13) Just after World War I this material apparently served as something new and precious with which to shock and defy the surrounding philistine majority. These and similar distorted and abnormal aims, rather than ordinary sexual freedom, seem to have played a dominant role in the literature that has been most honored during the last decade.

In such literature we seldom find men and women struggling with the complexities of love or simply enjoying, or being defeated by, vigorous natural passions and carnal lusts. Instead we are treated to the spectacle of androgynous young men in tortuous esthetic quests to determine whether they are male or female, or perhaps neither. (14) Not the ordinary desire of man for woman, but a persistent and disdainful misogyny dominates the work of many among our most successful writers. By some of these, refinements of algolagnia and even of urolagnia are presented in great detail and apparently with relish. (15) Often the pederast is sympathetically portrayed for us as a fictional hero in such a way as to leave the impression that he is to be admired, not despite these predilections but largely because of them. (16) Not only sadistic cannibalism but also a positive inclination to be the victim in this obviously undesirable and anything but romantic relationship has been offered as an esthetic treat for readers of special and reputedly superior sensibility. (17)

Similar morbid and perverse tastes have been prominent among small groups belonging to literary and artistic cults of the past. This is nothing new. But today those attracted by such interpretations of human life are voluble in their claims of support from science. Psychology and dynamic psychiatry, they insist, have demonstrated a natural and universal basis for the melancholy causes they espouse.

In order to deal with its subject this book must follow several themes concerning a number of topics which may appear superficially to have only remote relations. One of these themes is the currently popular preoccupation of many influential people, widely acknowledged as intellectually and esthetically superior, with what has long been regarded as sexual perversion, and with its broader and more pervasive overtones of life-rejection. Another theme consists of the extraordinary claims made by, and in behalf of, what is often called dynamic psychiatry, particularly the claim of discoveries in the unconscious through which basic human values are glibly overturned and because of which it is said to be imperative that man reorient himself to new and disturbing truths already thoroughly established by the methods of science. Since these themes are in fact deeply interrelated, I shall ask the reader's indulgence when I turn from one of them to the other.

Some of the items allegedly brought out from the unconscious by scientifically trained investigators are likely to tax the ordinary man's credulity. Among Freud's early co-workers, few were so honored and celebrated as Sandor Ferenczi, who repeatedly and promptly corroborated Freud's announced discoveries. Ferenczi also made discoveries of his own which were widely accepted and which are still respectfully referred to in textbooks and in psychiatric journals.

Among the most remarkable of these is Ferenczi's demonstration that the familiar sensations aroused in the male genital organ by sexual excitement are those of "unpleasure" and that the impulse to coitus has to be accounted for by unconscious desires in the man to work his way back into his mother's uterus:

There is above all the phenomenon of erection, for which a seemingly surprising explanation deriving from the maternal womb theory of genitality presents itself. I assume that the permanent invagination of the glans penis within a fold of mucous membrane (within the foreskin, that is) is itself nothing but a replica in miniature of existence in the maternal womb. Since upon an increase of the sexual tension accumulated in the genital the most sensitive portion of the penis (which, as already said, functions as the narcissistic representative of the total personality) is thrust out of its protected place of repose by erection, is as it were, born, the sensation of unpleasure (unlust) in the genital is suddenly distinctly increased; and this latter fact makes intelligible the sudden urge to restore the lost milieu by intromission into the vagina, or in other words, to seek in the external world of reality, this time actually within the female body, the hitherto auto-erotically satisfying place of repose. (18)

Ferenczi further reports the discovery that during sexual intercourse the woman's deepest intention is to amputate the male organ of her lover, and that the man, though he does not realize it, is seeking the same result. Though the man thinks he knows what he wants, he is, according to Ferenczi, actually doing the best he can to achieve castration. What he does achieve, according to this celebrated investigator, is a sublimated or symbolic castration. The contractions of the vaginal muscles, he admits, "seem to have as their purpose the aspiration of the semen and the incorporation of the penis," but he insists that there is "an intended castration as well."

Of the sexual orgasm in man Ferenczi speaks authoritatively:

... This discharge can be nothing else than the desire, in the sense of an autonomy, to cast off the organ under tension. From the standpoint of the ego we have already described ejaculation as such an elimination of material productive of "unpleasure"; we may assume a similar tendency also in the case of erection and friction. Further, erection is perhaps only an incompletely achieved attempt to detach the genital, charged with "unpleasure" of various kinds, from the rest of the body . . . one could suppose that the sex act begins as a tendency in the direction of the complete detaching of the genital and thus as a kind of self-castration, but is then satisfied with the detachment of its secretion. (18)

Those who care to see for themselves may, by reading Ferenczi's published work, readily check my assertion that no evidence at all is offered for his unusual concepts of the meaning of sexual intercourse. No wish or impulse or idea of this sort is ever brought out of the unconscious by specialized methods or otherwise. The claim rests purely on analogy. Though analogy is sometimes useful in our efforts to express ourselves, it has never been regarded by law, science, or common sense as a means of establishing evidence.

It is my contention that many distorted concepts of sexuality and pathologic interpretations of fundamental matters are being actively promoted today. In the name of liberalism or advancement, and usually with claims of support from science, perverse and absurd misevaluations are widely proclaimed by ardent followers, who, in a strange enthusiasm for the improbable and the uninviting, often succeed in ignoring the obvious. Let us briefly consider an example. Is it, or is it not, confusing to the public when a widely published psychologist engaged in the practice of "psychoanalytic therapy and marriage counselling" authoritatively informs his readers that men who strictly confine their sexual activities to women are abnormal?

In *The American Sexual Tragedy*, published in 1954, Albert Ellis announced that "if . . . a male in our culture engages in some homosexual behavior, alongside of his more socially acceptable heterosexual activities, we are hardly justified in calling him abnormal from almost any standpoint—since biologically, statistically and psychologically he is behaving in a normal fashion." (19)

He goes on to explain that if all of a person's sexual activities are carried out with partners of his own sex one is justified in regarding him as "neurotic" or "fixated." "If he merely prefers homosexual to heterosexual relations (as a man may prefer blondes to brunettes), that is one thing; but if he simply cannot, under any circumstances, engage in any kind of heterosexual behavior, then he is unquestionably disturbed, and hence 'abnormal' or 'deviant.'"

Similarly "abnormal" or "neurotic," Ellis informs us, are those men "who under no circumstances (even, say, if marooned on a desert island with other males for a long period of time) could permit themselves to engage in homosexual activity." (19)

Ellis is by no means ambiguous. He insists that "what is scientific sauce for the goose should also be sauce for the gander, and that exclusive heterosexuality can be just as fetishistic as exclusive homosexuality" (19)

Let us ask ourselves, is this sauce really scientific? If so, a revolutionary reorientation is perilously overdue for the present generation of children who are being deliberately encouraged by every means available to society toward that which Ellis says science has found to be abnormal.

To the psychiatrist, and indeed to the minister, priest, and rabbi, it is not at all remarkable to encounter in human beings sexual manifestations that are perverse and unfortunate; that, like disease in general, violate the basic premises of human aspiration. If the respected name of science is invoked as authority to mislabel such manifestations as normal, should this not prove of concern to all who believe the methods correctly designated by that abused term deserve better than to be identified with such methods as those that produced astrology, phrenology, and Dianetics?

It is my belief that a number of opinions popular and influential today are no more realistic or conducive to health or happiness than the ancient falsehoods that were told boys to discourage them from masturbating or the earnest conviction that a woman who is a "lady" should not be sexually passionate even in relations with her husband.

Out of theoretical and unverifiable surmises currently upheld in some schools of psychology and psychiatry, specious assumptions have emerged. Many of them promote unnecessary confusion in the immature; some, I maintain, constitute an insidious and unwarranted impeachment of orthodox sexual love.

If we define pathology as health, our search for health will be misleading. If we affirm that smallpox and typhoid fever are normal physiologic manifestations, can we consistently advocate vaccination or inoculation or even the following of ordinary laws of hygiene?

SOURCES

1. Ben B. Lindsey and W. Evans, *The Companionate Marriage* (New York: Boni & Liveright, 1925).

2. Ben B. Lindsey and W. Evans, *The Revolt of Modern Youth* (New York: Boni & Liveright, 1925).

3. V. F. Calverton, *The Bankruptcy of Marriage* (New York: The Macaulay Co., 1928), pp. 325–26, 329, 331.

4. F. Scott Fitzgerald, *This Side of Paradise* (New York: Charles Scribner's Sons, 1921), pp. 15–16.

5. Ernest Hemingway, *The Sun Also Rises* (New York: Charles Scribner's Sons, 1930).

6. H. L. Mencken, *In Defense of Women* (New York: Alfred A. Knopf, Inc., 1925), pp. 36–38.

7. Noel Coward, *Play Parade* (Garden City, N.Y.: Doubleday & Co., Inc., 1933).

8. Evelyn Waugh, *Brideshead Revisited* (1946), *Vile Bodies* (1946), *The Loved One* (1948), *A Handful of Dust* (1948) (Boston: Little, Brown & Co.).

9. T. S. Eliot, *The Cocktail Party* (New York: Harcourt, Brace & Co., 1950).

10. In T. S. Eliot, *Collected Poems* (New York: Harcourt, Brace & Co., 1936).

11. Reprinted by permission of the publishers, Abelard-Schuman, Inc., from *The T. S. Eliot Myth*, by R. H. Robbins; p. 76. Copyright 1951 by Henry Schuman, Inc.

12. F. J. Hoffman, *Freudianism and the Literary Mind* (Baton Rouge: Louisiana State University Press, 1945), p. 208.

13. *Ibid.*

14. Gore Vidal, *The Season of Comfort* (New York: E. P. Dutton & Co., Inc., 1949).

15. Tennessee Williams, *The Roman Spring of Mrs. Stone* (New York: New Directions, 1950).

16. Angus Wilson, *Hemlock and After* (New York: The Viking Press, Inc., 1952).

17. Tennessee Williams, *One Arm* (New York: New Directions, 1948).

18. Sandor Ferenczi, *Thalassa—A Theory of Genitality*, trans. by Henry Alden Bunker, M.D. (New York: The Psychoanalytic Quarterly, Inc., 1938), pp. 26–29.

19. Albert Ellis, *The American Sexual Tragedy* (New York: Twayne Publishers, Inc., 1954), pp. 80–81.

Chapter 2
A QUESTIONABLE POINT OF VIEW

Before proceeding further with several interrelated topics, let us consider a letter written by Sigmund Freud in 1935 and published in April 1951 in the *Journal* of the American Psychiatric Association under the title "Historical Note." The late Professor A. G. Kinsey obtained the letter and made it available to the *Journal*. (1)

Dear Mrs. ————:

I gather from your letter that your son is a homosexual. I am most impressed by the fact that you do not mention this term yourself in your information about him. May I question, why you avoid it? Homosexuality is assuredly no advantage, but it is nothing to be ashamed of, no vice, no degradation, it cannot be classified as an illness; we consider it to be a variation of the sexual development. Many highly respectable individuals of ancient and modern times have been homosexuals, several of the greatest men among them (Plato, Michelangelo, Leonardo da Vinci, etc). It is a great injustice to persecute homosexuality as a crime and cruelty, too. If you do not believe me, read the books of Havelock Ellis.

By asking me if I can help, you mean, I suppose, if I can abolish homosexuality and make normal heterosexuality take its place. The answer is, in a general way, we cannot promise to achieve it. In a certain number of cases we succeed in developing the blighted germs of heterosexual tendencies which are present in every homosexual; in the majority of cases it is no more possible. It is a question of the quality and the age of the individual. The result of treatment cannot be predicted.

What analysis can do for your son runs in a different line. If he is unhappy, neurotic, torn by conflicts, inhibited in his social life, analysis may bring him harmony, peace of mind, full efficiency, whether he remains a homosexual or gets changed. If you make up your mind, he should have analysis with me—I don't expect you will—he has to come over to Vienna. I have no intention of leaving here. However, don't neglect to give me your answer.

Sincerely yours, with kind wishes,
FREUD

Homosexuality appears to attract more attention today than any other distortion or deflection of the erotic impulses. Prominent and articulate apologists, as we shall note, defend it as unobjectionable and even praise it as an ennobling practice. The evaluation by Freud therefore deserves careful consideration.

If homosexuality is "nothing to be ashamed of, no vice, no degradation" and if "it cannot be classified as an illness," what then are we to call it? "A variation of the sexual development," Freud answers in his letter. Is this sufficient? Medical students and practicing physicians, after reading the letter, have asked *me* straightforward questions that I feel deserve straightforward answers.

Is it true that Freud came to the conclusion that homosexuality is normal? If it is normal and not a personality disorder, why should psychiatrists or other physicians attempt treatment of homosexuals? Why should efforts be made to prevent the development of homosexuality in children and adolescents?

What are the answers to these questions? It is a fact that Freud does not use the word "normal" in his letter. Can anyone maintain, however, that this is not the frank content of his statement? If so, what is the basis for his attitude? Whether or not Freud is pronouncing homosexuality normal, it seems clear that he means to give the impression that it is not particularly pathologic or regrettable.

It is true that the word "homosexuality" may suggest more than one single thing. To one man it may seem that Freud says it is "a great injustice and cruelty, too" to persecute as criminal feelings and reactions that are involuntary. Is there anyone who would not agree that there would be injustice and cruelty in punishing a person with inclinations toward sexual acts that to most seem detestable but who refrains from carrying out any act of this sort? On the other hand, will anyone say there is "no vice, no degradation" in the behavior of a scoutmaster who, interpreting his own impulses as normal and proper, persuades twelve-year-old boys into typical homosexual acts often defined by law as "against nature'? Is such behavior "nothing to be ashamed of"?

Apparently, the majority of psychiatrists today are convinced that environmental factors, particularly parental attitudes and other interpersonal influences, may do much to distort normal sexual development, and may in fact cause the person to become homosexual. Many believe that overdependence on the mother and hostility toward the father play a crucial part in the son's failure to develop the usual feelings for woman and for mating. Some psychiatrists feel that they have found the most convincing arguments for this belief in Freud's own work. (2) Those who adhere most closely to Freud's teachings express the most confident convictions on this point.

A former president of the American Psychiatric Association, Karl M. Bowman, recently wrote:

Freud felt that homosexuality is a disorder in psychosexual development. In each case of homosexuality, at any point, the development could have taken a different turn, if the situation had been different. (3)

A few years ago the *Journal of the American Medical Association*, in response to a letter that asked if homosexuality is thought to be congenital or acquired, made this answer:

... During psychiatric treatment it is learned that the homosexual has the usual heterosexual wishes and longings but these are repressed because of deep-seated fears of heterosexuality. Childhood sexual experiences of a fearful nature, especially parental attitudes which are prohibitive, threatening and punitive toward the normally developing sexuality (the expression of sexual curiosity and sexual play such as masturbation) may in the child shift the scale toward homosexuality. As such a child grows up he retreats from heterosexuality to homosexuality because of previous fearful associations with heterosexuality. (4)

Influenced by these viewpoints, parents take great care to avoid emotional attitudes and patterns of behavior that might warp the healthy psychosexual development of their children. Our entire educational system is designed to avoid situations that might distort erotic orientation in the young. Through social and recreational activities, child guidance efforts, and mental hygiene resources, elaborate and extremely expensive programs are maintained to help our youth escape every influence that might encourage or produce homosexual tendencies or other abnormal reactions.

Can our psychiatrists encourage society in these efforts if they accept as correct Freud's clearly expressed appraisal? If they continue to do so, can they hope to conceal their obvious inconsistency? They must, I think, either confess their disagreement with Freud's opinion, hard as this might be for some to do, or else reverse their position in some very practical matters. As psychiatrists they should be aware that it is neither wise nor healthy to profess one belief and to practice its opposite.

Sigmund Freud has become the most venerated figure in the history of psychiatry. At present, the influence of his opinions is predominant in professional journals and textbooks. Many novelists and dramatists have constructed characters and plots in strict accordance with Freudian theory. (5) This theory is often used by critics to interpret works of literature as diverse as *Hamlet* and James Joyce's *Finnegans Wake*. (6) It is difficult to pick up either a medical journal or such publications as *The Saturday Review* or *The*

New York Times Book Review without finding Freud cited as authority for opinions both plausible and implausible.

It is, however, the popular identification of any and every opinion expressed by Freud with science that becomes our concern
here. If Freud can be quoted in support of some argument, there
are many who are likely to yield the point as established by eminent authority. One prominent psychiatrist has written:

> Now it must be admitted that the enemies of Freud must be careful not to
> admit any single part of his discoveries to be valid, since one part is inter-
> locked with the other part, and if one admits that one thing is correct one
> is forced to admit the validity of the whole edifice. . . . If one admits that
> Anna, Freud's little daughter, dreamed of tasty food because she had no
> food all day on account of a bilious attack—that she wished for food and
> this caused the dream then one has to admit that all dreams are caused by
> wishes. (7)

This is not the time to enter into a general discussion of
Freudian theory or to attempt to assay its validity in detail or as a
whole. We are here concerned with the opinion of homosexuality
as expressed by Freud in the letter quoted above. This has led
many medical students who have read the letter to ask: "Is it true
that psychiatry has proved that homosexuality is normal?"

Is this opinion held by the majority of psychiatrists today? Is it
held by an enlightened minority whose discoveries will eventually
predominate? Is this, in contrast with lay ignorance and popular
prejudice, a scientific truth supported by evidence? I am quite certain the answer to all these questions is *no*.

Are there facts to support my unequivocal opinion on this? In a
matter so plainly self-evident, difficulties arise in any attempt to
present valid proof. It is obvious that the question of whether or
not homosexuality is an illness, a vice, or a normal and in no way
regrettable state of health, is not one that science can answer. I can
offer no more scientific evidence for this negative opinion than for
my belief, as a physician and as a human being, that we cannot
honestly say that it is normal and acceptable for fathers to have
sexual relations with their teen-age daughters. Science, as a matter
of fact, strongly suggests that such a practice would result in physically normal and healthy progeny. The fundamental issue is one
of values. Science, so long as it is really science, has nothing at
present to say about the matter of values. Do we look for scientific
proof to demonstrate that schizophrenia, asthma, or leukemia is
either an illness or undesirable? From science as it exists today, we
cannot obtain any answer to the question whether it is better to
kill the pneumococci that are making the patient ill or to let the
pneumococci kill the patient. Nor is there, to my knowledge, any
current *scientific* evidence that life is preferable to death. Common

sense, however, has a comment on all such questions that few care to challenge.

Though I cannot offer adequate evidence that science supports me in this disagreement with Freud's opinion, I hope I may, at least, avoid an error that is dangerously popular in argument about psychiatric matters. I hope I can avoid using such terms as "proved," "demonstrated," "so-and-so has clearly established," and so on, for what is no more than hypothesis, personal taste, analogy, manipulation of symbols, or speculation. I also trust that I can avoid misidentifying my own opinions, however strongly they may be supported by clinical experience, with scientifically demonstrated facts. Reasons for my disagreement with Freud's opinions are not hard to find. A number of them will be offered in the pages to follow.

SOURCES

1. "Historical Notes: A Letter from Freud," *American Journal of Psychiatry*, CVII (April 1951), 786–87.

2. Otto Fenichel, *The Psychoanalytic Theory of Neurosis* (New York: W. W. Norton & Co., Inc., 1945).

3. K. M. Bowman, "The Problem of the Sexual Offender," *American Journal of Psychiatry*, CVIII (October 1951), 250–57.

4. "Queries and Minor Notes: Homosexuality," *Journal of the American Medical Association*, CXXVIII (August 11, 1945), 1132.

5. Stuart Engstrand, *Son of the Giant* (New York: Creative Age Press, Inc., 1950) and *The Sling and the Arrow* (Garden City, N.Y.: Sun Dial Press, 1947); Eugene O'Neill, *Mourning Becomes Electra* (New York: Horace Liveright, Inc., 1931) and *Strange Interlude* (New York: Boni & Liveright, 1928); Robert Sherwood, "Reunion in Vienna," in *The Theatre Guild Anthology* (New York: Random House, Inc., 1936), pp. 752–822.

6. F. J. Hoffman, *Freudianism and the Literary Mind* (Baton Rouge: Louisiana State University Press, 1945); Ernest Jones, *Essays in Applied Psychoanalysis* (London: The International Psycho-analytical Press, 1923); Harry Levin, *James Joyce* (New York: New Directions, 1941); Patrick Mullahy, *Oedipus-Myth and Complex* (New York: Hermitage Press, Inc., 1948); C. Shrodes, J. Van Gundy, and R. W. Husband, *Psychology Through Literature* (New York: Oxford University Press, 1943); William York Tindall, *James Joyce* (New York: Charles Scribner's Sons, 1950).

7. Clifford Allen, *Modern Discoveries in Medical Psychology* (London: Macmillan & Co., Ltd., 1937), p. 113.

Chapter 3
ABSTRACTION AND ACTUALITY

Let us recall that Freud defined as sexual all types of affection and friendliness, all the interests and shared pleasures that may bring two people together in any form of positive social relation. This definition, held unmodified by Freud at the time of his death, automatically classes all human beings as homosexual in one way or another. A practical distinction is, however, recognized between the overt homosexual, who performs or is conscious of impulses to carry out sensual physical acts with another of his own sex, and the majority who, according to Freudian theory, have similar impulses which are unconscious and are defined as "instincts-inhibited-in-their-aims." In the normal adult these repressed homosexual instincts, disguised and sublimated, are said to express themselves in the ordinary interests and activities of friendship. (1, 2)

Later we shall have an opportunity to examine Freud's libido theory further and to question this definition of sex. Here it is sufficient to emphasize the point that Freud was evidently referring to overt homosexuality, to what the term ordinarily designates, rather than to the theoretical assumption. Otherwise the man whose mother appealed to Freud would have remained unaware of such impulses, and no such letter would have been written.

If we enter here into controversial discussion about what is or is not unconsciously felt or desired, we are likely to find ourselves in realms of hypothesis, dealing with concepts and verbal constructs that may be endlessly rationalized but that can never be brought to any practical or valid test. Let us not now become entangled with definitions of a libido, or try to determine how much or how incompletely it coincides with a postulated instinct called *eros*.

Rather, let us first consider some examples of homosexual behavior and try to relate them to the opinions expressed in Freud's letter. Let us turn our attention also to a few opinions about sex and love expressed by lay writers, and various other reflections of psychologic theory on the thinking of the general public. It is my belief that there are concepts and hypotheses popular in current psychiatric thought that promote confusion rather than enlightenment. These matters will be discussed in a later chapter.

Aristotle, despite all his prodigious philosophical efforts and accomplishments, is said to have died firm in his belief that men have more teeth than women. As Bertrand Russell has suggested, the great thinker could have avoided this error and also spared himself considerable tedious abstract reasoning by asking his wife to open her mouth so that he might count her teeth. (3) Whether or not this matter is correctly reported, let us try to profit by it and address our attention first to the actual behavior of people and to the results of their behavior. If we are to learn from clinical experience, we must not restrict our attention to mere terms such as "homosexuality, a variation of the sexual function, a natural libidinal component," and so on. Many of our terms are abstract. Some are vaguely and variously defined, so that in argument they can be molded and manipulated endlessly to prove or disprove this or that assumption at metaphysical levels. It is our task to examine as best we can the referents, the things we are talking about, as distinguished from verbal labels, and not to permit ourselves to be drawn off altogether from what is concrete and demonstrable. (4, 5)

Here is an actual and definite problem which confronted a certain physician in general practice. He recently wrote to me as follows:

Dear Dr. Cleckley:

May I have your psychiatric judgment of a local problem with which I have been confronted? I am practicing general medicine in a community of 5,000 which is the county seat for a county of 14,000. I mention these facts to you so that you may recognize that local issues with their reverberations can affect almost everyone in a town of this size.

Not long ago I submitted to the requests of a number of parents to ask their eleven- and twelve-year-old boys questions regarding contacts they had had and conduct they had observed in their sixth-grade teacher, a man. I knew the teacher only by sight, so that I could in no way be prejudiced by any inside knowledge. These boys told me stories which, to me, represented irregular conduct on the part of a teacher, and I reported my findings to the parents. I also wrote to the local School Board advising them that, if the stories were true, the teacher ought to have some action taken against him, beyond mere reprimand or reproof.

Much to my surprise, the Board took no immediate action and gave the parents little if any information as to what they intended to do. The teacher was retained. Both directly and indirectly I learned that the Board felt that one of the mothers was making every effort to get rid of the teacher because she had made a complaint about his beating some of the boys. The Board was annoyed that she appeared to be meddling in their affairs, particularly as it had not been her own boy who had been hit. It appeared to me that the Board had been so impressed with this mother's animosity toward the teacher, that they are unable to view the present case objectively. This I explained to them, and reiterated my advice as to what to do about the teacher.

Please understand that I am not concerned with this matter because I wish to vindicate myself, but because I believe that medically and morally I am right. However I feel that I need the support of expert, qualified opinion.

Here is the case with my assumptions, based as they are on the stories told to me by the three boys, in their own language:

All the boys agreed that the teacher had a habit of telling "dirty stories," although not actually in class sessions. One boy reported: "The teacher told us that on a certain island, the English had some donkeys. When the donkeys died off, they got asses. Then the Englishmen went about asking each other: 'How's your ass today?'" Another boy told that the teacher had warned him that he had better be careful when the doctor took out his appendix, for the surgeon's hand might slip, and he would get something else. Another boy told that the teacher had made the comment that the girls should be careful not to give birth to calves.

I advised the School Board, on the strength of these tales, that I considered no teacher is fulfilling his school responsibility when he tells his pupils stories of this type, and that I consider them unsuitable. When one of the members suggested that the boys probably hear worse than this at home, I replied that regardless of what one may think of so-called dirty stories at home, the telling of such stories and jokes by a teacher to young boys, in or out of school hours, is not only beneath the dignity of the profession, but actually a perversion of conduct.

When no action was taken, I wrote a second letter to the Board, in the hopes that I might move them out of their lethargy. In it, I offered the following definitions: "Perversion is an abnormal swinging away from recognized conduct expected of humans for that age and level, and is a deterioration rather than an improvement." Also, "Homosexuality is an eroticism toward those of the same sex and species."

All three boys agreed that the teacher has a special liking for boys in and out of school, and shows it by buying them treats and inviting them to his bachelor apartment in the evening. He often scuffles with them in the apartment. One boy related that he had been "tickled all over—just anywhere he wants to grab"—and admitted to his mother that he had been handled genitally in one of these tickling episodes. Another boy said he had been kissed by the teacher in a similar episode, and knew of others who had also been kissed. On another occasion, the teacher approached a boy who happened to be leaning forward with his elbows resting on a low table. Undoing the zipper of his trousers, the teacher bent over the boy, pressing his pubic region against the boy's buttocks, and making motions with his hips. He made no attempt to go further, but winked and spoke jokingly to the two other boys who were present and who took his action to represent some sort of sexually slanted horseplay.

I informed the Board that I do not believe these actions are just innocent sport, but that they look as if they had some motive, conscious or unconscious, and that it is of a homosexual nature. I pointed out that it is an abnormal thing to find a male teacher kissing boy students of any age. Medically my opinion is that such action is undoubtedly perverse and homosexual in its nature. I pointed out that roughing with a boy is different from tickling. Also that for a man to handle a boy genitally is a homosexual perverse act.

When the Board finally took action, it was to send a letter to the parents referring to the insinuations that they had been hearing about a certain school teacher. They told the parents that they had investigated and had decided to retain the teacher in his present position, hoping that nothing of the sort would arise again.

Contrary to the Board, I feel that the boys' stories are true, and that a different view of the problem should have been taken by the Board, despite their preconception that the whole thing is an outgrowth of the desire of one mother to get rid of a particular teacher.

Here are the questions I would now like you to answer for me (assuming, of course, that the boys' stories are true):

1. Do you approve of my deductions that this teacher is perverse in conduct and that some of the perverseness is homosexual?

2. Do you uphold my attitude as expressed to the School Board?

3. Would you consider the situation serious enough to warrant action on the part of the School Board against the teacher?

4. In your opinion, should the teacher be retained or dismissed?

5. If a psychiatrist were to see the teacher in question, is there any way that the psychiatrist can give a dependable diagnosis of the disease or symptoms without obtaining an adequate history? In the aforementioned case, I understand that the teacher was taken by friends to a psychiatrist and that the latter looked him over and gave him a clean bill of health, although no history of the episodes mentioned by the boys was given to the psychiatrist.

6. Assuming that a man is homosexually perverse, what is the best treatment and what is the prognosis? Also, can treatment, if any, be given locally, on the job?

I sincerely hope that you will be sufficiently interested to let me have the benefit of your reply. I have been here only about four years, and am considerably younger than you. Your judgment is going to mean a lot for or against me in my professional future. What I am looking for is to feel the support of a qualified man, if I am right; and I want to be set right, if I am wrong.

Very truly and gratefully yours,

————, M.D.

P.S. The teacher is 40 years old, well liked by his pupils, and reportedly good in class work. (6)

Now, what shall I, as a psychiatrist, reply to my young colleague? Shall I quote Freud's letter as authority and tell him that what this teacher does is "nothing to be ashamed of, no vice, no degradation," that his condition "cannot be classified as an illness" but should be considered a "variation of sexual function" shared by "many highly respected individuals of ancient and modern times . . . several of the greatest men among them"?

Why can I not make this reply to my questioner?

First, I have no qualifications as an expert to pronounce the deeds or the state of my fellow man as good or evil. Only as a layman could I, if I were to presume to do so, offer an opinion as to whether or not this teacher has "nothing to be ashamed of," or whether or not his conduct is free of "vice" and "degradation." So far as I know, about such questions as these Freud also could speak only as a layman.

Is there any psychiatrist who would differ with my opinion that it would indeed be a disastrous day for our country if physicians pronounced such a teacher as the one referred to above as normal and argued that he was well qualified for his work? Is there a psychiatrist who would knowingly permit his ten- or eleven-year-old son to be taught by a man whose sexual inclinations lead to this type of behavior, or be subjected to the influence of such entertainment in the teacher's apartment? If such there be, I can only say that he has not benefited by his studies and that he is himself psychiatrically ill.

But, the reader may interject, this argument is specious. Freud was not referring to such conduct as that of the teacher; he was referring to the abstract concept of homosexuality. Not all homosexuals are led by their impulses to attempt the seduction of children. We must not judge the innocent majority by the misbehavior of a few. This objection is indeed valid, if we confine ourselves to the abstraction and only to the abstraction. As with other purely abstract topics, debate could proceed endlessly and unprofitably. Abstractions, like Proteus, can take on any form. It is not difficult to validate one's claim about what can be defined or redefined at will and made to coincide with any claim.

Many serious and learned apologists for homosexuality have with excellent logic insisted that the invert, like the person with ordinary sexual impulses, should be judged or punished only by the effect of his conduct upon others. (7) The quest for heterosexual satisfaction leads sometimes to rape, seduction of minors, indecent conduct in public, and to various types of personally unfair or socially objectionable behavior. This is a reasonable argument and deserving of support, and no attempt will be made here to discredit it.

There is, however, another question that we must ask ourselves: Are homosexuals more likely than others to carry out acts and exert influences that society is justified in regarding as distasteful or dangerous? Where shall we look for a reliable answer to this question?

Karl M. Bowman has recently written:

The facts are that the majority of homosexuals are no particular menace to society. A small number of them, like those who are heterosexual, will attempt to seduce or sexually assault others or try to initiate sex relations with small children. . . . Homosexuals are no more open to seduction than are heterosexuals. (8)

An editorial in the *Psychiatric Quarterly* published the same year (January 1951) gives a different opinion:

The normal adult heterosexual presents few threats to the development of the child; he has presumably passed the stage where intercourse with children, sex play with children, exhibitionism to children, or peeping at children has attractions for him. The adult homosexual, however, is in a stage of arrested psycho-sexual development; he is not far above the child level—a matter not only of theory but one attested by empirical evidences. If most homosexual adults are attracted chiefly to other adults— which is debatable—many are still attracted to children; and more still are attracted to adolescents. The impulse to seduce is, like homosexuality itself, characteristic of arrested development. The normal child's danger is in seduction from occasional contacts with homosexual adults, and the effects of such contacts may not be inconsiderable. (9)

These contradictory opinions by experts certainly suggest that we do not at present have scientifically established facts by which we can statistically determine what proportion of homosexuals carry out socially detrimental activities and whether this proportion is greater or less than among the heterosexual majority.

Each of the aforementioned writers is expressing what his clinical experience has led him to conclude. Such a conclusion is not necessarily mere prejudice or guess. Judgment in many, perhaps in most, important matters must depend on what one's practical experience teaches is likely. For instance, the question of whether one's son would have a better chance for happiness growing up today in a typical American community or one in Russia must be decided, not on scientific evidence, but on just such a judgment.

My own experience as a psychiatrist, as well as my lay observations of my fellow men, seems to justify a rather strong opinion that in homosexuals a tendency to seduce and indoctrinate is very common, and hence real and dangerous. It has been argued that psychiatrists are likely to misjudge homosexuality because it is natural for them to encounter chiefly those homosexuals whose adjustment to life is least satisfactory. (7) This point deserves consideration. It should restrain us from sweeping generalizations and encourage us to be tentative in our conclusions.

Almost uniformly, homosexual patients I personally have studied have shown indications of promiscuity that in a mature heterosexual person could only be called distinctly pathologic. By no means have all demonstrated irresponsibility so obviously as the school teacher cited above, but a strong propensity for seduction, for the indoctrination and the initiation of the naive, has, in an impressive majority, been too obvious to be overlooked. Such propensity has furthermore often appeared strikingly incongruous with the person's general standards of behavior. The records of men whose general conduct could only be called reliable, dignified, and ethical, often showed repeated attempts to persuade or bribe pubertal boys to acts of pederasty, persistent efforts to convince bewildered and emotionally unstable youths that such acts and attitudes represent an emancipated and superior way of life. Even persons occupying distinguished positions in their communities have not been deterred from offering money and pleading with drunken sailors or disreputable drug addicts to submit to fellatio.

In the study and treatment of patients other than homosexuals, it has been an exceedingly common experience to encounter evidence of their personal contact with deviates who themselves did not seek psychiatric advice. Such reports indicate impressively a specific tendency to irresponsibility about sexual aims among homosexuals.

A few examples may be appropriate. Let us consider first a poorly educated, married man of low intelligence in his early twenties who sought treatment for anxiety and a number of somatic complaints. Among other events in his life he reported a recent bewildering experience with his former employer, one of the most successful businessmen in his town. While working after hours and alone at his simple job in a remote area of the warehouse, the patient was surprised to see the head of the firm approaching him. He was considerably more than surprised when this well-known church and civic leader peremptorily seized his penis, and shedding his customary dignity, insisted: "I want some of that." As the older man continued to pull and squeeze the genital organ, manipulating it through the worker's overalls, the young man thought in terror of his livelihood and of his wife and two small children whose support depended on his job. His employer continued the demands, perhaps threateningly, perhaps in plaintive cajolery—the younger man was too confused and embarrassed to discern clearly. The outlandish aspect of the boss in a role so completely inconsistent with dignity and manliness, as this simple laborer conceived of these qualities, so confounded him that he was virtually bereft of his wits. Somehow he removed himself from the scene, in the dazed realization that he had been far from smooth or courteous in his refusal.

Another patient, troubled with a speech defect and other symptoms usually classified as psychoneurotic, reported that in his late teens he had decided to study for the ministry. While visiting a denominational college where he planned to begin his training, a middle-aged clergyman of high rank in the church and in the college, graciously offered to guide him about the institution. This learned and, to him, awe-inspiring figure led him to a secluded hilltop which afforded a splendid view of the campus. Here he offered the prospective student counsel about studies and college activities and spoke inspiringly about the religious life. After quietly discussing lusts of the flesh and those temptations to which youth is said to be particularly vulnerable, he explained that some very religious men had devised methods among themselves to avoid the continuous and cumulative pressure of carnal desire. These were methods, he solemnly explained, that involved no sin with woman or any act that might defile her sacred purity. Though this particular church did not require celibacy of its clergy, he let the student realize that he personally believed that it was conducive to spiritual development. Even if the young man should eventually decide to marry, these other measures would be a safeguard to him during the years until he could be financially in a position to take such a step.

This experience was so disturbing that the patient decided not to enter that college, and eventually gave up his plans for the ministry.

In another case, a young clergyman of another denomination, while under treatment, expressed vividly painful emotion as, for the first time, he told of an event that had occurred shortly after he was ordained. An elderly church official, who had sponsored his career and contributed financially to his training, invited him to spend the night. The younger man was inexperienced to a remarkable degree. Overprotected by his widowed mother, he had been extremely zealous in his efforts to avoid anything even remotely associated with indecency, that might stimulate base or lustful thoughts. So great had been his devotion to this ideal that he apparently did not have any realistic conception of what might be an ordinary erotic act.

His older companion, who to him represented perhaps the most authoritative criterion of ethics on earth, spoke to him of the mysteries and paradoxes of intense religious experience. Then, in the guise of carrying out a beautiful but almost universally misunderstood rite of humility and spiritual communion, he performed fellatio on the youth, who, in shame, dismay, and paralyzing consternation, could at the moment find no acceptable way to resist or flee.

These incidents are not presented to imply that homosexuality or any sort of misconduct is prevalent among the clergy or among others who take their stand openly for righteousness. My own experience leads me to believe that both inverted and ordinary sexual irregularity is more rare among clergymen in general than among others. Any indiscretion or error of either sort will, if detected, attract public attention and be more widely broadcast as gossip in their case than in that of almost any other professional group.

I am personally acquainted with the three men whose homosexual acts have been cited. I know better quite a few others who have behaved similarly, sometimes over and over again. Although this opinion cannot be objectively proved or disproved, I believe most of them are sincerely ethical in all their other activities. In the area of sexual behavior, and there only, they commit deeds that are socially unacceptable and that appear grossly inconsistent with all the other aspects of their lives. Though I am not professionally qualified either to condemn them or to excuse them on moral grounds, I incline to the belief that they are less outrageously insincere than might appear. To my knowledge, some of them have demonstrated uncommon charity and courage, and have lived what nearly anyone would accept as truly good and admirable lives in all respects, except where sex is concerned.

I cannot, like Freud in his letter, tell others or myself that these people have "no illness." It is my strong conviction that their psychiatric disorder or personality handicap is genuine, and that it is not a trivial matter. The actions and attitudes of these people sometimes bewilder and harm others. They, too, are bewildered, and often become so disoriented emotionally that they cannot judge normally or adequately the regrettable effects of their behavior. Usually it has seemed to me that they cannot see or understand accurately the inconsistency between their sexual acts and their general beliefs and principles in other fields.

Nothing they do sexually seems to afford them real satisfaction, so they keep on seeking new and stranger activities. Though a kind of admiration or affection may accompany or prompt their sexual overtures, such feelings usually sour eventually into scorn or distaste for the object of desire. Moreover, in the biologically artificial situation they usually demand additional artificiality, often wanting the partner, although their impulses demand that he must be a male, to dress in woman's clothes.

The more we turn from philosophical preoccupations with unconscious homosexuality as an abstraction, from verbal manipulations of an assumed normal homoerotic libido, to the behavior of actual homosexuals and what we can learn from direct study of their inner reactions, the better we can understand what Kallmann meant when he wrote:

Psychiatrically it has been interesting to confirm . . . that the problems and attitudes of a sexually aberrant group look less wholesome in the twilight of gloomy hiding places than they do from the perspective of an ornamental desk or from a comfortable therapeutic couch. (10)

SOURCES

1. J. F. Brown, *The Psychodynamics of Abnormal Behavior* (New York: Mc-Graw-Hill Book Co., Inc., 1940).

2. Sigmund Freud, *An Outline of Psychoanalysis* (New York: W. W. Norton & Co., Inc., 1949).

3. Bertrand Russell, *Unpopular Essays* (New York: Simon & Schuster, Inc., 1950), p. 103.

4. Wendell Johnson, *People in Quandaries* (New York: Harper & Bros., 1946).

5. Alfred Korzybski, *Science and Sanity*, 2d ed. (Lancaster, Pa.: The Science Press, 1941).

6. Personal communication.

7. D. W. Cory, *The Homosexual in America* (New York: Greenberg, Publisher, 1951); André Gide, *Corydon* (New York: Farrar, Straus & Cudahy, Inc., 1950); René Guyon, *The Ethics of Sexual Acts* (New York: Alfred A. Knopf, Inc., 1948).

8. K. M. Bowman, "The Problem of the Sex Offender," *American Journal of Psychiatry*, CVIII (October 1951), 250–57.

9. Editorial, *The Psychiatric Quarterly*, XXV (January 1951), 156–57.

10. F. J. Kallmann, "Comparative Twin Study on the Genetic Aspects of Male Homosexuality," *Journal of Nervous and Mental Disease*, CXV (April 1952), 283–98.

Chapter 4
TEMPTATIONS AND OPPORTUNITIES

On the basis of clinical experience, I have expressed the opinion that a tendency to carry out acts that may endanger the normal development and adjustment of others is characteristic of homosexuality. I do not say that this tendency is universal. It could be argued theoretically that most people with inverted inclinations are as capable of refraining from any act that may harm the vulnerable as are people whose sexual desires are ordinary. No reliable statistical evidence is available to prove or disprove such an argument. All opinions must therefore be based on personal observation and study of what is necessarily a very small fraction of the total material; this and similar studies by other observers should prove of value. All opinions must therefore be tentative, for none can accurately or honestly claim the support of science.

If science could really demonstrate as fact that the homosexual, under similar circumstances and temptations, is no more prone than the heterosexual to carry out erotic acts undesirable to others and to society and that his acts are no more deleterious, physicians could happily and confidently reassure the community about many situations that arise in connection with homosexuality. But even if this most unlikely supposition were proved by evidence, some problems would still remain. Could we even then tell the parents of an adolescent boy that there is no reason why they should not let him be taken on a two weeks' camping trip by a homosexual scoutmaster or camp counselor?

Let us approach the matter in another way. Would anyone with good sense advise an unchaperoned camping trip for a teen-age girl with a young heterosexual male? I do not attempt to deny that there may be men sufficiently conscientious to resist the considerable temptations that might arise while bathing naked in the creek with a beautiful young girl, while sleeping with her alone night after night, or at any other moment during such an expedition. Any man who deliberately chose such a strenuous form of exercise of his self-control would, it seems to me, be better fitted for life in a monastery than as a counselor for adolescents. It may be granted that a few who conscientiously made such a choice might prove themselves suitable candidates for a monk's vocation. I am afraid that most would find a more appropriate environment in some psychiatric institution.

In the early centuries of Christianity, according to the records, it was not rare for very pious fathers of the Church to sleep with virgins. (1) Naturally, the only intimacies enjoyed were purely of a spiritual nature. This means of demonstrating a gift for celibacy is said to have been popular for some time. According to Bertrand Russell, "one eminently orthodox . . . divine laid it down that a confessor may fondle a nun's breasts, provided he does it without evil intent." (2) If we are to grant that those who followed such practices were normally responsive to erotic stimuli, we can only conclude that there were giants in those days! We do not find any evidence that these or similar exercises are advised today.

No remarkable imagination is required to see that the homosexual is inevitably subjected to temptations and opportunities that might prove too much even for St. Anthony. How many normal men—schoolteachers, physicians, taxicab drivers, or even clergymen—would be able to dress and undress daily with chorus girls, live in a dormitory at some woman's college, sleep with a great number of women, some of surpassing voluptuousness, and refrain from all erotic activity? After a few months of this, how much tranquility and peace of mind would be left to those who did refrain? Those able to refrain longest might find support for their endurance in loyalty to a wife. But homosexuals lack such incentive in their efforts to curb their sexual impulses.

I do not believe that the homosexual's feeling for other men is the same as a normal man's feeling for women. The reasons for this will be offered later. The analogy offered above does not compare situations which are identical. However, there can be little doubt that the homosexual is constantly subjected to sexual stimuli and to opportunities for promiscuous sexual acts almost unimaginable to the average man.

Another fact to be considered is that those who arouse the homosexual's desires are not automatically aware of the possibilities in the situation, as in even the simplest relations between man and woman. No woman is likely to undress in ignorance of what is likely to follow when she is alone with a man. Few girls, even at age ten, would get into bed with a boy or with a strange man. No stenographer would ride out to a lonely spot in the woods with her employer to spend several hours in the moonlight without thinking that he might at least try to kiss her. However, a twelve-year-old boy invited by his schoolteacher to go on a hike seldom has any prepared or familiar method for turning aside homosexual advances to which he may be exposed and which are likely to cause him deep bewilderment.

To my mind there are other important factors that influence the homosexual toward acts that society refuses to regard as acceptable. Despite his almost constant sources of erotic stimulus and of opportunity to make advances, the homosexual must carefully select those whom he will attempt to seduce. The girl who goes out on a date may not wish to be kissed, but she is not likely to be startled or in any other way seriously disturbed if the boy does make an attempt to kiss her. If he is overbearingly persistent she may take offense, but the chances are that a reasonably considerate effort, however enthusiastic, will be looked upon as flattering.

On the contrary, all men who are not homosexual will find themselves in a distinctly unnatural and distasteful situation if some friend or acquaintance, regarded merely as another fellow, should show signs of wanting to pet. Those with maturity and understanding may experience unpleasantness chiefly in discovering their acquaintance's misfortune and in the awkwardness of their efforts to avoid hurting his feelings. Some, however, are likely to react with plain disgust and a sense of outrage. Verbal insults, if not physical blows, may express the more inconsiderate man's reaction to persistent attempts. At best, the customary friendly relations of the two are spoiled. What most men regard as friendship does not thrive in such an atmosphere. Mature and well-adjusted men will have no part whatsoever in what the homosexual desires. In a heterosexual relationship, if a woman does not want to be seduced she may still participate, more or less passionately, in kisses and other erotic caresses short of intercourse. Can anyone imagine a normal man behaving similarly with a homosexual?

In most relations between men and women, some awareness of each other as reciprocally desirable on a distinctly sexual basis is apt to prevail. With no violation of strict propriety, no intention of advancing toward physical intimacy, the recognition and expression of such feelings are common and generally acceptable.

No matter how receptive the ordinary man may be to compliments, no matter how sadly in need of reassurance he may be, he cannot take satisfaction in the discovery that he is an object of erotic admiration or desire by another male. The chances are strong that he will find something unpleasantly ridiculous in this. No matter how well he may know that the invert will make no physical overture, he cannot take pride in a compliment of this sort. Only through a framework of the preposterous can he conceive of himself as being regarded by another male as sexually desirable.

Any man of reasonably natural orientation knows why the other man's incongruous and artificial role in any such compliment fails to arouse his enthusiasm. There is little need to search tediously in the unconscious for mystic explanations for this. Negative reactions toward what is biologically unnatural do not necessarily arise from guiltily concealed and specific cravings. If this were true, what a tremendous scientific demonstration could be made of man's guilty and secret thirst for sea water, of his unrealized but urgent and specific hunger for the straw, sawdust, alfalfa, and cactus that his repressions will not allow him to enjoy, together with or in place of steaks, or chops, or hamburgers.

The average child or adolescent, although aware of heterosexual activities and warned of their consequences, is usually quite unprepared for advances by the homosexual. For the homosexual, efforts at seduction among the immature probably offer a better chance of success, as well as less danger of insulting or violent reprisal. Since the classic days of ancient Greece, the mature or middle-aged invert has been moved by a specific and strong inclination toward the adolescent boy. At present this taste does not appear to be nearly so prevalent as in the Athens or Thebes of 2300 years ago. Clinical experience suggests, however, that this specific attraction is still notable. The naiveté and relative defenselessness of the very young and the peculiarly strong desire they arouse in many inverts are probably factors in promoting the invert's tendency to indoctrinate minors or, more precipitately, to molest them.

The girl child or adolescent, in addition to what she personally has learned about avoiding sexual exploitation by the male, can also find reasonable safeguards in customs, laws, and conventions that are basic in our social structure. Adolescent girls do not share locker rooms and showers with men. Parents, teachers, and others concerned with giving the very young a fair chance to develop judgment, mature attitudes, and sensible standards of behavior before being unduly influenced into traumatic sexual situations, have little means of offering such protection against the predatory homosexual. Like a wartime spy disguised in the uniform of the opposing side, he moves freely and undetected in the very areas from which he should be barred. He is accorded entirely unsupervised access to the immature of his own sex.

More fundamental than any of these influences in accounting for the prevalence of socially unacceptable conduct in the homosexual group are other characteristics that are, I believe, inherent in his erotic status. In my own clinical experience, evidence has been particularly impressive for the following features in homosexual erotic patterns:

First, they show a tendency to reject each other as worthy sexual partners, particularly as possible mates for a romantic and ideal union. Though able to give each other some sort of transient physical pleasure, and very prone to indulge in promiscuous activities, there is apparently a specific drive for what is intrinsically impossible, that is to say, for a normal heterosexual male partner. This discriminatory quality of impulse is, I believe, an important influence in the fact that homosexuals rarely find reasonable or lasting satisfaction in efforts at permanent union. Not being able to entice the really normal male into any sort of relationship, they are continually seeking new partners or victims among homosexuals who superficially appear somewhat virile, that is, among so-called "bisexuals" or psychiatrically confused men of questionable status who pass for normal. Often they are specifically driven to attempt the seduction of adolescents who, prior to the acts they hope to accomplish, perhaps represent for them an image of the male who is still heterosexual. If they succeed, he is not likely to remain an inspiring or an altogether acceptable object for what they call and think of as "love."

Second, the inability of the homosexual to conceive accurately of society's distaste for what to him seems desirable drives him to explain all negative feelings toward him as unwarranted prejudice. Unaware in his direct experience of what men and women can be to each other as mates, he has little means of contrasting his own, sexual experiences and longings and concepts of love with heterosexual life. Homosexuality is the best and most attractive way of life that he is able to understand through his own feelings and imagination, the best that he is able to know at first hand, to evaluate emotionally. Despite the frustrations and sufferings his sexual career brings, he is likely to choose this as an alternative—to nothing at all. He may therefore be far from insincere when he seeks to indoctrinate either the adolescent, or the older shy and bookish youth whose ascetic ideals and puritanical upbringing may have made him spurn heterosexual desire as ignoble lust. He may feel entirely justified in quoting poets and philosophers (and, alas, also psychiatrists) in his efforts to bring to younger or more unsophisticated persons the enlightenment and emancipation that he feels will enable them to express their real natures. He may tell himself that he is working to free others from what he regards as the prejudices, vulgarities, and smugness of a philistine society. Thus he may believe that he will enable them to enjoy something far better, something more like the rare Hellenic joys said to have been prevalent long ago in Athenian splendor. He can (correctly) cite Plato as authority in his argument that the sexual relations of grown men with boys is a nobler and more spiritual relation than that of man and woman. (3)

Finally, the man or boy who desires a girl still too young for marriage may be restrained from immediate and rashly hedonistic sexual acts by his hopes for a full, happy, and lasting union with her in the future which might otherwise be jeopardized. For the aroused homosexual there is no such future goal. Much as he may tell himself that an ideal, real, and lasting sexual union between males is not only beautiful but possible, he will fail to find within himself a genuine foundation for this belief. He may even tell himself that if he delays in the enlightenment and initiation of this youth, the vulgarizing, conventional, and unesthetic influences in society may blight the lad's now-radiant potentialities or susceptibilities, and stupid social forces make of him a dull philistine unable to accept and appreciate the rare intellectual and spiritual fulfilments of Greek love.

These are only a few of the pathologic attitudes, misconceptions, and antisocial motives that I have regularly seen, year after year, in homosexuals who, despite other admirable qualities, make themselves undesirable in various communities. In none of them have I seen convincing evidence of sexual aims expressed predominantly as love or in ways that could bring happiness to themselves or to others.

SOURCES

1. Homer Smith, *Man and His Gods* (Boston: Little, Brown & Co., 1952), pp. 262–63.

2. Bertrand Russell, *Unpopular Essays* (New York: Simon & Schuster, Inc., 1950), p. 80.

3. Plato, "Phaedrus," in *Dialogues of Plato*, trans. by B. Jowett (London: Oxford University Press, 1892), Vol. I, pp. 431–89; "The Symposium," *ibid.*, pp. 541–94.

Chapter 5
PARODIES ON A SEXUAL THEME

Despite the multitude of popular jokes referring to sexual disorder, the almost ubiquitous remarks familiar to everyone about "queers," "fairies," "pansies," and the like, there is reason to believe that general understanding of such disorder is limited and distorted. Any shoeshine boy or grocery clerk, or even the average teen-ager, probably has a fairly accurate notion of the usual physical acts carried out by homosexuals. Few people, however, except physicians and others who in their work must deal directly with such problems, have much opportunity to approach the profoundly pathologic situation that regularly, I believe, underlies such acts and the impulse to such acts. It is, of course, impossible to demonstrate scientifically the actual subjective feelings of any human being or animal. Direct clinical experience with specific persons does, however, give us impressions which are worth recording. The following are offered (let me emphasize at the outset) as impressions, not as proved facts.

It is my belief that only in specific detail and not in generalizations or abstractions can we usefully estimate human behavior or personality disorder. If we talk and think about "archaic attitudes," "immature practices," "deviations of libidinal impulse," and generalize at a distance about such assumptions as "the natural homoerotic component in all normal people"—if we confine ourselves to such vague concepts, we are likely to lose touch with basic clinical and social actualities.

Let us consider for a moment an assistant professor of sociology in one of the country's outstanding universities. This man has had a remarkable professional career. He is regarded as an outstanding scholar, a standard-bearer for causes often designated as "liberal," "modern," and the like. His classes are dramatically interesting, and his influence on students is said to be notable. He is reported to be able to stimulate "real thought" among undergraduates, in contrast to the activities of dull professors who merely convey information. His intellectual interests are versatile, and he is able to discuss the English novel, French poetry, psychology, and philosophy with groups of his students in such a way that many report that their more formal work in these fields appears dull and lifeless in comparison. He has published both poetry and fiction.

The letters from which we will quote below were written by this intellectually gifted man to a sophomore, a student of better-than-average academic ability, who in the past had been treated for superficially mild psychiatric illness.

Upon his return from military service in World War II this young student had found himself disillusioned and lacking incentive. Former standards and values by which he had directed his conduct, and which had shaped and stimulated his ambition, no longer impressed him as sound. Like other young men who have recently been hurt and disappointed by a woman, he questioned the possibility of genuine love between mates. He expressed mocking and cynical appraisals of marriage. As is not unusual with young people who have temporarily lost their bearings, almost any iconoclastic opinion automatically attracted him. He seemed to be groping for some new faith or standard, particularly for some ideology in sharp contrast to his whole former outlook. These developments had taken place in a person still remarkably unsophisticated for his age. Some features of his maladjustment suggest potential schizoid disorder.

The student addressed in the letters, perplexed and disturbed, had sought the advice of a more stable friend and confidant, who felt that the influence of the professor on the young man was extremely adverse. As evidence of this, the patient's adviser presented to me a number of letters written by the professor to the younger man:

Dear Jonathan:

Your letter just came, for which many thanks. I am so lonesome for you, and every word is good. I know you are awfully busy, and understand perfectly how hard it must be to write—with no privacy, no time, no materials.

You got my other letter all right, didn't you? If not, hunt it up. I wrote on the envelope "Personal," and to please hold, as addressee would call. I wrote it the moment I got the address, which was several days back.

Now, John, my Jean, let me mention these things:

1. Your closeness to me the first time you ever came over—that first night when I began to discover the grandest guy that ever lived. We talked and talked, laughed, got up and ate in the middle of the night, etc.

2. Your confiding in me and the trusting discussion of your love life and other affairs of importance to you.

3. Your fulsome correspondence when you first went to the summer camp

after I knew you. You wrote me a letter at the same time Frank wrote me a card. That meant a heck of a lot to me, and was the first step in readjusting my perspective on you.

4. That sacred night at the hospital when you turned to me for comfort, and laid your head in my lap in the darkest hour of your life, and talked out your feelings. At that moment I swore the deepest vow I ever expect to swear in my whole life. I swore that, though everything in the world attempted to intervene, I would *never* desert you, but would love you and do anything I could to serve you, so long as I should live. Yes, Jean. Yes, Jeanne. I promised you silently that I would be a friend to you no matter what ever happened, and would stick to you closer than blood, so help me God. I felt that I meant something to you then that nothing on earth or above or below could destroy. At that moment when you had a great loss, I swore that I would be such gain as I possibly could—and that as far as love-for-you went, you would not be the poorer.

5. That night you spent with me when Arnold and Fred were sleeping over at my house in the other room (the folks were away) and things were upset, and I asked you how you felt toward me, and you said: "How do you suppose a person feels toward his best friend?"

6. Up at the Heath's, the first night when you were so eager to have me sleep with you, and then when we were in bed *a la mode* you reached over toward me. I felt so wholly wanted. For you to reach first—is worth billions!

7. When you first wrote me long ago and signed "Love, John."

8. The wonderful night of May the 5th.

9. Last night when you said you'd still come over and spend the night, after you got married.

10. That time you said that other people seem dull after being with me.

11. When you told me you thought more of me than all your other friends put together. That *was* what you said the other night, wasn't it?

What right have I, lucky that I am to be your friend at all and to be with you, to be opening my mouth? I am afraid you might have mistaken my whole purpose as being critical. Ah, Jeanne. Perfect Jenny. Don't ever think that! There's not one slightest velleity in you that isn't good and swell and kind and better than anybody else. Nor is there anybody else in the world that knows it the way I do, both a priori and by experience. You are perfect, of course, and for that very reason you can't understand imperfection in others.

Since I opened my fool mouth to try to express this (in ways that looked critical of you, against whom I will not tolerate a single criticism from me, you or anybody else), may I on the other hand thank you from the very bottom of my heart, mind, etc., for those perfectly swell and pluperfect grand . . . acts of yours? These are just a *few* of the things that I could never, never forget or cease always to be grateful for and happy over.

And how I like to hear you speak of "my Billie" or hear you act possessive (that is, as if I belonged to you, which I do) about me or anything I have or do. I love it! Yes, I'm a Disciple.

I am missing you so much, John, ah, Jean, Jeanne. I was just thinking how non-existent I felt yesterday. While walking home through the woods in the grey twilight (my, how poetic—but the twilight was grey, it being a misty, sunless day). I felt like a shade in mythology—in abeyance, subjective, hypothetical. Since you have been gone, I have felt no purpose or motivation to do anything. Life is anemic. Now to bed, because I know that you will come back, and that there is nothing to worry about. But also—nothing good, just neutrally waiting to live again.

All this is by way of saying what must now forever and forever be the theme of my life, namely, how wonderful you are! My last words are already written, and my next to last, and so on backwards on to now; I love you Jeanne—Jenny—more than, I believe, anyone has ever loved anyone before. I love you not only psychologically, but ethically too. I not only *want* to love you, but I know that I morally *ought* to love you, too. Such a double feeling (duty and pleasure) are eternal guarantees, for what else is there to the conscious life of man that could oppose them? Nothing. You are heaven as well as earth, the universal as well as the particular, the end and the means, the good and the true and the beautiful, made one.

You are everything, Jenny-boy, that the most intense greed or ambition or selfish desire could want; you are also everything that love could inspire, or sacrifice, or wish to serve. You are fun and you are blessedness, you are Elizabeth and Venus, you are Christ and Babylon (so far as it is joy), you are Alpha and Omega and Pi also. You are mine. I love you in 4,000 different ways at once, and they are multiplying like yeast.

Yours truly, B

NIGHT THOUGHTS

Be not alone
if you draw breath.
No, choose a place
this side of death
that is your own;
for votive peace,
arcane release
from wind or rain.
Let fact outface such
creeds as say
we must apart
in state profane
consume our day.

Accept the bright
impassioned glow,
of Hellas born;
a Pagan choice,
the maenad's voice,
the Attic morn.
Let it be so.
Do not with trite
impeachment scorn
the nether flow.

In silence seek
the subtler way,
the stricter sight.
Eschew the weak;
the full delight
of urge obey.

Just another way of saying I love you, B

Dear John:
Please *don't* read this letter unless you can give it your *entire* attention for once. I can't talk unless you listen. If you are not going to read it carefully then please just throw it away and forget.

It's 2:20 A.M. now. I carried you home about an hour and a half or two hours ago. Ever since then I have been in bed trying to get to sleep. But I can't sleep. I keep thinking about you—the things you do and the things you *don't* do, the things you say and the things you *don't* say. I'm about to go nuts. Now, if you're still reading this, let me say a few things myself:
1. COMMUNICATION. For the love of Heaven, John, try to communicate with me when we talk back and forth. I can't seem to get anything across and neither can you. I don't seem able to get you to take the things I say *literally*. Please do that!! When I say something, you always act as if it were a metaphor or poetry or something that has to be taken with a grain

of salt. Can't you believe me when I use such-and-such an expression that I *literally* mean it?

2. FALSE KINDNESS. Damn it! Because you refuse to believe the things I tell you, you keep on doing things that look on the outside like kindness and consideration, but are really just as malevolent and harmful as they can be. For example, tonight you said that the reason you didn't come over for the night when I got sick was because you thought I needed the rest. I don't see how you could even flatter yourself that you are being "kind" when you do things like that. To give such a phony reason is to add insult to injury, because you know full well that I am actually (even physically) harmed more by staying up hours and hours worrying about you than otherwise. Both you and I know DARN well that it's driving me batty. If that's your intention, at least be honest about it—or else, or else—Jenny don't, don't do it.

To *you* peace of mind may not mean as much as physical comfort, but to *me* it means a hell of a sight *more*. When you feel that you just must ruin one or the other, *please*, in the future, let it be the physical comfort.

3. SILENCE. Please when and if things ever get balled up—talk to me. Don't wait until the last moment before we separate to say "Come out of the fog" or some such thing. If there's anything to be said, let it come out of both of us at the beginning; we can then enjoy the time we have together.

4. SOCIAL TRAPS. This, I think, is the supreme form of mental cruelty. To get somebody in a social situation where he *has* to smile and chitchat and smile again while he agonizes inside. I don't believe that there's any worse trick than this to play on someone. I know I *hate* to have to entertain in the doghouse—hell knows it's bad enough to be there without have to Pagliacci about it.

Well, John, that's that. I suppose I've made you mad, if I've had any effect whatsoever. But I've loved you so much and so long that I guess I got presumptuous in expecting any return or consideration. Don't think for a moment that this conflicts with my axiom that "John is perfect." You *are* perfect, but for that very reason you can't understand my imperfect attitudes. You're hurting the hell out of me, but only through a misunderstanding of kindness.

(I look at the clock, 3:22 A.M.)

Oh, John, perfect thing, the one principle that philosophy has taught me is this: Seek *ye* first the Kingdom of Heaven, and be content with nothing less. As someone said, after once knowing heaven, anything else is hell. And by following the rainbow, I did discover the pot of gold. Now I preach rainbows to everybody because I know that they are no myths. You are the gold, philosophy is the rainbow. Philosophy is directly responsible for my finding you.

Philosophy has already given me what I want. Now I am trying to make it help me in keeping you. Then, too, I want to be able to offer you something more than the love of a mediocre nobody. I want to be able to offer you the love of someone honored by others. The more I can make of me, why, the more I *am* to give to you! One of these days, you willing, we can be together in some arrangement that will allow us companionship plus the doing of our separate careers. We don't know what the exact details will be, but we can hope. Certainly, at our ages, life is not grooved.

I'm about to run out of news and tidbits, so I'll stop. But know that I
am thinking of you constantly, longing to see you, and loving you with a
great tidal wave.

Yours, B

The real name of the young man addressed in these letters is
John. Jonathan, Jean, and the rest are playful or affectionate distortions of the given name. The more intimate or enthusiastic the
writer of the letters becomes, the more frequently he seizes on pet
names that are distinctly feminine, such as Jenny and even the
paradoxical Jenny-Boy.

A charitable or tolerant observer might be inclined to say that
the writer is indeed expressing genuine love and deep human
need. However against the grain of biologic impulse and purpose
it may be for one man to seek in another man what men naturally
seek in women, some might presume that the feelings expressed
deserve respect as passionate human devotion. It might be held
that this man has found someone to whom he can offer the best
that is in him. However, many facts about the situation make such
an estimate extremely implausible, if not plainly absurd.

For one thing, a friend of the young man addressed in the letters has also been similarly approached by the professor. He, as
well as several other students, has received from him letters just as
extravagant. While in this alleged state of "love" for John, the
scholar in question has also sought to get access to the penis of
John's friend. On numerous occasions he is known to have attempted this with a half-dozen or more students. He often begins
by some high-spirited tussling or horseplay such as might naturally occur, or by casually pretending to demonstrate the effects of
massage. Inevitably he discloses his purpose, which is always to
obtain some sort of erotic contact which would be naturally attractive between male and female, but which, with another male, appears ridiculous and vividly repugnant to young men of ordinary
tastes. With those who did not in time fully grasp his intentions or
know just how to forestall him, he has eventually attempted fellatio.

Most of those approached in this manner react in such a way
that the older man does not make a second attempt. Some become
aware of his aims before an embarrassing situation develops and
manage to avoid him in the future. To several other students, who
like John are somewhat confused in their orientation and standards, he continues writing letters very similar to those quoted
above.

There is also a report that he clandestinely seeks out the company of a small local group of obvious sexual deviates whom he,
like the general public, disparagingly refers to as "queers," "fags,"
"fairies," and so on. A member of this group, an egregiously effeminate, unprepossessing, and affected youth, is said to have

caused the professor considerable difficulty and chagrin. At a sur-
reptitious gathering of the cult where women's clothes were worn
by those so inclined, and a rather open and general indulgence in
deviated acts took place, the prominent man gave or loaned the
other a ring that he was wearing. There are other reports indicating that the youth may have stolen it from him as he lay half-
dazed from drink or entranced by his activities with some other
male.

The youth, who was in the habit of flaunting his effeminacy and
who was ignorant, uncouth in manner, and generally regarded as
of a very low social status, was despised by the older man, who
inwardly refused to identify himself with the other members of
the group, all of whom he openly regarded with scorn. He was
perturbed and harassed when word reached him that his chief
sexual partner of the night was exhibiting the ring (which had his
family crest engraved on it) at homosexual gatherings, and boast-
ing that it represented a betrothal between them. It was understood that blackmail payments had to be made to salvage the ring.

So far as can be determined, John had not permitted the professor to carry out overt and complete sexual practices with him. The
older man had skilfully controlled himself and avoided forcing
such an issue. As a matter of fact, he often masked and even dis-
avowed all physical aims when his recurrent and sometimes subtle approaches threatened to cause a complete break between
them. From his attitude toward John, as well as toward others to
whom he expressed himself similarly, it seemed apparent that
what aroused the feelings he himself regarded as "love" was the
male whom he did *not* regard as distinctly homosexual.

It is difficult to see how real fulfilment for this man's aims is
possible. If, in the pursuit of what his specific tastes have caused
him to seek as a "mate," the other should respond as he wishes,
then the love-object would automatically and inevitably become
disqualified. Like the youth who stole his ring, the man who
proves himself a homosexual becomes for him an object of scorn
and contempt. There is, of course, little likelihood that anyone
who is free of serious emotional confusion, anyone in whom normal sexual impulses have matured, will ever participate in such a
relation with him. Among those who have psychiatric disability or
are too unsophisticated to understand adequately his aims, but
who appear to have, at least in some degree, a normal male status,
he continues, in a strangely cruel and pitiful travesty of erotic motivation, to seek that which he can never obtain.

The example of this academic figure is not designed to prove
that all homosexuals are similarly promiscuous or that all have a
comparably ambivalent feeling toward other well-defined homosexuals with whom they carry out physical relations. I am not
aware of any method available at the present time by which any

generalization about this group of persons can be proved. Rather, the example is offered as illustrating qualities and tendencies that I have found regularly, in various degrees, among a considerable number of homosexuals. In many cases a more kindly attitude is held toward other overt members of the group. Occasionally a predominantly positive affect for the "mate" may be maintained over considerable periods.

It is not my intention to regard as simply false the extravagantly expressed adoration and rapturous devotion. I would estimate these feelings as not entirely unmeant but apparently based on foundations so pathologically inadequate that they cannot sustain themselves. In my opinion the professor is as sincere as he is capable of being in this emotional area. All inverts that I have had the opportunity to observe have shown indications of complex self-contradictory elements inconsistent with the development of anything like the normal personal relations of sexual love. In many of these people the passion, admiration, and devotion expressed are, I believe, in a vague, transient sense real though usually not profound. These elements, furthermore, seem fused with opposite attitudes which eventually emerge to cause frustration and despair.

The obvious anatomical fact that homosexuals cannot have literal and complete sexual relations must not be overlooked. No genital intercourse in the true sense of the word can occur. Their final physical intimacies must necessarily be culminated in acts that are substitutive and biologically artificial. So too, it seems that in the broader personal aspects of the relation something is left out, something is distorted, the real goal cannot be reached. A basic un-naturalness, however vehemently it may be denied, is inevitable and seems inevitably to bring disillusionment and unhappiness. Committed to an original false premise with respect to the sexual object, all sorts of deviations and deflections of aim follow. The situation being intrinsically artificial, other artificialities are desperately seized upon and introduced, apparently to make the basic error less conspicuous.

Some, despite their inability to love women and a sharp sexual revulsion against women, want their love objects to impersonate the female. In gesture, in tone of voice, in feminine clothing and by the aid of lipstick, false bosoms, and other subterfuges, surprisingly accurate facsimiles are produced to excite other men whose excitement would miraculously subside should these figures actually be changed into women. Such impersonation is, however, complexly motivated. Seldom if ever is there lacking an impulse to caricature and somehow to mock the real female. Homosexuals also seek men whose superficial appearance is not only manly but coarse and overbearing and who cultivate what is regarded as the essence of supervirility, I have not, in contrast to some observers, found a sharp cleavage among homosexuals into two types, aggressive and passive, one consistently maintaining a "masculine" role and the other, a "feminine." (1) Both in the sexual acts performed and in the general personal attitudes assumed there is apparently a great deal of shifting toward each polarity and much complex metamorphosis of role through wide variations. The observations of Cory, who, himself an avowed homosexual, reports on these matters, coincide with the opinion just expressed. (2) Unable to accept fully either man or woman as mate, they seem invariably to demand an imitation. The artificiality itself seems to attract and at the same time to repel them.

The essential qualities of woman and man, though not easy to define satisfactorily, are, in the feelings of the ordinary person, quite distinct. Their roles in mating can be discerned, even by the most naive, as biologically appropriate. The gross facts of anatomy proclaim this as true. Intrinsic urges and aspirations, scarcely less obvious, inform both youth and maid of what each is naturally designed for. Only a severely pathologic distortion can account for confusion in what is ordinarily so plain, or for rejection of what is naturally felt as the essence of one's being. One boy may plan to be a soldier, another an engineer, still another might hope to be a poet or a chemist. In even the most modest youth, however, it is more basic to accept first, and to cherish, his identity as a male. The girl, too, whether she dreams of attaining the attributes of movie star, trained nurse, typist, or operatic contralto, dreams of attaining them as a female whose role as mate to man is primary.

Whatever bodily parts, endocrine secretions, and emotional characteristics man and woman have in common, they do not, unless psychiatrically disordered, encounter confusion about whether to seek a normal mate of the opposite sex or to pursue some of the many sad travesties of natural biologic behavior that constitute homosexuality.

The untranslatable idiom of these biologic axioms has apparently been lost by the homosexual somewhere in the course of his development. The signals of instinct that direct his erotic drives send him into blind alleys of mocking paradox, lure him mercilessly into the embrace of chimeras, dispatch him in desperation toward goals that do not exist. He suffers not only from a misdirection in the quest for a mate but also from a distortion of urgent inner needs for emotional realization of himself. His confused instincts demand what is not in nature and eventually reject in frustration whatever he does seize upon.

He cannot be a woman, nor can his partner. Neither could accept being a woman. Both would also reject the partner if he became a woman, even if this were possible. Yet they refer to each other as "she" and both are apparently struggling inwardly to be like woman and at the same time to be the opposite of woman whom they must impersonate in order to deride. Both want to be, emphatically, male; but each must reject the only way in which, erotically, this aspiration can be achieved.

What Theodor Reik reports of the inner fantasies of homosexuals seems to indicate an unadmitted or unconscious recognition of the artificiality of their relations, of the fact that they are not in reality mates to each other, but only substitutes.

In the realm of fantasy a man never goes to bed with a man or a woman with a woman. That is to say, one of the two men plays the part of the woman and vice versa. Of course a change of role is possible and even usual, but there are always—consciously or unconsciously—two persons of the opposite sex present in the fantasy. . . .

In other words, one of the persons in the homosexual union imagines that the other is a woman, but at the same time the true sexual identity is kept intact in the thought of the lover. The partner functions briefly and imaginatively as a woman, although the awareness that he is a man, an awareness temporarily submerged, remains. . . .

. . . the homosexual imagines that his partner is a girl, although he knows, of course, that the partner is a man. As for himself, he can play the role of a girl in his imagination, although he knows, in spite of the power of fantasy at his disposal, that he is and remains a man. It amounts, for the vividly imaginative, to a highly artistic, very brief bit of play-acting before oneself. The feelings of such a man must be very alike to those of the actress when, as Portia, she plays a male part. The acting can be that of a virtuoso, but it can never be without the awareness that it is acting. (3)

Homosexuals seem to be regularly driven by almost fantastically self-defeating aspirations. Though they dress in lacy lingerie they remain males, yet this artificiality is specifically sought. If the miracle of real transformation were possible, what could be more against the taste of both parties concerned? Both must struggle inwardly toward what is nonetheless repulsive. There is apparently no choice except for tragedy or absurdity—or perhaps for both.

Stirred by desires that prompt them to seek what does not exist, led by deviation into paths contrary to nature, they repeatedly grasp one unfulfilling substitute after another, regularly eschewing the real or the appropriate. For them it is not unusual to esteem the synthetic above the genuine, and to show predilection for whatever confounds or reverses the ordinary postulates of human feeling.

The very unsuitability or inappropriateness of the object apparently arouses in many inverts a specific attraction. In *Death in Venice* Thomas Mann pictures the venerable and renowned Aschenbach as being seized forthwith by an incredibly morbid lust for a fragile teen-age boy whose lack of health and poor teeth contribute to the perverse appeal. A fetid pestilence pervading the city seems to be greeted as a proper romantic background.

A similarly weird contrariness of taste has been expressed by decadent poets in lascivious and hopeless adulation for that unengaging freak, the literal hermaphrodite of Greco-Roman legend. Continually stimulated but always enlisted in quests that disillusion him, the deviate frequently identifies eros with its antithesis, confuses the natural aims of desire with distasteful amalgams of spite, ennui, and despair.

Failing so often to find any lasting satisfaction in efforts to mate with other homosexuals, many apparently, in a final and cruel turn of paradox, are attracted specifically toward a normal person of their own sex.

Such an account is, of course, too simple to give adequately the emotional disorientation and inner chaos of frustration that lie beneath the homosexual's erotic behavior. It is little wonder that some become bitter indeed and cynically damn life, and particularly love, in literature, in art, and in philosophy. It is also not surprising that others, less vigorous and enduring, restrict themselves to emotional shallows and banter about trivialities. Among the latter, sex and "love" are often dallied with casually, little personal emotion being ventured in the activity.

Though it was probably not his intention to do so, Cory well illustrates some of these reactions. Let us quote from his presentation of a scene in a *gay* bar:

. . . We will look up with the others as a new face appears in the door way, and we will hear a murmur:

"Look what's coming!"

"Isn't it gorgeous!"

This last comment is not in whispered tone. The inflection denotes desire, the tone defiance.

At one end of the bar, having beers, are three young queens; their eyebrows are plucked, their hair quite obviously bleached, and of course very wavy. Seldom seen in these bars, their presence is discouraged not only by the proprietors, but by the gay clientele. They gesticulate with graceful movements that are not so much feminine as caricatures and exaggerations of the feminine. They talk quickly, and their lips move in a manner not quite like the movements of either men or women. That can more aptly be compared to actors, seeking to imitate, yet not at all believing that they are play-acting.

"So, I told Margie [a man, of course!] that she'd just have to find herself a new apartment, because I wasn't going to put up with her carrying-on with my friends that way, and she got insulted and left in a huff."

"She said you raised a stink when she brought a friend home one night."

"She did? So you believed her?"

"I didn't say I believed any one."

"Well you can't believe a word she says."

The onlooker or eavesdropper is puzzled but the initiate is accustomed to the curious change in gender found in conversation of a few of the homosexual circles. Perhaps no other aspect of their lives is so amusing and, even to some inverts, so revolting. . . .

And yet after a few hours with groups of this sort, there is hardly a homosexual unable to say *Joan* for *Joe, Roberta* for *Robert*, although with trepidation and self-consciousness, perhaps even mocking himself: "She's nice," referring to a male entertainer.

A few gay young men, standing near the gesticulating group, listen to the conversation with amusement and contempt. "My how those faggots camp!" one remarks in a loud voice. A bleached blond turns and the retort is quickly forthcoming, "Are you jealous dearie, because nobody wants your trade?" (7)

It is not difficult to see how persons responding to the inner world of homosexuality seek to escape their major frustrations and despairs by devoting their attention to frippery and relative nonsense; or how others sometimes turn on the world in towering misanthropy. What impresses me as remarkable is that, despite all their inherent difficulties, some homosexuals succeed in accomplishing in their nonsexual activities much that is worthy of admiration.

SOURCES

1. Sandor Ferenczi, *Sex in Psychoanalysis,* trans. by Ernest Jones (New York: Basic Books, Inc., 1950), pp. 296–318.

2. D. W. Cory, *The Homosexual in America* (New York: Greenberg, Publisher, 1951).

3. From *Psychology of Sexual Relations,* pp. 46–47. Copyright 1945 by Theodor Reik. Reprinted by permission of Rinehart & Co., Inc., New York, publishers.

4. Thomas Mann, *Stories of Three Decades* (New York: Alfred A. Knopf, Inc., 1936).

5. Mario Praz, *The Romantic Agony* (New York: Oxford University Press, 1951), pp. 226, 318–20.

6. A. C. Swinburne, *Selected Poems of Algernon Charles Swinburne* (New York: Dodd, Mead & Co., Inc., 1928), pp. 77–79.

7. Cory, *op. cit.,* pp. 123–24.

Chapter 6
A SERMON IN PSEUDOSCIENCE

In popular fiction (1), in psychological treatises (2), and even in magazine articles (3), homosexuality has emerged as a rather prominent topic. In discussions among serious people, as well as among the frivolous, one hears many opinions expressed on the subject. It is no revelation when I state that the usual reaction, that of the average citizen, the great majority, is distinctly negative. My own impression of these negative reactions in the general public is that they represent not so much moral censure and indignation as immediate distaste, an unthought-out personal revulsion toward attitudes and acts that seem so plainly uninviting, so bizarre and unnatural. The general idea of two men trying to woo each other more or less as a man does a girl presents an aspect of the ridiculous so vivid to most that only after further consideration, or at least second thought, are questions likely to arise about the morality or immorality of the sexual acts that occur. For this I have, of course, no proof. It is an impression gained in approximately the same way that I have become convinced that most people with bald heads are adult males.

Many laymen who discuss the subject seriously, particularly those who are aware of current intellectual and artistic fashion, of the esthetic climate of our times, present opinions which emphasize the important creative work done by famous inverts and also what they often believe is evidence from psychiatry that, after all, there really is not much that is seriously pathologic about homosexuality. Such an estimate is often looked upon as progressive or scientific, in contrast with the errors of ignorance and prejudice. It has, in fact, become a fashionable viewpoint or article of faith among the self-consciously intellectual. This position has, apparently, become somewhat like a badge or membership card indicating that the bearer is qualified as a "modern" or "advanced" thinker.

Perhaps no shibboleth is so cherished today among "liberals" of this type as the point of view that it is "reactionary" to admit a negative evaluation of homosexuality. In a large southern city recently, eighteen inverts were arrested in the men's toilet of a public library and charged with offenses against decency. No penalty beyond those prescribed for a misdemeanor was considered by the court. Numerous cultured voices immediately arose to express comments such as these: "It's a shame to treat these people like common criminals!" "Our laws are archaic, brutal, and a disgrace to civilization," and so on. I could not help wondering how many representatives of the new enlightenment would have come indignantly to the defense if it had been nine men and nine women who had been arrested in such a place while carrying out sexual relations.

According to press reports, a distinguished British actor was arrested not long ago for "persistently importuning male persons" on the streets of London. He is reported as having said in court: "I am sorry; I cannot imagine that I was so stupid. I was tired and I had had a few drinks." Though convicted, he was let off with a fine of ten pounds. Five days later, at the opening of his new play at a packed London theater, the audience enthusiastically expressed its feelings by giving the actor six curtain calls. (4)

It is an old belief that sexual perversion thrives during the decadence of nations. Such a belief probably cannot be tested by the methods of science. No more statistical evidence for or against it is available today than a hundred, or two thousand, years ago. It is nevertheless interesting to read on the same page of *Newsweek* that carried the account of the celebrated actor's ovation another remarkable item. It is the story of a British soldier court-martialed and convicted of cowardice in action in Korea and dismissed "with ignominy" from the army. This man's desertion of his post apparently brought added danger to the lives of his fellows who held their ground. In addition to a dishonorable discharge he was sentenced to a year in prison. This sentence having been remitted, the young man returned to his home in Middlesbrough where he was publicly given a hero's welcome. "Special police had to be called out to hold back the cheering crowds. . . ."

There is much to be said for the impulse to refrain from condemning another who shows cowardice in dangers one has not himself experienced, as there is for declining to set oneself up to judge personally even the most deplorable of acts. Such a position, however, scarcely accounts for the demonstrations just cited.

Some laymen seem happy to embrace this faith in homosexuality as having been proved innocuous by psychiatry although they have little knowledge of the so-called proofs. In this they sometimes suggest others who are so ambitious to enter a far more exclusive circle of the cognoscenti that they laud the poetic, philosophical, and psychoanalytic wonders to be found in *Finnegans Wake*, (5) a book which they have probably never read, and whose every paragraph undoubtedly remains for them, as for most of us, unintelligible nonsense.

Let us examine briefly a few viewpoints on homosexuality recently expressed directly to me or encountered in print. Some of these illustrate what I believe is a serious and unnecessary confusion, a confusion not confined merely to the subject of homosexuality, but one which also promotes a general misunderstanding of sex and love. Before we investigate what real evidence there may be for these ideas and concepts derived from psychiatry or psychology and alleged to be scientific, it will be worth while to consider, first, their presentation to the general public and their possible influence.

This is a young man in his early twenties. While a student of the state university, he developed obvious manifestations of schizophrenia. Though remaining in good contact with his surroundings, he lost all interest in ordinary pursuits, sat inert in silence, and in what appeared to be great perplexity. Vaguely and apathetically, he admitted he was distressed. When asked what troubled him, he replied:

Well, among other things, there is the choice between a homosexual life and a heterosexual life. If I choose the heterosexual course, then I have to give up all the homosexual fulfilments of life. On the other hand, if I choose homosexuality, I must give up the pleasures of heterosexuality.

So far as could be determined, this youth had never experienced sexual relations with a girl or any abnormal relations with a man. He was, apparently, very little troubled with the conscious sexual drives that are a pressing matter to most unmarried men of his age. Nor had he, so far as I could learn, been struggling against deviate impulses. His statement seemed to be little more than academic. No real emotion invested the choice of alternatives he rather pedantically set up in words. It seemed almost as if, having heard of such a dilemma, he offered it as his own problem since his situation made it logical to assume that there must be some sort of a problem.

In a profoundly psychotic patient, many issues, plainly felt and normally evaluated by a person who is not ill, become confused. In the schizophrenic, attitudes, alternatives of conduct, and emo-

tional reactions to the simplest of human choices, to the most ax-
iomatic human standards, are often disturbed, sometimes
bizarrely distorted.

Though a schizophrene's bladder function is physiologically intact, he may retain urine until catheterization is necessary. He may
eat excrement in preference to ordinary food, or hold dead roaches
and cigarette butts in his mouth for hours. Because of his mental
illness, he may find nothing distasteful or uncomfortable in what
ordinary people regularly reject or seek to avoid. So, too, he often
finds no meaning and no incentive in what a nonpsychotic person
responds to without need of philosophical support. Normal persons seldom need to call upon reason or scientific knowledge for
guidance in such matters. In them, basic human evaluations and
choices are more deeply rooted in what might be called sociologic
and biologic postulates or premises.

It is, then, not remarkable to find this young man with
schizophrenia truly disturbed and confused about whether it is
preferable and normal for man to mate with woman or to seek
some substitutive activity with other men. Nor is it remarkable for
patients with a psychiatric disorder that leaves them unable to feel
what normal man feels for woman to be profoundly confused and
driven toward conduct that in the normal world would be repellent, incredible, and fantastic. This can be understood without assuming a hypothetically normal component of homosexuality
competing unconsciously with ordinary impulses in all human beings throughout their lives. I am ready to admit that there is such
an element in every case in which we discover it—not otherwise.

Indeed, the invert's choice of a sexual partner is so foreign to
any conscious inclination of the ordinary man, and the roles
sought with each other so incomprehensible and paradoxical, that
one can scarcely escape the suggestion that in these respects such
people are schizoid. The brilliant and, in most respects, "sane" patient with unquestionably schizoid attitudes and behavior in other
circumscribed areas of his personality functioning is familiar to
every psychiatrist. (6, 7)

Other observers have also been impressed by this point. In a recent study of identical twins, Kallmann says:

In addition, the specific psychodynamic significance of certain personality
deviations [in homosexual patients] has been emphasized by a group of
psychiatrically experienced investigators, especially by Bychowski, Hoch,
and Rado. The evidence of such special psychopathologic phenomena in
homosexual males is said to include general personality distortion with a
prevalence of schizoid or "schizo-sexual" disorganization as well as the
"obsessive" feature of insistence on pregenital or paragenital gratification
patterns. (8)

This term "schizo-sexual" seems appropriate, indeed, for choices of mate and role so odd and ordinarily so deeply against the biologic grain, for the tragic and fantastic emotional reactions between such partners.

Glover, also, in a careful study confined to homosexual students in a university, concludes:

Their indifference to fundamentals, their inertia, their fantasies and investiture of simple events with markedly exaggerated interpretation, their paranoid trends, emotional immaturity and well-known instability and suicidal ideas indicate a large schizoid element in their personality. (9)

Let us next consider a brilliant, spectacularly successful, and in many respects a very appealing woman who only recently expressed her viewpoints to me. She has earned considerable wealth in her own business, which she still directs, in one of the largest cities in the United States. Meanwhile she has achieved favorable recognition for both her painting and her writing. For a few months each year she teaches teen-age girls in a "progressive" preparatory school, motivated apparently by a desire to be of service and by her exuberant energy. This remarkable and sophisticated woman discussed psychiatric matters with me at length. She was not the typical or pretentious dilettante confused by a little learning. On the contrary, she had read, learned, and thought much on the subject.

She told me that she had lived for years as a homosexual. She cited psychiatric literature accurately and reasoned well. She knew several leading psychiatrists in the city where she lived and had been directed in her reading by these friends. Apparently she often discussed theories of dynamic psychopathology with them. During some months she had seen one professionally to develop her insight and augment her effectiveness in her chosen work.

She spoke of man as being bisexual, of every person as passing through a period of life during which it is entirely normal and natural to feel sexual attraction toward others of the same sex. She was confident that these opinions were supported by science. In making a comparison between homosexuality and heterosexuality, she concluded by saying: "After all, it really amounts to the same thing, doesn't it?" Despite the wish to be polite and an even more serious wish not to say anything that might in the slightest degree trouble this good and honorable person, I found no way to express honest agreement with such an opinion.

Attitudes such as these are naturally popular among people whose lives are complicated by homosexuality. A good many others have apparently become convinced that if this condition is not

precisely normal, scientific studies have at least shown it to be far
less serious a trouble than most people realize. Opinions of this
kind are often held more or less theoretically, chiefly about homosexuality as an abstract concept. Yet I have never found anyone
able to accept with equanimity the development of such qualities
in his own child, or to regard it as natural and benign.

Familiar as these ideas are to me, I was unprepared for a recent
incident reported to me by a young resident physician working in
psychiatry. With surprise and a somewhat humorous chagrin he
told me that a homosexual patient of his during his first interview
had solemnly asked him: "Is it true, doctor, that all psychiatrists
are *gay?*" When we consider some of the statements that appear in
professional journals, it scarcely seems remarkable to have a patient ask such a question.

Cory maintains that "as a matter of fact therapists have not hesi-
tated in bringing to the consciousness and encouraging homosexuality where it was basic and important to a patient." (10) In sub-
stantiation, he quotes two psychologists who report a patient suffering from anxiety and worry in connection with thoughts that
arose after he had been approached in seaports by youths who offered to perform fellatio on him: "The patient quoted the fact that
he could not accept the act as most of his companions did. He
could not comply yet he could not get the matter off his mind."
(11)

To the authors referred to, it became clear that the patient did
not consider one on whom fellatio was performed as homosexual,
although he regarded the one who took the oral role as a "fairy."
The authors conclude that this man's troubles have arisen from an
unconscious wish to be the oral performer, that "the anxiety attached to this inhibited wish generalized to the passive acceptance
of the act." They say: "If the therapist followed middle-class logic
in this situation his goal would have to be to make this sailor capable of passively enjoying fellatio." (11)

Cory correctly notes that these two authors do not state whether
this middle-class logic should be applied therapeutically. As
stronger evidence that "most professional psychiatrists . . . are actually encouraging homosexuality in those individuals who have
repressed it and who are suffering from the consequences of such
repression," (10) he quotes a well-known American psychiatrist.
The physician has been called to see a woman patient described as
"in her third depression." She had never been conscious of homosexual tendencies in herself, but had, on three occasions, broken
off her engagement to marry. The nurse in attendance was dismissed so that the patient might talk with her physician, who reported as follows:

The patient then told that she had discovered to her horror that she had an uncontrollable impulse to make sexual advances to the nurse. After some difficulty I persuaded her to admit the nurse to a three-cornered conversation about the matter. My reassurances not only calmed the patient, but, as subsequent events proved, gave the nurse courage to yield to her own consciously but timidly held homosexual inclinations. Without any connivance on my part, the two effected a permanent homosexual union. The patient got well. . . . (12)

The reader might well ask: "But don't most patients with depressive illness recover anyway?" He might also point out that this disorder can nearly always be cleared up promptly by electric treatments. Does any psychiatrist in practice today think that this would be more drastic than the measures recorded above?

From quotations such as the last one, it is easy to see how the layman or the medical student might get the impression that psychiatrists do industriously try to bring out homosexual tendencies in their patients and encourage those who come for treatment to perform pathologic sexual acts. Since the belief is held by many psychiatrists (13, 14, 15) that everyone has such tendencies, potentially and unconsciously, some might conclude that the psychiatrist's job is to enable all people to discover them and exercise them as natural and acceptable. I cannot believe that the writer quoted would carry out such a practice.

Clinical experience has not led me to believe that psychiatrists, by teaching homosexuals to accept their inclination as natural, can enable them to form happy and durable erotic attachments. The nature of the homosexual's drive does not appear to lend itself to the positive and lasting interpersonal relations and happy fulfilment which we regard as genuine love.

Many of the examples of inverted attitude and behavior cited by Cory are scarcely consistent with a sexual life of satisfaction and dignity. In the outlandish promiscuity of the "gay" bars and the "drags," a characteristic triviality of basic personal relations is reflected. Desire apparently must carry with it simultaneous distaste and peevish demands that sour any major joy. Cory says that when the psychiatrist eases a patient's repression against his homosexual impulses and enables him to accept them as good, he then, and often for the first time, may become able to accomplish the physical act of intercourse with women. He adds:

This does not mean that he ceases to desire men, but merely that he ceases to desire them to the exclusion of women. Marriage often becomes an attractive road. But such an adjustment can only take place in an individual who has been relieved of guilt towards his homosexuality, and who has hence learned to enjoy it, and therefore marriage will not replace the homosexual side of life, but merely complement it. (16)

Elsewhere the same author quotes a "gay" husband who speaks with his wife freely of his sexual exploits with a variety of men and boys. He does not hesitate to inform her about "when, where, with whom—everything but how—that's where I draw the line." (17) A woman who accepts her husband's male sex companions in her home is praised. This is what she cheerfully says to her successful male rivals: "I know what he needs and I know he's a better person if he has it. It's a weakness that has taken hold of some people. And I'm glad he finds pleasure with a friend like you whom he really likes." (18)

Are women supposed to find this status agreeable or acceptable? Is this what they are seeking in their marriages?

Cory also suggests that, if society would relax a discriminatory attitude, homosexuals attempting to live with each other permanently in relations simulating those of man and wife, "might adopt an orphan child or a nephew of an overcrowded and overburdened family." (19) How would such a lad be raised? What sort of influences would shape the development of his personality? Would any parent consent to this role for his small son? Would any psychiatrist advise it? If he were to do so, I can only say that he has drawn strange conclusions from his work. I do not think such a man would be qualified to practice medicine.

Here is a quotation from *The Folklore of Sex* which deserves attention:

In Paul Bowles' story in *Wake* magazine a thoroughly sophisticated college instructor, as well as a village full of British West Indian natives, is scandalized by the homosexual leanings of the instructor's son. In Nelson Algren's *The Man With the Golden Arm*, a hard-boiled police captain is shocked by a prisoner's saying that he has not been picked up for molesting a ten-year-old girl—but a ten-year-old boy. (20)

The implication, far more obvious in the context of the book than in isolated quotation, strongly indicates that it should be surprising to find a man, particularly a "sophisticated" man, upset because his son is a homosexual, and that the experienced police captain should be expected to find no particular difference between impulses that lead a man to make sexual advances toward a boy instead of a girl. I do not believe it is the task of psychiatry to promote any such sophistication as is here implied, or that psychiatry has discovered scientific reasons to regard the reactions of the instructor and the police captain as remarkable or erroneous. There is no psychiatric knowledge contradicting the awareness general among the lay public that sexual disorder is real, grave, and tragically regrettable. Such an assumption, however, is often reflected in contemporary comment.

I do not think that an appreciable number of practicing psychiatrists are truly confused about such matters. However, it would appear that in their speaking and writing, often with worthy motives, some of our group have promoted confusion in others.

Let us turn elsewhere in our survey. *Opus 21* by Philip Wylie, (21) though it is a popular novel, carries a recurrent theme of indirect but persuasive exhortation. This book can serve as an exquisite example of the misleading opinions that are sometimes offered to the reader as if they were the gospel of science. The author gives full credit to psychiatry for the remarkable message that runs through his book. This credit, I contend, does no honor to psychiatry. Reviewers speak of this novel as being "such devastating entertainment and enlightenment"; of the author as having a "basic perception about the sexual source of our ills." How these reviewers came to such conclusions deserves the attention of every psychiatrist.

In this story, which at times assumes almost the tone of an argumentative tract, the affairs of a good-looking young woman, Yvonne Prentiss, are discussed. She has left her husband after discovering him in abnormal sex relations with a male employed by him as a florist or horticulturist. Rol, the husband, is described as showing no interest in Yvonne. In her neglect and unhappiness she began to go out alone. He did not mind this. She then tried by more definite steps to make him jealous, but Rol showed only approval of what she seemed to be doing. She felt that he was actually encouraging her to go out with other men and, presumably, to have intercourse with them. (22)

Rol is a dilettante at botanical studies. He has been spending most of his free time with the male employee among his plants and flowers in the greenhouse. The presentation leads one to believe that the husband's interest is entirely absorbed in the other invert and that the activities in which his wife surprised them were a regular practice. The unhappy wife, Yvonne, is introduced reading the Kinsey Report at a New York bar. She explains that someone had told her that this work would demonstrate that Rol's behavior is by no means unusual among men. (23)

She is obviously desperate for attention from a man. This she makes clear to the narrator of the story, a character for whom the author uses his own full name. Her new-found acquaintance has more serious plans for Yvonne. He takes her out to dine and dance but chiefly to preach, through sparkling and glib badinage, some profound truths he has come by and which he seems to feel may offer her a solution to her problem. These are represented as having been worked out and grasped personally by the narrator from the discoveries of psychiatrists and psychologists. Although Freud is cited, the narrator seems to be even more impressed by the work of Jung. He tells Yvonne that a full psychoanalysis by Freud's technique will give anyone a tremendous shock about his own instinct life. Then he goes on to say that analysis by a Jungian will be likely to bring about even more profound enlightenment. Yvonne's escort muses about the important facts that he feels he has grasped through the application of these analytic techniques. He confesses to himself that he is afflicted with zeal to bring these to a more general attention and understanding. (24)

The facts, according to what Yvonne gathers from the repeated innuendoes, seem to make it clear that a woman cannot make love to a man adequately until she has realized that she possesses natural homosexual inclinations. Yvonne is not explicitly instructed by her escort to carry out any type of sexual exploit, but his conversation repeatedly implies that this important realization can be best obtained by some overt expression of these unrecognized inclinations. With men the situation is said to be similar. Each man must learn to take a woman's part in his feeling toward other men in order to understand the female libido and to satisfy its needs. This is a brief but accurate summary of what Yvonne is told in tantalizing morsels of enlightenment that the narrator interpolates into his effervescent patter.

The message seems at times almost to obsess the narrator. Even in conversation with Hattie, the madam of a brothel, he can't leave it alone. She comments on the wide appeal of Lesbian practices, implying that half the girls in the United States would participate in them if it were not for their lack of nerve. The narrator speaks of this latent inclination as being of great value, as, indeed, being a necessity if one is to understand his own sex. Psychologists, he says, have made this discovery. The philosophical madam shouts agreement. The narrator vigorously expresses delight in this splendid confirmation of his beliefs from a woman of such experience. (25)

Yvonne is subjected to an insidious and persistent campaign of enlightenment. In a night club two girls are dancing. Her escort explains that this is natural and also necessary if one is to dance well. You *must* learn both roles. So, too, with men. The best male dancers get that way from dancing together. (26)

Some readers may be a little surprised that the narrator is not himself tempted in this fiction to enjoy the sexual charms Yvonne seems to offer. He has already given the impression that his wife would have no serious objection if he did, that she might be amused, or, at worst regard it as of little consequence. (27) He has also told the reader that he would not like his own wife to be wanton, but would actually be made "sad" if toward the end of her life he learned that she had been strictly faithful. (28) Apparently he is ready to sacrifice any such pleasure Yvonne might offer him for the privilege of making her what he regards as normal and happy.

Gwen, a voluptuous professional woman from an expensive bordello, has come to the narrator's room; not, however, for the reason one might surmise. With her he is dancing the rumba. Yvonne, who has come in, expresses an interest in one of the steps. He suggests that Gwen show her how it is performed. The prostitute looks inquisitively at him and he nods archly. After they dance for a few moments, they simultaneously decide to change position, Yvonne taking the male role to lead Gwen. (29)

Yvonne soon takes the new dancing partner off to her bedroom where she apparently gets an adequate practical lesson to illustrate the "scientific truths of psychology" that her former escort has been trying to make her grasp.

Meeting him a little later she asks him what he would think of her if she were his wife. After a brief pause for meditation, he assures her that he would probably cherish her more than ever. She wonders why, and he explains that it is because she has been honest with herself. (30) The reader who is inadequately steeped in this psychology may find such attitudes hard to share.

Yvonne is enthusiastically pictured as seeing the light. In fact, it is hardly an exaggeration to say that she is made to appear as reborn. She literally shivers in ecstasy and with vivid delight shouts that she is, indeed, a new being. (31) The recently enlightened woman is described by her preceptor as having all her life miserably wasted marvelous potentialities. According to Gwen, she has been withering away, virtually perishing until now, from not recognizing her natural impulses, from not exercising the capacities she so recently demonstrated to the versatile entertainer who enabled her to find all this joy and understanding. (32)

Later the prostitute Gwen, through whom this swift and miraculous cure has been worked, commends Yvonne to the narrator, apparently for her heretofore unsuspected talents as a Lesbian. At this point the narrator seems about to launch again into his now familiar sermon. "A hundred and fifty million people," he begins, apparently intending to claim that all these must face, or have faced, the problem at last solved so splendidly by Yvonne. He is interrupted, however, by the prostitute who thinks his estimate of inversion is a little high. She suggests that a few million people may achieve by other methods the happy, natural orientation now enjoyed by the woman she has helped to redeem from misery. (32)

Yvonne's cure is complete. She now seems to find nothing objectionable in her husband's homosexual activities with the horticulturist and has made plans to return at once to join him in California. Over the telephone when she confesses to him her initiation into the world of sexual inversion, he shows intense jealousy —for the first time—and simultaneously becomes ecstatic. He urges her to come back to him, becoming almost frantic as he repeatedly shouts for her to hurry. (33) Yvonne, too, is in a blaze of joy. Expansively, she announces that she wants to have eighteen children, that furthermore she'd like for them all to become, like her husband, florists or horticulturists. The innuendo is almost unavoidable that she means to convey the idea that she would be pleased for them to discover homosexual impulses in themselves and not refuse to act on them. She seems truly euphoric as she emphasizes the new understanding she has achieved, of her husband and of herself. She claims to be full and complete now and is impatient at anything that might delay her from getting back to her husband. (33)

To the narrator she admits that she might continue homosexual activities along with this new bliss of marriage, and when he shows no sign of disapproval, she shouts that she can scarcely refrain from hugging him forthwith.

He playfully tells her not to give him too much credit and admits that the prescription he compounded for her is a dangerous one. In fact, he says he tried to evade the charge of responsibility for it but must now accept it. He modestly refers to the prescription as his "toxic monologue," but she praises it as an "elixir for the self-righteous." (33)

The narrator finally tells her that the "so-called sin" which is credited with effecting her cure is a dangerous remedy to try in America, that in other countries and other ages better understanding of its value might be expected. The reader is encouraged to believe that this couple will now be happy mates, the marriage a fine, healthy union. (33)

I do not know what Philip Wylie's purpose was in presenting this unrealistic picture of human relations. By many he is regarded as a professional cynic. Whether correctly or not, some of the aims sought in his writings have been compared to the effect achieved by the schoolboy who goes up close to the primmest little girl in the class, leers, and shouts at her an unprintable four-letter word. It could be argued that he accurately uses several dynamic concepts—bisexuality, normal homoerotic components of the libido, et cetera—and applies them literally to his fictional characters.

Though these concepts are popular today in theoretical discussion among psychiatrists and psychologists, they are not to my knowledge so applied by responsible therapists in the treatment of patients. Often those who express firm belief in such concepts are careful to point out that the terms in which they are stated must be redefined. We are, in effect, often told that when the word sex is used it must be taken as meaning not sex but something else, something far more broad and more vague. Whether or not it was his intention, Mr. Wylie has given a useful demonstration of confusions that can arise from the current practice of double talk in the psychiatric literature. It is a demonstration also of the folly that might result from a literal application of equivocally defined assumptions to the problems of actual life. As a satire on some of the language and thinking that floods our journals and textbooks it could, indeed, be helpful.

SOURCES

1. Truman Capote, *Other Voices, Other Rooms* (New York: Random House, Inc., 1948); Harrison Dowd, *The Night Air* (New York: Dial Press, Inc., 1950); Fritz Peters, *Finistère* (New York: Farrar, Straus & Cudahy, Inc., 1952); Gore Vidal, *The City and the Pillar* (New York: E. P. Dutton & Co., Inc., 1948) and *The Season of Comfort* (New York: E. P. Dutton & Co., Inc., 1949); Calder Willingham, *End as a Man* (New York: Vanguard Press, 1947).

2. D. W. Cory, *The Homosexual in America* (New York: Greenberg. Publisher, 1951); Albert Ellis, *The Folklore of Sex* (New York: Charles Boni, 1951); René Guyon, *The Ethics of Sexual Acts* (New York: Alfred A. Knopf, Inc., 1948).

3. Ralph R. Major, "New Moral Menace to Our Youth," *Coronet*, XXVII (September 1950), 101–8.

4. *Newsweek*, XIII (November 6, 1953), 44–48.

5. James Joyce, *Finnegans Wake* (New York: The Viking Press, Inc., 1939).

6. Hervey Cleckley, "The Mask of Sanity," *Postgraduate Medicine*, IX (March 1951), 193–97.

7. P. Hoch and P. Pollatin, "Pseudoneurotic Forms of Schizophrenia," *The Psychiatric Quarterly*, XXII (April 1949), 248–76.

8. F. J. Kallmann, "Comparative Twin Study on the Genetic Aspects of Male Homosexuality," *Journal of Nervous and Mental Disease*, CXV (April 1952), 283–98.

9. B. H. Glover, "Observations on Homosexuality Among University Students," *Journal of Nervous and Mental Disease*, CXIII (May 1951), 377–87.

10. Cory, *op. cit.*, pp. 188–89.

11. J. Dollard and N. E. Miller, *Personality and Psychotherapy: An Analysis in Terms of Learning, Thinking and Culture* (New York: McGraw-Hill Book Co., Inc., 1950), p. 420.

12. G. V. Hamilton, "Homosexuality as a Defense Against Incest," in *Encyclopedia Sexualis*, ed. by Victor Robinson (New York: Dingwall-Rock, Ltd., 1936), p. 334.

13. Franz Alexander, *Fundamentals of Psychoanalysis* (New York: W. W. Norton & Co., Inc., 1948).

14. J. F. Brown, *The Psychodynamics of Abnormal Behavior* (New York: McGraw-Hill Book Co., Inc., 1940).

15. Sandor Ferenczi, *Sex in Psychoanalysis*, trans. by Ernest Jones (New York: Basic Books, Inc., 1950), pp. 296–318.

16. Cory, *op. cit.*, p. 187.

17. *Ibid.*, p. 216.

18. *Ibid.*, pp. 217–18.

19. *Ibid.*, p. 231.

20. Ellis, *op. cit.*, p. 174. Quoted by permission of Charles Boni.

21. Philip Wylie, *Opus 21* (New York: Rinehart & Co., Inc., 1949).

22. *Ibid.*, p. 30.

23. *Ibid.*, p. 31.

24. *Ibid.*, pp. 89–90.

25. *Ibid.*, p. 118.

26. *Ibid.*, pp. 104–6.

27. *Ibid.*, p. 24.

28. *Ibid.*, p. 14.

29. *Ibid.*, p. 191.

30. *Ibid.*, pp. 243–44.

31. *Ibid.*, p. 245.

32. *Ibid.*, p. 293.

33. *Ibid.*, pp. 326–27.

Chapter 7
SUNDAY BELIEFS

Let us now examine the claim made by Wylie and by others that psychology and psychiatry have brought forward scientific evidence proving homosexual attitudes are natural and homosexual practices healthy and desirable. It is indeed true, as we have noted and I shall further demonstrate, that many psychiatrists and psychologists express themselves in such a way as to give this impression. In what is generally known today as dynamic psychiatry there are several concepts which, if interpreted in the ordinary meaning of the words used to define them, undoubtedly support these claims. Several points about these concepts deserve attention. First, the psychiatrists and psychologists who profess solemn belief in them insist that they use these terms to indicate not what these words have signified for years but something else, and often something not very much like the ordinary referent. Second, sufficient reasons for altering these definitions is said to lie in the discovery of unconscious impulses and desires which the ordinary person does not suspect but which are alleged to have been established by scientific evidence as normal in the life of every man and woman.

It is pertinent for us to consider some of the statements and claims made by professional people whom the laity regard as spokesmen for science. We should then examine some of the popular dynamic concepts—bisexuality, resistance, castration fear, a normal homoerotic phase of growth, instincts-inhibited-in-their-aim, and other items which have been used to support such arguments as that made by Philip Wylie. Let us also examine the methods by which these discoveries are alleged to have been made and established by scientific evidence.

A few years ago, when reports of homosexuals occupying positions of responsibility in our government aroused alarm throughout the country, I received a letter that had been drawn up by a
number of able and conscientious psychiatrists. It was suggested
that an official group of psychiatrists of which I was a member
give the public "some very simple and elementary scientific opinions" on the subject of homosexuality. (1) I had no doubt that the
intentions of the psychiatrists who made the proposal were admirable in every respect. They were unquestionably motivated by
a wish for fair play as well as by compassion. None of them, I am
sure, would regard actual homosexuality as anything less than a
serious personality disorder. After long experience as a psychiatrist, I wondered just what could be offered as a scientific opinion
on this subject. The statement that had been prepared, and that
some proposed should be made officially to the public, contained
these assertions:

The term "homosexuality" is usually interpreted by the average layman
to mean genital stimulation between two individuals of the same sex. Because sexuality is so closely linked with morals in our culture and since
"homosexuality" is officially a crime in most states and considered a sin
by some religious orders, this subject arouses great emotional feeling. . . .

   In contrast to this lay point of view, the psychiatrist most often uses the
term "homosexuality" to refer to one stage in the psychological and social
growth of the individual. It is used broadly to refer to the interest felt by
all persons in other persons of the same sex. In the course of normal development every child passes through a stage during the period of adolescence when his major interest is focussed upon persons of the same
sex. It is during this period that youth organizations thrive as expressions
of this normal stage of development. The normal individual progresses
through and beyond this stage to a preference for members of the opposite sex, with a choice of one of these for his mate. (2)

   Let us note first of all that the group of psychiatrists who were
questioned about the advisability of expressing this opinion to the
public apparently decided against taking this step. I have no
doubt that those who formulated the above statements sincerely
believed that genuine scientific evidence upheld them. But are
these statements correct? Do psychiatrists most often use the term
"homosexuality" to refer to a stage of growth during early adolescence when boys spend most of their time with each other, playing baseball together or going fishing, instead of having dates with
girls? If the term "homosexuality" refers chiefly to the ordinary attitudes and activities of this period, everyone, I think, will agree
that it is a usual and normal phase in human development. Was
this, however, the "homosexuality" referred to in the newspapers
and alleged to be prevalent in the State Department? Surely it will
be generally admitted that this is not what was reported by the

F.B.I. Let us ignore for the moment claims made by some that romantic relations involving sexual activity are common or even universal between adolescent boys. (3) Let us also defer consideration of the popular assumption that a specific desire for such sexual relations is regularly present at that age although the boys are not conscious of it. (3, 4)

At present we are concerned with what is more fundamental. I do not believe it is a fact that "the psychiatrist most often uses the term 'homosexuality'" to define the usual friendly relations of boys with each other prior to the stage when they are preoccupied with dating and courting girls. Be it noted that in the above quotation nothing is said about adolescent boys writing each other passionate love letters, or slipping off to kiss and pet in the moonlight. Nothing about this "major interest" that boys focus on each other sounds much like anything conveyed by such words as "sexual" or by such phrases as "being in love."

Suppose we grant as correct, despite its implausibility, the assertion that this is the regular psychiatric definition of homosexuality. Does that make the matter clearer? No special training in science, no gift of native wit, is needed to see plainly that the same term is being used for two separate and different referents. If we use this term as psychiatrists are said above to use it, are we talking about what the public thinks we are talking about when we address them? I do not see how we can in this way offer "scientific opinions" or even meet the minimum demands of common sense or candor. Any opinion we offer, whether true or false, will be on another subject. If we resort to what is plainly double talk, we can only promote confusion, among our listeners and among ourselves. (5)

In the English language, to be sure, there are many words which have multiple referents. If a general agreement were made to extend the meaning of the word "sex" in this way, it could be used to indicate the speed of light, what is now called a dish of scrambled eggs, or, if one chooses, a recently developed camellia. This would not however, make scrambled eggs the same thing as the speed of light, or the camellia. If we set out to describe a "pike," we may talk about the well-known game fish or about an archaic weapon. We cannot, however, make sense if we describe them both accurately and assume that they are identical. The histologist who writes a paper on epithelial cells would do science a disservice if he confined his observations either to the interior architecture of jails or to an investigation of subversive groups seeking to infiltrate the government. Even a man with the naïveté of Li'l Abner would protest if the lawyer he employed to examine records at the courthouse carried out the mission by playing jazz on the phonograph.

Some curious appraisals of human behavior have been pro-claimed and attributed to psychiatry. In the name of science, as-tonishing conclusions have been pressed upon the public. We all have ourselves chiefly to blame for the results of this if we do not take the trouble to avoid such obvious and unwarranted errors of reasoning. We will be shirking our responsibility if we fail to protest against conclusions so reached, no matter how learned or renowned the authority may be who supports them.

If we are to indulge in the privilege of extending definitions on the basis of resemblance, lack of resemblance, symbolism, or of some quality common to or opposite, in each referent, even the dullest of dialecticians could without great difficulty "prove" by this method that women have penises, that men give birth to ba-bies, that buzzards are an adequate defense against enemy air at-tacks, and that tigers fresh from the jungles of Bengal are safe and appropriate pets to bring into the nursery. In its efforts to learn more about human functioning and how better to treat personality disorder, psychiatry has an urgent and important task to fulfil. If in the process, however, we alter at will the meaning of the terms we use, it becomes wholly impossible to obtain scientific evidence for opinions we reach after studying patients by the use of any method. Bertrand Russell says:

Give me an adequate army with power to provide it with more pay and better food than falls the lot of the average man, and I will undertake within 30 years to make the majority of the population believe that two and two are three, that water freezes when it gets hot and boils when it gets cold, or any other nonsense that might serve the interest of the State. Of course, even when these beliefs had been generated, people would not put the kettle in the refrigerator when they wanted it to boil. That cold makes water boil would be a Sunday truth, sacred and mystical, to be professed in awed tones, but not to be acted on in daily life. (6)

I need no such army to establish these beliefs or any other, if I am granted the privilege of extending the accepted definitions of the words in which I state my case, of adding new referents at will. All obstacles to proof disappear magically if we are allowed to redefine our terms when facts contradict our hypothesis. If such beliefs about freezing water to make it boil were established, I fully agree that they would probably be held only as "Sunday truth, sacred and mystical, to be professed in awed tones, but not to be acted on in daily life."

So, too, I would call a Sunday belief the opinion cited above that the usual relations between adolescent boys are actually sexual. Whatever my colleagues might conceivably say to each other

about finding evidence that twelve- or thirteen-year-old boys typically behave toward each other as sweethearts, gaze rapturously
in each other's eyes, hold hands under the table, kiss long and ten-
derly, caress each other's flesh with panting ardor, I am sure none
of them would call such conduct normal, or approve of such conduct in their own sons, or in their patients. Psychiatrists realize, of
course, as ordinary human beings do, that evidence does not show
that ordinary boys actually do behave in such a manner. Popular
theory insists, however, that the boys *want* to behave in this way
but are not aware of their longings.

Brown, for instance, expresses what is often accepted as a dynamic concept well established by proof, when he writes: "In fact
it is doubtful if there is anyone who has never had a homosexual
libidinal attachment, although in many cases these do not lead to
overt behavior and in many others they remain unconscious." (7)

Apparently psychiatrists and psychologists insist that the boys
do not know their own minds about this, that they are fooling
themselves. They say, or at least imply, that a male adolescent or
pre-adolescent who honestly believes that the romantic stir and
sexual attraction he feels is directed toward the well-developed
blonde partner at dancing school is only deceiving himself; that, if
he knew his actual but unconscious choice and aim, he would realize that he preferred erotic physical contact and the role of a
suitor with his classmate, Butch, who shares his interests in football and fishing.

According to the prevalent theory, each boy in his unconscious
finds the other boy preferable to the girl, a natural choice as sweetheart, the normal object for sexual love-making at this age. This, I
maintain, is a Sunday belief.

The only evidence I have discovered to support it has been in
books, and here the evidence presented was obtained not by
bringing out and demonstrating any such feelings as those mentioned above from the patient's unconscious, but simply by re-
defining sexuality at will to include all friendliness between human beings, as, for example, any impulse that might lead two fellows sitting beside each other in a bus to exchange a remark about
the weather, or for one to offer the other a cigarette.

This is illustrated by Brown, quoted above to the effect that everyone has "libidinal homosexual attachments." Elsewhere in *The
Psychodynamics of Abnormal Behavior*, these attachments are thus
defined:

Now we have already seen how Freud considered heterosexual attachments between adults as only one specific instance of the general working
of the libidinal element of the life instinct. Libido, let us be reminded,

refers to that very general urge to come into close physical contact with other individuals. Not only is the adult heterosexual love relationship libidinal in nature but also parental love, sibling love, and the love of close friendships in the heterosexual as well as the homosexual sense. (8)

We are presented not with evidence from human behavior to support the opinion quoted earlier, but with a change in the definition of homosexuality to make it support the claim. In a footnote Brown adds that "actually the designation 'libido' should always be understood as referring to *libidinal* and *aggressive* impulses." (9)

If this additional extension is accepted, then the boys do not even have to like each other or to touch each other to confirm claims that they are behaving homosexually. If one gets mad at the other, and starts throwing brickbats at him, this, too, must be taken as evidence. Once this definition is accepted, everyone, of necessity, must agree. But what has been proved? It is nothing but a Sunday belief.

It is my contention that Sunday beliefs of this sort scarcely promote progress in psychiatry. Fortunately, however, they do less harm than they would if we tried to apply them practically. Despite the fundamental principle of psychotherapy that what is repressed and unconscious should for the patient's benefit be made conscious, I know of no physician who has ever proposed as a mental hygiene task that we undertake to help all these adolescents to know themselves better in this respect, that we enable them to express more satisfactorily what is so confidently pronounced as natural and normal. Even if we believe that the full sexual expression of natural erotic drives should be restrained, as we say it should be between unmarried boys and girls in their teens, why should we not let our young people at least know what their real drives are? If it is a normal and universal impulse, Jack and Butch might at least hold hands, send each other flowers, or in love letters express the sentimental aspects of their alleged unconscious infatuation.

I do not think that many of the teen-age boys or girls would be seriously endangered by psychiatric efforts to enlighten them along these lines. I fear, however, that anyone who, in the name of science, might set out to make our young people aware of their real nature and to convince them of such things about themselves would suffer embarrassment too extreme to justify the experiment. Sunday beliefs about these things are not likely to influence practice.

Let us look further to see what has been written on this matter. Here is another statement by Brown, about the period of puberty, which is typical of material that is to be found in current textbooks:

Revival of oral and anal interest . . . occurs. Children begin to show an interest in kissing and games like post office. They have a decided revived interest in anal stories and anal behavior. It is actually in the scout troop very often that the individual boy learns the four-letter Anglo-Saxon words. The threat of castration still lies heavily over the individual, however, and the first object choice is usually homosexual. (10)

If it is true that the first object choice is usually a homosexual one, one would expect in these games such as post office, to find the boys kissing each other instead of the girls. Is there any believer in libido theory whose faith is strong enough to maintain that such behavior is indeed customary? The creed demands, however, that one assume that the boys have this preference even if they do not know about it.

Brown goes on to say:

Most boys at this age engage either in mutual masturbation or social masturbation. By social masturbation is meant masturbation in the company of others. The fact that attachments are homosexual at this time is not due to any inherent biological nature, but rather is due to our social mores in segregating children at this age. (10)

While I fully agree that boys at this age often indulge in masturbation, I seriously question the statement that they regularly carry out such acts together and in groups. And when this does occur, it is far from common for them to regard each other as sweethearts. Nor do they so regard their own hands (in private masturbation), the milk bottle which may furnish the desired aperture, or even the obliging family cow that, according to reports, is occasionally utilized to make pubertal masturbation more realistic. Brown continues:

At first, there usually develops a feeling of antagonism towards the opposite sex. All of us remember the disdain with which we viewed the first of our "gang" to become "girl-crazy." All of us remember the embarrassment which we felt about our first puppy-love affairs. (10)

Who indeed does not remember these feelings? But who, even at the time, failed to see that he envied the boy who had the temerity to risk his sensitive feelings by actually venturing among the girls instead of just talking about them with other boys? Ordinarily the boy does not yet know his way around in such a world, and he fears he will look like a pretentious and ineffective jackass to his friends and to the girl when he first tries to put on the more grown-up manners, and even the minimum formalities required in teen-age dating. Feelings regarded as soft or sentimental normally accompany the boy's erotic excitement about the girl. He knows that these will promote ribbing, the good-humored but still painful mockery from his companions who have not yet got up their nerve to risk their very vulnerable feelings in such a venture. As long as the boys play chiefly together, it is customary to affect a tough-guy attitude toward "slush," "romance," "sweet-talk," and so on. Those who first dare to brave the world of dates and sweethearts know that they will be derided by the majority who are still too timid to take this step.

This shyness about girls usually, one might say obviously, must spring from the increasing intensity of heterosexual impulse. Similar diffidence and reluctant embarrassment are familiar at the brink of most ventures which offer thrilling and wildly desired possibilities at the risk of awkward failure when the stakes are high. Clinical experience leads me to believe that boys with real homosexual inclinations lack this typical embarrassment, as well as the concealed rapture of the normal boy. André Gide, according to a recent biographer, "assures us that he never felt the slightest physiological curiosity about the opposite sex." (11) This life-long homosexual writes:

Surrounded, during summer vacations at least, by children of my own age or a little younger, I took liberties with the little boys which never went below the belt; with the little girls I went to it in total heedlessness. . . . My modesty in the presence of men was excessive, and when my mother, on advice of our doctor, decided to have me take curative shower-baths (I couldn't have been more than twelve years old, then) the mere idea of having to show myself naked to a man made me sick with fear. If a woman had given me the baths I am sure I should have taken them without qualms. (12)

It is difficult for me to see how learned men can overlook such obvious factors in adolescent behavior and find it necessary to fall back for an explanation on a theoretical assumption of invisible homosexuality in all teen-age boys. Reverence for the theory (or dogma) must play a part in this, since there is no need for it in the easy task of explaining these adolescent reactions. Is it necessary to point out that because boys get out of their clothes together before going swimming we cannot assume that it is a sexual fascination with each other that keeps them out of the girls' dressing room? Is it a desire to hold hands on the sly and whisper flirtatious comments to each other that explains why, at their first dance, pubertal boys hang around together, for a while at least?

I think that the psychologists and psychiatrists who make such statements or draw such inferences in support of a revered hypothesis really do not believe them, in any practical sense. Let us return to Brown, who has been quoted several times above. We have noted his statement: "The threat of castration still lies over

the pubertal boy. . . ." (13) Earlier in the same book he defines castration as follows:

By the castration complex, psychoanalysts understand much more of infantile behavior than is shown in the fear of actual castration. The castration complex covers fears of all sorts of painful retaliation on the part of
the parents because of the sexual and aggressive wishes of childhood. . . .
Possessive love in the child leads to jealousy, which leads to imagined aggressions, which lead to the fear of punishment (castration as only one
form) for these imagined aggressions and fear of the loss of the love of the
one who is the object of the aggressions. The castration complex refers to
the whole behavioral situation. . . . Although actual castration may rarely
be threatened in our society, in some societies it is not only threatened but
practiced. (14)

It is not difficult to agree that actual castration is rarely, very
rarely indeed, threatened in our society. If this threat were the necessary cause of personality disorder we could use all our psychiatric hospitals for other purposes. Brown concedes the obvious
point that, after all, it is not a threat of castration but the well-
known parental and social influences that impel the growing boy
to restrain his sexual impulses. If it is not really castration that restricts the boy, then why keep on calling it "castration"? Who was
not aware long before he studied psychology or medicine, of these
other familiar influences that gain nothing but disguise in being
misdefined as castration?

Let us look at some other definitions offered by Brown: "Homosexuality refers to the choice of a member of one's own sex (biologically and anatomically) as a sex object," (15) he clearly tells us.
However, this is no longer clear when he adds: "Actually attenuated forms of homosexuality come out in all stag drinking parties." (16) His original definition dissolves in the claim that "in a
sublimated form, homosexuality also appears in songs like 'My
Buddy' and 'That Old Gang of Mine.'" (17) It would appear that
the chief sublimation is a process that occurs in the definition
rather than in the human impulse.

Since Freud for so many decades shocked the world by defining
as sexual many human activities not so regarded by others, it has
always seemed to me rather remarkable and a little amusing that
he, of all people, confidently proclaimed the period of childhood
between age five and puberty as a sexually latent period in which
conscious erotic impulses and interests subside or disappear. It is
still more remarkable that until his death in 1939 he was still expressing this belief (18) and that even now it is written down
solemnly in textbooks as if it were indeed a fact. (19, 20) Though
no physician or medical student with whom I have discussed this

concept ever failed to produce abundant recollections indicating
the opposite of latency during this period, it is only in recent years
that I have found in the literature of dynamic psychiatry any opinion at all expressing doubt about this curious item of faith. (21)

Even the relatively few definitions and opinions we have examined furnish adequate ground, I believe, for all the concepts that
Philip Wylie in *Opus 21* ascribes to psychiatry and psychology.
These are not, however, opinions based on scientific evidence. Nor
do they represent the real beliefs of well-adjusted psychiatrists. I
am confident that our illustrations have shown that such beliefs
are usually maintained by giving terms new referents; in other
words, by a kind of double talk. In the practical test, psychiatrists
do not act in accordance with such beliefs when the terms are
given their ordinary and real meanings. They are for most psychiatrists only Sunday beliefs. Mr. Wylie, in demonstrating a practical
application of such beliefs, may actually promote insight among
psychiatrists. *Opus 21* should stimulate all of us to say what we
honestly mean in straightforward English. It is our responsibility
not to name things in such a way that we contradict our real beliefs.

SOURCES

1. Personal communication.

2. Personal communication.

3. Philip Wylie, *Opus 21* (New York: Rinehart & Co., Inc., 1949).

4. J. F. Brown, *The Psychodynamics of Abnormal Behavior* (New York: Mc-
Graw-Hill Book Co., Inc., 1940).

5. Alfred Korsybski, *Science and Sanity*, 2d ed. (Lancaster, Pa.: The Science Press, 1941).

6. Bertrand Russell, *Unpopular Essays* (New York: Simon & Schuster,
Inc., 1950), p. 95.

7. By permission from *The Psychodynamics of Abnormal Behavior*, by J. F.
Brown; p. 379. Copyright, 1940, McGraw-Hill Book Co., Inc., New York.

8. *Ibid.*, pp. 181–82.

9. *Ibid.*, p. 185.

10. *Ibid.*, p. 202.

11. Harold March, *Gide and the Bound of Heaven* (Philadelphia: University of Pennsylvania Press, 1952), p. 37.

12. André Gide, *The Secret Drama of My Life*, trans, by Keene Wallis
(Paris: Boar's Head Books, 1951), pp. 31–32.

13. Brown, *op. cit.*, p. 202. By permission.

14. *Ibid.*, pp. 196–97.

15. *Ibid.*, p. 378.

16. *Ibid.*, p. 402.

17. *Ibid.*, p. 409.

18. Sigmund Freud, *An Outline of Psychoanalysis* (New York: W. W.
Norton & Co., Inc., 1949).

19. Otto Fenichel, *The Psychoanalytic Theory of Neurosis* (New York: W.
W. Norton & Co., Inc., 1945).

20. Ives Hendricks, *Facts and Theories of Psychoanalysis* (New York: Alfred A. Knopf, Inc., 1941).

21. Jules H. Masserman, *Principles of Dynamic Psychiatry* (Philadelphia: W. B. Saunders Co., 1956), p. 25.

Chapter 8
BISEXUALITY

Several popular concepts that have been mentioned are widely regarded as discoveries achieved by highly technical investigations into the unconscious. Among these is the concept of "bisexuality" with its accompanying assumptions of "normal and universal homoerotic components of the libido" and "instincts-inhibited-in-their-aims." Let us turn our attention to bisexuality.

Franz Alexander says in a recent textbook that "physiological and psychological bisexuality is . . . unquestionable in both men and women. . . ." (1) What is it that we are asked to accept as unquestionable? Common sense informs us immediately that no sane observer would maintain men are completely equipped with women's sexual organs as well as with their own, or vice versa. It is equally plain that men and women have many characteristics in common, anatomically, physiologically, intellectually, and emotionally. It is scarcely worth cataloguing facts so obvious. This, all will agree, is indeed unquestionable.

Who will deny that both men and women have arms and legs, eyes, a head, a gastrointestinal tract, and so on? There is, however, something about a girl's leg that makes it easy to distinguish from the leg of a man. Male and female appear to differ most sharply in anatomical aspect precisely in their sexual organs. In what are considered secondary sexual characteristics we also encounter features which should enable even a three-year-old child to tell a man from a woman. The woman, as everyone knows, has in her clitoris a small, sensitive sexual part that in some respects resembles the man's penis. The man, though he lacks large breasts, has at least nipples, which in a small, nonfunctional way correspond to the woman's.

These facts, however, offer no real support to any practical concept of bisexuality. So far, it is the sexual features that emerge as the specific differences between the two. It is known that the male and female develop from embryos that at early stages cannot be distinguished one from the other. In each—both the male and the female—we find some of the gonad-produced hormones which are characteristic of the other.

Men and women share many other features. Besides eating and sweating and breathing, those of each sex often enjoy going to the moving pictures, laughing at jokes, or, perhaps, playing tennis or canasta. Both usually have other common aims: to keep warm in winter, to have some fun, to be liked, and to enjoy the company of others who are pleasant. Just what, then, is meant by this popular term "bisexuality"?

Because there are, admittedly, male sex hormones in woman, and female sex hormones in man, is each thereby adapted sexually to take the place of the other? Obviously not. If either, because of personality disorder, attempts such a role, the unhappy results indicate anything but a true biologic adaptability. Does it mean that neither man nor woman can be satisfied in his or her own sexual status, but must always long for the other's? In psychiatric disorder, we do see such confusions. It is not, however, necessary to assume that everything which we are able to see in illness is normal and universal.

There is no evidence that the usual estrogen in man or the androgen in woman influences either one to need, consciously or unconsciously, to play the role of the other. If this were true, how easily it would afford an immediate solution for some of psychiatry's major problems and fully relieve all these people whose lives are blighted by what we call homosexuality. Many of the most intractably disordered patients of this sort have a normal endocrine status. This is not surprising in view of the fact that every psychiatrist has seen men with extremely virile physiques and typical secondary masculine features who are thoroughly inverted in their sexual life. So, too, there are numberless instances of women, successful as chorus girls or models for bathing suits, who have no sexual life other than that of Lesbianism. So far in this discussion we have not seen evidence for bisexuality or even been able to determine what this word is supposed to indicate. If it is, as Alexander says, "unquestionable," precisely what is it that we are to accept as unquestionable?

We need more information about the subject before we can agree or disagree. Fenichel, in his well-known treatise, says:

A certain amount of sexual feeling toward one's own sex remains in everyone as a residue from the original freedom of choice. . . . This freedom of choice may be ascribable to a biological "bisexuality" of man. However, this term does not have a definite meaning. (2)

So far, I can only agree that no definite meaning has been given; so far the term is almost without a referent. This is true except at one point. Fenichel has indicated that a "certain amount of sexual feeling toward one's own sex" is implicit in the proposition. We must next ask, what does Fenichel mean by "sexual feeling"?

Earlier he has said:

Freud combined the speculative and the clinical bases into a new instinct theory which states there are two qualities in the mind: a self-destructive one, the "death-instinct" (which can be turned against the outside world and thus become a "destructive instinct") and an object-seeking quality, striving for higher units, the eros. The objection that in reality there is neither a pure self-destructive nor a pure object-seeking behavior is overcome by assuming that the real mental phenomena are composed of various "mixtures" of these qualities. (3)

Who can deny that, according to this definition which he has accepted, Fenichel is entirely correct in saying such an eros prevails between man and man? Does it not prevail just as certainly between man and bicycle tires? It would be ridiculous to demand test by experiment or confirmation in clinical experience for what is self-evident. The proposition has already been proved in the definition. To illustrate with an analogy, I might say: "I hereby define leukemia as that disease, and the only disease, which inevitably responds to the treatment which I give, with full and immediate cure as the result." Granted this definition, I could easily and with perfect logic demonstrate beyond a doubt things about leukemia heretofore never dreamed of by physicians—perhaps not even by schizophrenes.

Whether or not we accept such a definition of eros, we soon encounter other statements by Fenichel:

In certain situations where there are no women, for example, at sea or in prisons, men who under other circumstances would have remained normal establish homosexual relationships. This is called accidental homosexuality and proves that latently every man is capable of this object choice. Normally a man prefers women as his sexual objects; if women are not available, however, men are his second choice. (4)

Why should this be brought forth to prove what is already proved in the definition? Apparently Fenichel has forgotten the definition he accepted and uses the term now for something more specific.

No doubt our great-great-grandfathers were not unaware of the fact that enforced sexual deprivation is likely to cause pressure from sexual impulses. If two prisoners in their isolation manipulate each other sexually, does that prove that either of them has made a specific sexual love-object of the other? Does anyone assume that such relations are necessarily those of sweethearts? What sort of flirtation precedes, what sort of personally romantic feelings accompany these relations? No doubt these things differ greatly with the various persons so engaged. Though many prisoners are far from normal erotically before their incarceration, I am inclined to believe that most of these homosexual activities are efforts to make masturbation more realistic, rather than the result of specific object-choice. Some appear also to represent bullying efforts to achieve dominance, colored by immature sexuality and concepts of virility.

As psychiatric consultant to a very large prison I have had some firsthand acquaintance with this matter. Frequently the attitude of one participant is primarily that of dominating or bribing the other to comply in a relatively impersonal method of obtaining physiologic orgasm. I have seen little or nothing to suggest that men who enter prison with ordinary sexual orientation think of anything but the unavailable female, whether they masturbate with their hands, avail themselves of a knothole, or manipulate their genital organ against or within the body of another man. Who will say that such incidents *prove* that latently every man is capable of an actual *choice* of man as a mate? By such reasoning we might prove that the flesh of his dead companion is a second natural choice to a beefsteak for an explorer who is literally starving. So, too, we might attempt to prove sea water a second choice but a physiologically acceptable substitute for fresh water, by citing the actions of sailors, who after remaining for days in lifeboats on the ocean without ordinary drinking water, have drunk sea water to their disaster.

The influence of Wilhelm Fliess on Freud, and particularly the former's indirect contribution to currently popular concepts of bisexuality, deserves attention. This physician, who specialized in diseases of the nose and throat, apparently dominated Freud's thought for a considerable period of time. According to Ernest Jones, "The really passionate relationship of dependence extended from 1895 to 1901." This distinguished follower and biographer of Freud writes:

. . . for a man of nearly middle age, happily married and having six children, to cherish a passionate friendship for someone intellectually his inferior, and for him to subordinate for several years his judgment and opinions to those of that other man: this . . . is unusual, though not entirely unfamiliar. But for that man to free himself by following a path hitherto untrodden by any human being, by the heroic task of exploring his own unconscious mind: that is extraordinary in the highest degree. (5)

Fliess, to whom Freud, after some reluctance, granted priority in originating and developing the prized concept of bisexuality, must have been a remarkable figure. Apparently endowed with more imagination than critical judgment, Fliess described periodic nasal swellings which he attributed to menstruation in both female and male. He soon convinced himself that in them lay the cause of neurosis. Since there are often 28 days between the beginning and 23 between the end of one menstrual period and the onset of the next, these two numbers assumed magically pseudoscientific significance for Fliess as he pondered over them. Manipulating the figures freely, subtracting one from the other, arbitrarily adding or multiplying, he began to derive explanations of illness, to unearth natural laws, and boldly to predict events in the future.

This man, who was Freud's sole confidant in scientific matters and the strongest influence on his thought for more than ten years, not only worked with the methods of numerology but also enthusiastically extended the researches on planetary influences begun centuries before by medieval astrologers. As a basic premise to support his accumulating conclusions, Fliess maintained the assumption of a bisexuality which he insisted he had discovered to be characteristic not only of all men and women, but of each living cell. Letting his magic number 28 represent the feminine component and the number 23 the masculine, he assumed the presence of a corresponding female and male chemical substance for each. From laws of periodicity derived from these obliging numbers, Fliess devised methods of treatment, foretold the onset of illness, explained the motions of the heavenly bodies, and confidently prophesied Freud's death at age fifty-one. (6) (Freud lived to be eighty-three.)

Of Freud's attitude toward this weird body of thought during the 1890's, Jones reports:

One cannot doubt that he did accept it for many years, strange as that must appear; the evidence is decisive. He tried to explain in terms of the fatal 23 and 28 the difference between the two "actual neuroses" he had separated, and he also suggested that it was the release of a male 23 material (in both sexes) that evoked pleasure, that of a female 28 material, "unpleasure". . . When Fliess's calculations of the sexual periods later extended into the cosmos, Freud went so far as to bestow on him the title of "the Kepler of biology". . . (7)

As late as August 27, 1898, Freud wrote:

Yesterday the glad news reached me that the enigmas of the world and of life were beginning to yield an answer, news of a successful result of thought such as no dream could excel. Whether the path to the final goal, to which your decision to use mathematics points, will prove short or long, I feel sure it is open to you. (8)

Most of Fliess's postulates and imaginary discoveries, which are more alien to both science and common sense than those on which the familiar chiropractic and naprapathic systems are founded, were finally rejected by Freud. The concept of bisexuality which Fliess, without recourse to evidence, devised and presented to him was retained and defended as a basic postulate of analytic theory. Freud seems never to have seriously questioned its validity during the four remaining decades of his life. (9, 10, 11)

Did Freud actually find evidence of this bisexuality in his patients? Was he able by his analytic method to discover in the unconscious manifestations of a normal and universal homosexual component of the libido, a real and specific but unsuspected choice and longing for physical relations generally regarded as perverse with a person of one's own sex? If objective evidence for this was discovered, Freud apparently neglected to report it anywhere in his voluminous works. These pages abound in confident affirmations about homosexual instincts-inhibited-in-their-aims. We do not, however, find evidence that such instincts were ever brought out and revealed by analysis, or by any other method, in people of normal sexuality, that they could ever be demonstrated in awareness.

In the final summary of his life's work, *An Outline of Psychoanalysis*, Freud states: "Analysis shows that in every case a homosexual attachment to an object has at one time been present and in most cases persisted as a latent condition." (11) For this conclusion, to the best of my knowledge, no evidence is offered either in this book or elsewhere.

In one of Freud's most celebrated reports, one that is often referred to as the "Schreber Case," (12) we find this statement:

Generally speaking, every human being oscillates all through life between heterosexual and homosexual feelings, and any frustration or disappointment in the one direction is apt to drive him over into the other. We know nothing of these factors in Schreber's case . . . (13)

And we find this said about the patient, Schreber:

It is easy to understand that the mere presence of his wife must have acted as a protection against the attractive power of the men about him; and if we are prepared to admit that an emission cannot occur without some mental concomitant, we shall be able to supplement the patient's emissions that night by assuming that they were accompanied by homosexual phantasies which remained unconscious. (13)

As Walters has recently pointed out in an impartial and admirably thorough study of Freud's report on this case, (14) the
conclusions reached by Freud are assumed at the beginning and
inserted arbitrarily into the material. Many psychiatrists and psychologists have maintained that in the Schreber case Freud's analysis reveals strong evidence for his claims of universal bisexuality,
of omnipresent normal homoerotic components of the libido. The
material quoted above shows the concepts which were assumed
and which regularly determined his interpretations.

Note that Freud states with full assurance:

. . . if we are prepared to admit that an emission cannot occur without
some mental concomitant, we shall be able to supplement the patient's
emissions that night by *assuming* [italics mine] they were accompanied by
homosexual phantasies which remained unconscious. (13)

On what grounds can anyone, without claiming divine guidance, assume that Schreber's reported emissions were accompanied by homosexual phantasies? Freud's reasons for this assumption are not given. How can anyone be confident that he has determined the nature of "phantasies which remained unconscious" in
a person who was awake, much less in one like Schreber, who was
asleep? The implausibility of all this is further compounded when
it is recalled that Freud stated that he had never met nor seen the
Senatspräsident, Herr Doktor Daniel Paul Schreber, of whom he
writes and about whom these assumptions are made. Nonetheless
Freud says:

. . . I think it is legitimate to base analytic interpretations upon the case
history of a patient suffering paranoia (or dementia paranoides) whom I
have never seen but who has written his own case history and brought it
before the public in print. (15)

With due respect to science, can the statement be made that we
know Schreber even had the seminal emissions he reported? The
statements of a patient with schizophrenia may or may not be accurate. Who will affirm that they are a proper basis for anything
put forth as an item of scientific proof? This question, however, is
trivial in comparison with the need for some evidence to support
the claim that we can *assume* that these emissions reported by the
psychotic patient were "accompanied by homosexual phantasies
which remained unconscious."

This is by no means an unusual example of the type of evidence
and reasoning to be found utilized many years later by those who
insist that they have scientific proof for various conclusions of excessive implausibility. Let us grant that Freud's study of Schreber
contains much that is interesting and helpful. Perhaps many of his
conclusions do apply to patients with paranoid disorder. I main-

tain, nevertheless, that none of the material in the report can be looked upon as scientific evidence.

Elsewhere Freud offers another pertinent statement: "In the light of psychoanalysis we are accustomed to regard social feelings as a sublimation of homosexual attitudes toward objects." (16) Are we to assume that he means all social feelings? Then it follows, with no need of further evidence, that two men playing tennis or four women playing bridge or canasta are, however much our resistance makes us deny this, indulging in homosexual relations. We may call these relations sublimated, to be sure. But this would not deny the assumption that unconsciously their more fundamental aim is to satisfy the "normally homoerotic components" of their libido in acts of perversion. Scholars with advanced degrees from universities have proclaimed their conviction that this is true.

Let us consider an additional statement by Freud on this subject:

We have to conclude that all feelings of sympathy, friendship, trust and so forth which we expend in life are genetically connected with sexuality and have developed out of purely sexual desires by an enfeebling of their sexual aim, however pure and non-sensual they may appear in the forms they take on to our conscious self-perception. To begin with we know none but sexual objects; psychoanalysis shows us that those persons whom in real life we merely respect or are fond of may be sexual objects to us in our unconscious minds still. (17)

If Freud's work, or any other work, presented valid evidence that all these commonly recognized feelings could be traced back to an origin in repressed but specific impulses toward sodomy, fellatio, or cunnilinguism with someone of the same sex, there would be substantial grounds for such a claim. In lieu of evidence we find merely a preliminary assumption of these instincts-inhibited-in-their-aims. Then obvious manifestations of interest or cordiality are pointed out, arbitrarily defined as sublimations of a universal but unconscious homoerotic component of the libido, and used in a specious process of reasoning to support the original assumption.

In the last quotation from Freud above, we have a general definition of what is meant by instincts-inhibited-in-their-aims. Let us look at some specific and concrete examples in life and see how this cumbersome term applies to them. If we grant that a father's interest in his three-year-old son is really sexual (and homosexual), and at bottom nothing else at all, we have an example of an instinct-inhibited-in-its-aim. So, likewise, if the ten-year-old boy likes his dog, we must assume that he feels this way *only* by virtue of the fact that the dog is really and fundamentally the object of a physically sexual aim. He is inhibited from carrying out this aim genitally, and his desire to carry it out is concealed from the boy by repression. Of course we must accept it as an aim-inhibited heterosexual desire if the dog is a female, otherwise we are dealing with a homosexual component of the libido.

But what about the dog and the dog's libido? It is generally believed that dogs love boys. Do not Freud's words "all feelings of sympathy, friendship, trust and so forth" apply also to what the dog feels? It is hard, even for those who detest dogs, to maintain that the affectionate pup has no liking at all for his little master. Surely there is some positive affective relation, or at the very least an interest on the part of the dog. Is this also a sexual instinct-inhibited-in-its-aim? If so, we must wonder what inhibits it. Who will tell us that the dog also grew up under a fear of castration and that this has made him inhibit his aim? Has it also made the dog, like the boy, unconscious of the real aim? These are similar problems, and I see no reason why the libido theory, as used above, should not be applied to them.

Still other questions lie before us. How about the soldier's love for his country? If we say this love is certainly free of elements ordinarily regarded as sensuous, we are still confronted by the fact that the soldier regards his country with positive feelings of some sort. Shall we call them "interest"? If so, where did this interest come from? We have been informed by Freud that "all feelings of sympathy, friendship, trust and so forth . . . have developed out of purely sexual desires by an enfeebling of their sexual aim." It has also been positively stated that "to begin with we know none but sexual objects." If we accept the proposition that eros includes all of human impulse except one other instinct, that of death, I think we must, perforce, conclude that the soldier's feelings for his country are also instincts-inhibited-in-their-aims. What would he do if these instincts had not been adequately inhibited, or, perhaps, not inhibited at all? A schizophrenic patient once informed me that he was, at that very moment, carrying out sexual relations with the Universe, but I was able to get only a vague impression of his technique. Just how, then, are we to imagine the patriotic soldier as proceeding if he should set out to accomplish overtly such sexual aims with such an object?

Those who accept as a philosophical belief the hypothetical origin of all affection, friendliness, loyalty, respect, and interest from a unitary libido, and feel that a useful purpose is served by labeling as sexual all human activities except purely destructive activities, always, if they are sane, make practical distinctions. All recognize a most important difference between the man who seduces his five-year-old granddaughter and the grandfather whose affection for her remains an instinct-inhibited-in-its-aim. If it does anyone good, if it satisfies needs for loyalty to a creed, there may be little harm, for people who choose to do so, in calling things that differ so profoundly by the same name. All activities and all objects can be shown to have some features that are authentically similar.

I do not think that any member of the American Psychiatric Association would be unhappy to know that his son went fishing with another boy or was at the moment playing in a football game with a number of teammates. If, in loyalty to the libido theory, he tells himself that such conduct is homosexuality, he will, I am confident, find it immensely different from other activities for which he might use the same term. Is there any member of the association who would regard as less than tragic and horribly regrettable the discovery that his twenty-five-year-old son (or his fifteen-year-old son) was seeking erotic pleasures and romance (or its grim caricature) in passionately kissing, fondling, and "petting" other men or boys? Even if such instincts were inhibited-in-their-aims sufficiently to restrain the son from completing such acts as fellatio or sodomy, it is my impression that the psychiatrist, or any normal parent, would nevertheless react with alarm. If the inhibitions prevented all physically erotic contact with other males, I think the parent would not be happy to know that his son was exchanging with another boy the sort of love letters ordinarily inspired by a girl.

At this point the familiar story of "The Emperor's New Clothes" by Hans Christian Andersen emerges by free association in my awareness. The monarch, desiring particularly resplendent robes of state, paid great sums to two fraudulent weavers who, in hope of enriching themselves unduly, have told the emperor that his outfit will not only be the most sumptuous ever conceived, but that it will have an additional and unique feature. They convince him that these clothes will be invisible to any person unfit for his office or incorrigibly stupid. In this way, they point out to their ruler, the garments will not only make him into a veritable peacock of imperial elegance, but also will enable him to detect and eliminate all the ineffective office-holders in his realm.

Most readers are, perhaps, familiar with this tale, but I cannot forbear to continue with this brief summary. When clothed and bedecked on the great day, the emperor of course dare not admit that he himself sees no robes at all, or that he feels no garments against his skin. Rumor of the magic properties has spread throughout the city and over the entire countryside. Our emperor, his countenance proud and serene, his stride stately, leads the procession for some little distance down the chief avenue of the capital. Everywhere there is a hubbub of admiration and awe. At last a very small child (for only such a one would dare) breaks the solemn silence with a shout: "But he has nothing on!"

Under similar circumstances, even those who lack the reputed innocence of a little child sometimes feel like making a similar outcry. The academic and endless debates of the scholastic philosophers also come to mind, particularly those learned and heated discussions about the number of angels who could dance on the point of a needle. After listening long enough, it is hard to refrain from shouting: "Bring on your angels and let us see!"

Thus, too, with this hypothetical homoerotic component of the libido. When argument about it and assumptions about it continue on and on, when proof of what common observation makes extremely implausible is confidently announced, when universal truths are continually derived from such philosophizing, when all this looks as if it is to go on indefinitely—it is then, perhaps, proper to request that this protean entity be brought within actual scrutiny, or at least that we be told how so much has been learned about it.

"It is," Nicole writes, "to libido trends that have . . . become non-sexual that Freud has applied the name of instincts-inhibited-in-their-aims. Other psychologists, however," Nicole states succinctly, "have preferred to call them 'interest.'" (18) It is scarcely necessary for me to add that I think "interest" is the more accurate term.

On philosophical grounds there may be good reasons to argue that all human feelings, strivings, impulses, and activities, all biologic manifestations whatsoever, originate in one or the other of two primal sources; that from these two homogeneous but separate entities evolve all the reactions of adult life. It might also be argued that everything evolves from ten, or ten thousand, such original elements, or from one. If one single element is assumed, we can draw a useful analogy from embryology.

Beginning as the microscopic fertilized ovum, the unicellular zygote, the relatively huge and immensely diversified human fetus grows and develops within the uterus. After birth this continues, and at length we have the human adult—all from one original cell. In this adult we know that the skin and also the cerebellum have come from the same layer of embryonic cells, the ectoderm. Though what is now cerebellum was once ectoderm, just as the skin was ectoderm, few find it profitable to call the cerebellum ectoderm or to insist that the skin and the cerebellum are really identical. No one, so far as I know, insists that this is the only correct and scientific practice.

We have genuinely adequate evidence, not just hypothesis, that all our organs, tissues, and parts were once the unicellular zygote. Bone, pancreas, hypothalamus, hand, eyeball, red blood cell—everything that constitutes an organism—came from this identical source; was, if we care so to phrase it, at one time zygote. What is now the foot was once part of the zygote; so, too, the hair, the tongue, and the adrenal glands. Despite this fact which can be demonstrated objectively to anyone's satisfaction, I have never heard anatomists define an eyeball as a bone-inhibited-in-its-aim. Nor do we encounter arguments to prove that the nose is a latent rectum, or that the teeth are actually repressed components of the kidney. Even if anatomists and physiologists could interest themselves in such a debate, the surgeon or the dentist would be little influenced by such philosophy in practical efforts to extract a tooth or perform an appendectomy.

SOURCES

1. Franz Alexander, *Fundamentals of Psychoanalysis* (New York: W. W. Norton & Co., Inc., 1948), p. 104.

2. Otto Fenichel, *The Psychoanalytic Theory of Neurosis* (New York: W. W. Norton & Co., Inc., 1945), p. 329.

3. *Ibid.,* pp. 58–59.

4. *Ibid.,* p. 330.

5. Ernest Jones, *The Life and Work of Sigmund Freud* (New York: Basic Books, Inc., 1953), Vol. I, p. 287.

6. *Ibid.,* pp. 287–318.

7. *Ibid.,* p. 304.

8. *Ibid.,* p. 298.

9. *Ibid.,* Vol II, p. 281.

10. Edith Buxbaum, "Freud's Dream Interpretation in the Light of His Letters to Fliess," *Bulletin of the Menninger Clinic,* XV (November 1951), 197–212.

11. Sigmund Freud, *An Outline of Psychoanalysis* (New York: W. W. Norton & Co., Inc., 1949), p. 31.

12. Sigmund Freud, *Collected Papers* (London: Hogarth Press, Ltd., 1943), Vol. Ill, pp. 387–470.

13. *Ibid.,* pp. 429–30.

14. O. S. Walters, "A Methodological Critique of Freud's Schreber Case," *The Psychoanalytic Review,* XLII (October 1955), 321–42.

15. Freud, *op. cit.,* p. 388.

16. *Ibid.,* Vol. II, p. 243.

17. *Ibid.,* p. 319.

18. J. E. Nicole, *Psychopathology* (Baltimore: The Williams & Wilkins Co., 1947), p. 19.

Chapter 9
PORTRAIT OF A LADY–
NONOBJECTIVE STYLE

To the end of his life, Freud maintained his assumption that the libido, defined by him as the energy of the sexual instinct, is always masculine. Consequently he could not account for any positive manifestations of sexual feeling or any voluntary sexual activity in the female except by making another assumption—that all such feelings and activities in women arise from a masculine component of their nature. If woman is sexually responsive only insofar as she is in part male, it would seem logical to conclude that women who show pronounced masculine features will be ideal sexual partners. I am not aware of any evidence that extremely hirsute and virilized women who seem to prefer a man's social role have proved more ardent than the lovely and voluptuous women who represent for most men what is specifically feminine. In fact, if such a conclusion is correct, men are regularly and curiously misled by their tastes.

In his final summary of psychoanalytic findings, after mentioning "the great enigma of the biological fact of the duality of the sexes," and concluding that "psychoanalysis has made no contribution towards solving this problem," Freud refers to "the fact, long suspected, that no individual is limited to the methods of reaction of a single sex but always finds room for those of the opposite sex, just as his body frequently bears, alongside the developed organs of one sex, the stunted and often useless rudiments of the other." (1) Freud continues:

. . . For the purpose of distinguishing between male and female in mental life, we assert an equivalence which is clearly insufficient, empirical and conventional: we call everything that is powerful, and active "male" and everything that is weak and passive "female." The fact of psychological bisexuality embarrasses all that we say on the subject and makes it more difficult to describe. (1)

This appears to me to be a philosophic abstraction indeed, a peculiarly metaphysical assumption. It does not seem to be a reasonable conclusion about actual men and women, or about males and females of any species. It is not even a plausible caricature. As an empty, armchair generalization, it might serve the confirmed misogynist who feels the need to taunt some woman. I can conceive of no practical or possible confirmation of this definition in the world we encounter through our sense perception. Certainly most men do not seek such passiveness in women as a desirable characteristic during sexual intercourse. Try applying Freud's definition to a tigress whose cubs are threatened or to a male rabbit pursued by a (female) beagle. Of course, if we accept the definition, we can and must call the tigress male (or predominantly male). The rabbit, despite its fame for male copulative prowess, must be pronounced a female. This appears to me to be a fair and accurate application of Freud's statement. I agree that the definition is insufficient and is, indeed, embarrassed by facts.

In his efforts to define what is sexually female and to distinguish this from what is sexually male, Freud seems to ignore the obvious fact that both men and women as human beings have much in common. As mammals they share what is shared also by squirrels, elephants, and whales of each sex. Surely we must recognize what is shared biologically by each sex in a species before we can see where to look for differences that are specifically sexual.

By confining his ultimate distinction to qualities plainly and characteristically shared not only by mankind regardless of sex, but also by mammals, reptiles, fish, and even by many invertebrates, Freud completely misses all chance of hitting upon anything like a definition of actualities.

Let us assume academically that only women have legs and only men have arms and that this constitutes their basic sexual distinction. Let us take as a proved absolute that arms are masculinity and accept as an article of faith that legs are femininity. Then our observations of people will immediately drive us to the conclusion that all males are in part sexually female, all females in part sexually male.

After such an arbitrary splitting apart of what perceptual experience reveals as homogeneous, we are forced in all subsequent examinations to give specious reports. These word-made inconsistencies then demand a second false assumption to bring us back to the world of common sense.

Patrick Mullahy, author of *Oedipus — Myth and Complex*, a book that sets out to summarize several dynamic theories of psychiatry, does not feel that this definition quite satisfied Freud. He explains:

The first meaning of the conception of masculinity and femininity desig-nating activity and passivity is for Freud the essential one and the one which he says has significance for psychoanalysis. And it agrees with his conception of the libido as "lawfully" and regularly of a masculine na-ture, whether in man or woman, whose object may also be either the man or the woman. Even when the libido is diverted to a passive aim it is al-ways active, always masculine. (2)

Many so-called feminists have rivaled Freud here in an opposite direction of illusion, ascribing all human virtue to woman and in-sisting that any merit found in the male must arise only from his luck in sharing some of her gender. Two quotations from *Modern Woman: the Lost Sex*, illustrate this:

The female is the race. . . . The lowest prostitute is yet better that the best of men . . . The female among all orders of life, man included, represents a higher stage of development than the male. (3)

Many of those who insist that all positive qualities are confined to one sex or the other are not able to see much charm in hetero-sexual mating. It is perhaps worthwhile to note that few of these women who vehemently denounce masculinity and extol the su-periority of the female are likely to impress the average person as particularly feminine. Some of them scarcely seem like women at all. The following statements are typical:

There is a sex war just as there is a class war. . . . I will incite this meeting to rebellion. Be militant each in your own way, I accept the responsibility for everything you do. . . . As indicating the extent of the present sex-re-volt we see a type of woman arising who believes in a state of society in which man will not figure in the life of woman except as the father of her child. . . . If young women, or perhaps those not so young, were to apply the sheer logic of common sense to life's contemporary complication, they could indeed summon many telling arguments for the homosexual way of life: it is the most remarkable method of simplifying the burdens of ex-istence in an age when these burdens have become truly intolerable, that can be imagined. (3)

But let us return to Freud, who apparently insists on the oppo-site and equally implausible absolute. Since the libido is hypothet-ical it may, unlike objective entities, be described any way one likes. This insistence, however, that, even when found in woman, libido is masculine, can hardly fail to evoke memory of early the-ologians who contended that woman has no soul.

Let us quote again from Mullahy's *Oedipus — Myth and Complex*:

However, Freud does not, in the end, think that active and passive can be said to be the ultimate differential traits of mankind. The fact that little girls can have plenty of aggressiveness was soon observed. And men for various reasons often manifest passive characteristics. (2)

What is meant by the statement that this fact was "soon observed"? Before, or after, such a definition of the female was devised? Can anyone doubt that this observation was made earlier than Neanderthal times by every child, or that it is embarrassing to receive the report of such a truism? It is worth remarking upon only when one tries to apply Freud's peculiarly unrealistic definition of woman. Mullahy continues:

For these and other reasons, Freud was never able to find, in any unequivocal fashion, any psychological characteristic that would clearly differentiate masculine and feminine. But his conclusions that women are a "riddle" is, even from a logical point of view, very curious. (2)

Men have said, sometimes in jest and often in earnest, that you simply cannot understand a woman. Much more difficult, however, than any actual woman is this bizarre verbal artifact set up in the region of metaphysics with which Freud has chosen to grapple. Apparently this bloodless and invisible nymph never quite satisfied him. Without modifying his definition of female as passivity, Freud nevertheless offers an ingenious scheme for telling boys from girls in actual life on this planet. Apparently in order to make this subtle distinction, he agrees to call women those "who are characterized as manifestly or preponderantly female by the possession of female genitals." (2) This, it seems to me, is the point from which any intelligent three-year-old child starts. No evidence of bisexuality has been obtained—except in a definition that Freud could not himself apply to anything in human experience. This at least brings us back to actual woman. And, should we so choose, we can prove her role male if we can catch her in lively activity— so long as we forget that Freud had to forswear this in practice.

So much difficulty in defining what is feminine and in distinguishing this from what is masculine might reasonably suggest caution. Undoubtedly a concept more realistic than one of femininity identified simply and totally with inertness is needed before attempting to find proof of abstruse and unconscious elements sexually female in the male. A better picture of woman as woman must be furnished before we can profitably search for her where she may be concealed in man. If we take Freud's word for it, that every passive characteristic is female, then, of course, all males immediately prove themselves part woman. Suppose, on the contrary, we accept Freud's other rule and recognize as women only those who have female genital organs. Following these instructions, we find nothing really bisexual in a practical sense about either man or woman.

It is difficult to understand how Freud could have hoped to explain biologic manifestations far simpler than woman by such a method. A scarcely less plausible definition might be made by saying that respiration is the function of the male only. Then, since we observe that women also breathe, we are driven to conclude that every woman is part male. Why should this diligent clinical investigator, widely regarded as one of the greatest in medical history, have turned so far from the actualities of experience to set up such unlikely hypothetical abstractions, and then have lost himself in tedious and unprofitable manipulations of metaphysical artifacts?

Having defined all human beings (and apparently all mammals) as sexually part male and part female, it was, to be sure, pertinent for Freud to explain just what this maleness and femaleness was, in a sexual sense. Only after we understand clearly what each essence is, and in what respects each differs from the other, can we test the claim that in man and in woman both essences are universally found. Wandering far from what can be directly tested, the most influential of all psychiatric investigators chose a peculiarly unrealistic absolute, and insisted that it be accepted as the definition of femininity. Psychiatric speculations and pronouncements of this sort impress me as having much in common with estimates by Empedocles, Anaximenes, and other early Greek philosophers about whether the essence of all matter is fire, or water, or air, or some other hypothetical monad. (4, 5) If we are trying to improve our understanding of actual woman, there are grave doubts about the practicality of such methods.

What definitions shall we, then, propose to identify satisfactorily the female monad and the male monad, and to distinguish between these imaginary entities? None at all. Such an approach to this problem would not be more likely to give a real solution than meditations by Thales and Heraclitus (4, 5) on the ultimate nature of the material world were likely to produce the steam engine, the radio, the jet plane, antibiotics, or air conditioning. I am convinced, furthermore, that at a practical and working level, the average teen-age boy, the factory worker who may just have finished grade school, already know far more in their own feelings and reactions about the femaleness of woman than philosophy can intellectualize. Aside from obvious points of anatomy, he has an excellent, and I think a rather accurate and genuinely felt, awareness of what a girl is like personally, and how she differs from a boy. Even the very unsophisticated know enough, unless their development has been marred by psychosexual disorder, to distinguish the girl at a hundred paces and to recognize her clearly as the uniquely appropriate sexual object.

It strikes me as remarkable that scholarly and laborious efforts should be directed toward estimating "maleness" and "female- ness" on the basis of traits and qualities arbitrarily chosen and as- sumed, more or less on hearsay, to constitute essential differences. An interesting article in a magazine for women is illustrative. Here we find a popularized report of conclusions reached by psycholo- gists and psychiatrists who have attempted to rate men (and women) according to the degree of masculinity (and femininity) shown by special tests. Let us try to be clear as to just what is be- ing estimated in such investigations. The following are given as the criteria according to which a Male-Female rating (M-F index) was determined:

The typical masculine personality is aggressive and domineering. There is little room for sympathy and sentiment. Physically the body is large, strong and muscular. The voice is deep and booming. . . . Femininity is marked by a passive and submissive nature. Physically the feminine indi- vidual is small and weak. The voice is soft and melodious. Such individu- als are tender, sympathetic and sentimental. (6)

With masculinity and femininity thus defined, it is not surpris- ing that the tests, however faithfully and scientifically performed, gave some curious results. Men of the "cave-man type" were sometimes found to show a very feminine M-F index. Policemen as a group revealed themselves as particularly feminine. The most feminine period in a woman's life turned out to be when she was in the eighth grade. Rather oddly, marriage made women grow more masculine, and lots of children caused both husband and wife to grow feminine. Some husbands were found to have M-F indexes which rated them as more feminine than their wives.

Undoubtedly these tests accurately measured what they were designed to measure—that is to say, the combination of pointless truisms and unrealistic suppositions that had been put into the definitions of what is male and what is female. Accordingly, the obvious inadequacies of the definitions, and not anything either new or pertinent about the sexes, are what is reflected back in the results of the investigation.

It is misleading and unprofitable to assume that various quali- ties or reactions, conscious or unconscious, in men must be called "feminine" until we have evidence that many of these qualities and reactions are not those common to humanity. As already men- tioned, the fact that both men and women have feet, hands, the need of food, and the inclination sometimes to drink a cocktail, has never been used as an argument for the bisexual theory. What, then, is offered in support of this theory by the fact that men and women also share the capacities of being at times aggressive and at other times compliant, of enjoying a stiff game of tennis, feeling compassion, acting with courage, speaking in a loud voice, and appreciating symphonic music?

SOURCES

1. Sigmund Freud, *An Outline of Psychoanalysis* (New York: W. W. Norton & Co., Inc., 1949), p. 89.

2. From *Oedipus—Myth and Complex*, by Patrick Mullahy; pp. 44–45. Thomas Nelson & Sons, New York. Copyright 1948 by Patrick Mullahy.

3. F. Lundberg and M. F. Farnham, *Modern Woman: The Lost Sex* (New York: Harper & Bros., 1947), pp. 454, 458.

4. Will Durant, *The Story of Philosophy* (New York: Simon & Schuster, Inc., 1933).

5. J. G. Hibben, *The Problems of Philosophy* (New York: Charles Scribner's Sons, 1898).

6. George Kisker, "How Feminine Can You Get?" *The Woman,* XXII (May 1949), 38–42.

Chapter 10
ADOLESCENT HERO WORSHIP

It is plain that many social influences shape and distort concepts and ideals of virility and womanhood during human growth and maturation. Let us rather consider these influences than strive at once for metaphysical explanations. Let us briefly note here a few relatively simple items of commonplace experience.

The average pubertal boy has striven for years to live up to the gang's standards. He has learned throughout this period to accept willingly some bumps and jolts on the football field, to take a few risks and scares in climbing trees, and not to show too much concern about the elegance of his attire. In this milieu of his it is probably more a virtue than a vice to have some dirt showing at times under his fingernails. He has no doubt come to enjoy handling earthworms and baiting them on fishhooks. His pleasure in this may well be related to his awareness that little girls usually recoil from such an act. Often this recoil is prompted less by the earthworm itself than by her choice of a reaction that is traditionally feminine. The pressures of the parental world in general have, on the contrary, been steadily exerted toward making the little boy conform to reasonable standards of neatness, politeness, safety, nonviolence, and compassion. Since he has little experience and maturity to enrich his judgments, he sees many choices only as two-valued, that is, either-or absolutes. (1) If he appears to be fastidious about getting dirt on his hands or clothes, if he is too squeamish to utter a few profane or inelegant words, he is likely to be branded as a sissy or called chicken. On certain occasions some show of compassion may be allowed without loss of face as a straight, reasonably hard guy, but one must be very careful not to indulge in the sort of sentimentality and softness that is thought of by the boys as distinguishing the female.

In a thousand ways, by ten thousand incidents, he is taught a lot about the attitudes, manners, idioms, and behavior that, in the eyes of his fellows, characterize the boy in contrast to the girl. He has thoroughly learned that playing with dolls, or indulging in any activity chiefly associated with girls, would be a major departure from his role—his role as one who is male by a small boy's normal standards. He must thoroughly identify himself with this basic immature core of male-image before he can dare to grow or extend his being into larger and more complex patterns of masculinity. He must make his foundation secure before he can afford to add to it. I do not think it is accurate to say that the new attributes he must acquire, the more complex reactions he must learn, are specifically feminine characteristics. They appear, rather, to be characteristics not really identified with either sex but with a basic human maturity shared equally by men and women.

Despite the postulated "latent period" (2) he has, long before puberty, been well aware of distinct and unambiguous genital excitability and has felt what the adult world terms "lust" or "evil thoughts" about girls. If he has avoided personal intimacy with them, it is not because they failed to stimulate his erotic feelings but because intimacy with them might, in his eyes, constitute joining the girls and thereby proving himself not much of a male. Perhaps he has had genital exploits with girls; but if so, they have probably not been experiences of shared personal devotion. It is unlikely that they have fostered attitudes that could be called romantic. At this stage a distinctly negative personal evaluation may arise toward any girl willing to participate.

The chances are that the average boy has experimented with masturbation before puberty. If he has carried out genital stimulation with other boys, it has been in an atmosphere where the boys are talking about girls—which ones will do what; in rather coarse, aggressive terms, bragging or speculating on what they themselves have done sexually or would like to do sexually to girls. Clinical experience leaves me with the impression that such mutual masturbation is rare. Talk in vulgar terms about sc . . . g or f . . . g girls, and so on, however, appears to be almost universal. Only in serious psychiatric situations does the preadolescent or adolescent boy regard another boy as anything even remotely resembling a sweetheart.

The adolescent, on reaching the age for having dates with girls and trying to establish a romantic relation with one of them, is still equipped only with jejune concepts of masculinity and confused orientations about love and sex. He still has to learn that it is not unmanly to risk his pride and sentiments in personal relations with a girl. It is not entirely easy for him to give up any item of the childish and incomplete maleness he has acquired in his role of a small boy. He is for a while afraid to risk any modifications of this concept in efforts to acquire the broader, less black-or-white, and far more complex and more real masculinity demanded of the mature male. The girls tempt him; but fears of blundering, of appearing as an affected fool or a tongue-tied lout to the girls and to the boys, restrain him and prompt him to deride the dating and dancing activities of his fellows. He is in a transition period where he has to reorient himself and find new and less superficial criteria for the ideal of manliness.

Traits popularly regarded in adult life as distinctively feminine or masculine are not always clear-cut and reciprocally exclusive. The boy of twelve or thirteen might name courage, endurance, toughness, and boldness as masculine and, as feminine, mercy, fear, sensitiveness, shyness, a concern with what is beautiful, and so on. It is unlikely, however, that any boy at this age will go so far afield into unreality as Freud did in his metaphysical definition.

In the behavior to be observed in actual people, I find little evidence for assuming that qualities such as those just listed have much to do with distinguishing the male from the female. The most masculine and courageous men known to me have usually been men of extraordinary gentleness and compassion. Many of them impress me as experiencing in an extreme degree both fear and shyness. The most feminine of women in real life are not characterized by a lack of courage, nor do they regularly show more real concern for what is beautiful than men do. This indicates to me that all these qualities are those of the human being rather than sexually distinguishing characteristics. No bisexuality need be postulated. All reasonably observant adults must realize that at puberty the concepts of these qualities are often, if not usually, distorted, exaggerated, and sometimes paradoxical.

For instance, the cowardly braggart may seem supremely masculine to a teen-ager; so, too, the frigid, callous, scheming flirt may appear as the essence of what is sexually passionate in the female. Scarlett O'Hara in *Gone With the Wind* (3) is an excellent example of how even in maturity such a confusing appearance is often maintained. Many traits puerilely conceived of as distinguishing what is male from what is female can be found equally in each sex. The situations in which a woman most often shows industry and courage may differ from those in which men are typically pictured. Only a very foolish observer could deny, however, that it is not in her nature so to behave. Unlike such traits, the basic reaction of knowing that one is a woman and needs a man as a mate, and vice versa, is not vague or confused except in psychiatric disorder and sometimes in psychiatric literature. Even in the adolescent any serious confusion on this point is a very grave manifestation indeed.

It is scarcely surprising that adolescent concepts of male and female contain a residue of once useful but now artificial distinctions held over from earlier years during which both the little boy and the little girl were groping their ways with caution. No matter what they have been told, adolescents still lack the emotional experience to foresee accurately the more mature social roles as male and female toward which the years are taking them.

In contrast to efforts to explain all social feelings and all human interests by the roundabout hypothesis that they are sexual-instincts-inhibited-in-their-aims (chiefly perverse aims) is Adler's conclusion that love "is only a special case of sociability." According to Nicole:

Adler would consider sex as another, more intense, form of friendship, and not friendship as a modification of sex. Consequently, he repudiates entirely the notion of sex-love leading—via homosexuality—to communal feeling. (4)

This viewpoint, though scarcely original, certainly coincides better with common-sense observation. It comes far nearer accounting for demonstrable human behavior, and it does not require a metaphysically postulated monad which defies adequate definition and which must be assumed on faith as existing in the unconscious.

Theodor Reik, one of Freud's early and prominent followers, is unable to accept the dogma that feelings of tenderness, affection, interest, and love come only from sexual drive. Extensive experience with analytic method brought Reik to the conclusion that love and sexual desire, far from being identical, emerge from different sources, that they may or may not combine. He believes it is plainly erroneous to insist that affection and interest are only sublimated or disguised manifestations of impulses which are unconsciously sexual. He speaks of Freud's libido theory as

. . . the amazing misinterpretation psychoanalysis has presented to the world. Here Freud made a magnificent mistake. Fertile, but not creative, many of his pupils, following in the footsteps of their master, have made psychoanalytical literature the richest source we possess of misinformation about sex and love. (5)

Reik does not hesitate to emphasize the errors introduced by unjustified extension of the term "libido." He says:

. . . It originally meant the energy of the sex-drive, and nothing else. For Freud it also took on the meaning of the emotional power of affection and tenderness directed towards a person, towards several persons, and even towards abstract ideas. Freud had, like Procrustes in Greek mythology, an inclination to extend and to stretch a term until it fitted his idea. Such behavior is comparable to the attitude of the stubborn opponent with whom Abraham Lincoln had once to argue:
"Well, let's see," said Lincoln to this farmer, "how many legs has a cow?"
"Four, of course," was the quick answer.
"That's right," said Mr. Lincoln. "Now suppose we call the cow's tail a leg. How many legs would the cow have?"
"Why, five of course."
"Now, there's where you're wrong," argued Lincoln. "Simply calling a cow's tail a leg does not make it a leg."
Similarly, calling love and tenderness a form of sex does not make them sexual. Identifying affection and sex by using the same name for both does not make them the same.
Freud, however, warned his followers and students not to take the word sex in the old literal meaning of the term. He tried again and again to convince them that in psychoanalysis all the feelings of affection and devotion are included in the new meaning. For some time he preferred to speak of "psychosexuality" in order that he might not be misunderstood to have meant the primitive sex-desire. The attempt was vain. The word proved stronger than Freud's will to change its connotation. This deep-sea fisher threw a wide net into the ocean of the human soul. He hoped to catch too many big fish in a single haul: sex, love, tenderness, friendship. But what he netted was only sex. The others escaped through the wide meshes of the net . . . He skirted around the problem of love in assuming that it was an appendix to sex. Thus he really made an effort not to get to the problem but to get rid of it. The effect is not so much to solve the question as to keep it under cover. To the psychoanalysts affection appeared to be only a poor facsimile of sexual desire. They had no difficulty in by-passing the problem; their theoretical blinders prevented them from seeing it. The few who were aware of its existence hoped that it would disappear if they permanently looked away. An original idea could not be inserted, even edgewise, into their consolidated system. Love is sex minus sex and that is all. (6)

Actually we know that sexual acts and relations frequently occur not only as expression of the "more intense form of friendship" ordinarily called "being in love," but without the presence of even a mild but real friendship. Surely, few will argue that friendship necessarily accompanies the sexual satisfaction obtained by men in visiting houses of prostitution, or that the woman in earning her fee is likely to develop toward a transient client personal feelings that merit such a term. Who can doubt that sexually sensuous and genital satisfactions are often sought first

by the immature male either with embarrassed indifference toward the partner as a person, or with puerile ideas of quasi-virility
and impulses to dominate, that cause him to regard her as being
despoiled, a sort of victim seduced by his competitive prowess?
Such attitudes often persist in a pathology of adult sex-and-love
relations.

These nonaffectionate, essentially competitive, and personally
derogatory attitudes are more accurately reflected in common
phrases than in ordinary description. Such remarks are often uttered in words that make very plain the lack of any feelings either
affectionate, or friendly, or even respectful. Even the verb "love"
seldom indicates regard or affection in such usage. The very fact
that our oldest and strongest terms for sexual intercourse (for
which "making love" is the most familiar euphemism) serve also
regularly as synonyms for "cheat," "swindle," "foul up the
works," and the like, is significant. These terms are also among the
most popular to convey outrage or extreme insult. The real meaning of *snafu*, and the conversation in World War II novels, (7) are
illustrative. Though the words "f . . . you," if spoken in wrath, may
start a fight, they, like "son of a bitch," are in some groups used
paradoxically on occasion to express affection in a rough, unsenti-
mental idiom. (8) Other words not literally indicating sexuality,
aggressiveness, or treachery, may through the context of a phrase
be used to express these things. "They sure did it to John Brown,"
may be a way of saying that some people trusted by Brown callously and deceitfully swindled him out of valuable possessions.
The remark, "That fellow sure did it to Mary Brown," may convey
not only that he had sexual relations with her, but imply also that
he slyly and callously took advantage of her with an attitude of
personal indifference or contempt.

The manifestations of sexual desire without affection or devotion, and even with accompanying hate or contempt can, of
course, be accounted for by the libido theory. One can assume that
eros is adulterated by its opposite, the destructive instinct, in various proportions of mixture. There seems, however, no need, aside
from a partisan need to gain support for the theory, to insist on
such interpretations. Actual observation reveals people seeking
genital satisfaction with or without love and respect for the partner, with almost infinite degrees and kinds of interpersonal attitudes. So, too, we see great variations of feeling, distaste, liking,
indifference, respect, devotion, tender regard in the relation of
people to objects poorly designed to arouse or to satisfy any sensuously sexual aim. A fifteen-year-old girl may hold in affectionate respect her grandmother, or the mare she has raised from a
tiny colt; an angler may really crave the spinning reel and rod he
cannot afford and also highly regard the canoe to which he has for

years devoted affectionate care. A lonely widow might find pleasure in the lively little parakeet for whose welfare she develops a true consideration. Is it reasonable to assume that all these familiar items of human experience can be accounted for *only* as disguised expression of an unconscious desire for genital relations? Is it not more likely that man, and other mammals, are motivated by more than the two urges, for sex and for death, postulated by Freud?

I do not think that efforts to explore the unconscious, however assiduous, will lead to a real discovery of evidence, in the examples just mentioned, for the instinct-inhibited-in-its-aim. The evidence that has been offered lies in a redefinition of terms to support the assumption.

As the male matures, his sexually sensuous aims are more likely to arise from (or to join naturally) strong and positive personal feelings toward the sexual object, with affection, devotion, adoration, and the like, which might be called intense and specialized forms or developments of friendship and affection. So, too, these more broadly personal attitudes and relations may grow out of or join what was at first chiefly a self-centered sensuous aim. Considering the immense variety of human attitudes and reactions, it does not seem necessary for practical purposes to insist on either sex-sensuality or social feeling as a philosophical monad from which the other evolves. The real sexual love of those happily mated appears to be not merely an additive mixture of intense friendship, plus special devotion and adoration, plus true pride of each in the other, plus sensual sexuality, but, instead, something more like an integration of these and other affective components into what is different from, and more than, a sum of the parts. The gaseous elements, hydrogen and oxygen, uniting to form water become an entity that is not like any gas at all. So, too, the human affective elements that participate in real love cannot separately or in mere addition account for the properties and the nature of this unique experience.

At this point, a distinction strongly emphasized by Freud despite implications of the libido theory deserves attention:

Freud warns us not to confuse identification with "object choice." In the first case the boy wants to be like his father. But "when he makes him the object of his choice, he wants to have him, to possess him," as his sexual object. (9)

Not only common sense but also this plausible and useful point made by Freud is sometimes overlooked by those who can see in hero-worship and friendship only the manifestations of an instinct-inhibited-in-its-aim. The real but unconscious aim assumed is, of course, that of homosexual physical relations.

A rather striking example of confusion about such matters can be furnished from Ellis' *The Folklore of Sex*. In this the author points out the popularity of magazines devoted to weight-lifting and body-building which display "almost nude pictures of well-muscled males" and assumes that this popularity must indicate homosexual interest. (10) While it is not unlikely that such magazines and pictures may appeal to the homosexual, can anyone be so blind as to ignore the typical boy's reaction? This, of course, is to find some way of developing himself into a paragon of physical virility and thus be sexually desirable to the girls. To my knowledge, no one has yet said or implied that the average woman's interest in magazines and advertisements displaying cosmetics, new styles in dress, voluptuous models posed in sheer nightgowns or lacy lingerie, indicates Lesbian rather than normal inclinations. A sophistication which prevents one from recognizing what is so obvious can be misleading.

These things are thoroughly understood by most teen-agers, by the fellow at the filling station, the bricklayer, and the lad at the supermarket. The attitudes of such people are, one might say, based on little academic knowledge or scientific experience. This, of course, is true. Such an orientation is so basic and the stimuli determining it so plain that no book learning at all is necessary to establish it.

Those whom the ordinary boy seeks to emulate, to choose as models, as objects of hero worship, perhaps are the father of the boy, and other males whom he admires and indeed loves. He wishes to be like them and to do as they do; not to have them in such a relation to himself as he wants to have his girl. Nor does he seek any role with them even remotely approximate to the role in which he places his girl in relation to himself. In normal situations, an unusual or extreme degree of attachment or devotion between friends of the same sex is not an indication that, if the friendship continues to develop, these two people will begin to feel lascivious impulses toward each other or to seek each other as sexual mates.

Any man, except one with serious psychosexual disorder, would in fact, if driven by erotic deprivation or any other influence that might block his natural sexual aims, be inclined to seek almost any other substitutive activity than perverse relations with an admired and devoted friend. What could appear to an ordinary man more preposterous than for his best friend to begin making eyes at him like a flirtatious girl, or to show signs of that specific interest in his body that is naturally stimulated in men by the body of a woman? A sad and unprepossessing caricature of friendship is here superimposed upon the grim caricature of a situation for love-making.

The reasonably healthy pubertal boy may idolize Mickey Mantle, Tarzan, General Robert E. Lee, Jack Dempsey, Abraham Lincoln, or perhaps Superman. Such personalities, currently real, historical, or imaginary, do not appeal to the boy as those with whom he longs to have a date with opportunities for kissing and petting. Most remarkable evidence would be necessary to show that the teen-age boy really has this wish unconsciously but simply cannot realize it. The degree of his hero worship obviously does not indicate the strength of concealed impulses to relate himself to such figures as a sexual mate. The masculine features of his ideal figure do not, except in a perversion of ordinary response, stimulate him toward effeminacy. It is to be like this male image that the hero worshipper yearns, like him, to seek a woman as mate. The more he can be like Superman, or perhaps like Dick Tracy, the more his girl will admire him. The deep intimacy and loyal devotion of the old friend who puts his arm around the shoulders of another man, does not in healthy human relationship mask a real but unconscious longing to lure him into a passionate kiss, or to carry out genital or any other sort of activity with him such as men naturally desire with women. It is difficult to understand how learned men can be persuaded by metaphysical argument to ignore so much that is familiar in human experience, and seek unnecessary explanations for the obvious in implausible postulations unsupported by evidence.

Never, in the study of any patient, have I encountered a specific object-choice for a person of the same sex in preference to one of the other sex, an active pursuit or acceptance of the person of the same sex as a sweetheart, except in those who plainly showed personality disorder that was serious indeed. This is not to say that everyone who in adolescence has suffered from such a profound confusion is doomed to major psychiatric illness for life. Though auditory hallucinations, psychotic depressions, genuine delusions, and other symptoms are serious, we all know that these, too, occur in people who may recover and lead happy and effective lives.

SOURCES

1. Alfred Korzybski, *Science and Sanity*, 2d ed. (Lancaster, Pa.: The Science Press, 1941).

2. J. F. Brown, *The Psychodynamics of Abnormal Behavior* (New York: McGraw-Hill Book Co., Inc., 1940), pp. 198–202.

3. Margaret Mitchell, *Gone With the Wind* (New York: The Macmillan Co., 1936).

4. J. E. Nicole, *Psychopathology* (Baltimore: The Williams & Wilkins Co., 1947), p. 30.

5. From *Psychology of Sexual Relations*, p. 19. Copyright 1945 by Theodor Reik. Reprinted by permission of Rinehart & Co., Inc., New York, publishers.

6. *Ibid.*, pp. 16–17.

7. Norman Mailer, *The Naked and the Dead* (New York: Rinehart & Co., Inc., 1948).

8. Richard Tregaskis, *Guadalcanal Diary* (New York: Random House, Inc., 1943).

9. From *Oedipus—Myth and Complex*, by Patrick Mullahy; p. 40. Thomas Nelson & Sons, New York. Copyright 1948 by Patrick Mullahy.

10. Albert Ellis, *The Folklore of Sex* (New York: Charles Boni, 1951), pp. 173–74.

Chapter 11
THE DYNAMICS OF ILLUSION

The popular "dynamic" concepts we have been discussing continue to exert profound and peculiar effects on psychiatric theory. The definition given by Hinsie and Shatzky in their *Psychiatric Dictionary* apparently reflects full faith in "bisexuality, the normal and universal homoerotic component of the libido," and in other assumptions we have discussed:

homosexuality (al'i-ti). *n*. The state of being in love with one belonging to the same sex. Up to the early part of the twentieth century, this generally meant a form of sexual perversion. Thus, C. H. Hughes (*Alienist and Neurologist*, 24, February 1903) defined it as a perverted sexual desire for someone of the same sex. With the development of psychoanalysis, however, there came to be less emphasis on sex proper and a correspondingly broader connotation assigned to the term sexual. Today genital relations between members of the same sex is called homogenitality; when the relationship is sexual, but not genitally expressed, the term homosexual is employed. When the relationship between them, while very close and erotically bound, is well sublimated, the term homoerotic is used. (1)

Are we to understand from this that homosexuality, though once considered a form of sexual perversion is now recognized as normal? If we broaden the connotation of the term "sexual" and apply it to all forms of friendliness do we thereby make the "perverted sexual desire for one of the same sex" less abnormal? We may do what we like with words, but this, unfortunately, does not miraculously transform their referents.

"Homogenitality" is apparently used to distinguish inverts who carry out such acts as fellatio or sodomy from those who perhaps restrict themselves to kissing and petting ("homosexuality") but recognize a specific sensual attraction toward those of their own sex.

The third term, "homoerotic," implies that all other very friendly relations are based on a libidinous or lascivious attraction which, remaining unconscious, is sublimated or expressed in disguised and attenuated modalities.

According to Freud's libido theory, it is, as we have noted, impossible to account for any real friendship between two males, or the reciprocal personal concern and interest of two females, without assuming it to be this sort of sublimation. Full faith in libido theory demands this drastic redefinition of sexuality. Some confusion, as we have also noted, arises when by this extension of definition we verbally identify two such diverse groups as the inverts discarded by the State Department and all normal teen-age boys. If this theory is established by scientific evidence, then there is good reason to argue for such a redefinition, and for a drastic revision of ordinary concepts of human relations. If, on the other hand, facts do not adequately support the theory, it seems reasonable to suggest that the theory be altered.

Let us consider the sort of evidence that has been offered, and particularly let us examine the methods by which these unconscious feelings and inclinations, alleged to be present in all people, are discovered and identified. Surely no fairer example of these methods could be obtained than from the major articles in Freud's *Collected Papers*. Ernest Jones, their editor, writes that "all Professor Freud's other work and theories are essentially founded on the clinical investigations of which these papers are the only published record." (2)

Freud's long report published under the title *From the History of an Infantile Neurosis* (3) can, I believe, be taken as a typical example of this work. In it a dream recalled by the twenty-six-year-old patient as having occurred when he was four years of age is confidently interpreted. The chief conclusions reached about this patient appear to be based fundamentally on this interpretation. Freud reports the entire dream as follows:

I dreamt that it was night and that I was lying in my bed. (My bed stood with its foot towards the window; in front of the window there was a row of old walnut trees. I know it was winter when I had the dream, and night-time.) Suddenly the window opened of its own accord, and I was terrified to see that some white wolves were sitting on the big walnut tree in front of the window. There were six or seven of them. The wolves were quite white, and looked more like foxes or sheep-dogs, for they had big tails like foxes and they had their ears pricked like dogs when they are attending to something. In a great terror, evidently of being eaten up by the wolves, I screamed and woke up. . . .

The only piece of action in the dream was the opening of the window; for the wolves sat quite still and without any movement on the branches of the tree, to the right and left of the trunk, and looked at me. It seemed as though they had riveted their whole attention upon me. (4)

Freud draws from this dream a number of conclusions by interpreting its various items symbolically. From its association with a few fairy tales familiar to the patient in childhood and with some not particularly extraordinary early memories he devises an astonishing explanation of the patient's illness. Freud confidently states that the dream reveals in considerable detail an experience the patient was subjected to approximately two and a half years earlier, when he was eighteen months old. Fragment after fragment of the dream is used by Freud to derive proof that the infant at that time saw his parents while they were having sexual intercourse. He is quite confident that the dream reveals that the parents had intercourse three times in succession while the infant observed them and also that the *a tergo* position was chosen for their activities. He maintains also that the patient, at eighteen months of age, was so affected by this scene that he had a bowel movement as a pretext to make an outcry and interrupt the parents in their still enthusiastic love-making. In this interpretation the number of the wolves, which the patient recalled as being six or seven, is regarded as an effect of the dreamer's unconscious processes to disguise what he had really seen—that is to say, the two parents. The fact that the dream scene is quite stationary and the wolves make no movement is accepted as evidence (by reversal) for vigorous coital activity by the amorous couple. The appearance of keen attention noticeable in the dream-wolves who stood in the tree, according to Freud, indicates an intense and absorbing interest on the part of the infant in what he was watching. The fact that the four-year-old boy experienced fear of the wolves in his dream is said by Freud to represent a terror experienced earlier by the infant at the sight of his mother's external genital organs when seen as an infant of eighteen months. The interpreter assumes without question that this alleged sight contributed to the belief that the mother had been mutilated sexually. From these points Freud reaches the confident conclusion that when the boy at four years of age had the dream he was suffering from a profound dread of castration by his father. The fact that the wolves who appeared in the dream are remembered as having particularly long tails is considered sound evidence of an opposite state (taillessness) and hence a substantial confirmation of this disquieting dread. This preoccupation is said by Freud to have been the chief deterrent to this four-year-old boy's dominating impulse, assumed to be a specific and strong yearning for his father to carry out upon him sexual relations *per* *anum.* In the entire report no item of objective evidence is offered to support these conclusions. Freud appears, however, to be completely convinced that all this is correct and adequately established. In fact, he insists that his whole study of this case must be "all a piece of nonsense from start to finish, or everything took place just as I have described it above." (5)*

If today one does not find it easy to accept such methods as this as scientific or these conclusions as really plausible, should it be assumed that an unconscious pathologic resistance is distorting the sceptic's judgment, that unconscious prejudices of his own prevent him from recognizing adequately proved facts? When a method so elastic is employed can we not easily come by it to virtually any conclusion that we might choose? Though the use of symbolism and analogy may indeed be useful in formulating hypotheses, an unsupported appeal merely to symbolism or analogy can scarcely be regarded as a means of establishing valid evidence. If such assumptions are made about what is in the unconscious but what is never made conscious, then surely something more substantial than analogy must be offered to demonstrate or corroborate them. Can we not accurately say that such methods can be used in such a way as to constitute a dynamics of illusion?

It may be said that in condensation the real supporting evidence cannot be adequately presented. This, I admit, is true. It is only when examined in detail that the nature of such evidence can be fairly judged. The full report must be read to see how support for each implausible assumption is sought in making additional assumptions that are often still more implausible. Proof is not adduced by carefully gathering evidence in small items, until out of these individually inconclusive or only suggestive data there emerges a reasonably strong and progressively accumulating indication of plausibility. On the contrary, the more Freud seizes upon to support his amazing claim about the Wolf-Man, the more truly incredible everything becomes. A fact, however small, can lend some little weight to an argument. Additional speculations, and assumptions piled upon assumptions, only compound improbability and at last approach the limits of the preposterous.

**** Years after the original publication of this paper Freud added a number of additional pages. In these he entertains the possibility that the astonishing experience which he has attributed to the infant might not have been an actuality. After a good deal of debate about this he seems again to conclude that his original interpretation of the dream was after all correct. He nevertheless insists that, even if the events he was led by the dream to believe had occurred at age eighteen months were actually derived later from fantasy, the four-year-old boy's specific impulses for the father to carry out acts of sodomy upon him and his intense fear of castration are still to be regarded as valid. (6)

It does not seem surprising that Freud, before announcing the significance of this dream about wolves by a four-year-old child and presenting his construction of what he claims happened two and a half years earlier, in infancy, should write: "I have now reached the point at which I must abandon the support of the analysis. I am afraid it will also be the point at which the reader's belief will abandon me." (7)

After assuming all the details mentioned above about an alleged scene witnessed by the patient at age eighteen months, Freud asks only for provisional acceptance of his claim. He promises to allay all doubts with evidence as the discussion progresses, and also to tell later how the infant finally interrupted his parents. Nothing recognizable as real evidence is brought forward; we get only further assumptions on the basis of faint resemblances and arbitrarily used symbolisms. Even faint resemblances are not always needed to reach the desired conclusions, since the distinct lack of a resemblance is also accepted as proof equally valid.

Freud does not, however, neglect his promise to tell us how the infant interrupted his parents. Some forty pages afterward he writes:

I have already hinted at an earlier point in my story that one portion of the content of the primal scene has been kept back. I am now in a position to produce this missing portion. The child finally interrupted his parents' intercourse by passing a stool, which gave him an excuse for screaming. (8)

Years of analysis of the patient apparently never brought out one shred of memory to confirm this alleged episode imagined by Freud in such vivid detail. No facts are offered to support the contention that, on this or any other occasion, the patient ever saw his parents having intercourse. Freud does not even report evidence of this as a conscious fantasy. He says, however, of the additional assumption that the infant brought the activities of the parents to an end by defecation: "The patient accepted this concluding act when I had constructed it, and appeared to confirm it by producing 'transitory symptoms.'" (8)

Many years later, Freud still expressed absolute conviction that his analysis of this patient's dream proved beyond doubt that he labored under the fear of castration. In *The Problem of Anxiety* he states:

The Russian's fear of being eaten by a wolf contains no suggestion of castration, it is true; through oral regression the idea has been removed too far from the phallic stage; but the analysis of his dream makes any other proof superfluous. (9)

This I think is a fair demonstration of the methods by which alleged evidence has been obtained for the belief in universal castration fear, for the assumptions of bisexuality, of a normal homoerotic component of the libido, and for many other major articles of the currently popular creed of "dynamic" psychiatry. These articles have become so reverently cherished that many insist the definition of relatively simple and familiar terms must be altered so as to coincide with them and offer a specious verbal confirmation.

I have mentioned the elasticity of the methods by which Freud drew his remarkable conclusions from the dream of the Wolf-Man. Studies published today in our best and most respected psychiatric journals afford interesting demonstrations of this elasticity. Reasoning also by analogy, assuming that either similarities or dissimilarities justify identification, learned investigators present evidence of even more remarkable discoveries within the unconscious. Some of these reports "clearly reveal" through dream interpretation a psychic trauma sustained three or four decades earlier when the dreamer was an embryo. Sometimes the trauma is found to have been caused by the embryo's fear of the father's penis during intercourse of those who were eventually to become the patient's parents. These reports explain "dynamically" how such an alleged event has caused the patient's illness and, without hesitation, announce the relief of symptoms effected by such explanations. Let us quote from Peerbolte's article in *The Psychiatric Quarterly*: (10)

In the matter of pre-natal traumata the author experienced some resistance against accepting the possibility the unborn child could react to pre-natal sexual intercourse. This resistance, however, had to pass when a female patient told this dream; "I am in a church, all is good. But then Christ enters. He has a wooden leg and I become extremely afraid of the rhythmical clashing of His foot on the floor." (11)

According to the interpreter of this dream: "The wooden leg may be associated to the swollen foot of Oedipus."* He states, however, that on a deeper level it represents the penis of the dreamer's father and indicates that during intercourse with her mother, while the patient was an embryo, she was traumatized emotionally by its invasions. He seems to have little or no doubt that "the extreme anxiety and the disturbance of silence and security (in the dream) indicate a prenatal experience in this case." Final confirmation for this conclusion, the investigator seems to feel,

---

**** Even a person with a mediocre imagination, it seems to me, might by similarity or contrast associate the wooden leg with hundreds or even thousands of other things.

emerges when "interpretations of this dream in this way caused the anxiety to disappear at once." (11)

The same medical observer explains at some length the romantic nuances of a love affair each embryo has with the placenta. The placenta, dream interpretations lead him to believe, always takes the male role regardless of the sex of the embryo. Evidence for these early adventures is regularly discovered in the dreams of adult patients. (12, 13)

Peerbolte reports further details of his investigations:

> If abortion is threatened by accidents during gestation, one of the most important questions is whether the placenta is damaged and to what extent it is hurt. When accidents occur, one may discover, in dreams, the reactions of the unborn child. In one case the injury to the placenta was symbolized by a fur garment with a rip in it. . . . In another case, there was a nightmare in which a leak of water into a room indicated an unsuccessful attempt to produce abortion. (11)

This rip in the fur garment and the leaking water are, to be sure, as suggestive of an injury to the placenta as the details of the Wolf-Man's dream are to the remarkable experiences and reactions Freud ascribed to him at the age of eighteen months.

Fodor, also reporting in one of our most responsible medical publications, offers young physicians who seek knowledge of psychiatry an account of the existence and the psychic activities of a bodiless, immaterial being. This so-called "double," revealed by dynamic methods, is, we are told, a sort of immaterial twin of the opposite sex which all living people possess. When a male zygote is conceived, what about the potential female that might have been, had a different spermatozoon reached the ovum first? Though bodiless, she is reported as being quite active and as exerting a remarkable influence on her biologically real brother all his life. By dream interpretation the therapist receives important communications from the "double" through the unconscious of the living patient. (14)

In "The Search for the Beloved," Fodor informs readers of *The Psychiatric Quarterly* that "occasionally, a dream of defiance will point to the lost self as having a dream life of its own, in which fantasies of liberation, tragic resignation, or revenge are dominant motives." (15) Reasoning along such lines, the investigator demonstrates the basic psychodynamics of illness, offers proofs and explanations of bisexuality, and confidently clarifies other matters.

Let us return to Peerbolte as he discovers prenatal experiences from what his patients dream several decades later and from them confirms the findings of Fodor as readily as Ferenczi and Abraham confirmed those of Freud. Here is the dream of a young woman:

Now I am with a lot of other people in what appears to be an airship moving in space between the earth and the sky. We are going somewhere, but the destination is unknown. The moon or a similar object, is, however, quite visible from the space ship. There is something wrong with the moon. I see it with a dark shadow spreading from the right-hand side to the middle. It looks rather similar to the real shadows on the moon, but this is only one shadow and is very dark and clear in outline. A substance is flowing out the shadow part and into the sky surrounding it on the right. This is discoloring the sky's texture. I am very much concerned about it. I wish to speak to someone and I describe the moon as being angry, with some disturbance inside it which threatens our safety. Nobody seems very interested but me. Throughout the whole of this journey I go in fear of the disturbance on the moon getting worse and something happening then that will kill us. (16)

Peerbolte has no difficulty in seeing precisely what all this means. He writes:

This dream depicts the prenatal state; the moon obviously symbolizes the placenta—the dreamer's double, the male who cannot afford to pay for her food. [In an earlier part of the same dream the lady had gone into a store with an unknown man who offered to buy food for her.] As already mentioned her mother had had an automobile accident in the sixth month of pregnancy; and in this dream, the injury to the placenta is symbolized by the threatening shadow on the moon. The substance flowing out of the moon must mean blood. (This patient had produced several dreams in which the color orange had indicated blood, a mixture of red and hazel.) It is notable that she depicts the moon as angry. Here is the source of her aggressiveness. (16)

Notice how these explanations emerge—how readily and how absolutely free of doubt. We are told forthwith that "the dream depicts." The moon "obviously" symbolizes the placenta. The substance flowing out of the moon "must" mean blood. Are these methods fundamentally different from those used by Freud in his discoveries about the Wolf-Man? In both we find an explanation of cause and effect by free and confident interpretation of dream symbols, by the identification of A with B because of some similarity, or fancied similarity, or because of a difference. Freud sought in his interpretation evidence for castration fear, for bisexuality, for Oedipal conflicts, for anal eroticism, and for homosexual desires in the son for his father. Fodor and Peerbolte are looking for intrauterine experiences and by the same methods have no difficulty in discovering them in the dreams of their patients.

In fact, the very dream that Freud used to convince himself that his patient at eighteen months of age witnessed all those details of intercourse between his parents lends itself just as readily to an analysis supporting the claims of Fodor and Peerbolte. Why, for instance, should not the big walnut tree represent a penis? And because of its size, why not the father's penis? The dreamer is lying in darkness and silence within a bed. Might this not indicate a fetus snug within the womb? The foot of the bed points toward a window. Who can say that this aperture giving outlet to the closed room does not suggest the opening through which birth occurs? The long foxlike tails of the wolves plainly resemble the umbilical cord, and, at the same time, can be used to confirm our assumption that the tree symbolizes a penis. The long noses of the wolves obviously give further support to this interpretation, if any were needed. To Freud, the number of the wolves, *six* or *seven*, indicates a distortion effected unconsciously by the dreamer's resistance. This, he declares, is designed to conceal the fact that it was *two*, the mother and father, who were observed in the sexual act.

Would it not seem equally reasonable to say that the number, *six* or *seven*, might point to the month of gestation? Its uncertainty can still be said to indicate the work of repression in response to a traumatic experience. Surely this sudden opening of the window, through which emerges an image of the huge tree (and a walnut tree at that) might indicate that the intrauterine fetus was disturbed by the paternal penis as it entered the vagina to agitate and threaten him at close range. The terror inspired by the dream-scene is indeed appropriate. The immobility of the wolves, as Freud emphasizes, is a reversal indicating vigorous activity. This is far more applicable if we grant that it was as a fetus that the dreamer actually got shaken up by the motions of coitus and the repeated intrusions of the father's male organ. Who can doubt that such a trauma was sufficient to play an important part in the uncertainty as to whether the symbolic wolves numbered *six* or *seven*? Who would deny that this ambiguous figure may conceal a smaller number, perhaps *one* or *two*, that will establish the first or second month (or hour) of fetal life as the date of this highly significant event? Would not resistance to the idea that a very early embryo (or a zygote) might retain, through preverbal mechanisms, the affective record of such an experience, act to distort the figure toward something more plausible at conscious levels? By furnishing, in the manifest content, material suggesting six or seven months as the age of the fetus, the dream-work discloses its subtlety.

Perhaps we are still too superficial in our exploration. Surely the wolves themselves exquisitely symbolize spermatozoa. They are animals which, like the protozoa, sweep on to the hunt, vigorously active and in multitudinous packs. The rapacity of the wolf is proverbial. Attacking his victim with savage jaws, he chews his way into the flesh. So, too, with the spermatozoon. He drives boldly at the inert and helpless ovum with an assault that tears into her flesh. The unusually prominent tails on all the dream wolves faithfully represent the most characteristic feature of the spermatozoon, its conspicuous caudal appendage.

"They were looking at him with strained attention." Freud could only fit this element of the dream into his interpretation by assuming that it was "twisted completely round." (17) The strained attention with which the dream wolves stared at the dreamer do not, he decided, represent attentiveness on the part of the parents, whom he says they symbolize, but on the part of the dreamer who, at the age of eighteen months, was studying his parents so assiduously.

Let us leave these relatively superficial levels of infantile experience and, without bias, consider the phenomena of conception. Now what do we find? Could such strained attention ever apply more accurately than to the searching spermatozoa? Fired by primeval urge, utterly dedicated to biologic mission, they sight the victim, or somehow sense its proximity. What attention could be more totally devoted, more rapt, than that given by the successful spermatozoon as it rushes toward the ovum!

At this point, like Freud, I fear that there is danger of parting company with the reader, or with his credulity. Nevertheless, I must continue, for we have now come upon the heart of the matter. Has not our interpretation led us to a means of placing the traumatic experience precisely? No longer need we speculate among possibilities and probabilities. Any question of this crucial event having occurred when the dreamer was a fetus of six or seven months becomes absurd. We need entertain no more surmises as to whether the penis so fearfully threatened an early embryo or a unicellular zygote. It is assuredly the still unfertilized target, the trembling but helpless ovum, and this only, which in agonized anticipation could so perceive the approach of the wolfish invader.

Any residual skepticism must yield as we consider the wealth of corroborative detail. The dreamer's ambiguity in recalling the number of wolves in the tree becomes quite clear when we realize that no ovum facing assault by so many is likely to maintain the poise necessary to make an accurate count of the half-dozen or so leading assailants now closing in for the kill.

"The fear of being eaten by the wolves," (17) Freud has emphasized, dominates the affect of the dreamer. While we do not deny that this intense emotion may also refer to the universal castration fear, surely none will doubt that the dreamer's terror of being *eaten by the wolves* much more accurately represents the ovum's reaction to the spermatozoa, those ravenous *assassins*, as one of them, in advance of all competitors, is now about to quench its cannibalistic and primordial libido in the ovum's passive protoplasm.

Freud reports that when he explained to the patient how his act of defecation interrupted the parental coitus, "transitory symptoms" developed and that this seemed to confirm the interpretation. The opportunity to make such an objective test is not available to me. Suppose someone could be persuaded to accept as his own experience my alternative formulation, and relive it emotionally. Would he not be likely to produce a similar confirmation?

A few small difficulties remain, it is true, but they should not be obdurate. Some thought arising from unsuspected depths of our resistance might argue that in ordinary acts of eating it is the assailant who consumes the prey, but in fertilization it is he himself who undergoes incorporation in the body of the other. This simple reversal, effected by the vigilant forces of repression, should not trouble us after Freud's convincing demonstrations of the mechanism in such transpositions as the stillness of the wolves indicating the vigor of action in the primal scene, the long tails indicating taillessness and castration, and so on.

As every child knows, the term "wolf" is also used colloquially to convey the idea of a rapacious male, one likely to pursue and, if possible, to effect a penetration of women. While this connotation reflects perfectly the fertilization, there is no reason not to conclude that it also demonstrates the ovum's preliminary traumatic fright caused by intrusions of the penis into the vagina. Such a conclusion becomes almost inescapable when we recall the prominence of the walnut tree, a marvelously expressive symbol of the male genitalia. Is it not sufficiently plain that the helpless ovum, bullied and buffeted as intercourse begins and already frightened sufficiently, experiences new and really formidable terror as the deadly and swift spermatozoa emerge as if shot with furious intent from the threatening object?

Important corroboratory inferences may be drawn, if that should prove necessary, from the final three letters of the word "walnut," which have in vulgar use a highly significant anatomical referent. And who can deny that the initial letter, *w*, when separated into its two components (*v*) represents the legs of a woman with knees spread suggestively apart? Add now the fact that this same letter stands first in *woman, wife, womb, whore,* and even in the German *Weib,* and what reasonable doubt can remain of the dreamer's essential bisexuality, of the already dangerously repressed homoerotic component of his unconscious libido?

Our interpretation should not be taken as contradictory to

Freud's. It in no way decreases the likelihood that such events as he described took place in the patient's eighteenth month of life, or that the infant so reacted to them. We have merely pursued the matter further, and have attempted by approximately the same methods of analysis to go deeper into the latent content of the same dream.

In all seriousness, however, it is interesting to note that D. E. R. Kelsey has reported discoveries made through hypnoanalysis that coincide marvelously with what has just been presented through our alternative interpretation of the Wolf-Man's dream. The British investigator gives us numerous details of intrauterine adventures recalled by patients under hypnosis. With one of these patients he apparently had little difficulty in exploring the period we have just discussed. Of this patient, Kelsey reports:

Eventually he reached his conception, in which he saw himself as the ovum being raped, rather than wooed, by the over-anxious sperm of his over-anxious father. Though I have phrased this rather jocularly, I am in fact in earnest about its significance, though time does not permit me to go into this topic at length. Suffice it to say that following this session still more improvement was noticeable. . . . In short, since we recovered this material he has turned from an apparently hopeless therapeutic prospect into a promising one. (18)

Like the works of Fodor and Peerbolte already mentioned, this report suggests the thought that psychiatry might benefit from a sobering influence. Weird cults of pseudoscience and magic healing have for generations attracted followers. The metal rods of Elisha Perkins, the psychic techniques of Mary Baker Eddy, and the fabulous machine of Albert Abrams all offer historical testimony to human gullibility. (19, 20) In the comic books, in science fiction, or in tracts distributed by the I AM society (21) or The Institute of Mental Physics, (22) comparable revelations are familiar. The publication by established medical journals of such discoveries by such methods impresses me as quite another matter, and one that deserves attention.

To those who take seriously these investigations of embryonic experience by dream interpretation or hypnosis I suggest that they acquaint themselves with the cult of Dianetics. To those who are confident that Freud offers scientific evidence for his conclusions about the Wolf-Man, I make the same suggestion. According to Ron Hubbard, the founder of this new "science of the mind": "The creation of Dianetics is a milestone for Man comparable to his discovery of fire and superior to his inventions of the wheel and arch." (23)

Like Fodor and Peerbolte, Hubbard goes on to describe methods which reveal a fetus' or a zygote's emotional life. By Dianetics he discovers its reaction to quarrels of those who are to become its parents. When he demonstrates in an adult the memory of music played at a light opera attended by his mother a few hours after his conception, Hubbard has, I admit, offered little if anything more remarkable than what has already been quoted from responsible medical journals. The progress of Dianetics has been swift. By improved methods, its founder has now investigated personal experience during prior existence not only in this world during earlier millennia, but also on other planets, billions of years ago.

I should like to propose that all young physicians beginning the study of dynamic theories popular today in psychiatry, not be allowed to ignore the cult of Dianetics; that, rather, they be compelled to note carefully its discoveries and its methods.

Perhaps Dianetics has an unspoken message for psychiatry, a message unintentional but profound. When sacred dogma has been rendered inaccessible to direct test, is it not possible that insight may eventually emerge if we patiently observe this process of *reductio ad absurdum*?

SOURCES

1. L. E. Hinsie and J. Shatzky, *Psychiatric Dictionary* (New York: Oxford University Press, 1953).

2. Ernest Jones, editorial preface to Freud's *Collected Papers* (London: Hogarth Press, Ltd., 1940).

3. Sigmund Freud, *Collected Papers* (London: Hogarth Press, Ltd., 1943), Vol. III, pp. 473–605.

4. *Ibid.*, p. 498.

5. *Ibid.*, p. 530.

6. *Ibid.*, pp. 531–34, 575–78.

7. *Ibid.*, p. 507.

8. *Ibid.*, p. 558.

9. Sigmund Freud, *The Problem of Anxiety* (New York: W. W. Norton & Co., Inc., 1936), p. 38.

10. M. L. Peerbolte, "Psychotherapeutic Evaluations of Birth-Trauma Analysis," *The Psychiatric Quarterly*, XXV (October 1951), 589–603.

11. *Ibid.*, p. 596.

12. M. L. Peerbolte, "Some Problems Connected with Fodor's Birth-Trauma Therapy," *The Psychiatric Quarterly*, XXVI (April 1952), 294–306.

13. Peerbolte, "Psychotherapeutic Evaluations of Birth-Trauma Analysis," 600.

14. Nandor Fodor, "The Search for the Beloved," *The Psychiatric Quarterly*, XX (October 1946), 549–603.

15. *Ibid.*, p. 579.

16. Peerbolte, "Psychotherapeutic Evaluations of Birth-Trauma Analysis," 598–99.

17. Freud, *Collected Papers*, Vol. III, pp. 513–15.

18. D. E. R. Kelsey, "Phantasies of Birth and Prenatal Experiences Recovered from Patients Undergoing Hypnoanalysis," *The Journal of Mental Science*, XCIX (April 1953), 216–23.

19. Martin Gardner, *In the Name of Science* (New York: G. P. Putnam's Sons, 1952).

20. H. W. Haggard, *Devils, Drugs and Doctors* (New York: Harper & Bros., 1929).

21. Carey McWilliams, *Southern California Country* (New York: Duell, Sloan & Pearce, Inc., 1946).

22. E. J. Dingle, *Borderlands of Eternity* (Los Angeles: Econolith Press, 1941).

23. Ron Hubbard, *Dianetics* (New York: Hermitage House, 1950).

Chapter 12
WHERE KNOWLEDGE LEAVES OFF

Many other implausible conclusions are currently offered in the name of science but with no evidence except what sophistry can derive from symbolism and analogy, and from carefree assumptions about "unconscious fantasies" that are never brought to awareness or otherwise exhibited. Among these, and held by many as having been irrefutably established by the methods we have just examined, is the belief that every male child experiences fears of castration when he has a bowel movement, and, furthermore, that from the flushing of the toilet he is almost certain to conclude he, like the feces, will be discarded by his parents. Occasionally a realistic clinician questions such dynamic concepts. Bakwin, in *The New England Journal of Medicine*, asks:

Can one really believe that normal child development is as hazardous—as tragic—as it is depicted by this author? Can one really believe that flushing a toilet is a traumatic experience for a child?

He goes on to emphasize a point of great significance:

But an essential difference exists between the erroneous practices of general medicine and the fallacious teaching of child psychiatry. The concepts of general medicine have been built up slowly and laboriously through repeated testing in clinic and laboratory. Theories that are unproved or are not susceptible to proof are accepted tentatively, if at all, and are discarded when found to be false. Many of the concepts of mental health, on the other hand, rest on a theoretical substructure that is considered inviolate. The tendency, here, is to discard or disregard the data if they do not fit the theory, or to distort the data to fit the theory. (1)

Another physician has recently called attention to some of the effects of theoretical concepts on parents who have been impressed by authoritative claims. Of one of these parents he writes as follows:

The mother is a trained nurse, energetic, intelligent, and somewhat over-awed by doctors and their knowledge. During her training, she had some lectures on psychiatry, and she carried away from them the firm conviction that to spank a little boy produces irreparable harm to his psyche "because little boys are afraid of being castrated." So concerned is she with this that she will not permit herself to use scissors in her three year old's presence and has several times cautioned her friends about talking about knives or cutting things in his presence. . . . The father is puzzled by her theories, but since they come from acceptable authority he isn't greatly concerned with them. . . . (2)

Today celebrated psychiatric authors "plainly demonstrate" by methods widely proclaimed as scientific that the chief reason human beings came in time to wear clothing lies in the ever-present influence of a "castration fear" of which they all remain unconscious. Not for protection against the weather, primarily, we are told, or for purposes of adornment, did primitive men and women first don bearskin coats or grass skirts. According to high authority, the real motivation lies deeper, in a universal but unconscious terror felt by each male that a jealous father will amputate his penis. Concealing his genital organs with apparel offers him, it is claimed, a slight measure of protection from this inescapable anxiety. The female (unconsciously), believing herself already dismembered as a punishment for (unconscious) incestuous aims, hastens to cover her mutilation and veil her shame. (3)

Much of the reasoning and investigation classed as dynamic depends upon verbal constructs which can be readily manipulated by the accepted rules to furnish a bogus proof for virtually any assumption the human imagination might contrive. Malcolm Cowley, an outstanding man of letters, comments wisely on this point in discussing bold psychologic explanations of literature. He cites the example of a doctor of philosophy who urges that high school teachers of English give their students the popular dynamic interpretation of novels and poems:

To make the interpretation easier, Dr. Wormhoudt explains that the book [*Ivanhoe*] presents vivid examples of oral and anal eroticism, homosexuality, and both the Oedipus complexes, positive and negative. He adds that the destruction of Torquilstone Castle, set afire by the discarded Saxon mistress of Reginald Front-de-Boeuf, "enables Scott to express most forcefully the climactic experience of feminine orgasm." The students will be edified.

In another essay Dr. Wormhoudt explains Keats' "Ode on a Grecian Urn." The poem, he says, is an example of regression to the oral level of sexuality and the urn itself is "the counterpart (mouth or cup) of the Muse-mother from whose fountain-breast the poet derives the unconscious identification of words—milk. In his conflict with the talking breast the poet raises an aggressive defense. It is not true that I am dependent on mother's breast for sounds—liquid, I can supply myself. The compulsive flow of words in poetic inspiration is the result of this unconscious mechanism." (4)

Unlike some of our most articulate psychiatrists today, the intelligent critic, without hesitation, recognizes such appraisals as "silly." Another of his comments is particularly germane:

Many of the reports are subtle and stimulating, but others, for all their abstruse language, are essentially as simple-minded as the scribbles on the wall of a school house toilet. Of course this is a post-graduate school and most of the students wear Phi Beta Kappa keys, but some of them, emotionally speaking, are still eleven years old. (4)

This I believe is an important point. For all its polysyllabic jargon, the reigning scheme of popular dynamics constitutes an amazingly rigid and stereotyped process by which the same stilted and tiresome answers are always ground out. However complex, rich, marvelous, or profound the material of human experience may be, it is mechanically reduced by this rule of thumb to unvarying banal and implausible equations. Similarly, the chiropractor applies limited and unrealistic techniques to the diverse problems of pathology, and with the same monotonous regularity, these techniques lead to the discovery of spinal subluxation and neural pressure.

Though only a small percentage of psychiatrists are qualified as psychoanalysts, many others derive their concepts and methods chiefly from Freud. The term "dynamic psychiatry," now extremely popular, usually implies viewpoints and therapeutic techniques predominantly influenced by Freudian theory. A number of physicians who emphasize their "dynamic" orientation, but who are not trained as analysts, accept as unalterable fact original Freudian concepts which some thoroughly qualified psychoanalysts today find obviously incorrect. A. C. Oerlemans, in his excellent *Development of Freud's Conception of Anxiety*, clearly points out the implausibility and even the absurdity of basic concepts that are still devoutly defended as truth by some analysts, and by many more psychiatrists not so qualified. (5)

The enthusiasm of Freud for methods which he felt were opening new and astonishing depths of knowledge may account for amazing credulity and dogmatism in a very great man. Docile acceptance today of the conclusions offered in his study of the Wolf-Man justifies a sad astonishment. Learned men continue, however, to cite these "findings" as scientific evidence worthy not only of belief but also of reverence. This, I maintain, however pious the motivation, is a disservice to Freud and to what he sincerely sought to achieve.

Jules H. Masserman, a well-qualified Freudian analyst, makes several important observations in his *Principles of Dynamic Psychiatry* which deserve our consideration at this point:

As already indicated, many psychoanalysts, even when radically deviant at some points, have shown a general tendency toward an ultra-conservative cultism; moreover, when they are challenged on this score, their theoretic assertions have tended to become even more defensively polemic and dogmatic.* Outmoded concepts are clung to in the face of later clinical observations, not because the original formulations have proved to be heuristically advantageous, but because Freud or some authorized disciple proposed them in writing which, apparently, must be quoted by chapter and verse as a basis for reverent hermeneutics. This is particularly evident in the apparently cherished handicap of a fanciful and out-worn terminology, much of which has lost its original meanings and become confused, vague or ambiguous. So also is there an implicit re-emphasis of the role of sexual conflicts as constituting the primary etiology of the neuroses, despite the fact that most progressive analysts, in their private thinking, no longer attempt to maintain this theoretic position. (6)

Masserman points out that Freud early in his work concluded that the symptoms of his hysterical patients were caused solely by repressed sexual impulses and unconscious incestuous fantasies.

Dora's behavior [referring to a patient reported upon in detail by Freud] would now be analyzed much differently and more completely in terms of conflicts other than purely sexual ones. (6)

Freud presented these conclusions quite positively and regarded them as proved. Disagreements with his interpretation he dismissed as products of resistance. (7) Masserman continues:

Unfortunately when this single discovery was met with incredulity or derision from his Viennese medical colleagues, Freud himself became defensively insistent on the "sexual roots" of all neuroses; moreover when he, Abraham, Jones and others disclosed the important roles played by actually quite disparate "pre-genital" drives, such as "oral incorporation" or aggressivity, he labeled these "erotic" also and regarded them as more primitive forms or stages of "libido." Many analysts, misled by this ambiguity of the terms "pre-genital erotism" and "libido," then continued to over-emphasize the role of sexuality in all behavior disorders whether sexuality in its usual sense was demonstrably concerned or not. (6)

Many leaders in American psychiatry who value the influence of some dynamic concepts seem to recognize the dangers of accepting theoretic constructs without reservation and announcing them as proved facts.

It was clearly apparent at the Conference that there is a considerable respect among medical educators for the part played by selected, competent, and broad-minded psychiatrists in the education of good physicians. It was not nearly so evident, and indeed it may be doubted, whether there is a comparably high regard for psychiatry as a body of scientific principles and working hypotheses. (8)

*** In a footnote at this point, Dr. Masserman explains that "such tendencies are not exclusive to psychoanalysts, but may be found in the enthusiastic protagonists of any school."

This quotation from the report of a 1951 Conference on Psychiatric Education is encouraging. Referring to a large number of statements submitted to the Conference, in which various psychiatrists set forth their opinions about the "actual body of knowledge and theory to be communicated to students in psychiatry courses," the Committee concluded:

Some of these statements have been given in Chapter IV. As may be noted there, the terms used were rather broad and general; they were the labels on large packages so to speak, rather than bills of lading listing the contents in detail. (8)

No falsehoods are so misleading and dangerous, in my opinion, as those mixed with valid principles and useful facts and offered under a single identifying term. Falsehood, dogma, or superstition, standing alone on its own merits and under its correct name, can be examined fairly and at length usually recognized. A child taught the religious rule of conduct "Do unto others as you would have others do unto you," who is enjoined also to kill witches (9) and encouraged to handle poisonous snakes as proof of his faith, (10) if he accepts all three of these items as the genuine will of God, is likely, on the contrary, to encounter peculiar difficulties. (11, 12) Referring to "dynamic" theory, the Committee reports:

Stirred by these events there has occurred within the ranks of psychiatry a series of schisms and revolutions, and there still are rather widely divergent opinions, passionately proclaimed and passionately attacked. A body of principles and theories which may be designated as the psychodynamic aspect of psychiatry is still in the process of development. . . .

The formulation of psychodynamic principles in psychiatry, for teaching purposes, has tended therefore to outrun the validation process. For example some of the bolder dynamic hypotheses, such as the libido theory of Freud, have not been of a character that made feasible prompt scientific validation or rejection. Many teachers of psychiatry have been troubled by the problem of the medical student who has been prematurely indoctrinated in some abstract system of psychodynamic hypotheses, and who needs special help in working out a more realistic integration of facts and concepts. (8)

Meanwhile, a good many implausible speculations are being announced as sober fact and, in this guise, are used to amaze the public and perhaps to confuse many who are groping in emotional insecurity.

Though writing as an ardent protagonist of Freudian theory, which is today the chief basis for what are generally called dynamic concepts in psychiatry, J. F. Brown says:

To mention only one other important need of clarification of Freudian concepts, let us take the idea of reaction formation. Reaction formation, as we have seen, consists in turning behavior into its diametrically opposed form to protect oneself against anxiety and to strengthen repression. Squandering money is to be considered as a sublimated form of spreading of feces; hoarding of money is called a reaction formation against this type of behavior. It is easy to see that by allowing opposite behaviors to be accounted for as the continuation and reaction formation of the same basic mechanism there is little possibility of bringing Freudian theory to disproof. From the standpoint of modern operational logic, a theory must be expressed in such a way that it may be proved. This is surely the case with the Freudian theory. On the other hand, from the standpoint of modern methodology, the evidence or experiment which is designed to prove the theory must be one which could have a possible negative outcome and so disprove the theory. At the present time, many of the concepts of psychoanalysis are undoubtedly developed in such a way that only proof and not disproof is possible. . . . The criticism which we made of the concept of reaction formation is applicable to many of the other Freudian mechanisms. (13)

This is a statement of fact that I believe no psychiatrist should ever forget or neglect.

Valuable as these methods may be, at present they obviously have an intrinsic and peculiar potentiality for misuse. They lend themselves to the purposes of casuistry and rationalization as freely as to honest investigation. Since almost any hypothesis, however implausible or absurd, can be supported logically by manipulations of the most popular hypotheses of dynamic psychiatry, it is everyone's grave responsibility to use these hypotheses only with rigid care and honesty. This responsibility is further magnified by the fact that no assumption, however wild, can be disproved within the framework of these methods. It is obvious that here it is necessary to remain tentative in drawing conclusions and not to shun common sense. In seeking validation for our hypotheses, let us particularly avoid the popular method of assuming that it can be obtained by extending, distorting, transforming, or conveniently ignoring the actual meaning of the terms in which we state our case. This is one of the oldest and most obvious forms of casuistry. If we juggle with words, and with facts, so loosely and romantically, is it surprising to find confident announcements, in the name of science, that tax credulity? Let us bear in mind that the methods we have been discussing are still of such a nature that by them anyone can "discover" or "clearly demonstrate" any conceivable absurdity—and in any person. If psychiatrists persist in so using these methods and arguments, they will have the privilege of joining the astrologers, the phrenologists, and those consecrated men who, over the centuries, devoted themselves to the practice of haruspicy. (14)

Oliver Wendell Holmes, speaking long ago but recently quoted in the *Journal of the American Medical Association*, emphasizes a point that deserves the attention of every psychiatrist today:

The best part of our knowledge is that which teaches us where knowledge leaves off and ignorance begins. Nothing more clearly separates a vulgar from a superior mind, than the confusion in the first between the little that it truly knows, on the one hand, and what it half knows and what it thinks it knows on the other. (15)

SOURCES

1. Harry Bakwin, "The Aims of Child Rearing," *The New England Journal of Medicine*, CCXLVIII (February 5, 1953), 227–31.

2. G. R. Forrer, "Parlor Psychiatry," *The Psychiatric Quarterly*, XXVIII (January 1954), 126–33.

3. Edmund Bergler, *Fashion and the Unconscious* (New York: Robert Brunner, 1953).

4. Malcolm Cowley, "Psychoanalysis and Writers," *Harper's Magazine* (September 1954), 87–93.

5. A. C. Oerlemans, *Development of Freud's Conception of Anxiety* (Amsterdam: North Holland Publishing Co., 1949).

6. Jules H. Masserman, *Principles of Dynamic Psychiatry* (Philadelphia: W. B. Saunders Co., 1956), pp. 94–95.

7. Sigmund Freud, "On the History of the Psychoanalytic Movement," *Collected Papers* (London: Hogarth Press, Ltd., 1940), Vol. I, pp. 287–359.

8. *Psychiatry and Medical Education: Report on the 1951 Conference on Psychiatric Education* (Washington: American Psychiatric Association, 1952), pp. 97–100.

9. Exodus 22:18.

10. Mark 16:17–18.

11. Wendell Johnson, *People in Quandaries* (New York: Harper & Bros., 1946).

12. Alfred Korzybski, *Science and Sanity*, 2d ed. (Lancaster, Pa.: The Science Press, 1941).

13. By permission from *The Psychodynamics of Abnormal Behavior*, by J. F. Brown; pp. 246–47. Copyright, 1940. McGraw-Hill Book Co., Inc., New York.

14. Andrew Salter, *The Case Against Psychoanalysis* (New York: Henry Holt & Co., 1952).

15. Oliver Wendell Holmes, "Knowledge," *Journal of the American Medical Association*, CXLVI (June 23, 1951), 698.

Chapter 13
RESISTANCE

The term "resistance" has emerged several times in our discussion. Freud used this word to designate the reluctance patients showed in bringing up and discussing painful and humiliating experiences during the process of analysis. This resistance, he believed, often utilized the mechanism of repression to remove or to withhold from consciousness impulses or memories which the patient found it particularly unpleasant to accept and admit as his own. When many physicians continued to reject some of Freud's chief concepts he at length came to the conclusion that their inability to accept what seemed to him adequate proof must also be a product of resistance. If a psychologist today does not concede that Freud's interpretation of the Wolf-Man's dream satisfactorily demonstrates that at eighteen months of age this patient observed his parents perform sexual intercourse three times successively in the *a tergo* position, one way of accounting for this skepticism is to assume that some disturbing but now forgotten experience, perhaps an experience to some degree similar, has compromised his ordinary ability to judge impartially. If a psychiatrist cannot accept as adequate the evidence Freud offers for his claim that at age four this patient was intensely motivated by a specific desire for his father to practice sodomy upon him, and was restrained in these inclinations by a fear of castration, he must be prepared to defend himself against the argument that similar (unconscious) desires and fears are determining factors in the dissident opinion. So, too, the critic who cannot accept the popular concept of universal bisexuality lays himself open to suspicions that an unrecognized homosexual tendency within himself, probably one of more than ordinary magnitude, is playing an important part in his alleged failure to accept evidence and react to it normally.

Brown is only repeating an argument used thousands of times before when he makes this statement in his textbook *The Psychodynamics of Abnormal Behavior*:

Today we find two types of individuals who are inclined vehemently to reject the Freudian theory of psychosexual genesis. The first group includes all those who know nothing about it, and their rejection is quite normal and easily understood. On the other hand many psychologists and even some psychiatrists are still denouncing the Freudian theory in a polemical fashion. They are exhibiting the well-known factor of "resistance." Even those psychiatrists who are quite ready to attribute infantile sexuality to others usually show resistance when they undergo psychoanalysis themselves. (1)

Brown himself mentions another excellent reason that might account for disagreements about psychiatric theory in a passage from his book quoted on pages 115–16. He now appears to be ignoring completely the point he made so clearly there.

We have noted that Peerbolte, who reports discoveries of intrauterine emotional experiences through interpretation of the dreams of his adult patients, spoke of having to overcome resistance to the idea that this was possible before he could succeed in his task. So too, Fodor, the pioneer worker in this field, had preliminary difficulties; he reports that "it was against strong resistance that certain facts of dream life gradually forced themselves on my attention." (2)

Both these investigators confess that at first they experienced doubt that an adult's dream could accurately and reliably portray prenatal experiences. Skepticism disappears as the distorting influence of resistance is overcome, and neither has any further difficulty in finding ample evidence from such dreams that intercourse between the patient's father and mother while he was a fetus, or perhaps some damage to the placenta, or some disturbance of emotional relations between fetus and placenta, caused psychiatric difficulties not yet overcome in adult life. (3, 4) Note that these psychopathologists do not here speak of remaining simply unconvinced until sufficient evidence has been accumulated to afford proof. Instead, they seem to feel that it is chiefly a matter of overcoming resistance in order to see the evidence clearly and evaluate it properly. After the resistance is conquered there is no difficulty in discovering all the things just mentioned, or even in recognizing which dreams are not those of the living patient but of the bodiless "double" who was never conceived. As we have noted, interpretation of these reveals the feelings and attitudes of the "double" which apparently are independent from those of the physically real patient.

Fodor concludes, furthermore, that telepathic communication between the mother and the unborn fetus has been demonstrated —from dreams occurring thirty or perhaps forty years later, to the erstwhile fetus. (3) Peerbolte reports that he found indications of telepathic communication shortly after birth. "From a purely scientific standpoint, without any philosophical prejudice," he discusses the activity of "an extra-personal form of libido" that might account, he thinks, for this telepathy. "It would be attractive," Peerbolte adds regretfully, "to propose a theoretical connection between this 'cosmic libido' and the eventually independent form of libido. . . ." (5) Reluctantly he declines to go further, "since, as a research worker, the author is averse to theoretical speculations. . . ." It is interesting to note his apparent conviction that, having overcome his resistance, he is now a neutral observer uninfluenced by theoretical assumptions.

It is pertinent here to return for a moment to the articulate lay author, Philip Wylie, to whose work reference has already been made in Chapter 6. We have remarked on the fictional situation in which the author of *Opus 21* describes the cure of a woman who was unhappy because of her husband's neglect and his practice of homosexuality. We have noted that this cure was allegedly effected by her indulging in Lesbian activities with a prostitute, thereby learning to accept such inclinations in herself and in her husband as healthy and entirely natural. (6)

In his book, Wylie also warns us against proclaiming too freely the truths he has disclosed, because of the formidable ignorance and prejudice he is trying to combat. It is possible, he announces in a soaring lyric monologue, for doctors of philosophy to speak of these truths in obscure scientific language, and to publish the evidence for them in heavy technical books. One must not, however, he warns us, say much about them in ordinary language or to ordinary people, because the public is not prepared to accept the understanding they would bring. This prejudice, he tells the reader, causes each person to suppress and conceal from himself the sort of impulses that Yvonne at last discovered within herself. Without them, he maintains, men and women could never understand each other. He speaks of such impulses as universally present during adolescence and strongly implies that in everyone at this age they are directed specifically toward those of his own sex, and that only because of public opinion does the adult repudiate them. When they are expressed openly, in feelings or in acts, they are ferociously condemned. The sole reason for this, according to the monologue in *Opus 21*, lies in the fact that the condemned impulses are shared by every disapproving critic. Each is aroused to suppress in another what he is endeavoring to keep suppressed in himself. The reader is enjoined to remember that disapproval of these inclinations regularly indicates their presence and is told that this will enable him to understand what is the matter with anyone who reacts to their manifestations with definite distaste. (7)

It is, first of all, interesting to note how readily Wylie seems to assume, as if this were a demonstrated fact, that in adolescence boys universally seek boys, and girls seek girls as mates or sweethearts. About the earliest, forgotten years of life, it is possible on better grounds to argue that we may have been motivated by impulses unrecognized in adult years, impulses which are not now available to conscious memory because of repression or because memory was not at that time capable of retaining them. To assume the universality of such a spectacularly pathologic and unfamiliar state in adolescence—which nearly all of us remember very well—is indeed an assumption that urgently demands proof.

We need not at this point, however, comment further on theories of bisexuality and the practical applications of such theories as they are demonstrated fictionally in *Opus 21*. Let us instead give our attention to Wylie's apparent conviction that all who disagree with what he says on this subject are necessarily motivated by homosexual tendencies within themselves, which they are ashamed to admit. He seems to have absolute confidence that there could be no other valid basis for objection. If others are not convinced by what has convinced him, then it is because their powers of observation and logic have been disturbed by these unrecognized tendencies. If others react with different feelings to what he proclaims as so natural and delightful, then it is to be assumed that their reactions should not be regarded as normal judgments but can be dismissed as products of resistance. The fact that it is specifically uninviting, and not a little preposterous, for the ordinary man to think of himself in a role with other men that is the natural role of man with woman is not recognized except in the confident assumption that these reactions prove that the person is at heart responsive to homosexual appeals. According to what seems clearly to be the message of *Opus 21*, one can automatically assume this to be true in every case.

Even those who have not heard of resistance will probably agree that what is generally spoken of as prejudice may sometimes explain why a person cannot accept good evidence but will ignore it to persist in a comforting belief that it would disturb. Such defects in human judgment were well recognized long before Freud. When one imputes resistance or prejudice freely to those who disagree, he is, however, making use of a dialectic that has the proverbial attributes of a two-edged sword. If a man is indeed still suffering from fears engendered by the belief that his father was likely to castrate him, and is not conscious of their source, it is reasonable to say that he might be unduly reluctant to accept facts that would make him aware of such a childhood preoccupation. On the other hand, he might be more susceptible than another to arguments that such beliefs and fears are universal and that he, therefore, has no reason, because of his personal difficulty in this matter, to feel isolated or singled out in an unpleasant situation.

Is it, or is it not, also possible for unconscious resistance, or prejudice, to develop when a man (however reasonable and learned he may be) confronts information that he sees, or thinks he sees, will threaten the validity of a cherished article of belief on which he has based the major efforts of his life? If this is true sometimes about political or religious beliefs, can it not also be true about beliefs one has become convinced are based on scientific evidence? The bitterness which criticism of some dynamic concepts has provoked may be pertinent to this last question.

Clinical experience in psychiatric practice as well as ordinary experience with people affords many examples that suggest that the selfish man may be particularly prone to decry selfishness in others, that the habitual liar may openly crusade against the sin of falsehood. I myself have been impressed by the association of sexual insecurity or quasi-virility with a personally vindictive attitude toward the deviate, with the impulse (or the boast of intention) to handle any approach by a *queer* with physical violence. Almost gloatingly some people with characteristics suggesting potential homosexual tendencies seem to exult in the thought of being solicited perversely by a *fairy* so that they might "knock his teeth down his throat." There is, of course, no scientific proof that unrecognized abnormal tendencies regularly cause unusual harshness of judgment toward the practicing homosexual. Yet clinical experience leads me to believe that they sometimes contribute significantly toward such an attitude. These reactions have been familiar for centuries and can scarcely be regarded as a discovery of dynamic psychiatry.

On the other hand, there is no valid evidence to support the rationalization that mankind's chief, or only, basis for finding perversion distasteful must necessarily lie in one's own unconscious desire for perverse practices. Nor is there reason to believe that the parent who is distressed and dismayed to learn that his son has robbed the bank can be motivated only, or chiefly, by the wish that he himself had beat the boy to the act. Such rationalizations not only lack supporting evidence but, to gain acceptance, require more than ordinary credulity in any person of normal feelings. Let

us briefly examine other examples of behavior rejected by the ordinary human being as distasteful, unacceptable, or perhaps as
horrible and perverse.

Some years ago, in a southern city, the local newspapers were
filled with accounts of the murder of a seven-year-old girl. There
was evidence indicating that the grandmother and other members
of the family had engaged a derelict to do away with the child for
a fee of $75. Much sordid detail was presented. In all this there is
nothing to suggest a sexual motivation in any of those involved.
The child's relatives, according to the man accused of carrying out
the murder, actually haggled about the price. Naturally, there was
horror and indignation and disgust from the public at this shocking deed.

Does any psychiatrist believe that the ordinary person's distaste
for such treatment of a child arises primarily from unconscious
impulses to treat a child or children likewise? Must we assume
that the horror and revulsion aroused by such perverse attitudes
toward this child can be accounted for only by unadmitted and
envious approval? Dynamic theories of the unconscious could be
manipulated, it is true, to "prove" such an assumption. If, however, psychiatry becomes so intrigued by such manipulations of
hypotheses that it jumps to such conclusions, it will, I think, be appropriate for the layman to look elsewhere for help with his emotional problems. It would be a strange learning, indeed, that could
make anyone overlook the obvious reasons why such behavior
provokes sorrow and disgust and indignation.

Regional newspapers also reported the activities of two men
who were arrested for soliciting other men and completing arrangements for them to have sexual relations at a cheap price with
women who served as prostitutes. The fact that the wives of these
two men were among the women prostituted, were, indeed, the
first chosen when business was slack, is likely to provide a distinct
feeling of revulsion. Whatever the psychiatrist has learned from
theories of psychopathology or in his clinical experience, it is certain that he, too, will feel revulsion for such attitudes and such behavior. If this example appears too remote, let him react to this situation with his son as one of the men, or his daughter as one of
the women. It is true that the psychiatrist may be able to find distorting and crippling influences in the life of a man that would account for his becoming what is often called a pimp, perhaps even
for his attitude toward his mate being so perverse; but it would be
a strange psychiatrist indeed who would not find such behavior
pathologic and tragically distasteful. Is there a person who cannot

find other reasons for his reactions before having to fall back on the assumption that, unconsciously, he too is seriously motivated to do the same thing?

Teen-age drug addiction is a subject that has aroused much attention in the public press. Some commentators have demanded that legal steps be taken to mete out capital punishment for dope peddlers who, at first, hand out drugs to children and then extort from them large sums for the drugs that they have begun wildly to crave, but cannot obtain without resorting to crime and prostitution. If we accept the argument being discussed, we must, I suppose, conclude that our only, or at least our fundamental, reason for strong negative reaction against the practice of initiating children into disastrous dope addiction comes from our own unrecognized and unconscious desire to lead them to addiction ourselves. Does such an argument deserve serious comment? Aside from any such theoretical casuistry, I believe that there are reasons any normal person can find within himself that explain the alarm, repugnance, the concern of the normal layman about such matters.

Who will apply here the popular dynamic rule that he who responds with intensely negative reactions to such conduct thereby discloses his unconscious longings to emulate it? Has psychologic theory produced disciples so zealous that they ignore all that is obvious about the natural sources of this indignation and disgust in order to derive their explanation from a single, narrow dogma? If so, one can only suspect that they must ignore too much of human experience to participate in it significantly.

We all have seen indications which convince us that people are often unaware of the very motives within themselves which they particularly criticize in others. Unless we are very obtuse, the chances are that we have discovered such reactions in ourselves. I am, however, confident that psychiatrists in general have enough common sense not to assume that there are no other motives or reactions that produce strong dislike or revulsion. Let us trust that most psychiatrists can be relied upon to realize this, just as most internists can be relied upon not to conclude, because the malaria parasite causes fever, that every illness must arise from this organism and from this only.

Long before the development of present theories of psychopathology, it was no secret that when "the lady doth protest too much" she may be attempting to conceal her real motive, and the false humility and oily courtesy of a Uriah Heep or the bold front of the cowardly braggart is certainly familiar to everyone. From such observations one is scarcely justified in assuming that there is no such thing as an honest expression of grief, or a manifestation of real indignation, that courtesy and humility have no existence except in pretense and that courage cannot be genuine.

It is a pathetic misuse of psychiatric experience, and a traduction of common sense, to assume that man is inevitably, regularly, or generally devoted—unconsciously—to everything that he finds distasteful, unnatural, or unattractive.

SOURCES

1. By permission from *The Psychodynamics of Abnormal Behavior*, by J.F. Brown; pp. 182–83. Copyright, 1940. McGraw-Hill Book Co., Inc., New York.

2. Nandor Fodor, "The Search for the Beloved," *The Psychiatric Quarterly*, XX (October 1946), 559.

3. *Ibid.*, pp. 549–602.

4. M. L. Peerbolte, "Psychotherapeutic Evaluations of Birth-Trauma Analysis," *The Psychiatric Quarterly*, XXV (October 1951), 589–603.

5. M. L. Peerbolte, "Some Problems Connected with Fodor's Birth-Trauma Therapy," *The Psychiatric Quarterly*, XXVI (April 1952), 303–5.

6. Philip Wylie, *Opus 21* (New York: Rinehart & Co., 1949).

7. *Ibid.*, pp. 352–53.

Chapter 14
THE NOBEL PRIZE AND
THE NEW HELLAS

Mention has been made of several appraisals of homosexuality that clash with generally accepted standards and values, and with the primary concepts on which law over the centuries has based its judgments. These appraisals were derived largely from psychiatric theory which, as I have tried to show, might in its present status be so interpreted as to support almost any thesis, however plausible or fantastic. Let us now consider a judgment derived from other sources and expressed by a writer widely regarded as of colossal stature among the intellectuals of our century.

Perhaps no author since the fall of the Roman Empire, has more frankly defended and praised homosexuality than did André Gide. Unlike writers such as Walt Whitman and Proust, who present deviated reactions to life indirectly or in disguise, Gide—in *Corydon*—openly contends that it is natural and normal for males to choose each other sexually. (1) To ordinary ears an argument about this is likely to seem contrived and artificial. Man's choice of woman is by impulses and biologic reactions too fundamental to need or seek support from reason. Yet Gide is very serious. It is plain to anyone who reads *Corydon* that the writer is not mischievously trying to see just how far the credulity of mortals can be stretched, or how outlandish a premise a persuasive and articulate man can induce his more naive listeners to swallow as fact.

Since André Gide was in our own time awarded the Nobel Prize for literature, we cannot shrug off his opinions without careful examination. There is no intellectual distinction more impressive than that conferred by the Nobel Prize. In all civilized nations

it is accepted as evidence that the chemist or physicist so re-
warded and acclaimed before the world has contributed brilliantly
and significantly to progress in his special field of science. Those
who gave the world the sulfa drugs and penicillin were given the
Nobel Prize in medicine. Their work has revolutionized medical
practice, and saved untold tens of thousands from death. The importance of what is contributed in scientific work is an obvious criterion for this supreme award. That it be sound and reliable is an
even more fundamental criterion. If sulfa drugs or penicillin did
the patient no good, or were more likely to do harm than good, it
would have been absurd, indeed, to reward their discoverers with
the Nobel Prize.

Harold March, a recent biographer of Gide, referring to this triumph, writes:

The apotheosis came in 1947 with the award of the Nobel Prize for literature; his enemies, still numerous, were reduced to impotence, and for the
augmented band of his admirers, he became an object of veneration
whose lightest word was piously preserved like the nail paring of a saint.
(2)

One might think that literary work deserving the Nobel Prize
must first of all be soundly rooted in the basic values of human
life. To merit such recognition as this the work should also contribute something remarkable, should offer some fruits of wisdom
and insight not already available to the ordinary person. *Corydon*
is of course only one of many books written by Gide. No one
could reasonably contend that the prize was awarded to him
chiefly because of it and its message. It is, however, true that homosexuality, in various degrees of disguise and distortion, appears as an insidious theme in many of his major works. Even
when a homosexual viewpoint is least obvious, the peculiar disillusionment, the rejection or reversal of ordinary human reactions
and basic values, that seem so often to be part of this deviation,
permeate his most acclaimed writings.

It may be argued that the truth or value of art and literature is
more difficult to prove than the truth or value of a scientific
achievement. All, however, must agree that the Nobel Prize at
least establishes the fact that an important jury representing contemporary civilization has expressed its judgment favorably.

What is the substance of a literary masterpiece? There are many
who say that the artist and the poet do not necessarily offer precise rules for living, that they do not, like the didactic teacher or
preacher, attempt to explain life and to counsel mankind. Most
psychiatrists would probably agree that the deepest lessons in life
come in a less direct manner than by deliberate verbal instruction.
The child seems to learn more about truth, love, kindness, man-

hood and womanhood from the actual behavior of his parents than he does from anything that they can tell him. Many would agree that the poet or the artist expresses himself best not when he offers a set of rules but when he reflects or somehow conveys what cannot be preserved in mere copybook maxims.

According to Matthew Arnold, a great book is the precious life-blood of a master spirit. Does not the authentically great writer preserve his unique experience as a person and in his book so embody it that others may feel something of it and learn by it even after his own life has ended? Neither *Hamlet* nor the "Ode to a Nightingale" offers us specific instruction. *Paradise Lost* may at times attempt to persuade us about theological matters by argument that suggests a sermon. Most who find *Paradise Lost* a great poem, however, are less influenced by its direct philosophical argument than by other qualities.

Let us grant, then, that the worth of a poem or a piece of literature cannot regularly be proved in court or demonstrated scientifically. Does it follow that great and genuine art has no meaning, that it has no hearing on good and evil, on disease and happiness, no immediate relation to human life? Is human pathology equivalent, by true literary standards, to health? I do not think so. Would any but those who take an extreme position in the dubious cause of "art for art's sake" deny that a literary work of the highest order, or of any appreciable validity, for that matter, must reflect what is true, worthwhile, and significant about human experience?

Van Wyck Brooks impressively demonstrates what happens to some who seek in art the approximation of a religion unrelated to biologic existence. He shows us Ezra Pound turning away in disgust from what he regarded as the subject matter of previous poets—from love, anguish, hate, evil, mercy, and so on. Committed to a program of avoiding any echo of what had been said before by others, he addresses himself to what is either too vague to be named, or to what, some might say, is too trivial to matter. (3)

So, too, Gertrude Stein, claiming that she and her followers were "creating the twentieth-century literature and art," attempts to follow the rule that "the matter is of small importance," that nothing is to be considered but the method and form. (3) She speaks of "nice wars" and "wars that are not nice" with what seems to some a queer detachment from human decency and to others a pathetic gesture of purposeless effrontery. In what has been called an attempt to separate words from sense and what seems also to be an effort to make art that has nothing to do with life as we know it, Gertrude Stein became a legend the world over for such utterances as "Pigeons on the grass alas," "Toasted Susie is my ice cream," "Honey is funny," "Chicken, a dirty bird, a dirty word, a dirty third," "A rose is a rose is a rose." Somewhat charitably, I would say, Van Wyck Brooks refers to these gems as "bread-and-milk baby talk." (3)

Many of us will agree that Gertrude Stein, having dispensed "with subjects . . . had little to say." (3) I do not feel myself qualified to offer an expert opinion on the artistic worth of such literature as that produced by Ezra Pound and Gertrude Stein. It does appear, however, that these qualify as bona fide examples of art for art's sake, art, or so-called art, that stands apart from biology and all the essence of human feelings and values. The fact that Ezra Pound was tried in our courts for treason to his country during war and also pronounced psychotic at St. Elizabeth's Hospital does not necessarily, I suppose, offer final evidence that his work does not merit its current recognition as great poetry. Instead of attempting judgment in an area that impresses me as probably nonexistent, that is, a scale of art values known to man but unrelated to living, I can but say that, as a human being, I find no substance here sufficiently definite to support further comment.

In contrast to such efforts at avoiding any reference to life as we live it, André Gide expresses himself frankly and clearly about what is real and familiar. He does not hesitate to give us his opinions, to express his taste, and to instruct us about matters that are far from abstruse.

Let us turn to what he has to say. In *Corydon*, Gide does not use narration to demonstrate, nor does he express himself in metaphor. He allows rather pale and unconvincing characters to carry on an argument. The thesis thus plainly advanced by the author is that homosexual activities are normal, fine, healthy, and indeed superior to the love of man and woman.

Gide uses many arguments. He often refers to the behavior of animals. He appears to have been much impressed by a male dog who, in the confused activities and strivings of a typical group attending a bitch in heat, carried out some of the motions of coitus with another male dog. (4) The emphasis put on this by a man awarded the Nobel Prize merits more than ordinary astonishment. Is there any child ten years old who has not observed male dogs carrying out blundering and forlorn preliminary steps toward mating with other male dogs, or with the knees of human beings, or with female dogs which, out of season, are entirely negative to such an approach? With a distinct relish, as if he had discovered something extraordinarily important and peculiarly gratifying, Gide reports this observation.

Nearly any day, in my own house, I could show him a small female fox terrier mount a male pit-bull and exercise herself in a frankly sexual way. The big dog, in his stoic manner, quietly suffers these efforts but in no way responds to them sexually. The male bulldog also has sexual impulses. Responding to them in an eager but vague search for his goal, he often grasps the leg of a man or woman with his front feet, and carries out motions in the general direction of copulation. His understanding of what will satisfy him is indeed imperfect. In some respects, however, it might be said that the dog is less confused than the argument offered by Gide. Once the biologically appropriate mate is near the dog, he is no longer vague or blundering.

This sort of fumbling exploration among dogs is scarcely to be taken as evidence of homosexuality as we see it in practice among human beings. A similar fumbling is common in the child. It would be tedious and unprofitable to follow in detail the whole argument of *Corydon*. Behavior is reported in dogs, other mammals, and even in fowls, which the author interprets as indicating that it is "natural" for males to choose males in preference to females for sexual purposes. Nearly all the reports cited indicate no more than that animals, like adolescents, may at times seek some substitutive masturbatory genital stimulation when the opportunity to complete the sexual act with a real mate is unavailable. A few observations cited by Gide suggest that animals long isolated from the opposite sex may persist in confused, quasi-erotic genital activities with each other. More recent studies of animal behavior referred to by Guttmacher offer much more convincing evidence that rats, after long frustration in sexually segregated groups, may develop abnormal loss of interest in heterosexual mating. (5) Others have reported not only homosexually deviated activity but also "prostitution and masturbation to orgasm" in chimpanzees and monkeys. (6)

Data of this sort loom small indeed against the regular and plain biologic facts available in almost infinite multitude to anyone who observes domestic animals or fowls. That confused sexual gropings along unrewarding paths occur in other species than ours, that actually pathologic choices of behavior may be produced by abnormal circumstances, or may perhaps occur spontaneously does not invalidate the biologic accuracy of the impulses that direct the ordinary cat or rooster. Gide's solemnly mobilized arguments from animal behavior to show that homosexuality is "natural" make little or no sense unless we take the word to mean that such things do occur. By this definition, pulmonary tuberculosis, two-headed calves, cannibalism, hernia, congenital blindness, and schizophrenia are also "natural."

A remarkably wise and compassionate observer, himself a homosexual, writes with an insight apparently undistorted by Gide's bias—a bias which apparently leaves him unaware of the obvious:

Most men are heterosexual. Every country lane and city street at evening gives the lie to the suggestion that there is serious competition between natural and unnatural love. . . . Indeed one wonders how anyone who has ever picked his way among the omnipresent lovers of this romantic world can possibly doubt the complete normality of the emotions which control the lives of most men and which survive, supreme and proud, above even the most disastrous waves of human affliction. (7)

In defense and in praise of homosexuality, Gide advances other arguments. He takes pains to specify that he is not speaking of "inversion, effeminacy and sodomy." (8) Of just what then is he speaking? Admiration is explicit and implicit in every reference he makes to "Greek love," which, he says, "has nothing whatsoever to do with effeminacy." (8) Despite these implausible statements, the fact remains that homosexuality among the Greeks, according to all reports, was what the word "sodomy" legally and medically defines today. The term "normal homosexuals" (9) is frequently employed, but what sort of sexual activities between men Gide regards as normal is never disclosed in *Corydon.*

The art and civilization of ancient Greece are repeatedly offered as proof that homosexuality is admirable and superior. The mouthpiece for this argument, Corydon (represented as a physician), is made to say:

And I maintain that the peace of the home, the honor of the woman, the dignity of the family and the health of every man and wife were more effectively safeguarded by the Greek way of life than by our own. . . . I think that a friend, even in the fullest Greek sense of the word, is a better influence on an adolescent than a mistress. (11)

Arguing that homosexual activities promote courage, manliness, and superior qualities among men, he says that if these activities are denied "you must make men into saints; for otherwise physical desire will cause them to misuse their wives or defile young women." (12)

It seems strange that anyone should speak of a husband's making love with his wife as a misuse. It is not likely that normal wives will find that this accurately reflects their own feelings.

Corydon's companion, who in the dialogue makes stilted replies, now objects, saying: "So, according to you, it is to save the woman that the boy is sacrificed." (12)

**** According to March, Gide elsewhere explains that it is pederasty which he distinguishes for his praise. This term ordinarily includes both sodomy and fellatio between the adult male and the child or pubertal boy. (10)

Corydon insists that "the passionate attachment" of boys and young men to older men, whether or not these older men carry out complete homosexual acts with them, is far more conducive to true virility and proper development than heterosexual love:

I say that this love, if it is profound, tends towards chastity—but only, it goes without saving, if physical desire is reabsorbed into it, which simple friendship can never achieve—and that for the boy it can be the greatest incentive to courage, work, and virtue.

I say, too, that an older person [man] is better able to take account of the troubles of an adolescent than any woman, even one expert in the art of love. Indeed I know certain boys too much addicted to solitary pleasures, for whom I consider an attachment of this kind would be the surest remedy. (13)

Other remarkable opinions are expressed. Pliny is quoted to support the contention that young men are "more attractive than attracted," that is to say, more inclined to be courted by an older man than to feel sexual desire for woman.

Who can agree with this statement that boys under twenty-two years of age do not feel much sexual desire for girls? How many teen-age youngsters are there who could be talked into agreeing with this man of world-renowned intellect?

Corydon is quite confident in stating that if "some older person is to fall in love with [the youth] then I believe it is best for him that this person should be a friend of his own sex." This belief, Corydon emphasizes, was "shared by a civilization which we studied two days ago [ancient Greece] and which you [the companion set up by Gide to answer Corydon] refuse to admire except for its shell."

The point is belabored as Corydon continues:

I think this friend [an adult homosexual] will jealously watch and guard him, and himself exalted by this love, will lead him to those marvelous heights, which can never be reached without love. If alternatively he falls into the hands of a woman, it can be disastrous for him. One has alas! all too many examples of that. But since at this tender age, he would still not know how to make love in any but the most indifferent manner, it is fortunately not natural for a woman to fall in love with him. (13)

Let us consider some of these statements. We must bear in mind that they are opinions of a man who has been stamped as a great intellect by civilization's highest official literary award, but is this wisdom? Are we offered counsel by him that is reliable and conducive to sound personal and social health? Many poets, novelists, and other literary figures refrain from giving direct instruction. Gide, in this work, does not. He tells us frankly what he regards as good and bad and what we ought to do.

We are informed that it is particularly virile for a teen-age boy to subject himself to what is officially termed sodomy by an older man. Even if such acts are not completed, the personal relations and emotions, the reciprocal attitudes between the man and the young boy who feel that way about each other are pronounced eminently natural and highly conducive to the development of spiritual excellence. What do teen-agers think of that? Is there any principal or teacher in a high school who would say that this is correct? Does any one have evidence that such procedures promote the development of virility? Since the insubstantial character, Corydon, is labeled a physician, it is appropriate to ask: Is there a physician who thinks that this is advisable or normal?

Are there any older people, men of thirty or forty, who agree that relations of this sort would be a naturally romantic experience? What would a normal man of thirty-five find it natural to say to the teen-age boy in support of their becoming sweethearts? What idea of himself, of his biologic and social role, would a boy develop under such sexual and spiritual guidance by his elder? What sort of figures would occupy his imagination as models of the manhood toward which he is to grow?

What do the wives of grown men think of this proposition? Do they agree that their husbands can be more manly and encourage more virility among teen-age boys by such practices? Would they welcome this arrangement to avoid being "misused" by husbands who now make love with them? What man or woman is there who can conceive of this as naturally passionate or romantic? Or as elevating, or as spiritual?

Such proposals might simply be discarded as unworthy of consideration were it not for the fact that they are made by so eminent a writer. Upon this man the intellectual world has placed its highest stamp of approval. It is hardly surprising if ordinary people presume that this approval supports Gide's judgments in general. He, himself, said that of his works he most valued *Corydon*.

The first edition of this book in English was published in 1950, decades after it first appeared in French. It is impossible to avoid the suspicion that the influence of Kinsey's report and the subsequent wave of enthusiasm about pathologic sexuality may have had much to do with its presentation to the American public. In his preface to the new edition Gide says:

. . . I would certainly have renounced the Nobel Prize rather than retract any single one of my writing. . . . *Corydon* remains in my opinion the most important of my books . . . if I had to rewrite it today I would do so in a far more affirmative tone. . . . I have come to realize that I was far more right than at first I dared to believe. I knew that the book could wait. Its hour, in France at least, has not arrived. In America perhaps it has? The publication and circulation of the *Kinsey Report* allows me to suppose and hope so. (14)

Despite Gide's exalted position, the ordinary person may find it difficult to imagine just what is meant by the virility to which he refers. However modest about his own powers of intellect, the common man is not likely to take Gide's word that homosexual experiences are "a better influence" than the love relation between man and woman.

In addition to sexual acts between men and boys generally regarded as "acts against nature," Gide applauds the personal attitudes and orientations promoted by males turning romantically toward each other instead of toward sweethearts. He insists that boys and older men who fall in love with each other instead of with girls or women, though they deny themselves the final goal of their desires, are nevertheless fortunate. In comparing "one strong desire, whether satisfied or not, with another," he acclaims the homosexual experience as morally and spiritually superior, more esthetic and elevating. (15)

Suppose we draw a sharper focus on this judgment of Gide's. The daily life in Periclean Athens or in the Thebes of Epaminondas and Pelopidas can be known to us only by fragmentary reports of distant happenings among persons long dead. What we are able to imagine about personal relations and the actualities of emotional life there can scarcely be more than generalizations and abstractions. Living people who surround us today are more concrete and accessible to study than the Hellenic shepherds and sculptors of two and a half thousand years ago whom Gide bids us regard. Of the records that have come down to us, many were composed by homosexuals of that time.

Let us ask ourselves how we respond to scenes nearer home such as the following: A prep school where it is natural for masters stirred by impulses toward sodomy to gaze with lyric physical desire into the eyes of teen-age boys? A place where personal notes suffused with hot sexual passion are slyly passed between the history teacher and the star halfback, notes reflecting all the rapture, longing, despair, and nameless delight of sweethearts who remain within the bounds of physical chastity, but in other ways express their burning love? Does the basketball coach steal away in his convertible with the lad who won the biology prize? Later, parked in the moonlight, do these two say to each other what might be said by some boy and girl in the first flush of sexual love? In this picture are to be assumed all the ardor and excitement, the sighs, the tears, that anyone would consider natural in the case of the boy and girl.

Let us grant that the coach and the boy, like many biologically more appropriate couples, refrain from what they would regard as ultimate fulfilment. Even scrupulously chaste couples usually hold hands, kiss, embrace; and many allow themselves caresses and intimacies still more stimulating. If these boys regard themselves as the natural objects of courtship for their elders, how are they to be taught to develop their charms and graces? How shall they respond to the desires that Gide says it is so natural for them to evoke? In the heterosexual world, a college girl, for example, no matter how virginal and morally upright, is likely to be pleasantly stimulated by a discreet but appreciative glance from the professor, although she knows that he will not feel justified in revealing more of his reaction. What form of behavior does Gide recommend as appropriate for the expression of "normal homosexuality," which he regards as so fortunate a situation for the young boy or man?

In clinical experience today and in what is recorded of the "boy love" of ancient Greece, the older man usually caricatures the male suitor, the youth falling into some bizarre travesty of the feminine role. If the superficial mimicry or burlesque of woman's characteristics is inconsistent with what Gide tells us is most natural for male youth, what does he feel should be their inner subjective response? In his supposedly ideal situation, just what are they to regard themselves as aiming at? What would he have them try to be or to become?

All the characteristics of woman, whether in outer accessories of adornment or in the inmost essence of her being, fit naturally and with human dignity into the process of courtship and mating. If we try, in imagination, to put the boy or young man into such a picture, replacing the girl, it is hard to see, whatever Gide may say of "virility," how anything compatible with the minimal requisites of inward identity as a male can survive. In major psychiatric disorder the greatest confusions may arise, and tragically incongruent roles may be sought. Like all disability and illness, such distortions demand respectful compassion. Whether the sexually disordered male dons female attire or whether, like many, he assumes the outer manner of a "tough guy" and despises the very sight of a "fairy" who flaunts effeminacy, it is only by the most obvious perversion of judgment that his status in the role idealized by Gide can be termed "male" or "virile."

Only when we look at such a picture, and not at speculative concepts of ancient Greece, can we truly evaluate Gide's teachings. Do we find this an acceptable portrayal of normal life? Does anyone want his son, his nephew, or the friendly little fellow across the street, to grow up in such a way? Will anyone volunteer to tell us just what Gide finds in such a proposition that is elevating or natural?

The methods of science cannot be used to prove or disprove the worth of Gide's taste and judgment here. Are there abstruse rules or truths in art and esthetics to support Gide's teaching? Is he perhaps aware of mysterious spiritual values to which the ordinary man is blind? I cannot help thinking that any such "esthetic truths," visible only to the elect, must, if they exist at all, be too remote from human life and human feelings to bear relevantly on ordinary human conduct.

Gide argues vehemently that the orientations, relations, and standards just discussed should not merely be tolerated but should be accepted officially as a natural and biologically conventional way of life. Corydon devoutly urges such a change "for God's sake and for the good of the state." (15)

To such a proposal, physicians and teachers of youth should have some reaction. This is the unequivocal judgment of a writer regarded by our most distinguished critics with reverent admiration, of an intellect certified, one might say, as among the greatest of our century. Should ordinary citizens and parents be too humble to challenge such a judgment? Should we assume that our distaste for Gide's proposal can be explained only by our limited capacity for artistic values? Or by our blindness to some superior esthetic standard that is plain to greater spirits? Or, perhaps, by resistance caused only by our unadmitted longings for the relations praised by Gide?

SOURCES

1. André Gide, *Corydon* (New York: Farrar, Straus & Cudahy, Inc., 1950).

2. Harold March, *Gide and the Hound of Heaven* (Philadelphia: University of Pennsylvania Press, 1952), p. 4.

3. Van Wyck Brooks, *The Confident Years* (New York: E. P. Dutton & Co., 1952), pp. 435–45, 561–77.

4. Gide, *op. cit.*, p. 76.

5. Manfred Guttmacher, *Sex Offenses* (New York: W. W. Norton & Co., Inc., 1951), pp. 19–20.

6. C. S. Ford and F. A. Beach, *Patterns of Sexual Behavior* (New York: Paul B. Hoeber, Inc., 1952).

7. Anomaly, *The Invert* (London: Baillière, Tindall & Cox, 1948), pp. 57–58.

8. Gide, *op. cit.*, pp. 193–94.

9. *Ibid.*, p. 145.

10. March, *op. cit.*, p. 172.

11. Gide, *op. cit.*, p. 148.

12. *Ibid.*, pp. 134–35.

13. *Ibid.*, pp. 150–51,

14. *Ibid.*, pp. xi–xiv.
15. *Ibid.*, pp. 147–51.

Chapter 15
FUGITIVES FROM EROS

As pointed out by Cory, homosexuals speak of themselves as lead-ing the *gay* life. The same author, in a chapter entitled "Love Is a Wonderful Thing," maintains that homosexual relations are full of joy, romance, and fulfilment. Many of the incidents cited in his book do not, however, confirm such an estimate of the results when men attempt to make love with each other. Cory admits that promiscuity is prevalent in such relations. (1)

Edward Carpenter, whose favorable opinions on the subject have for decades been noted, is quoted by Wickham as follows:

The question is not whether the [inverted] instinct is capable of morbid and extravagant manifestation . . . but whether it is capable of a healthy and sane expression. And this it has abundantly shown itself to be. (2)

I agree that this is, indeed, the question, but what of the an-swer? On what evidence does Carpenter base his enthusiastic af-firmation? Outstanding triumphs in literature, sculpture, painting, and in other arts, it is often pointed out, have been achieved by people generally regarded as homosexual. These triumphs are not necessarily evidence that inverted sexual instincts find a healthy and sane expression in personal relations, that they bring love and fulfilment to mates of the same sex. The surrounding world has in-deed been impressed by morbid manifestations of homosexuality, but few if any such relations can be found that command general respect. Is this distinctly negative attitude of the majority due merely to prejudice? Or is there something intrinsically pathologic about the invert's eroticism that prevents his establishing relations comparable with the accepted and respected love between man and woman? Let us proceed with a few observations before going further into these questions.

In the popular novel *From Here to Eternity*, Jones presents two penniless soldiers, picked up by relatively affluent homosexuals from whom they are glad to accept free drinks. As the evening progresses, after considerable disagreement and friction, one of the soldiers says to one of the hosts:

If you guys like being queer, why don't you be queer with each other? Instead of all the time trying to cut each other's throat? If you believed that crap about true love you've been putting out, why do you get your feelings hurt so easy? . . . Why do you always pick up somebody who ain't queer? (3)

The soldier, while the hosts are out of earshot, says to his fellow: "I've heard a lot of talk about 'great love' between homos, but I ain't never seen it. I think it's more like hate, probably." (4)

In this brief scene, several points are touched on, which bear on the real problems of every homosexual that I have ever observed. They do not seem able to confine themselves to each other as sexual partners. What they call "love" is apparently not a good translation of what this term means in heterosexual feeling. They often show a specific tendency to mock and deride each other for showing the very qualities that they share with each other. Often their choice for an ideal, or even a genuinely desirable, love-object, in contrast with a more or less scorned pickup, is directed paradoxically toward the unattainable—characteristically, in men, toward the normal male.

The opinion has been often expressed that ignorant or hostile attitudes on the part of society cause all or most of the homosexual's difficulty. In all cases that I have personally studied, the factors intrinsic in the erotic impulse and attitude impressed me as more fundamental in the maladjustment. A real source of the homosexual's unhappiness arises from his inability to find any mate that can be genuinely or consistently loved. It is this, far more than persecution by society, that accounts for the wretched unhappiness or the flip promiscuity so typical of the sexual life of inverts. Among the more serious of the group this often promotes cynical disillusionment, beliefs in a duplicity of nature or fate, a rejection of ordinary human goals and of the simple interests and enthusiasms that enrich ordinary human existence.

Not only in great cities but even in villages, these emotionally crippled and unfortunate people have ample opportunity to live with each other as mates. It is remarkable how little the community bestirs itself to interfere with them. And yet, hate, spite, pettiness, mockery, gross and casual infidelity to what would be basic in relations between man and woman, appear to be the rule in such attempts at abnormal union.

A typical example is furnished by a particularly intelligent Lesbian. Among other fine abilities and desirable human qualities, she has the appearance of a pretty and sexually attractive woman. She is in fact remarkably endowed physically, having such glamor that she invariably arouses attention in men, and sometimes hopes that are never to be realized. After study and treatment by me and later by a psychoanalyst to whom she had been referred many years ago, this woman established herself in one of the nation's large cities. She has become financially successful and prominent. Paradoxically, she has achieved this status through her charm and her appeal for men as an entertainer in a very high-class night club. As a talented dancer, a sultry singer, she is able to suggest subtly that she is as responsive to the male as most men are to her.

She has no difficulty at all in attracting suitors and enjoys this as a game and as a concomitant of her work. She knows and uses like a virtuoso every gesture and tone in the vocabulary of flirtation, every catch of the voice, every erotic nuance of feminine motion or posture. Men often think they sense in her a smoldering passion of breathless intensity and often suspect it is particularly adapted for or directed toward them in person. It is thus not difficult to understand her success in her profession.

Despite her fame and fortune, she finds life not only petty and rather pointless, but at times bitter indeed. Totally without normal response to the male, she lives her real life among Bohemian groups where deviation is accepted as the standard of enlightenment. Time after time, during the course of casual and utterly promiscuous Lesbian activities, she has considered herself truly in love with another woman. On such occasions the two sometimes set up an establishment and attempt to live as mates. Experience has taught this patient to accept such projects as inevitably doomed. Disillusionment is usually swift. No positive and meaningful union can occur, no valid happiness can materialize. Carping, fantastic jealousies, absurd and childish demands, mistrust, small and large acts of bitterness, make their appearance. There is much grim and gloomy talk about how passion fades, how lovers inevitably betray, how fate makes all dreams false.

In speaking of the experience that came nearer than any other to affording a temporary illusion of love and fulfilment, this girl described a brief relationship with an older and wealthier woman who had taken her on a sort of honeymoon trip to South America. She admitted that, even from the start, each had been jealously watching every reaction of the other in uneasy anticipation of derisive rejection. Each had vied with the other in petty demands for proof of utter and eternal devotion and each had fretted and carped at the other, no matter what either did. She herself remained, she reported, carefully on guard in order to be the first to break away into some plain and mocking infidelity with another woman. Thus she was able to avoid the role of being herself discarded and humiliated. She had apparently beaten the other woman to the punch, so to speak, and broken off the affair with what was to her as near an approximation to "romantic" memories as anything that she could ever attain. Having been the one who acted first seemed to leave a perversely sweet savor that she almost poetically cherished.

This remarkable woman is not spiteful and frivolous in any of her behavior except that concerning sex and what she, for the want of better knowledge, thinks of as "love." Except in this specific emotional area, she does not seem untrustworthy, superficial, or shallow. Never finding satisfaction that is personal or genuine, she is, one might say, driven, or at least continually prodded on, by an oddly virginal unfulfilment into new and ever unrewarding liaisons. I would not say that behind her longings, her seekings, there is none of the warm and real stuff of love. There is much to indicate that she has a sort of embryonic capacity for this, perhaps even in high degree. It cannot, however, embody itself sufficiently in the ambivalent Lesbian situations ever to be quite born, to become solidly real. Her potentialities for genuine love, nascent again in each new effort to mate, apparently bring suffering enough to set off adaptive and protective reactions that soon bleach them of warmth and seriousness.

Though this woman's sexual history strongly suggests general irresponsibility and the stunted emotional status of one intrinsically callous and petty, I think it is the pathologic restriction to a biologically inappropriate role in mating that curtails her erotic activity and fulfilment to such frustrating shallows. There is much more to her than can be given in relations not naturally designed for sexual love and happy mating. The psychiatric disorder that has tragically distorted this major human drive from its healthy goal has fixed it upon a course that leads inevitably into biologic mirage.

Edmund Bergler, a prominent psychoanalyst who has for years devoted his work especially to sexual problems, says:

As far as homosexuals remaining together for any length of time, their quarrels—especially in jealousy—surpass everything that occurs, even in the worst heterosexual relationship. They simply act out the mechanism of "injustice collecting." . . .

Sometimes homosexuals assert that they are completely "happy," the only thing bothering them being the "unreasonable approach" of the environment. That is a conventional blind. There are no happy homosexuals, and there would not be, even if the outer world left them in peace. The reason is an internal one. . . .

A man who unconsciously runs after disappointment cannot be consciously happy. The amount of conflict, of jealousy for instance, between homosexuals surpasses anything known even in bad heterosexual relationships. (5)

Typical of what I myself have regularly encountered in a large number of homosexual patients, particularly in those with superior ability, is this striking inability to work things out happily, or even in tolerable unhappiness, between themselves, no matter how little society intrudes, no matter how favorable the general circumstances.

Bergler further says:

Secondarily a "philosophy" is created by the homosexual to bolster his unconscious defense. He "approves" of his homosexuality because it camouflages well the facts he runs away from. . . .

He cannot escape, though, other reverberations of that conflict; in his personality he is the classic "injustice collector." Hence he constantly feels "unjustly treated." (5)

A striking example is afforded by the relations between two brilliant, technically trained men, men of almost thirty, who are both instructors in a metropolitan university. For months these two have engaged in abnormal sex practices together. They consider themselves lovers and each has avowed that only from the other has he been offered real understanding, or anything else that makes life worth living. Eloquently and articulately they protest their love for each other, quoting the poets of all times and nations, ascribing to each other physical charms more consistent with such mythological sirens as Helen of Troy or the pagan goddess Astarte than with the masculine actualities. They philosophize about the rare nature of their oneness, the pure honesty of their love, the spiritual development each has induced in the other.

Despite such avowals, however, in actuality they carp at and deride each other, fly into pouts of distrust and recrimination. Neither can refrain from hurting and frustrating his alleged mate. No issue is too trivial to serve as grounds or pretext for a quarrel. Each quarrel leads to petulant rages and vociferous accusations, eventually to silent and sulking despairs. Outlandish and even impossible pranks of infidelity, with bus-boys, bellhops, letter-carriers, and so on, are imagined by each one whenever the other is out of sight. Wrangles over alleged and real acts of unfaithfulness drive one or the other "out into the night"; whence he eventually returns, sometimes to open arms, sometimes to cold scorn, or to new sarcastic demands for proof of good behavior during the absence.

They abase themselves to each other as if to demigods but soon either may be railing at his idol as a "bitch," a "slut," or a whorish "queen." They boast pitifully of their union as a beautiful, clean relation and think of it as rare if not unique. When separated, they write notes to each other capriciously confessing sexual activity with others and driving one another into despairs and rages of impotent jealousy.

After a recent quarrel about sundry infidelities one of these intellectuals was beaten up in the streets and seriously injured by some man in a slum whom he accosted and sought to engage in perverse activities. The other of the enamored pair meanwhile was arrested in a tourist camp for attempting to carry out on a twelve-year-old boy, despite the child's refusal, what the legal charge described as "a detestable and abominable act against nature."

If persons of this type could really find sweethearts and mates and if meaningful love between them could be achieved, there is little reason to believe that they would be a serious problem to society. What they did would then be their own business and theirs only. Parents would not have to worry about the danger of their molesting children and would, it seems likely, leave them in peace and continue to treat them respectfully. Most homosexuals, however, apparently are unable to find satisfactory relations among themselves.

It is not difficult to see why, in their unhappiness, they rationalize their complex and profound problem into a belief that society is the chief cause of their troubles, that they are misunderstood and persecuted. Often the argument is that society does not appreciate the artist, the truly creative spirit, and that accordingly this intellectually and esthetically superior person must expatriate himself or withdraw into some cult of those with similar attitudes. Here he often icily bemoans the vulgarity or materialism of the herd, calls attention to his exalted standards and voices his distaste, in verse or prose or conversation, for the normal attitudes and aims of those not sexually disordered.

Again I declare that I am not qualified to evaluate what real artistic worth the bulk of nonobjective painting and noncommunicative writing currently held in high regard among the esthetically elite may or may not have for true devotees. No doubt many normal people find genuine pleasure and meaning through a highly cultivated discernment or appreciation in what to the unsophisticated appears merely as chaos or nonsense. Particularly difficult or contrary forms of art also seem to offer the sexually disordered person a refuge from the ordinary standards and values to which he is unresponsive.

In the cryptic symbolism and intricacies of literature or music that is unintelligible to the general public he may find meaning, or if not meaning, at least grounds for allegiance to the mere quality that excludes those who do not understand him and whose feelings are to him incomprehensible. Uncomfortable and forlorn at the level of majority reactions and feelings that he cannot share, he is naturally drawn to the *avant garde* movement with its exclusive cult of devotees who, like him, defy the outer philistine world. This participation in an esthetic withdrawal affords cultural aloofness and may support efforts to identify his sexual peculiarities with superiority of intellect or spirit. In this position of loveless isolation, ennui, and cynicism, he can better rationalize the pathos of his fate into a supercilious disdain for natural human interests. If psychiatrists or others succeed in convincing the public that homosexuals are indeed normal, these negative attitudes will appear as mere foppish and voluntary affectation. Knowledge of a genuine infirmity should diminish all expression of disrespect.

Not all attempts at permanent union among homosexuals are so transient as those of the beautiful Lesbian, or so stormy as that of the two university instructors, mentioned above. A greater durability and a relative immunity from major and uproarious dissension between partners is, apparently, sometimes purchased at the price of wholeheartedness. When the two are content not to seek in each other very intense fulfilment or to demand a close approximation of personal mating, they may, it seems, enjoy for longer periods some measure of companionship plus some pleasure in their sexual activities.

An example of this is afforded by the benign, middle-aged man, often nearer neuter in his sexual status than vigorously homosexual, who supports and protects a younger companion more obviously effeminate than himself. Such relations follow many patterns but sometimes a sober and moderately affectionate atmosphere may prevail despite jealousies, little tiffs, and fusses about trifles that are not really womanly, or feminine, but effeminate. Often such a pair in their approximation of a marriage for security strain little at high passion for each other, avoid spending much time in *gay* bars, and partake sparingly, if at all, of extravagances at the *drag* or at other gatherings where inversion is flaunted. (1) Some promiscuity, particularly in the younger male, is perhaps inevitable. Jealousy and suspicion without grounds can scarcely be avoided. Such unpleasantnesses in some partnerships of this sort may be sufficiently well tolerated to postpone separation for a considerable period. The hand of the older man which generally holds the purse strings seldom becomes careless or impetuous, but he is apt to allow his protégé some little indulgences. The protégé is often specifically averse to jobs that would make him self-supporting and usually dabbles at some sinecure where little more than an appearance of employment is maintained.

Situations of this sort which I have had opportunity to observe, though they offer only limited rewards to the participants, often avoid the bitter and sometimes tragic farces and horrors that befall homosexuals who, in violent sincerity, try to force their union into greater depths, into more ambitious relations that become progressively more unnatural and painful and impossible. Those who settle for small stakes and content themselves with relatively trivial goals in each other do not, so far as I can observe, achieve anything comparable to happiness between man and woman. They do, I believe, achieve the best that is available in homosexual relations. In none of these affairs have I ever observed confirmation of the opinion quoted by Edward Carpenter: "Happy indeed is that man who has won a real Urning for his friend—he walks on roses, without having to fear the thorns." (6)

Many observations have contributed to this impression: that the more earnestly a homosexual strives for full and genuine love, for a partner who he hopes can be to him all that a responsive, passionate, and utterly devoted woman can be to a man likewise committed to her without stint or reservation, the more surely will his disillusionment be severely traumatic and disastrous.

A young man of genuinely fine character whom I treated years ago for suicidal depressive illness will serve as an example of a large series who have illustrated this for me clinically. His splendid integrity, his superior social and personal attributes, had been proved over many years in behavior that need not be here recounted. Few men I know had more manfully sustained sorrows and hardships, more consistently shown dignity, compassion, and understanding in all his relations except those specifically sexual. I emphasize these points because some of his sexual activities may seem to falsify my estimate of his character.

This man, moved intensely by inverted sexual impulses since he completed grade school, had for years resisted numerous opportunities to commit homosexual acts. Though he had at length succumbed to this temptation and participated in such relations with numerous men, he had not until recently formed any serious personal attachment with another man. For some months he had been sharing an apartment with this new-found "friend" who apparently awakened in him profound needs never before suspected.

He felt there could be no happiness to equal that of living with this man as a mate in permanent and unreserved union. Up to this time he had, as a sincerely religious man, felt shame and remorse for his transient and casual exploits with other homosexuals.

The new love-object had helped him to accept his homosexuality as "natural" and at first the future loomed magically bright. His feelings for the other man were intensely romantic and he felt he could commit himself utterly to the union. Typically, he felt proud that the mate was "bisexual." The latter had been able to complete intercourse with women but had no specific interest in them, sexually or otherwise.

It was not long before my patient was grieved and all but devastated by his mate's casual infidelities with a number of men and boys. In the aftermath of stormy scenes in which he offered forgiveness, the other proposed to help him achieve also a status of "bisexuality" by teaching him the art of representing himself to women as a lover and giving him sufficient emotional support to carry out with them sexual acts that for him were unappealing.

It is difficult to understand how this intelligent and earnest man, so normally oriented in other matters, could have been talked into this proposition in the name of true love between himself and his male partner. The fact that he could reflects much of the self-contradictory chaos and savage paradox on which homosexual concepts of love appear to be based.

The patient eventually succeeded in carrying out, one might say, the motions of copulation with a woman. He apparently found nothing attractive about her, erotically, and much that was repulsive in his role, but he did achieve technical success through homosexual phantasies of forging thus a new bond with the other man. A woman, whose husband traveled and left her alone for long periods, and who must have been a person of uniquely obliging nature, lent herself to the project. If not in the literal name of fidelity in love, at least in some sadly perverse conception of it, the two men, in addition to their ordinary homosexual acts with each other, developed a new technique of mating.

Both men went to bed with the woman, whose amiability apparently knew no bounds. Each had genital relations with her in succession. Neither man, however, remained idle awaiting his turn. It was customary for all three to participate in a general effort at sexual stimulation and cooperation. In giving me an account of these events, the patient stated emphatically: "The woman meant nothing, to me or to him. She was merely a vehicle for us. A sort of medium through which we felt each other. She was nothing more." Actually he did not regard the woman with simple indifference. He truly despised her as something foul and unnatural which somehow served a purpose in promoting the illusion that his relations with the other man were made more complete and more important.

Dissatisfaction, and curiously enough jealousies, arose even during these triangular practices. They became unbearable to the patient, when, instead of a woman, his mate insisted from time to time in bringing in various other males to share their sexual intimacies. Their nightly episodes became more turbulent and, for the patient, progressively more tormenting. The partner's own feelings of jealousy were minor in comparison and apparently acceptable to him as a choice seasoning for these affairs, but his ill temper and vexation about other matters waxed constantly.

After a wild altercation, during which blows were struck, and my patient seriously injured his "beloved," the former temporarily abandoned his partner, fled to another town and threw himself into varied homosexual dissipations. He was genuinely disturbed because he knew that he had barely avoided a decision to kill the other man. He was well aware that he could easily have done this with his hands and that he had narrowly escaped obeying the impulses that urged him to proceed. Soon a reconciliation took place, only to be followed by similar misunderstandings, and for the patient, but not for his partner, by heartbreaking grief and confusion.

Though the partner was articulate in speaking of immortal bonds, the consecrated relations of those mated spiritually, and so on, he showed little hurt in comparison with my patient, who had tried to give so much more of himself in a relation that could not fulfil his high hopes. My patient, a serious and sincere person, tore his feelings in a vain effort to make something genuine of what is impossible. Finding himself close to murder and to suicide, he still hoped something could be worked out, but finally decided to give up relations with his "friend" who lightly wondered why the other man should get himself so worked up about what had happened.

It has often been said that psychiatrists and other physicians are not in a position to estimate fairly the results of homosexuality, since they see professionally only those who come, or are sent, because of illness or maladjustment. (7) On similar grounds, the impression of the judge or the lawyer is often challenged. However clearly and regularly these defects in homosexual relations disclose themselves to us in clinical experience, we are not warranted in claiming that such evidence is scientific proof that all such relations are similarly unfortunate. Such evidence is, however, impressive and deserves consideration in opinions based on extensive experience.

Among others, as we have noted, André Gide has insisted that homosexuality is grossly misjudged because a minority of homosexuals, afflicted with irrelevant abnormalities which might be found in any group, attract undue attention. He protests:

If you don't mind we will leave aside the inverts. The trouble is that ill-informed people confuse them with normal homosexuals. . . .
  In any case, degenerates, and sick and obsessed people are to be found amongst heterosexuals as well. (8)

If we are permitted to take Gide himself as an example of the so-called "normal" homosexual, we have a remarkable opportunity to evaluate accurately the type of love he has praised so highly. Few literary figures have left intimate records so revealing as his own.

Gide's enthusiastic affirmation in *Corydon* of rare spiritual values, of joys between homosexual lovers, of passion that is more elevating and more beautifully personal than anything between men and women, is, I fear, sadly contradicted by confessions in his *Intimate Journal* (9) and elsewhere. "As soon as desire enters into it," we find him stating, "love cannot hope to last." (10) Of recent homosexual relations he reports: "The latest adventures I have pursued have left me an utterable disgust." (10) Referring to what, in *Corydon*, he was to insist is the most beautiful form of love, he writes thus: "I well know that today, more restless, alas, further advanced in debauchery, I could not remain a mere contemplator as I then could." (10) These thoughts and words are curiously incompatible with what Gide has elsewhere preached of Greek love. (7)

His recent biographer, March, quotes him as writing late in life:

No shame as a result of facile voluptuous pleasure. A sort of vulgar paradise and communion on a low plane. The important thing is not to attribute to it too much importance, not to feel oneself polluted; the mind is not at all involved any more than the soul, which doesn't pay too much attention. But in the adventure an extraordinary amusement and pleasure accompany the joy of discovery and of novelty. (11)

Apparently he is here referring to the same relations which he has boldly proclaimed to the public as a crowning glory of man's spirit.

In this discerning biography, *André Gide and The Hound of Heaven*, March describes a meeting of Gide with Oscar Wilde and Lord Alfred Douglas in Algiers:

To Gide, Wilde seemed at this time to be a man under the cloud of an impending destiny: his laugh was loud and strained, his wit brittle, almost tragic. "I have gone as far as I can in my direction," he said, "I can go no farther. *Something* must happen." As for the egregious "Bosy" [Douglas], Gide failed to find him as beautiful as he appeared to the infatuated eyes of Wilde. He was brutal, cynical and made atrocious scenes which Wilde endured meekly and with a look of dumb suffering. (12)

This picture does not seem to bear out Gide's confident assurance in *Corydon* that "a friend in the fullest Greek sense" is ideal to bring out the best and noblest in a young man. Such a relation, in contrast to nonsexual friendship, we must remember Gide insists, can be "for the boy . . . the greatest incentive to courage, work and virtue." (13)

According to Gide's personal records, Wilde and Douglas led him

. . . on a round of dubious cafes where hashish was smoked and where the principal attraction was beautiful boy musicians. In one place a languorous flute player caught Gide's attention. "Dear," whispered Wilde, "would you like the little musician?" Choked by emotion, Gide managed to articulate "Yes." Some arrangements were concluded with a hideous go-between, and to the accompaniment of the diabolical laughter of Wilde they wound through dark alleys and brightly lighted squares to the disreputable hotel where Gide spent the night with the flute player. (12)

I suppose the personal reactions to his sexual acts quoted earlier and the episode above must be what Gide refers to as "normal homosexuality" and what he seeks to contrast with "inversion," "degeneracy," and so forth.

Gide's relations with his wife deserve particular attention. Throughout his entire life he maintained that he loved her with superlative devotion. On their wedding journey he repeatedly abandoned her for hours while he engaged in homosexual practices with boy prostitutes. He regarded his own love for his wife as too spiritual and elevated to permit consummation of the marriage. He assumed that his obvious sexual relations with numerous unloved boys during this curious honeymoon were kept from his wife by some obtuseness, "which," he writes, "permitted my pleasure without too much remorse since neither my heart nor my mind was engaged in it." (14)

During the course of this strange honeymoon journey Gide, on the train with his bride, notes that three school boys are in the next compartment. He writes:

They had half-undressed themselves, the heat was provocative, and alone in that compartment, they simply raised hell. I heard them laugh and tussle. At each of the frequent but brief stops of the train, leaning out of the little side window which I had lowered, I could touch with my hand the arm of one of the three boys, who amused himself by leaning towards me, from the neighboring window, and lent himself to the game, laughing. I enjoyed delicious tortures in stroking the downy amber flesh he offered to my caress. My hand slipping along his arm, rounded his shoulder. . . . I sat panting, palpitating and pretended to be absorbed in reading. Madeleine [the bride], seated facing me, said nothing, affecting not to see me, not to know me. (15)

Later when he and she were alone she said to him in a tone which he regarded as containing "still more sadness than blame, 'You had the look of a criminal or a madman.'" (15)

Years later Gide writes on the anniversary of their marriage:

I don't know which is the most atrocious: to be loved no longer or to see the person you love and who still loves you cease to believe in your love. I have not succeeded in loving her less, and I remain near her, with bleeding heart, but without words. (16)

While marveling at his wife's failure to be the proudest and happiest of women because of the great and sincere adoration he feels that he offers, Gide occupies himself with his homosexual pursuits decade after decade. According to March, who is both compassionate and strict about facts:

. . . his standard course had been night-wanderings undertaken in the half-recognized hope of seeing and trailing some youth, preferably ragged and with the air of not being a disciplined and functioning part of the social machinery. Sometimes the hope was fulfilled, more often not; but in either case the result was physical exhaustion, disappointment and further restlessness. . . . sometimes his desires seem to have found their target, and his only melancholy is at the thought of the transitoriness of experience. On a warm spring night of 1905 he writes: "My brain is clear, not frivolous, my flesh in repose, my heart firm. I should make an admirable lover tonight." (17)

Gide is apparently without anything approaching ordinary ability to see why the sort of "love" he offers his wife does not make her happy, why she does not recognize it as something to rejoice in and prize as a reward beyond the lot of other women. He is utterly without comprehension of her act when at last she burns his letters to her. He writes as follows:

She did it, she said, right after I left for England. Of course, I know she suffered atrociously on my leaving with Marc, but did she have to take revenge on the past? It is the best of me which disappears, and which now will not counterbalance the worst. Over more than thirty years I had given her (and still was giving her) the best of myself, day after day, throughout the briefest absence. . . . I could have killed myself without effort. (18)

Gide apparently has no real grasp of why a normal woman would not consider herself fortunate in the possession of a husband who never completed the marriage and who spent many hours away from her even on their wedding trip, in perverse activities with boy prostitutes. After many years of such relations, when he left her to go abroad with a young "friend," he finds it beyond his comprehension that his wife should burn the letters which he regards as a rare and superlative romantic testimony to their incredibly beautiful love. As a literary embodiment of this love he hoped to bequeath them to generations yet unborn. To an illiterate moron much would be plain that to this man of towering intellect remains a cruel enigma.

He often seems to feel he has given her the most ideal and perfect love imaginable; that only a cruel perversity has prevented her from joining him in acclaim of what he has bestowed upon her. (19) As he beats his breast in despair at her incomprehension and cruelty, her failure to appreciate her role with such a husband and lover, he shows something that March describes thus:

It is impossible to ignore the egotism in his sustained play for Madeleine's sympathy after the loss (day after day of weeping in the chimney comer, with occasional hopeful glances to see how she was taking it) and his eager seizing of the opportunity to blame somebody else for what was chiefly his fault. . . . (20)

His friend, the poet and diplomat Claudel, wrote:

Gide is fascinated by mirrors. His *Journal* is only a series of poses before himself. When one looks at oneself one always poses. From this point of view his *Journal* is a monument of insincerity. (21)

Who can fail to agree with the humane and scholarly biographer when he says:

Sex—the natural kind . . . came to arouse in him a repulsion which he took for virtue. . . .
The tortured history of his sex life is certainly no recommendation of his separation of love and desire. (22)

Can anyone find in the life of this celebrated man a recommendation of homosexuality? All that Gide reveals of his inner life is entirely consistent with the impression of homosexual affairs obtained from clinical experience.

Glover, in a recent and very discerning study of personality traits in homosexual students at a university, brings out points that are fundamental. This statement made about his own cases applies uniformly to those which I have observed:

These people represent a parody and a paradox in emotions; in a sense they burlesque love as a heterosexual knows it and yet they are a continual tragedy of failure to find either sex gratification or a person through whom they may enjoy continuously that measure of sex gratification they attain. . . . There is a narcissistic selfishness in their disregard for people as a whole. . . . A general disdain of inheritance and social values of law, religion and the betterment of mankind. . . . All feel distinctly inferior though their facade may be one of superiority. (23)

SOURCES

1. D. W. Cory, *The Homosexual in America* (New York: Greenberg, Publisher, 1951).

2. Harvey Wickham, *The Impuritans* (New York: Dial Press, Inc., 1929), p. 106.

3. James Jones, *From Here to Eternity* (New York: Charles Scribner's Sons, 1951), p. 390.

4. *Ibid.*, p. 386.

5. Edmund Bergler, "The Myth of a New National Disease," *The Psychiatric Quarterly*, XXII (January 1948), 66–88.

6. Edward Carpenter, *Love's Coming of Age* (New York: Vanguard Press, Inc., 1928), p. 127.

7. André Gide, *Corydon* (New York: Farrar, Straus & Cudahy, Inc., 1950).

8. *Ibid.*, p. 145.

9. Harold March, *Gide and the Hound of Heaven* (Philadelphia: University of Pennsylvania Press, 1952).

10. *Ibid.*, pp. 182–84.

11. *Ibid.*, p. 368.

12. *Ibid.*, pp. 79–80.

13. From Corydon, pp. 147-51. Copyright 1950 by André Gide. Published by Farrar, Straus & Cudahy, Inc.

14. André Gide, *The Secret Drama of My Life* (Paris: Boar's Head Books, 1951), p. 39.

15. *Ibid.*, pp. 40–41.

16. *Ibid.*, p. 90.

17. March, *op. cit.* pp. 133–35.

18. Gide, *The Secret Drama of My Life*, p. 77.

19. *Ibid.*

20. March, *op. cit.*, pp. 383–84.

21. *Ibid.*, p. 382.

22. *Ibid.*, pp. 37–38.

23. B. H. Glover, "Observations on Homosexuality Among University Students," *The Journal of Nervous and Menial Disease*, XCIII (May 1951), 381–82.

Chapter 16
TRAVESTY AND DISAPPOINTMENT

Though homosexuals show, in some respects, a strong affinity for one another, this feeling is continually adulterated and contradicted by what appears to be an odd but specific distaste that each manifests toward his fellows. They haunt "gay" bars, gather at the "drag," join each other in exclusive groups where effeminacy is proudly flaunted. Yet, as Cory so clearly shows, they bickeringly deride each other as "faggots," insult each other with petulant accusations of "camping," that is, showing obvious homosexual characteristics. One aspect of their affinity suggests that it is accepted as a union of pariahs. Another indicates that it is taken to be a natural confluence of the elect. Some attitudes of homosexuals suggest that each finds, or tries to find, his anomaly a proud distinction in himself, but an absurdity in all his fellows.

"I want to get it straight with you from the beginning, Doctor," a patient almost sixty years old emphatically told me, "I want you to know I'm not a *queer*! In fact I'd never heard of such a thing as a *queer* until a few months ago."

This patient, a former schoolteacher, frankly discussed decades of promiscuous homosexual activity with scores of boys and men. Married, the father of grown children and several times a grandfather, he had left home some months earlier. During this time he had lived in an apartment with a nineteen-year-old boy who worked and supported him. He himself meekly kept house and served as a sexual partner.

His companion, an unstable lad of violent temper, constantly suspected him of infidelities and made raging scenes, particularly accusing him of sexual traffic with an eighth-grade boy who lived in the apartment across the hall. So annoyed did the younger of the two become about this that he insisted on locking up the old gentleman in the apartment, keeping him there in isolation until he himself returned from his work at the end of the day. My patient was submissive to this as well as to occasional but sound beatings for alleged unchastity. He smiled as if in a quiet but triumphant satisfaction at his success and desirability in a role so strange to an ordinary man that it is difficult indeed to imagine the attributes in which he found himself flattered. After forty or more years of such a life, this well-educated man could see no possible reason for classing himself with those whom he disparagingly called "queers."

So, too, it seems remarkable that homosexuals, so eloquent in describing a sexual love of man for man as natural and glorious, should dress themselves, or their mates, in evening gowns, nylon stockings, and feminine finery. If it is a man they desire, why do they dress the man as a woman? Behavior at the "drag," such as that reported in Cory's book (1) and described to me by patients, does not appear to substantiate John Addington Symonds' opinion of homosexual love as "in its origin and essence masculine, military and chivalrous . . . clearly neither an effeminate depravity nor a sensual vice." (2)

This appears to me unrealistic. Everywhere in homosexual feeling we meet paradox and ambivalence. Describing homosexual men at such a "drag," a party and dance where many wear women's clothes, Cory writes:

. . . Some can be spotted from afar. They trip over their skirts and their shoes. They are clumsy, gawky, uncomfortable. Others require close scrutiny and a few can never be identified with certainty. . . .

At midnight, the striking of the drum, the flashing of the lights, and the floor is cleared. The parade of the queens will take place. Every male in female attire who so chooses may get in line. The gowns are mainly on the lavish side, with here and there some striking simplicity. But mostly one sees flowing skirts, flamboyant colors, an ostentatious overdressing. Many wear wigs, while others have scarves skillfully tied around their hair. There are no visible crew-cuts among them.

One by one they march to the platform, each stopping to pose like a model. Each turns around, shows form and figure to the judges and the audience, smiles coyly, listens for applause, and then descends. Perhaps the march continues for an hour. After the first few rounds of applause, the audience gives only a cursory clapping, except for an outstanding costume or an extremely effective impersonation.

Now and then the judges halt the march and examine more closely, seeking conviction that this is impersonation and not fraud. No woman may compete with these men who have faced the competition of women all of their lives.

Then the awards, with the queen being crowned, and second and third prizes given, followed by applause and protest, and by more dancing, drinking, flirting, weeping, long into the hours of the night. The time of departure draws near. Some part, alone and lonely, wishing to remain, although anxious to forget the evening. Others make their way out with the friends or lovers with whom they came. Some leave in the company of new-found friends. For them, the evening of adventure remains to be explored. The night is young and does not end even when the sun comes up in the morning. (3)

Would Symonds insist that this type of behavior and these attitudes are in "essence masculine, military and chivalrous"? That which attracts the typical homosexual apparently at the same time revolts him. He often insists on his disgust with anything even suggesting a "swish" or a "fairy," while accepting within himself as natural and desirable the very tastes and reactions by which he defines these terms of opprobrium for others. He may even speak of homosexuality as if he denied in it anything sensual, and at the next moment acclaim its sensuality as supreme and supremely desirable. Of such relations between men, Symonds writes:

The passion which grovels in the filth of sensual grossness may be transformed into a glorious enthusiasm, a winged splendor, capable of rising to the contemplation of eternal verities and reuniting the soul of man to God. (2)

Despite this apparently ascetic approach to homosexuality, we find the scholarly Symonds expressing almost mystic rapture about physical contact with Swiss peasants among whom he lived. He is particularly impressed by this remark of an ignorant gymnast, which he quotes:

"You can only learn to love men whose bodies you have touched and handled."

True as I believe this remark to be and wide-reaching in the possibilities of application I somehow did not expect it from the lips of an Alpine peasant. (4)

At one moment Symonds' ideal appears to be his burly servant and guide, Christian Buol, who, apparently, "enabled him to bring into practice those ideas of comradeship and democracy which had drawn him to Whitman." (5) But again we find him turning with esthetic and erotic admiration to such an effeminate figure as Antinous, "that beautiful equivocal boy, an Emperor's Ganymede." (5)

Bragman, in his admirable study of Symonds, sharply illustrates the unfortunate paradox of repulsion and attraction so familiar in homosexuality. Symonds writes of men loving boys in "pure wedded lives of Achilleian honour," of golden dreams about a young man who, having glided to the poet's side, "kissed my lips . . . kissed my cheeks." Symonds writes also of a shepherd whom the star Hesper informs of the joys and beauties of boy-love. The star "gives him the vision of a god who would take a youth for a lover;

and promises him a place in the heaven of male lovers, if he keeps faith with his beloved," etc. (6)

Yet, as Bragman shows, this poet and scholar reviles the very physical contact he calls so noble: "Where the treatment of passion in poetry," Symonds writes, "has the object of showing vice to be odious, I think great lengths are allowable." (6)

Despite dreaming of an immortality promised to shepherds by gods for fidelity, he also writes a "plea against the necessity of permanence in love" insisting that transience adds beauty to homosexual affairs. Symonds describes one of his works on the theme as intended "to describe by way of allegory the attraction of vice that fascinates and is intolerable; with its punishments of spiritual extinction or madness in this life." (6) From this work Bragman quotes:

> . . . In what dark abyss
> Of thy deep counsel dwells the black decree
> Whereby, O God, such shapes of blessedness
> Must sink beneath the scurf and barren spume
> Of lust unlovely, loathed and lustreless. (7)

These men, who often refer to each other as "she" and call John "Jenny" or "Joan," insist that their sexual status is the essence of manliness. Edward Carpenter even offers proof in this remarkable quotation from Jaeger:

Among the homosexuals there is found the most remarkable class of men, namely those whom I call super-virile. These men stand, by virtue of the special variation of their soul material, just as much above Man, as the normal sex man does above Woman. Such an individual is able to bewitch men by his soul aroma as they—though passively—bewitch him. (8)

If among homosexuals there are not only "queens" who try fantastically to imitate women but also these specimens of "super-virility," one might conclude that here lies the opportunity for a suitable match. Surely these will delight each other. This may be so in books, but apparently not in life. (9) As a matter of fact, just as the imitator of woman suggests not what is really feminine but a pathetic travesty, so, too, these others suggest less a supervirility than a pseudovirility, often a bizarre and far from manly parody of the actual male.

I would not say that in all phases of life either the obviously effeminate type of homosexual or those of extremely masculine or athletic appearance necessarily lack such attributes as courage, stoicism, and aggressiveness popularly regarded as characterizing the male. Some of both types have shown these qualities admirably in military action. (10) Nor are women really lacking in these virtues. Women's present-day role in courtship seems to make her generally prefer an escort who is at least a little taller than she is. The girl, as a rule, wants the boy to call and ask her for the date. She will not be pleased if her dancing partner expects her to lead. It is his social role to get out of the car first and open the door for her. No one is so foolish as to think that the girl could not, if she wished, get out first and help the boy over the curb. It is indeed strange that anyone who has had the chance to observe mammalian life as long as a child of ten has, could conclude that the female is feminine only insofar as she is inert and lacks courage. It is stranger, far, that psychiatrists could be persuaded to accept such a definition!

Like ordinary men and women, both the obviously effeminate and the apparently supervirile homosexual can sometimes show in most of their activities those virtues often regarded as specifically manly. It is in the special role of mating where we find neither type, nor any type of homosexual, appearing as really feminine or really masculine. What we do find is only a grim and merciless caricature—of the male, of the female, and of the mating.

Whether obviously effeminate or otherwise, inverts show a specific tendency to choose, instead of another homosexual, the real male—the one love-object most unsuitable, in all creation, and most unwilling to comply. To this ordinary male, the homosexual's inclinations are incomprehensible. To him the proposal appears not so much evil as preposterous. It is little wonder that his astonishment has given our language the term "queer."

Further comment on this specific inclination will be made later. Let us note now that even in this choice the homosexual is confused. The nearest he can come to a romantic concept for his mate is, typically, the normal male. This ideal is automatically unobtainable. If it could be attained, the ideal would in the very act of fulfilment be ruined, would lose its peculiar charm and value. Blind to the ordinary stimuli, the basic biologic signals, the homosexual flounders around in situations where every appeal soon contradicts itself; where that which seems most promising turns out inevitably to be a fraud.

Even Cory, a homosexual who writes to prove such relations between men are natural and can bring happiness, honestly admits:

... the inner resistance that many homosexuals display toward their own tendencies is reflected not only in a resentment and contempt, frequently unconscious, of their partner, but a hatred of him, for without the partner, the individual would not, or could not, be indulging the desires he secretly despises. (11)

Though this intelligent and sincere author seems vastly more aware of this fundamental situation than such rapturous literary glamorizers of homosexuality as Gide, Edward Carpenter, or John Addington Symonds, he argues that this disgust and contempt are not intrinsic to the inverted relation but artificially implanted by society's unjust appraisal.

Numerous examples from clinical experience as well as from the lives of such men as André Gide and Oscar Wilde indicate to me that the more thoroughly his unusual impulses are accepted as natural, the more promiscuous and petty is the invert's sexual life, and the less like genuine and happy love his attitude toward his partners. For neither Cory's contrary view nor mine is there available today any statistical proof.

Cory writes:

When the latter [shame and conflict within] is present, there will frequently be an abnormally large amount of hatred for the sexual partner. A homosexual harboring such hatred does not wish to combine sex and affection, but to separate them. He wants to sleep with strangers about whom he cares not two pence, and then discard them, only to seek new strangers for the next experience. . . . The homosexual who is inclined to fight against himself will resent his partner, and this pent-up feeling will sooner or later manifest itself, either in such obnoxious treatment as to cause the partner to withdraw from the relationship, or in a voluntary withdrawal of the individual himself. He is not likely to forsake the homosexual life, but merely the partner. (11)

In the psychiatric theory that homosexuality is caused by a flight from incest and the fear of castration, Cory finds reasons that lead him to admit that the male partner may not for many homosexuals be the real love-object, "the ultimately desired, but only a substitute for . . . something else. . . ." Whether or not in this theory is to be found the sole cause, or important causal factors, of the disorder, all my experience confirms the impression that a satisfying mate is not found, that real love is not attained. This has been vividly obvious not merely in many such relations studied, but in all. The sister of a homosexual quoted by Cory emphasizes a feature so regularly found in these relations that, whether or not it can be proved literally universal, must be recognized as at least extremely characteristic:

"At first," she said, talking about her brother, "I pitied him, and felt that the tragedy of his life was his inability to establish a permanent relationship with a woman. Today I have a slightly altered viewpoint. I regard it as the tragedy of his life that he cannot establish a permanent relationship with a man." (12)

Clinical experience, as well as the inner personal reactions reflected in literature, convince me that this is because man is not,

anatomically or otherwise, suited to mate with man. What is, even
to the simple, so obviously unnatural cannot really be proved natural by any amount of philosophical legerdemain. The pathologic
influences, psychological or physical, that so tragically distort
man's basic drive toward mating until he is forced into the preposterous choice of another man instead of a woman, do not leave the
indescribably complex and almost magic nature of that drive otherwise unaltered. On the contrary, it is not only deflected in direction but chaotically transmuted in quality or structure, woefully
disintegrated, tangled and fouled with impulses and aims that
show themselves clearly as pathology of love. The relations between biologically incongruous pairs are not often primarily those
of love.

Poets such as Oscar Wilde and his esthetic "friend," young Lord
Alfred Douglas, talk and write ecstatically of the beautiful satisfactions of their relationship. Evidence at Wilde's trial, however, despite tremendous obstacles in the way of obtaining such public
testimony, was indeed convincing that his "love" was by no
means confined to the allegedly adored one, but had also been expressing itself in diverse techniques, not precisely lyric, with a
wide variety of male prostitutes, guttersnipes, pimps, and other
specimens from the London slums. (13, 14) In the homosexual orientation, none of this apparently contradicted Wilde's conviction
that his adoration for Douglas was both pure and stupendous. In
letters to the youth he marvels that "those red rose-leaf lips of
yours should have been made no less for music of song than for
madness and kisses" and insists that "your slim-gilt soul walks between passion and poetry." (15)

When asked at the trial to define what the young lord had
meant when he wrote of the "love that dare not speak its name,"
Wilde launched boldly into panegyric:

The "love that dare not speak its name" in this century is such a great affection of an elder for a younger man as there was between David and
Jonathan, such as Plato made the very basis of his philosophy, and such
as you find in the sonnets of Michaelangelo and Shakespeare. It is that
deep, spiritual affection that is as pure as it is perfect. It dictates and per-
vades great works of art like those of Shakespeare and Michaelangelo,
and those two letters of mine, such as they are. It is in this century misunderstood, so much misunderstood that it may be described as the "love
that dare not speak its name," and on account of it I am placed where I
am now. It is beautiful, it is fine, it is the noblest form of affection. There is
nothing unnatural about it. It is intellectual, and it repeatedly exists between an elder and a younger man, when the elder man has intellect, and
the young man has all the joy, hope and glamour of life before him. That
it should be so the world does not understand. The world mocks at it, and
sometimes puts one in the pillory for it. (16)

All this sounds spiritual indeed, and no doubt elevating, as Wilde puts it in words. A more accurate idea of the realities of this Platonic enchantment is conveyed by incidents recorded by his admirer, André Gide. One of these we noted (on page 149) when Wilde generously acts as a procurer to obtain the sexual services of a young Arab musician for Gide, and along with his golden boy Douglas, accompanies the two to a sordid hotel, mocking and deriding Gide with "diabolical laughter." Why should he be derisive of what he hails as the noblest form of affection? Apparently Wilde, like the world, "does not understand" this spiritual relation which, he says "is as pure as it is perfect." March reports:

Shortly after this night Wilde left for London where his fate awaited him. Gide, anxious to shake off Douglas, set out for the deliriously remembered Biskra. But on the way, at Setif, a telegram from Bosy [Wilde's enthralled and radiant Platonic mate] urged him to wait; he was on his way with his latest fancy, a sixteen-year-old Arab boy. Gide, always liable to irrational reactions and curious about the boy, waited, and later accompanied Douglas and his companion to Biskra. (17)

In a world where such relations are not distinguished from genuine sexual commitments it is not difficult to see how strange ideas develop about "love." Decades later Douglas apparently still thinks of his attachment to Wilde as having been a pure devotion. At least he wrote: "I really was crazy about the man. . . . The truth is that I really adored him." (18)

Few more cynical appraisals of love between man and woman exist than those glittering in Wilde's numerous epigrams:

There's nothing in the world like the devotion of a married woman— it's a thing no married man knows anything about.
The proper basis for marriage is a mutual misunderstanding.
In married life three is company and two is none.
A man can be happy with any woman as long as he does not love her.
One should always be in love. That is the reason one should never marry.
The difference between a caprice and a life-long passion is that the caprice lasts a little longer.
When one is in love, one always begins by deceiving oneself, and one always ends by deceiving others. That is what the world calls romance.
When a man has loved a woman he will do anything for her, except continue to love her. (19)

Hesketh Pearson, Wilde's discerning biographer, points out that such observations as these could not have been based on his experience with his own wife. (14) There is every reason to believe that she was consistently devoted, and that she offered him love which a normal man would have found eminently gratifying. It must be plain to anybody what these sayings reflect. They are, after all, observations not of women, or of relations in which women are concerned. So often the brilliantly cynical comments of a literary homosexual are thus projected in disguise as judgments of normal life. These accurate descriptions of his own situation are often given in terms that refer to what he has no means at all of investigating personally, to what he, of all people, knows least about.

Wilde, in *De Profundis*, continually whines and scolds Douglas. His carping, arrogant accusations and reiterations of bickering complaint demonstrate in his vaunted attachment a bitter core. This sense of outrage and betrayal, and the pettiness, are grossly inconsistent with his earlier lyrical affirmations. They do, however, precisely echo the attitudes that clinically observed homosexuals so often develop towards those whom they select as mates. (20)

Bitter, dispirited, and perverse reactions of this sort are often mistaken by the immature as some genius's discerning evaluation, not merely of his own sexual disorder, but of life itself. The modest, introspective young student of the humanities may actually suffer considerable confusion before he dares accept his own unassuming judgment as more accurate than that of a loudly acclaimed poet and man of letters, of the greatest Athenian philosopher, and of a Nobel Prize winner. Should it be discovered that the genius whose works he is studying was a homosexual, what will our undeviated but sometimes still insecure and dangerously impressionable adolescent make of announcements that psychiatry or psychology has proved *scientifically* that homosexuality is normal? Is it possible that some groping and confused teen-agers may be persuaded to accept as esthetic gospel sad and cynical reactions to a specific illness?

Innumerable portrayals in fiction of homosexual attitudes and relations exemplify the precise features that so regularly emerge in clinical study. Though fictional characters and fictional behavior cannot be offered as evidence for opinions that derive support from direct experience with patients in the practice of psychiatry, this material can validly be used to illustrate what has been actually observed but cannot readily be kept for demonstration like a slice of pathologic tissue on a slide, or a solution in a test tube. The reader who wishes for detailed, and in my opinion, accurate portrayal of the profound differences between homosexual attachments and normal love can find this in many books readily available.*

**** A few relatively new and popular novels worth mentioning are: Jocelyn Brooke, *The Scapegoat* (New York: Harper & Bros., 1949). Truman Capote, *Other Voices, Other Rooms* (New York: Random House, 1948). Harrison Dowd, *The Night Air* (New York: The Dial Press, Inc., 1950). Fritz Peters, *Finistère* (New York: Farrar, Straus & Cudahy, 1951). Gore Vidal, *The City and the Pillar* (New York: E. P. Dutton & Co., 1948). Evelyn Waugh,

Though Cory objects to some of these books because they portray the path of homosexual mating as a dead-end road or as one inevitably leading to such tragedies as murder or suicide, they faithfully reflect the very features that have regularly distinguished this relation as I have encountered it in my psychiatric practice. It is quite true that the majority of such relationships do not lead to murder or suicide. All, however, according to my experience, fall far short of love or major fulfilment. Like those portrayed in the novels, all are marked by fierce or petty contradictions of desire and spite, praise and derision, sensuousness and boredom, extravagances of endearment hybridized with glib or bitter mockery. The widely differing patterns of unhappiness described in these novels, like those observed in the lives of my patients, are patterns of unhappiness or of exquisitely cynical superficiality in relation to what is erotic. When sorrows and frustrations of major proportion are less prominent, the results of such a union are still rich in petty torments of disdain and jealousy that often extend beyond the borders of absurdity.

SOURCES

1. D. W. Cory, *The Homosexual in America* (New York: Greenberg, Publisher, 1951).
2. L. J. Bragman, "The Case of John Addington Symonds," *American Journal of Psychiatry*, XCIII (September 1936), 390.
3. Cory, *op. cit.*, pp. 131–32.
4. Bragman, *op. cit.*, p. 393.
5. *Ibid.*, p. 392.
6. *Ibid.*, pp. 375–98.
7. *Ibid.*, p. 396.
8. Edward Carpenter, *The Intermediate Sex* (London: George Allen & Unwin, Ltd., 1935).
9. Sandor Ferenczi, *Sex in Psychoanalysis*, trans. by Ernest Jones (New York: Basic Books, Inc., 1950), pp. 296–318.
10. J. D. Campbell, "Psychiatry and Mobilization," *Journal of the American Medical Association*, CXLVI (May 12, 1951), 87–93.
11. Cory, *op. cit.*, pp. 136–37.
12. *Ibid.*, p. 140.
13. H. M. Hyde, *The Trials of Oscar Wilde* (Edinburgh: William Hodge & Co., Ltd., 1948).
14. Hesketh Pearson, *Oscar Wilde: His Life and Wit* (New York: Harper & Bros., 1946).
15. Hyde, *op. cit.*, p. 112.
16. *Ibid.*, p. 236.
17. March, *op. cit.*, pp. 79–80.

Brideshead Revisited (Boston: Little, Brown & Co., 1946). Calder Willingham, *End as a Man* (New York: Avon Publishing Co., 1947).

18. Pearson, *op. cit.*, p. 237.

19. *Ibid.*, pp. 103–4.

20. Oscar Wilde, *De Profundis* (New York: Philosophical Library, Inc., 1951).

Chapter 17
ERRANDS OF SISYPHUS

No simple explanation can adequately answer the fictional soldier who asked: "If you guys like being queer why don't you be queer with each other?" (1) I have already expressed the opinion that male homosexuals, perhaps not universally, but characteristically, are erotically attracted not merely by men but especially and specifically by those who are, or appear to be, clearly normal, quite free of inversion.

For many years I wondered why this peculiarity, which emerged so often in my own patients, is not emphasized, why it is, in fact, never to my knowledge mentioned in psychiatric literature. I have elsewhere reported this observation and discussed some of the patients who revealed so vividly this particular predilection. (2) It seems to me that clinical evidence of this is impressive.

Psychiatrists have apparently ignored this feature of homosexuality, but it has been remarked upon by others. Though not explicitly discussed, it is well illustrated in Gore Vidal's novel, *The City and the Pillar*. (3) Marcel Proust, who so thoroughly, and I believe so accurately, described the odd intricacies of behavior and inner perversities of feeling among this group, is clearly aware of its presence and of its importance. Referring to male homosexuals in general, he writes:

. . . lovers from whom is always precluded the possibility of that love the hope of which gives them the strength to endure so many risks and so much loneliness, since they fall in love with precisely that type of man who has nothing feminine about him, who is not an invert and consequently cannot love them in return; with the result that their desire would be forever insatiable did not their money procure for them real men, and their imagination end by making them take for real men the inverts to whom they had prostituted themselves. (4)

This opinion is not, of course, a proof by science. I believe, however, that any psychiatrist who cares to look will be likely to find considerable evidence supporting it in his patients. Those who have studied Proust's life feel that he himself was undoubtedly a homosexual. (5, 6, 7) He says that the paradox he describes is hidden usually from inverts by an illusion and that any attempt to dispel this illusion will anger them. (8) He repeatedly emphasizes his point, writing again of

. . . those who, the exceptional character of their inclinations making them regard themselves as superior to the other sex, look down upon women, make homosexuality the privilege of great genius and of glorious epochs of history, and, when they seek to communicate their taste to others, approach not so much those who seem disposed towards it (as the morphine maniac does with his morphia) as those who seem to them to be worthy of it, from apostolic zeal, just as others preach Zionism, conscientious objection to military service, Saint-Simonism, vegetarianism or anarchy. . . . (9)

It is true that the invert, in his search for a male person, will often put up with other inverts. But, according to Proust

. . . he seeks out essentially the love of a man of the other race, that is to say a man who is a lover of women (and incapable consequently of loving him). . . . (10)

It is doubtful if any writer has ever so adequately as Proust rendered the paradoxical elements of homosexual aim and desire. The pompous coquetry between Charlus, a fat, middle-aged nobleman, and the young tailor whom he despises but chooses for a sexual partner, is deeply revealing. Contempt infuses itself into the very lust by which the older man is attracted. So perversely unlike ordinary feelings are those of Charlus that it seems the disgust itself has become the essence of desire, not merely a conflicting and competing emotion but its nuclear identity. The sexual act of voluptuous detestation is consummated in an emotional key— less of love, or even of hate, than of inane farce. Before he has had time even to catch his breath, the scholarly nobleman plies the tailor with questions about other men who might satisfy his sexual whims. Be it noted that Jupien the tailor is regarded as a uniquely suitable partner. Charlus makes it plain nevertheless that he expects his newly discovered favorite to serve him also as a pimp and that this is an integral feature of his passion. Immediately after their initial consummation of "love," Charlus hastens to ask:

You don't know anything about the man who sells chestnuts at the corner, not the one on the left, he's a horror, but the other way, a great, dark fellow? And the chemist opposite, he has a charming cyclist who delivers his parcels. (11)

It seems likely that the Baron is counting on his new mate not only to serve him as a procurer in further exploration but perhaps also to assist in various exploits of "love-making."

The tailor coyly replies: "I can see you are completely heartless." Soon, however, he yields to all requests, fascinating his lover as he says, "Aren't you naughty . . . all right you big baby, come along!"

Charlus continues imperturbably:

If I hark back to the question of the tram conductor, . . . it is because, apart from anything else, he might offer me some entertainment on my homeward journey. For it falls to my lot, now and then, like the Caliph who used to roam the streets of Bagdad in the guise of a common merchant, to condescend to follow some curious little person whose profile may have taken my fancy. (11)

Like so many who can contemplate the female as a sexual partner only with abhorrence, the Baron must still try to dispute nature and by language force the detested femininity in some way upon the male he pursues:

So as not to lose the trail . . . I spring like a little usher . . . into the same car as the little person herself. . . . If she changes her car I take, with possibly the germs of the plague, that incredible thing called a "transfer" . . . as an antidote for the boredom of returning home by myself I should rather like to make friends with a sleeping-car attendant or the conductor of an omnibus. Now don't be shocked. . . . (12)

Referring to "young gentlemen" whom he contrasts with common tradesmen, such as his charmed listener, he expresses another reaction characteristic of inverted sexuality:

As soon as, instead of leaving my letters unanswered, a young man starts writing to me incessantly, when he is morally at my disposal, I grow calm again, or at least I should grow calm again were I not caught by the attraction of another. (12)

It is difficult to see how this sort of talk could be taken as love-making by the listening Jupien. The charms of the Baron, however, for him are specific. His reaction at first sight is described as stopping to "stand quivering in ecstasy before a stoutish man of fifty." (13)

These brief quotations give only a faint suggestion of the unpleasant, unloving, and outlandishly unhappy attitudes that are integrated into every erotic impulse of this intimately portrayed character. It is significant that Charlus' learning and his powers of intellect, when directed in other channels, are not only impressive but immense.

The degree of confusion, the total lack of ordinary affection, portrayed in the Baron de Charlus' sexual affairs may be more extreme than what is usual among homosexuals. But the attitudes he shows in exaggeration toward the object of sexual desire have never failed to emerge in some degree in all relations of this sort that I have observed.

Both the nature of the love-object forced upon them by their feelings, and the contradictory elements of aim and role in all such affairs, seem to forestall real mating. Daphne, pursued for sexual reasons by Apollo, is said, on being attained, to have turned into a bush or a tree. A change not entirely dissimilar apparently occurs to the homosexual's mate. And he, despite a hopeful ardor like the god's in pursuit, at the moment of triumph seems himself to share the miraculous and unhappy transmutation.

The homosexual's specific attraction toward the normal person of his own sex, so clearly emphasized by Proust, is also noted and carefully considered by the author of *The Invert*. (14) This little volume, written by a male homosexual who uses the pseudonym "Anomaly," is probably the most realistic presentation available of the personal reactions, the peculiar status and the complicated problems of a serious person trying to make the best adjustment possible despite his grave disorder. No attempt is made to glorify homosexuality as a superior passion or as a natural human need. With courage and superb dignity, the distortion of basic impulse is recognized as a misfortune. "Anomaly" offers no glib solutions. He does not join the popular chorus and proclaim that antisexual prejudices in society and persecution constitute the chief cause of all the problems which those like himself must face. (15–20) Instead, he offers a wise understanding, genuine and hard-earned, which should be helpful not only to those similarly deviated, but also to their perplexed and distressed families. The homosexual who can accept the insight offered by this book and live by it is likely, I believe, to find satisfaction far more real than in what attracts him to the gay bars or to aloof, esthetic circles where pale nihilistic scorn for the ordinary is languidly whipped up. In this anonymous writer's viewpoint the healthy man, no matter how distasteful to him homoerotic characteristics may be, will find a charity and manliness that he cannot but respect and envy. Such respect as "Anomaly" deserves and commands will, I believe, do more to dispel unkind mockery and hostile generalizations in the heterosexual world than all efforts to prove "scientifically" that homosexual inclinations are natural and normal in all people.

This serious commentator reports:

As I gained the confidence of individual inverts, they almost always told me that they had a particular friend, or at least, that they wanted some one as a friend. They usually assured me that this friend, or hoped-for friend, was "completely normal." Whatever the conditions, extent or

depth of these unusual friendships (they were as often as not quite innocent), it was evident that from the invert's point of view a prime condition
for their existence was that the other party must be a hundred per cent
MAN.

Whatever may be the pseudo-amorous relationship of one invert with
another, the invert-invert relationship is neither complete, satisfactory,
nor compelling. Listening to the often indiscreet gossip of inverts, I noticed that their serious emotional interest centered in normal males; not in
another invert. . . . I noticed that visitors to invert rendezvous were often
men about whom not a trace of the tell-tales of inversion was evident. Indeed both they themselves, and their particular friend (they were usually
introduced, or to be more exact "produced," by an invert friend) were
quick to assure one that they were competent males with regulation susceptibilities to feminine charms and with normal attachments of a wife,
sweetheart or mistress, or a more promiscuous devotion to women.

I was told that in prison some inverts found friends, and even protec-
tors, among the toughest and most masculine inmates, and did not by any
means seek solace from one another. (21)

In discussing books by homosexuals, the author of *The Invert*
mentions some which give lurid descriptions of "loud (or shrill)
invert groups." Though he questions the taste of these works, he
says those who wrote them "know what they are talking about;
they make it quite clear that in the most uninhibited circles *inverts
do not pursue or desire their own kind.*" (22)

He again emphasizes this opinion:

If by "homos" is meant "same," I find that so-called homosexuality is usually nothing of the sort, but that it indicates the existence of polarity between those whose sexual psyche is essentially different. One must strip
the invert of that accidental disguise which makes him physically the
same as the normal male, and observe his psychic nonconformity, which
is at once his cross and in a sense his capital. Having done this, one has
rounded the circle to find oneself faced with the almost inescapable conclusion that all *psychosexual attraction is essentially heterosexual.* (23)

It is difficult to see indications here of a hypothetical component
of the libido normally directed toward objects of the same sex, and
universal. If such a natural component existed, ordinarily repressed and inhibited in aim, would it not, on emerging from repression, direct males to other males most similar to themselves?
Would it put upon them the impossible task of trying to find between each other the real points of biologic differentiation by
which man and woman become sexual mates? What we see is a
tortuous mimicry of heterosexuality, a quest for the opposite polarity—but a quest in barren fields.

Homosexual erotic acts are efforts at adaptation whereby those
handicapped by the loss or serious impairment of a natural function try by substitutive acts or choices to approximate this function. The man who has lost both hands may with his feet or toes

learn to write or to play a musical instrument. Few, however, achieve with their toes the full range of function that is a natural capacity of the human hand. An artificial leg is chosen by a person who has lost his real leg. A colostomy may preserve life by performing the minimal functions of the anus. It is, however, a poor substitute, not an adequate or natural equivalent. So, the homosexual must seek some unnatural substitute and attempt some approximation of normal erotic behavior.

Perhaps this selectivity described by Proust and by "Anomaly" is not universal in homosexual choices. I have encountered it so often, however, in my psychiatric practice that I cannot ignore it as a major factor in the inmost emotional difficulties of homosexuals. What appears to be, in erotic relations, a wilful perversity, a deliberate preference for rejection or destructiveness, may, instead, be the influence of such a specific inclination not well recognized by the person whom it nonetheless motivates.

If this is correct, it contributes a great deal toward explaining the frustration, ambivalence, and promiscuity already noted. As I have mentioned, it may also play an important part in the choice by so many inverts of young boys who are still normal. Various other compromises and approximations are apparently utilized to achieve an illusion of the ideal. Often the homosexual may by bribes induce psychopaths to comply, sometimes even those who are quite free of any specifically inverted inclinations. The psychopath may be willing to play this role, in what to him is masturbation in a silly way, for small rewards, or sometimes just for the hell of it. Though he may be heterosexual in all his sensual inclinations, he lacks the normal personal responses to sexual love and adequate evaluation of this and of nearly all other serious matters. He may even find it a sort of joke to watch how the "queer" seems to get so worked up about it. (24)

Female prostitutes apparently get little or no sexual satisfaction from their work, but no shortage has, over the centuries, developed in their ranks. No doubt there are, besides typical psychopaths, other maladjusted, asocial types, living on the fringes of human dignity and not quite within the law, who for pay will join in sexual practices that do not hold any intrinsic attraction for them. These approximations of a male with really normal feelings apparently are preferred by many inverts to partners like themselves.

One psychopath with whose many problems I tried to deal over a long period of time picked up considerable money now and then by prostituting himself to a wealthy and prominent homosexual. He did not like the job, and in fact seldom resorted to it unless pressed by financial problems; but it served as one of the many ways, most of them ingenious and illegal, in which he could get money promptly and without regular work.

Among his fellow inverts, the so-called bisexual has a special distinction. Any homosexual who can accomplish the act of intercourse with a woman might, in a superficial sense, be called bisexual. I have not, however, known any man, capable of mature and substantial erotic interest in a woman, who also chose men for sexual relations. Usually the act with the woman means little, even as sensual stimulus, and is chiefly utilized to promote the illusion of real bisexuality. This illusion, in turn, promotes for him the further illusion that he is normal. Experience leads me to agree entirely on this point with Bergler, a prominent psychoanalytic investigator, who writes:

Some homosexuals are seemingly "bisexual"—that is to say, slight remnants of heterosexuality can be detected. These remnants guarantee, for some time, erective potency in a lustless coitus. Nobody can dance at two weddings at the same time, not even the wizard of a homosexual. Equal distribution of libidinous drive between homo- and heterosexuality does not exist because homosexuality is not a drive but a defense mechanism. The so-called "bisexuals" are in reality homosexuals with a light admixture of potency with unloved women. (25)

By virtue of the fact that these remnants of heterosexuality make the "bisexual" appear to other inverts more like a normal man, he is especially sought after, and often taken more seriously than others in the homosexual world. In discussing their problems, many patients emphasize with pride the fact that their current or most prized sexual partner is of this type. Recently while recounting to me quarrels and problems with his favorite, a successful man who is ordinarily the picture of dignity actually began to pace the floor in his excitement as he repeated over and over again: "You see, John is a *bisexual*! He is *really* bisexual!" Despite his chagrin and distress about the recent alienation, he was inclined to boast about this, apparently with feelings not unlike those that might prompt a social climber to miss no occasion to remind others that his daughter had married an earl or a millionaire.

Though it does appear that the degree of unsuitability has a real and positive correlation with the homosexual's choice of a love-object, I think that this is but one influential factor rather than a sole or primary cause of his failure to find love and happiness in erotic situations.

The basic reactions of male and female in love, so clearly felt within by the normal, are apparently not well understood by the homosexual, no matter how brilliant or sensitive he may otherwise be. Drawn only toward inappropriate objects, he furthermore approaches them with aims and intentions pathologically different from those of real mating. Disappointed and unfulfilled in each new relation, he is driven toward extremes of promiscuity. In unique bewilderment and in frantic repetitive persistence, he continues in efforts that sometimes suggest the futility of trying to wring blood from turnips, to make bread from stones, or to quench parching thirst in the emetic and impotable waters of the Dead Sea.

SOURCES

1. James Jones, *From Here to Eternity* (New York: Charles Scribner's Sons, 1951), p. 390.

2. Hervey Cleckley, *The Mask of Sanity* (3d ed.; St. Louis: The C. V. Mosby Co., 1955), pp. 319–41.

3. Gore Vidal, *The City and the Pillar* (New York: E. P. Dutton & Co., Inc., 1948).

4. Marcel Proust, *Remembrance of Things Past* (New York: Random House, Inc., 1932), Vol. II, p. 13.

5. L. Bagratuni, "The Illness of Marcel Proust," *The Oxford Magazine*, LXXIV (June 7, 1956), 23.

6. D. W. Cory, *The Homosexual in America* (New York: Greenberg, Publisher, 1951), pp. 157–66.

7. Harry Levin, introduction to *Letters of Marcel Proust*, ed. and trans. by Mina Curtiss (New York: Random House, Inc., 1949).

8. Proust, *op. cit.*, Vol. II, pp. 3–26.

9. *Ibid.*, p. 17.

10. *Ibid.*, p. 25.

11. *Ibid.*, p. 9.

12. *Ibid.*, p. 10.

13. *Ibid.*, p. 22.

14. Anomaly, *The Invert* (London: Baillière, Tindall & Cox, 1948).

15. Cory, *op. cit.*

16. Albert Ellis, *The Folklore of Sex* (New York: Charles Boni, 1951).

17. Albert Ellis, *The American Sexual Tragedy* (New York: Twayne Publishers, Inc., 1954).

18. André Gide, *Corydon* (New York: Farrar, Straus & Cuclahy, Inc., 1950).

19. Reno Guyon, *The Ethics of Sexual Acts* (New York: Alfred A. Knopf, Inc., 1948).

20. Philip Wylie, *Opus 21* (New York: Rinehart & Co., Inc., 1949).

21. Anomaly, *op. cit.*, pp. 179–80.

22. *Ibid.*, p. 182.

23. *Ibid.*, p. 187.

24. Cleckley, *op. cit.*, pp. 412–16.

25. Edmund Bergler, "The Myth of a New National Disease," *The Psychiatric Quarterly*, XXII (January 1948), 66–88.

Chapter 18
IS SOCIETY SO HARSH?

There have been many recent complaints that society is unfair and brutal to the homosexual. It has even become popular to explain the unhappy results of abnormal behavior as being caused entirely or almost entirely by society's distaste for it. (1, 2, 3) This argument is usually restricted to a defense of homosexuality but occasionally other types of behavior generally regarded as perverted and unnatural are similarly explained. (4)

In summation: sexual "perversion" is so universally condemned and deliberately suppressed in American society that very little frank, sly-dog, or ribald undercover enjoyment of it is permitted. When it does express itself, it generally does so in an anxiety-ridden, morbid or ridiculously exaggerated, way (e.g., the mincing manners and garish display of Greenwich Village homosexuals). This may be one reason why, while adultery, fornication, whore-mongering and other immoral sex outlets are utilized by millions of fairly normal Americans, homosexuality, sado-masochism and other abnormal sex practices, when they are habitually and exclusively used as modes of sex participation, are so frequently concomitants of seriously neurotic behavior. It may not be sexually perverted acts which make a society sick or decadent, but society's own mores which by their expressing unduly harsh attitudes toward certain sex acts, render the acts "perverted" and "abnormal" and thereby encourage their habitual or exclusive employment by many of society's neurotic members. (5)

Is society really so brutal and stupid in its attitudes toward sexual disorder? Just what is it that deviated people demand of society?

In a sentence quoted above, "sado-masochism" is included with "homosexuality" as a way of behavior toward which society is said to lack tolerance and acceptance. Are we to ask of society that it applaud, or tolerate, or greet as something acceptable, the act of a sado-masochist who disembowels an eleven-year-old girl in the name of carrying out an acceptable variation on the theme of normal love? The author just quoted would not, I am sure, ask this. Society does not accept, or respect as normal expressions of sexuality, the acts of a man who pays little girls to let him whip them, moderately or mildly until he achieves an orgasm. Is it, then, this prejudice of society and not the perversion itself that we should chiefly blame for the "morbid exaggeration" of sadistic expression into the act of murder? Should we therefore encourage people to express sadism in less drastic acts of perversion so that the more extreme disasters resulting from it may be avoided? I find no support for this attitude in what I take to be psychiatry.

Let us put aside such obvious matters, and consider the reiterated complaint that the homosexual's difficulties arise from persecution by society. In his book, Cory presents many arguments for a more tolerant attitude toward those who are deviated. I have seen very little hostility or disrespect shown directly to homosexuals in any community. At work, those with obvious characteristics are as a rule treated with friendly politeness. In social gatherings, many are welcomed whose tendencies are well known to the group. In fact, I have been strongly impressed by the willingness of what I would call the ordinary person to overlook this peculiarity in all aspects of life not directly pertaining to sex. It might be said that unless the homosexual himself brings out his aberrant inclinations and deliberately confronts his fellows with them, they will not be remarked upon, and he will usually be treated just like other members of any group. It is only the specific manifestation of his erotic inclinations, either openly and aggressively or within the proprieties that limit normal heterosexual expression, that is rejected as distasteful by the social group.

It has often seemed to me remarkable that society takes such pains not to persecute or even embarrass the homosexual. There are laws, it is true, on our statute books which, if invoked, would punish severely people carrying out acts that are considered "against nature." Until quite recently, in the state where I live, the penalty for sodomy, on the books, was a prison sentence of ninety-nine years. But what other laws are so little enforced?

I have not been impressed by any actual penalties meted out to those who indulge in such behavior. I have observed legal action brought against homosexuals only where abnormal relations had been forced upon children or they had otherwise been seduced in situations that I believe even the most charitable and understanding of parents would resent and would consider a tragic experience for the child.

What seems notable to me is not that society is so vindictive and "prejudiced" but that people naturally outraged at such dealings with their children could be so compassionate. In nearly all instances of this sort with which I am personally familiar, the parents of the child so misused agreed to drop the charges, sometimes on condition that the deviated offender remove himself from the immediate environment.

In addition to patients with this disorder, I have observed in all communities familiar to me many other persons generally recognized as homosexuals. So far as I have been able to observe, these people are not regularly shunned or humiliated by others. It is in fact one of the most remarkable examples of tolerance and compassion known to me that in large cities and also in small towns persons of this sort are treated respectfully, accepted in clubs, invited to weddings, dinner parties, etc., and often elected to office in civic, fraternal, and religious organizations. They are not boycotted in business, or insulted even indirectly by those whose most basic feelings are repulsed by what they represent in their erotic outlook. The derisive terms and uncomplimentary jokes so often heard about homosexuality are, it seems to me, directed toward tastes and practices that the majority involuntarily react to as ridiculously incongruous, as queer. It is usually not toward the victim of the disorder but toward the symptoms that negative feelings are expressed. Such jokes and terms may not be justified but they are often less unkind than they appear. I have been impressed, on the other hand, by the care and tact with which most people avoid telling such jokes or using such terms in the presence of anyone who, they suspect, might be homosexually inclined.

Albert Ellis speaks of homosexuality as being forced to express itself in "an anxiety-ridden, morbid or ridiculously exaggerated way (e.g., the mincing manners and garish displays of Greenwich Village homosexuals)." The expressions of homosexuality impress the public as morbid, to be sure, and everything about such attitudes and relations, when perceptible, is likely to appear not only garish but bizarre and distasteful to the normal person. Many features intrinsic to the disorder, when publicly displayed, are simply not attractive to others.

I have before me a brochure advertising a famous night club in a large city. It is embellished with photographs of what appear to be good-looking and definitely sexy girls. In large print it is announced that these are really pictures of "the most beautiful boys in America." What this club affords is not, to be sure, relished or admired by the public, but like many others of its kind it is allowed to flourish.

Cory, appealing for respectful acceptance of the homosexual's erotic tastes and behavior, presents the reader many scenes from homosexual gatherings. Even brief excerpts are illustrative. A man who took advantage of the mother-in-law's visit to slip away from his wife and rejoin the gay world has greeted two males in a bar, calling them "a couple of crazy love-birds."

They laugh heartily. "That reminds me," says the newly arrived married man. "Last month I was travelling with one of the kids from my office. Jackie—he's a swell kid—the most beautiful face you ever saw in your life and the campiest' thing you ever laid eyes on. So I went into a hotel in Portland to find if they had a room, and he went to park the car. I asked for a double room, and the clerk asked if I would register for myself and my wife, so, I says, no myself and my husband."

Again they laughed, although no one believed the story. He was relating to them what he might have liked to say. (6)

At a private apartment some of those who had enjoyed themselves earlier in the bar gather to continue their pleasures:

The lights are turned low, and a few young men dance with each other to the tunes coming from a record player. There is a general division into couples, on chairs, couches, even on the floors. But a few do not participate in the pairing off. They remain alone, perhaps wishing they were able to seek or ask for a partner, or perhaps just tired of this constant partner-seeking and exchanging. . . .

"Tomorrow's Church, and I have to get up early," a lad might be saying, while he has one arm around a friend's shoulder, the other hand holding a drink. . . .

. . . Two youths in a corner are kissing, several men are dancing. . . .

"Oh for the Navy, the good old days in the Navy. Plenty of lovers and you never had to look for a job!"

"Why don't you reenlist if you liked it so much, dearie?"

"Listen darling, if I could get my old captain, I sure would. All you need in the Navy is a pretty face and a captain with hot pants."

"There you go bragging again. I suppose you had the admiral, too?"

"Let me tell you about me and the admiral." (6)

Aside from the point that all this talk about the Navy, like the boast of the *gay* husband, probably expresses wish-fulfilment rather than fact, such scenes naturally invite questions.

Just how, we ask, does the deviate want us to react to his behavior? It seems to me that most people are quite willing to let homosexuals do what they want to do, so long as they confine their aims to adults who are similarly inclined. Is it possible or reasonable to expect the ordinary man to do more? I fear it is a little too much if the deviate demands a more active empathy or participation in his attitudes, such a fellow-feeling, for instance, as is implied in "All the world loves a lover." Such impulses and goals are foreign and instinctively distasteful to the sexually normal person. The most one can do is to step aside and wish the deviate well in aims one cannot, whether one wishes to do so or not, regard as

---

**** The most effeminately behaving.

alluring, or natural, or romantic. Is it remarkable if those who do not share such impulses and such orientations think of them as "queer," "outlandish," and the like? How else can one expect such behavior and such attitudes to be regarded by an ordinary person?

Even those who most earnestly believe that freely chosen homosexual activity between adults should not be sought out and mocked by others or punished by the law will hardly find themselves able to cheer at the kind of scenes described above or bless them as socially desirable. Those thoroughly able to respect homosexuals for abilities and other personal qualities deserving of respect find more difficulty in respecting as a healthy form of sexual love these erotic relations and their results. The inner ideal, the concept of self chosen or sought by the homosexual in these relations, is not clear, or even quite imaginable, to others. It is difficult for the outsider to focus on any distinct erotic status or role or attainment, such as the role of male or of female, on which he might offer compliments or felicitations such as those evoked by an announcement of the engagement of a happy couple. The average person is seldom able to see in the liaisons between inverts anything that he can recognize as a happy achievement, or about which he can honestly offer congratulations. The ordinary man would fear that he might be insulting if he tried affably to commend a homosexual acquaintance on being the "campiest thing" he'd seen in quite awhile.

The Kinsey report on males (7) has often been cited by those who insist that society persecutes the homosexual cruelly and without reason, particularly by those who seem to feel that all or most of the fault in the relations of this minority to the larger group lies in a blind prejudice of the majority against what the others regard as natural. Let us note briefly a few points, and only a few, about the celebrated study and conclusions that have been drawn from it.

In my mind there are serious doubts that any series of questions can be depended on to make people reveal with scientific accuracy a true account of their sexual activities. Immemorially, and I think correctly, such inquiry has been considered more likely than that in any other area of human experience to elicit either boastful exaggeration or remarkable understatement and distortion. Every psychiatrist must realize how often sexual histories become modified as examination and treatment continued. No matter how zealously Dr. Kinsey and his co-workers have tried to test the answers given, or how conscientiously the statistics were compiled, we still have only the record of what certain people say they have done. This, as Knight has pointed out, is not always the same as a record of what people actually have done. (8)

It has been said that the report should be entitled, not *Sexual Behavior in the Human Male* but *Sexual Behavior in the Human Male Who Wants To Talk About It*. Among homosexuals there seems to be an intense desire to have their status established as normal. Such a desire might influence a disproportionate number of the group to volunteer and so in frankness and good faith contribute statistics not truly representative of the American male. The careful investigator, Kallmann, writes:

> It may be borne in mind . . . that Kinsey's data on overt homosexuality apply to men distinguished by their willingness to cooperate with an investigation of ordinary sex behavior. . . . (9)

The more inverts might succeed in having their acts registered in a catalogue designed to record what is customary and natural, the more support can be furnished for their claims that their erotic life is normal. I have no way of knowing how much or how little such tendencies are reflected in Kinsey's conclusions. In this connection Bergler says:

> The chances are that many volunteers, though *consciously* inspired by noble intentions, had some less altruistic *unconscious* motives. Among these, one could suspect, were many homosexuals who gladly used the opportunity of proving by volunteering, that everybody has homosexual tendencies—thus seeking to *diminish their own inner guilt*.
>
> Moreover, the clinical fact remains that the circle of friends of neurotics consists almost exclusively of neurotics. Hence the second and third "crop" of volunteers must have consisted of too many neurotics, too. (10)

Bergler and others (8) have pointed out that no consideration is given by Kinsey and his co-workers to what various acts meant to the people who reported them. The subject who once as a twelve-year-old boy participated in mutual masturbation with another boy is classed as having chosen a "homosexual outlet," even though both were specifically and passionately dreaming of girls, and though either would have preferred the vagina of a calf to the male hand as a means of stimulus. His act enters the statistics as an item identical with the act of a "queen" in black lace underwear who records an incident of specifically chosen fellatio. It is true that the forty-year-old man who reported the single episode at age twelve will be listed as "predominantly heterosexual, only incidentally homosexual," while the "queen" may be classed "exclusively homosexual." The "queen" may be so classed, but not necessarily. Because of a few essentially distasteful copulatory successes with women undertaken to convince himself and fellow inverts that he is "bisexual," a rating of "predominantly homosexual, but incidentally heterosexual" may be earned; or perhaps even the rating of "predominantly homosexual but more than incidentally heterosexual." (11)

According to Legman:

The deepest and worst error of the Kinsey report is in its presuming to study human beings while scientifically rejecting every aspect of their lives which is specifically human. (12)

Despite these points, Kinsey's statistics seem to have led many to the conclusion that 37 per cent of American males are proved to be at least in part homosexual. Some have assumed that this in turn proves that homosexuality is normal and should be so regarded by all. Kinsey and his colleagues are themselves apparently among those so convinced, for they say:

In view of the data which we now have on the incidence and frequency of the homosexual, and in particular on its co-existence with the heterosexual in the lives of a considerable portion of the male population, it is difficult to maintain the view that psychosexual reactions between individuals of the same sex are rare and therefore abnormal or unnatural, or that they constitute within themselves evidence of neuroses or even psychoses. . . .

The homosexual has been a significant part of human sexual activity since the dawn of history, primarily because it is an expression of capacities that are basic in the human animal. (13)

M. F. Ashley-Montagu's comment on such reasoning is worth noting:

The most stupendous fallacy which runs through the whole work is the authors' implied assumption that the normal is equitable with a large quantity . . . there are . . . millions of persons with criminal tendencies in the United States, but their mere quantity makes them neither normal nor natural. (14)

Legman also finds it difficult to accept such conclusions, arrived at by "equating maximum with optimum" and pronouncing as natural even "expressly antibiological behavior like homosexuality." He thus expresses his objections:

Conscious, perhaps, of the stupendous lack of proof behind this irrelevant generalization, Professor Kinsey betrays his uncertainty as to what homosexuality is really all about . . . by fortifying this subject with the greatest number of tables, the swoopiest charts, the most concentrated bold-face type, and the only breakdown into numbered levels that he accords any sexual act. Behind this fourfold statistical safeguard, one presumes he feels safe in his ignorance. (12)

Bergler, who has made an excellent criticism of this famous study and its part in creating dangerous and absurd illusions, objects to Kinsey's claim that the sooner we learn to regard homosexuality as normal the "sooner we shall reach a sound understanding of the realities of sex." This highly qualified psychoanalyst concludes his paper, "The Myth of a New National Disease," with these remarks:

"Sound understanding of the realities of sex" is not furthered by creating the myth of a new national disease of which 50 million people are victims. Nor is "sound understanding" increased by labeling disease as health in the name of an equally mythological "heterosexual-homosexual balance." (10)

Kinsey's tendency to wander off into value judgments that seem very unrealistic in the light of ordinary human experience is illustrated in this opinion:

Interpretations of human behavior would benefit if there were a more general understanding of basic mammalian behavior. On the present issue, for instance, it is to be emphasized that in many species of mammals the male ejaculates almost instantly upon intromission, and that this is true of man's closest relatives among the primates. Students of sexual activity among chimpanzees, for instance, report that ten to twenty seconds is all the time which is ordinarily needed to effect ejaculation in that species. Far from being abnormal, the human male who is quick in his sexual response is quite normal among the mammals, and usual in his own species. It is curious that the term "impotence" should have ever been applied to such rapid response. It would be difficult to find another situation in which an individual who was quick and intense in his responses was labeled anything but superior, and that in most instances is exactly what the rapidly ejaculating male probably is, however inconvenient and unfortunate his qualities may be from the standpoint of the wife in the relationship. (15)

Karpman (16) among others has said that the potentiality for every sexual abnormality exists in every human being. This may be true. There is equally good reason to believe that potentiality for every type of crime and for every type of psychosis is also within every human being. Certainly it would be difficult to argue convincingly that the most healthy man did not have some susceptibility or potentiality of developing almost any kind of physical illness or disease.* It would scarcely be profitable or accurate, however, to assume because of this that there is little or no difference between serious illness and health, between psychosis and sanity, between any sort of crime and ordinary social behavior.

Too much, perhaps, has already been written about the Kinsey report. I have no wish to enter extensively into a general discussion of it. As regards the report itself, I need only say that the statistics very unrealistically reflect homosexuality as it appears in psychiatric practice and in the ordinary experiences of life.

A few applications of the statistics are worth attention. Karl M. Bowman, a very prominent American psychiatrist who apparently

---

**** I say "almost any," for otherwise the meticulous might point out that a healthy man has no appreciable susceptibility to ruptured tubal pregnancy, or the woman to carcinoma of the prostate.

accepts Kinsey's figures, concludes that "there would seem to be little or no chance of keeping our Government free of overt homosexuals." Such efforts, he says, are based on "some of the wish-fulfilment thinking, dissociated from reality, that we see in schizophrenic patients." (17)

He goes on to point out that Kinsey's figures on the incidence of homosexuality if applied to members of Congress and male Civil Service employees would show that 192 male members of Congress and 525,279 male Civil Service employees are homosexuals. Are all these, he asks, to be classed with those discharged from the State Department as poor security risks? Given sufficient faith in the Kinsey statistics, and in so applying them, it would be easy to "prove" also that over one-third of the members of the American Psychiatric Association are homosexuals. I hardly think there is anyone who believes this to be a fact.

The authors of a sensational book, *U.S.A. Confidential*, (18) give the impression that homosexuality is indeed prevalent. They express alarm and suggest that increasing homosexuality threatens our nation with decadence and disgrace and impotence. I am confident that most people share my belief that a progressive increase in homosexuality in our country would be unfortunate and, eventually, disastrous. I am not acquainted with any psychiatrist, whatever theoretical attitude he might hold, who does not share this belief. I do not, however, think we have real evidence to show that "our entire nation is going queer." (18)

But suppose that convincing evidence of this were indeed available? Could any psychiatrist find in theories which establish homosexuality as relatively normal the confidence to speak out and declare: "You have nothing but your own prejudices to fear"? Would he then be able to add, "In the name of science, I can assure you that all is well"? I very much doubt it.

SOURCES

1. D. W. Cory, *The Homosexual in America* (New York: Greenberg, Publisher, 1951).

2. André Gide, *Corydon* (New York: Farrar, Straus & Cudahy, Inc., 1950).

3. Philip Wylie, *Opus 21* (New York: Rinehart & Co., Inc., 1949).

4. René Guyon, *The Ethics of Sexual Acts* (New York: Alfred A. Knopf, Inc., 1948).

5. Albert Ellis, *The Folklore of Sex* (New York: Charles Boni, 1951), pp. 175–76. Quoted by permission,

6. Cory, *op. cit.*, pp. 126–27.

7. A. C. Kinsey, W. B. Pomeroy, and C. E. Martin, *Sexual Behavior in the Human Male* (Philadelphia: W. B. Saunders Co., 1948).

8. R. P. Knight, "Psychiatric Issues in the Kinsey Report," *Sex Habits of American Men*, ed. by Albert Deutsch (Englewood Cliffs, N. J.: Prentice-Hall, Inc., 1948), pp. 59–70.

9. F. J. Kallmann, "Comparative Twin Study on the Genetic Aspects of Male Homosexuality," *The Journal of Nervous and Mental Disease,* CXV (April 1952), 283–98.

10. Edmund Bergler, "The Myth of a New National Disease," *The Psychiatric Quarterly,* XXII (January 1948), 66–88.

11. Kinsey *et al., op. cit.*

12. G. Legman, introduction to Norman Lockridge's *The Sexual Conduct of Men and Women* (New York: Hogarth House, 1948), pp. 29–30.

13. Kinsey et al., *op. cit.,* pp. 659, 666.

14. In *About the Kinsey Report,* ed. by Donald P. Geddes and Enid Curie (New York: The New American Library of World Literature, 1948), pp. 59–60.

15. Kinsey *et al., op. cit.,* p. 580.

16. Ben Karpman, "The Sexual Psychopath," *Journal of the American Medical Association,* CXLVI (June 23, 1951), 721–26.

17. Karl M. Bowman, "The Problem of the Sex Offender," *American Journal of Psychiatry,* CVIII (October 1951), 250–57.

18. Jack Lait and Lee Mortimer, *U.S.A. Confidential* (New York: Crown Publishers, 1952).

Chapter 19
CRUSADE TO NONSENSE

We have noted André Gide's defense of homosexuality and his enthusiastic estimate of this aberration as a superior way of life. Other types of sexual behavior generally regarded as pathologic also have their champions. In fact, contrariness has often been applauded for its own sake by discontented intellectuals who, apparently, find the familiar biologic goals distasteful. There are many styles in which life can be rejected, in which love can by portrayed in bitter and unhappy caricature. Those who come forward to enlighten us on these subjects usually seem to regard themselves as exponents of a precious freedom, as liberal thinkers who boldly dare to strike off our shackles and guide us on the road to truth and bliss.

In certain discussions where science is allegedly invoked to "shatter savage and superstitious taboos," "to set eros free," and the like, truly amazing conclusions are reached. They are often proclaimed to the reader in a tone of authority. Examples that impress me as representing the *reductio ad absurdum* of this practice abound in *The Ethics of Sexual Acts* by René Guyon. (1) The author is not a physician. He is presented in the introduction to the second printing of an English translation of his book as a Doctor of Laws, as a profoundly wise and vigorous crusader against "anti-sexualists" and "professional moralizers," and indeed as "today's foremost sex-philosophical writer." (2)

There is hardly an author anywhere with qualifications comparable to those of Guyon, who not only writes from a vast personal experience but is also a philosopher, a world traveller and a student of human behavior, fully familiar with the main roads and the by-ways of passion. (2)

This relatively old shocker was reprinted in haste under stimulus of the Kinsey report, twenty-four years after its original publication. The physician who writes an introduction evidently believes that Kinsey's work has confirmed with scientific proof most, if not all, of Guyon's opinions. He writes:

... it is amazing how frequently Kinsey's cold objective figures bear witness to the truth of Guyon's assertions and tend to support his ideas, which at times may seem extreme. (2)

The same physician informs us that

Neither Guyon nor Kinsey can find justification for the terms "normality" or "abnormality" in the sexual life of man. (2)

He also warns us:

Both Guyon's and Kinsey's books are high explosives. They are likely to blow sky-high many of our most sacred notions. What arguments can the anti-sexualists and professional moralizers—forever on the warpath against men like Guyon—advance against Kinsey's figures and charts? ...

Faced by Guyon's disconcerting candor (and also by Kinsey's unimpeachable figures) even the liberal-minded scientist, believing himself quite free of prejudices, may suddenly discover that he too has retained childhood inhibitions and that his reasoning is impaired by some deeply embedded, ecclesiastical taboos and subconscious repressions. (2)

Guyon has a great deal to say and he goes at it with commendable zeal. According to the writer of the introduction, Kinsey stands closely behind Guyon, ready to back up this early crusader with "science."

In the work of Guyon itself, we are offered a "mechanistic theory of sexuality." By this theory the author repeatedly "proves" that any and all means by which ejaculation can be attained are equally "natural." "A sexual object," he announces, "is not essential or indispensable for the full satisfaction of the sexual sense. For this purpose, any one mechanical process may be as good as any other, whether this process involves the use of an object or not." (3)

After some argument to establish what he maintains is the perfect normality of various immature, incomplete, or pathologic acts, Guyon states:

This being so, if the anal, oral and sexual mucous membranes are all equally suited to play their part in the mechanical process, they are all of equal value, and it is no more necessary to delimit these specific zones than to compare their relative efficacy. ...

In reality, all this amounts to nothing more than that the anal and oral zones behave like the genital zone. . . . This behavior derives its value from the fact that the cavities in question have all more or less the same form; but we know very well that in onanism the prehensile members [hands] show themselves quite capable of creating an artificial cavity which serves the same mechanical purpose. (3)

By his "mechanistic theory of sexuality," Guyon "proves" that exhibitionism, incest, and all the activities of homosexuals are healthy and equally satisfactory expressions of biologic impulse, entirely normal and commendable. (4)

With enthusiasm Guyon cites a play showing "a father, his sons and two daughters, who are thrown upon a desert island, and there practice incest with a happy naiveté which affords a healthy lesson to those who believe in conventional scruples." (5) If we grant Guyon's assumptions that "the sexual sense aims only at its own proper satisfaction and has no real concern with the nature of the object employed," (6) I suppose it follows that the father and brothers might cheerfully take turns with daughter or sister. If Dad should keep one waiting because he takes too much time with sister, why worry? One's own hand has been "proved" by the "mechanistic theory" to be in every respect as natural and suitable a means of sexual fulfilment as making love with any girl.

The psychiatrist who reads Guyon's remarkable arguments may, like myself, recall one or more seriously ill patients who, as teen-age girls, were induced by their fathers into loveless and perverse sexual relations. If so, he may recall the harmful effects from such relations as worth bringing to the attention of the author in question. In his exposition, however, we do not deal with persons or with human feelings but with philosophical abstractions and a surprisingly mechanical account of physiology which is, one might say, not only subhuman, but submammalian. If it is a prejudice that makes psychiatrists share the common man's revulsion for such relations as that of a father seducing his daughter, I for one confess it is a prejudice that I am not eager to relinquish.

The author of *The Ethics of Sexual Acts* insists that a man who seeks sexual satisfaction with other men is behaving as normally and naturally as one who is drawn to women. He compares such a choice to the preference one person might show for a pear instead of a peach, or for "green to violet among colors." He apparently feels that these natural variations of taste need little explanation:

All that our present knowledge permits us to say is that a similar individual peculiarity makes some prefer homosexuality, others heterosexuality; while occasional homosexuality corresponds to the case of a lover of pears who now and then indulges in a peach, although it is not actually his favorite fruit. (7)

Noting that most show preference for a partner of the opposite sex, this amazing authority admits with surprise that this "may go so far that some prefer solitary onanism to homosexual satisfaction." (8) He assures us that it is pleasant and natural to have company or the services of an assistant or two in making love:

. . . so long as love is not concentrated on one particular person, and it is merely a mechanical stimulation that is sought, we often find that three or more persons participate in the same act, of whatever nature this act itself may be. There are many men who prefer the presence of a second woman, and prostitutes, who are well aware of this, often spontaneously make some such proposition. . . . It goes without saying also that its justifiability is never called into question by those who have rebelled against repression and have deliberately rejected it from their system of sexual ethics. (9)

Applying his mechanistic theory, which he apparently feels is the final test of science, Guyon goes on to "prove" that pederasty, necrophilia, and coprophilia are in no way distasteful, regrettable, or inferior to what "prejudiced" people regard as the sexual consummation of love, that these pursuits are natural expressions of eros, entirely normal even if a little unusual. (10)

Defining necrophilia as "the violation of corpses" and coprophilia as "the licking of excrement," this emancipated guide assures his readers that there is "no point in labelling [these sexual preferences] with terms of obloquy." (11) Guyon apparently withholds his approval from such forms of necrophilia as "a bandit or soldier engaged in the sacking of a town and who kills and violates at the same time, without stopping to notice whether his victim is or is not already dead as the result of his treatment." (11) Though he does not condone murder in conjunction with any sexual deed, he says of necrophilia and of coprophilia:

. . . The psychology of these extraordinary acts can be explained as a simple manifestation of *preference*, and cannot be looked upon as "morbid," since it has a perfectly natural source. (11)

Let us consider further the attitudes and aims of a person who chooses necrophilia as the ideal way of making love. According to Guyon, all methods are equally normal. Brill, in his study of necrophilia, reports:

Necrophilic acts are very often accompanied by a disfigurement of the body. . . . For the corpse is totally helpless and defenseless, so that any act may be perpetrated on it. . . . Decomposition, stench, coldness, play a part in this perversion. . . . The idea of violating a corpse or to have carnal relations with a lifeless person frequently evokes in some people lustful feelings, and some obtain gratification through mere imagination, symbolic necrophilia. . . . Bloch . . . thinks that stench plays a large part in this perverse gratification. (12)

It is difficult for me to grant that Guyon really believes what he so plainly says. Is he so engaged with philosophic theory that he completely loses touch with the human actualities his words literally indicate? Surely this seems more likely than the alternative, namely, that Guyon really appraises such basic matters in the way he says he does, and thus evaluates life.

In a genuine test of experience, how, let us ask, would he compare such alternatives as these? Alternative one: a man and wife who have been happily married for ten years, make love, each giving all to the other, not only in physical, sensuous offering and acceptance, but also in utter commitment of love and trust, and living each for the other. Or alternative two: a meek and profoundly miserable little man who was arrested in a rural community for flagging down truck drivers on the highway and begging them to let him practice fellatio on them. Apparently he sought no personal relation other than that of his mouth with the other's penis. He was usually denied, cursed, and insulted by the drivers who had no inclination to participate in such behavior. Even when accorded the privilege he humbly requested, this man was nearly always treated with contempt by the man accosted. The scorn, derision, and the occasional blows he received, were apparently relished by him as part of the abnormal fulfilment he sought. The occasional truck driver who accommodated him seemed motivated in part by curiosity and in part by the immature notion that one's own virility is enhanced by another male's degrading and submissive act.

I am inclined to believe that Guyon became so absorbed in his reasoning and in his zeal to rout the Puritans that he lost all concrete realization of what he was talking about.

A case reported in detail by Boss (13) furnishes another example for testing Monsieur Guyon's philosophy. Let us note only a few items of this unusual man's "love-making":

. . . When he grew up, his school work prevented him from spending much time in the stables, but the distant smell of stables was sufficient to provoke his excitement. At the age of 14 to 15, he began to masturbate more than ever and he needed the mental picture of defecating cows to produce excitement. These masturbation phantasies disappeared after he had seduced a young maid in his parents' home when he was 21. However, he was completely impotent towards the girl until she submitted to coitus per anum. As soon as he felt a lump of feces in the rectum, "contact was made" and the height of sexual excitement was attained. He stresses that it had to be a well-formed piece of feces, not just mush, which could not really be felt. . . . (14)

After marrying a lady of excellent family he can enjoy with her only the relations described thus:

When I penetrate deeper and deeper into my wife's rectum and when I finally touch a piece of well-formed feces, I feel as if I had reached her core, the place where the heat is so great that I melt. One would also melt in the center of the earth. . . . A piece of feces by itself, my own or somebody else's in a public toilet will already excite me very strongly. . . . The female body, except for the bottom part seems to me like some sort of material, it is like a lifeless statue. Skin or genital parts mean nothing to me. All that is finished, formed, rigid. Life begins inside, deep below the skin, within the intestines. Whenever I find feces, it seems to set me on fire. Feces are not dead. They are the beginning of everything. They are warm, and everything can be made from them, they can still be molded. After all, what is man if not an earthworm, made of dirt? (15)

The wife, long made miserable by these rather unusual attentions, began "after a few years to suffer from a serious inflammation of the rectum with large anal rhagades."

This disease became so painful that any perverted activities were made impossible. The man, however, was impotent without the coprophilic technic. He was so distressed when he had to give up his sexual gratification that he became more and more quarrelsome. He began to nag his wife, to tyrannize her and to make home life quite unbearable for her. Therefore she was much relieved when her husband began to travel, and it was a great help to her that he used to return from these excursions in a much better mood. Soon he confessed the reason for these trips. He would go to places where he was not known and there he would visit the public men's rooms of the railroad stations in search for pieces of feces. Then he collected them, wrapped them up carefully and carried them around with him, thus experiencing sexual-orgastic relief. When his wife heard this, she became afraid that he might be discovered and came to see us for medical advice as to whether she should not tolerate coprophilic practice despite her pains rather than run the risk of having him found out. (16)

All this certainly corroborates Guyon's mechanistic theory of sex on the point that orgasm can be reached without a partner. This somewhat less than original claim we can grant. Note how this husband's peculiar satisfaction from his contact with the products of defecation far exceeds any sexual interest in his wife, or in any woman. According to Guyon, as I understand his argument, this man and his interests should be regarded as normal, and in no way or degree perverse or pathologic or biologically inferior to the status of a man who takes delight in his bride. It is my humble conviction that nothing in psychiatric experience upholds such evaluations.

For many pages Guyon continues his impassioned argument, insisting that

Every mechanical means of producing sexual pleasure is normal and legitimate; there is no room for moral distinctions between the various available methods; all are equally justifiable and equally suited to their particular ends. . . . The personal characteristics of the sexual partner have nothing to do with the physiological manifestations of sexual pleasure itself; the importance attributed to these characteristics is a matter of convention. . . . (17)

Such reactions to such choices scarcely provoke comment or rebuttal. Let them stand as appraisals to be evaluated by the reader in the light of his own feelings. It is worth noting that Guyon continually emphasized the *morality* of various acts generally regarded as uninviting. It is my belief that normal people refrain from homosexual activities, coprophilia, necrophilia, and the like, not so much because of moral laws as through absence of incentive.

Patients whose disorder causes them to seek or to desire such activities are not treated by the physician with contempt and derision. As seriously ill people, they deserve respectful compassion. This, however, is not to say that a normal physician is able to accept such activities or impulses as any more natural, or as any less deplorable and unprepossessing, than other normally oriented people.

Although Guyon, like some others with similar convictions, cites Freud to support many of his arguments, he makes it plain that he considers even Freud a slave to benighted and "antisexual" taboos. He says:

It is unfortunate, that psycho-analysis has not taken up a more definite attitude in dealing with this conflict, but has on the contrary, shown a regrettable tendency to follow in the old paths. . . . Every time that psychoanalysis, in its pathological and therapeutic discussions, uses the word "perversions" to designate certain sexual manifestations of whatsoever kind, it contradicts the whole spirit of its own conclusions and discoveries, and is guilty of the old errors of the psychiatrists. (18)

Note that here Guyon includes sexual manifestations of whatsoever kind. The author goes on at some length in *The Ethics of Sexual Acts*, congratulating Freud for pointing out that the child often commits acts considered distasteful and perverse in adult behavior. He also reproaches Freud for not realizing or admitting that infantile interests and confused immature sexual gropings are also to be considered true and full expressions of what is best and most natural in adult sexual behavior:

He ought to have said, that the fact that these acts are carried out *naturally* by the child compels us to the view that such acts are not "perversions"; the term in question is one which has been wrongly attached to these acts, when they are performed by the adult. . . . (19)

. . . the "sexual pervert" has no real existence, nor any proper place in the nomenclature of disease . . . these are not pathological cases; they are, on the contrary, people who have remained in much closer touch with nature, truth and health than those who, willing or otherwise, have succumbed to repression. . . . In the interests of psycho-analysis itself we cannot therefore follow psycho-analysts in their division of sexuality into two classes: normal sexuality . . . and abnormal sexuality or "perversion.". . . Freud has, of course, employed figurative expressions to establish a theory in support of this distinction . . . but we must not allow them to lead us into fundamental errors of principle. . . . (20)

And we have surely good grounds for wondering how it is that the artificial has been regarded as normal by the psycho-analysts, who, above all others, have understood the true nature and importance of the neuroses which this condition, through its concomitant repressions, has produced. (21)

In the firm belief that it is enough merely to offer these opinions of Guyon's to the reader, I refrain from arguing about them at length.

This point may perhaps be worth noting: It has become the rule in psychiatric literature to use terms such as "immature" or "archaic" in referring to pathologic sexual conduct or even psychotically destructive activity in the adult. Such euphemisms may avoid implication of disrespect or condemnation of a patient, attitudes which all agree are out of place in medical relations. But sometimes real confusion is promoted by insistently implying that any and every sort of criminal or pathologic behavior is normal for the immature. One commentator recently stated that "any act which is expressed while growth is taking place is in itself relatively unimportant." (22) Does he mean that it is relatively unimportant if a seventeen-year-old boy brains his mother with an axe? Of course he does not mean this. Why, then, should he say what he does not mean? The danger of the euphemisms employed sometimes distinctly outweighs their value.

It can hardly be said that scientific evidence has demonstrated that the conduct of a man who strangles a five-year-old girl or another who induces a ten-year-old boy into sodomy is determined by motives and evaluations identical with those normal in the child or infant. If such a hypothesis is ever proved, or if we grant it for the purpose of discussion, another matter cannot be ignored. Immature cells in the embryo are universally present and are regarded as normal. They participate in the infinitely complex growth and evolution of an adult person from the fertilized ovum. Such cells are similar in many biologic characteristics to cells sometimes found in the breast of a grown woman, in the prostate gland, or in the lung of a man. Though correctly termed immature, such cells in the adult body are pathologic. They are not compatible with health or with the continuation of life. Pathologic, indeed! They are the cells of cancer.

Let us return to Guyon. It is of interest that he carefully avoids all reference to personal relations in developing his mechanistic theory of sexuality. One might be led to believe that this evangelical author is unaware of man and woman as human beings, or even as animals. Through most of the book he shows no concern for anything remotely related to the love and warmth and understanding that each seeks in a mate. Apparently some comment has to be made on this presumably inconsequential matter, so a chapter is finally offered on "Individualized Love." (23)

It is a remarkable comment. After such hospitable treatment of fellatio between men, sodomy, incest, and pederasty, and such un-equivocal acceptance of coprophilia and necrophilia as dignified and natural erotic practices, it might surprise some readers to see that this authority can find nothing important or desirable in the normal love of passionate and devoted mates. He asks:

... who can deny that homosexuality and incest, to take only these two typical forms of the so-called aberrations, enjoy exactly the same possibili-ties of passion, the same paroxysms of joy, the same jealousies and tor-ments, in a word the same characteristics as the most usual forms of inter-sexual love? (24)

Who can deny this? Should we not instead demand: Is there any physician who has qualms about denying it? If so, let him give thought to possible sexual relations between father and daughter which are favorably compared by Guyon with those of a married couple. Let him remember the tragic or miserable situations so common among his homosexual patients, their inevitable failure to find anything equivalent to a real sexual mate. The torments and jealousies I grant as inevitable consequences of homosexual relations. Indeed they have appeared in my patients to become very soon the chief consequences. To my way of thinking, how-ever, these are not the natural or the desirable fruits of a love rela-tion.

In this chapter Guyon demonstrates in a remarkable degree the misanthropic viewpoint seldom inconspicuous in those who inter-pret the expressions of sexual disorder as equivalent to biologic mating. In rejecting the most serious and enthralling aspects of erotic experience he demonstrates in a particularly malignant form the very antisexuality against which he so vehemently preaches. He assumes that man and woman cannot, however intense their transient illusion, love and trust and continue to desire each other specifically. Quoting from literature and from history, he pays an academic respect to what he is sure must be a romantic myth, to the concept that mates can ever achieve a sexual relation that is genuine or rewarding. This man, hailed as a seer and prophet of carnal passion, apparently cannot conceive of reactions sufficiently robust to sustain themselves even for a little while.

To the pleasure-seeker who wants a woman for an hour and to the lover who seeks a wife, the author of *The Ethics of Sexual Acts*, rather grudgingly, one might say, grants some exercise of selec-tion. He implies that for a moment the man or woman may actu-ally be deceived into thinking it is of importance to be personal in such a choice. In this connection he writes the following:

It has to be admitted, that individualized love is clearly a failure. . . . The possession of the same woman—the eternal spouse—blunts all pleasure and charm in the fact of possession. . . . Even among the most passionate the fire of love becomes extinct. . . . An indissoluble union, which, through inexperience may have been entered into lightly and unthinkingly enough, may thus become a veritable hell for people of a certain nature. . . . In truth, individualized love dies a natural death, at first by the mere fact of possession, and then through satiety . . . and this is true in the most sincere of lovers. . . . Permanent cohabitation between a man and a woman is the greatest mistake that can be committed in the name of love. We may look on it as an excusable error on the part of the young and inexperienced but scarcely pardonable among those who have had time and opportunity to understand human life and human nature. . . . It compels them to experience in common the coarsest and most unromantic sides of life, the inelegant postures of sleep, . . . the unpleasant odours of the human body . . . and indeed in nearly every case a prolonged union ends in disillusionment. . . .

But why insist? Which of us who has loved long enough has not known the disappointments of individualized love? Let the reader look into his own heart. . . .

The reasons for this failure of individualized love are clear enough. They can be summarized under a single heading: individualized love claims to be in accordance with human nature, but is not really so. . . . Thus men and women of today are coming to be less deceived by the promises of individualized love; they do not deny that it exists, but, if we may be allowed the expression, they see through it. . . . Sensible people also learn from experience either to love no one or to love everybody . . . for this is the logical outcome of our actual experience of human values. . . . (25)

These scattered excerpts speak for themselves, and help us understand some of the other appraisals which ignore so much that is plain and fundamental in ordinary human experience. If one reads the entire chapter, he will find therein an accurate picture of what those who lack the capacity to find a real love-object so often project into a universal rule which they assume holds for normal mates. If this affords unfortunate personalities some measure of comfort in their frustration, it might be unkind to deny them such an anodyne. Such viewpoints, however, are scarcely those to offer to the immature in the name of science and enlightenment.

It is particularly interesting to note how the writer who so vehemently defends sodomy, incest, and coprophilia as natural and sexually inviting practices, concludes that in "individualized love" a man and woman will inevitably find the odor of the other distasteful.

This superchampion of "sexual freedom" can accept as noble and happy manifestations of eros almost every unnatural, distasteful, damaging, and unloving activity that emerges in psychiatric disorder; but he seems almost to shudder at the thought of mates finding in each other love and fulfilment that is true and lasting. Happy, normal love between man and woman seems to strain Guyon's powers of tolerance. Could he be tempted to use for this, and for this alone, his discarded and detested term "perversion"?

SOURCES

1. René Guyon, *The Ethics of Sexual Acts* (New York: Alfred A. Knopf, Inc., 1948).

2. Harry Benjamin, introduction to Guyon, *op. cit.*

3. Guyon, *op. cit.*, pp. 295–96.

4. *Ibid.*, pp. 312–35.

5. *Ibid.*, p. 329.

6. *Ibid.*, p. 326.

7. *Ibid.*, pp. 333–34.

8. *Ibid.*, p. 331.

9. *Ibid.*, p. 320.

10. *Ibid.*, pp. 299–348.

11. *Ibid.*, pp. 336–37.

12. A. A. Brill, "Necrophilia," *Journal of Criminal Psychopathology*, II (April 1941), 436–37.

13. M. Boss, *Meaning and Content of Sexual Perversions*, trans. by L. L. Abel (New York: Grune & Stratton, Inc., 1949), pp. 55–61.

14. *Ibid.*, pp. 56–57.

15. *Ibid.*, pp. 58–59.

16. *Ibid.*, pp. 57–58.

17. Guyon, *op. cit.*, p. 344.

18. *Ibid.*, pp. 272–73.

19. *Ibid.*, pp. 274–75.

20. *Ibid.*, pp. 279–80.

21. *Ibid.*, p. 288.

22. Oscar B. Markey, "A Study of Aggressive Sex Misbehavior in Adolescents Brought to Juvenile Court," *The American Journal of Orthopsychiatry*, XX (October 1950), 719–31.

23. Guyon, *op. cit.*, pp. 349–75.

24. *Ibid.*, p. 355.

25. *Ibid.*, pp. 362–71.

Chapter 20
ART, ILLNESS, AND PROPAGANDA

In the letter written by Freud quoted in Chapter 2 he points out what has often been emphasized, that many persons who achieved great and lasting fame were homosexuals. In support of this there is certainly abundant historical evidence. Nor is evidence lacking that other artists, poets, and philosophers who have been recognized as geniuses suffered from hallucinations, delusions, and other manifestations of frank psychosis. William Blake, Schopenhauer, Tasso, Strindberg, Van Gogh, Ezra Pound, and Nietzsche are a few among many who might be named.

Some of these as well as other artists, neither homosexual nor frankly psychotic, have, whether true geniuses or not, reflected in their works some extraordinarily abnormal appraisals of life. Though Schopenhauer may have been well versed in philosophical esthetics, his opinion that women are less attractive than men remains merely a personal reaction. If he saw the typical female figure as that of an undersized human being in which the hips are too broad, even the simplest schoolboy is likely to wonder why they should seem so to this unhappy philosopher. Strindberg very often presents human relations as they are characteristically felt by patients with paranoid schizophrenia.

Tolstoy, in "The Kreutzer Sonata" (1) and elsewhere, expresses very positive convictions that sexual love, even in marriage, is evil and degrading. "In this abuse," he declared, may be found "the key to all the suffering hidden in the enormous majority of families." (2) He refers to complete and perpetual abstinence in the following excerpt:

"He that is able to receive it, let him receive it," that is, let everyone aspire never to marry, but having married, let him live with his wife as a brother with his sister . . . the Christian ideal is one of love of God and of one's fellow man, a love incompatible with sexual love or marriage which amounts to serving one's self. (2)

Such opinions naturally make one wonder about the real nature of what Tolstoy refers to as love, and what unhappy attitudes must have played a part in his sexual relations. The activities he so vigorously rejects as unworthy he apparently continued to carry out for decades after his condemnation of them. (3)

I am not qualified to judge as an expert the final worth of art or philosophy produced by creative workers with sexual disorder, or of those with schizophrenia and other psychoses. Many may feel that the productions of such geniuses are more valuable to humanity, or in the eyes of God, than normal reactions to life, or sanity, in the persons who achieve them. It can be argued that a system of philosophy, a volume of poetry, or a collection of paintings constitutes a more genuine and worthwhile fulfilment of the human being than life without major and permanent psychiatric disorder. These are not matters accessible to proof or disproof. I have doubts, however, that there are many parents who would not find it tragic for a child to lose his normal biologic orientation even for the reward of achieving what might be widely acclaimed as success in music, literature, painting, the ballet, and so on.

If, as I believe, people with sexual disorder are, by their disorder, seriously curtailed in meaningful and major fulfilment of love in this life, it is not difficult to see how this might serve as a strong influence in turning them to art as a substitute for life itself. The common preoccupation of sexual deviates with the various forms of expression by which man is said to communicate his personal reactions and evaluations, must be obvious to any physician or social worker, or other person in close contact with such deviates. Inability to achieve valid or positively satisfying goals in deeply personal relations of human love might very well make it almost inevitable for the more talented and energetic deviates to devote their lives to art as an alternative.

Among the ignorant and the immature it is often assumed that a concern for symphonic music or for poetry may be taken as a sign of effeminacy, or an earmark of the sissy or the "queer." Even in universities, the term "esthete" has often been resorted to as a euphemism for persons with sexual aberration. One of several unfortunate effects of this popular association is that it may cause normal youth to turn from serious interest in music and poetry and so lose much that is unique in communicating feelings that may be as normal, virile, and unaffected as any known to mankind. Unfortunate as this is, it is doubtful if anyone really familiar with the subject will deny that the proportion of homosexuals identified with various arts, from the ballet to interior decorating and the designing of clothes and costumes, appears to be significantly large.

In some advanced schools of unintelligibility it has often seemed to me that, both among creative workers and among particularly highbrow and exclusive cults of admirers, strange sexual attitudes even seem to predominate. Scientific evidence for or against this is not available, so it is here offered merely as an impression. To bring up again an analogy that has already been used, I would say that the reasons for my opinion are similar to my reasons for believing that most people with bald heads are adult males. I do not say that a majority of creative artists show abnormal sexual attitudes; only that there are artistic cults and circles in which such attitudes are surprisingly common.

In his article, "The Sexual Gentleman's Agreement," (4) published in the magazine *Neurotica*, Alfred Towne presents the argument that cliques of deviates play a considerable part in literary and artistic criticism and in the shaping of taste for what is intellectually fashionable. Not only in abstruse art but even in popular movies, the homosexual, according to Towne, is sometimes presented for admiration as a type, and homosexual attitudes are applauded. This, he points out, is often done without letting the audience realize what it is applauding. Mr. Towne expresses the opinion that it will not be advantageous to the American boy, if a new legendary figure, akin to Paul Bunyan, Davy Crockett, or Jesse James, is created reflecting homosexual attitudes and reactions, and perhaps eventually becoming a sort of folk hero or quasi-idol. The personalized images or concepts of folklore, he says, are those that people feel are accurate or ideal representatives of themselves. Heretofore none of these in our country have, as Towne puts it, "been effeminate pillars of the community."

Some of the arresting points made by Towne in his very discerning article will emerge in a few quotations:

The first thing we see is that the intelligent, average American who, thirty years ago, frowned on nothing so much as "sissiness" and "the fairy," has been in the last five years or so, exposed (if he reads) to a fairly large dose of the he's-more-to-be-pitied-than-censured approach to the homosexual problem. The list of novels alone that deals with this aspect is too long to bear reproduction. Add to this the growing amount of popular and clinical non-fiction on the subject and you have a small mountain of material.

It is safe to conclude that there has been a change of attitude. The recent wave of excitement and interest among intellectuals over the writings of the young French homosexual, Jean Genet, is a good, if extreme, example of this change. Genet is a flashy, mystical writer who might be called a homosexual Henry Miller. His one translated novel, *Our Lady of the Flowers,* sells for $35.00 under the counter, but its buyers and praisers are not confined to homosexuals. The first serious treatment of Genet was in *Partisan Review* in April, 1940, in an article entitled "The World of Jean Genet," written by Eleanor Clarke. In this seven-page piece, which concretized what had been heretofore only isolated interest in Genet and called him "one of the most gifted prose writers of this generation," there is little mention of the total, recurrent homosexual content of Genet's work. For a woman to seriously eulogize Genet in print might be some nadir of the ludicrous if it did not grotesquely illustrate the alarming degree to which a subtle traduction of sexual and critical values has proceeded. Is it somehow indiscreet for the non-homosexual to mention that three hundred and fifty pages of minute descriptions of homosexual love (in the most unabashed language) may be interesting or well-written, but is also extremely distasteful to him? Judging from Miss Clarke's article, and others assessing similar work, it would seem to be so.

But it is not only with such overt examples of homosexuality as a theme for popular or highbrow art that we must deal. People buying these books, for instance, know what they are getting and, presumably, buy them for that very reason. Where the phenomena of homosexuality are brought right out in the open, the non-homosexual at least has the chance to orient himself before exposure. The problem raised by Belvedere* is that most people who watch his antics don't know what he is. His character and his incidental predilections are left intact; it is only the fact of his specific sexual anomaly that has been excised. Thus it is those books, movies, magazines etc. where it is not clearly labelled for all to see—that raise the delicate and difficult question: what pervasive influence, subconscious or otherwise, does a steady diet of homosexually-motivated art have upon the non-homosexual? (4)

This, I believe, is a basic point. In such straightforward books as *The Homosexual in America,* (5) *The Invert,* (6) *The City and the Pillar,* (7) *Finistère,* (8) or *Corydon,* (9) every reader knows what is being discussed. So, too, in the "Symposium" (10) and in "Phaedrus" (11) there is no effort to conceal the real subject.

In contrast, Walt Whitman, presented to every school child as one of our greatest poets, is also usually presented almost as an apotheosis of masculinity. The lusty and earthy passions of which he sings, the panting and sweating of those who make love, are explained as products of the naturalness of that rough and vigorous he-man. So the children are told. When Walt Whitman writes that he will establish democracy in "the institution of the dear love of comrades," probably not one in a thousand of his readers today has the slightest idea about what sort of love or what sort of comrades he is talking. (12)

After Whitman, who had been described as "a dandified journalist" in his earlier days, adopted a new role, he wrote, anonymously, in praise of his own work to this effect:

**** In the moving pictures, *Mr. Belvedere Goes to College,* etc.

Very devilish to some, and very divine to some, will appear the poet of these new poems, *Leaves of Grass*: an attempt, as they are, of a naive, masculine, affectionate, contemplative, sensual, imperious person to cast into literature not only his own grit and arrogance, but his own flesh and form, undraped, regardless of morals, regardless of modesty or law. (13)

It is only in very recent years that the ordinary adult reader has had much opportunity to learn that Whitman was anything but the vast, natural, unpretentious male figure so familiar to the high school student. Edward Carpenter, John Addington Symonds, André Gide, and other literary advocates of homosexuality have made of him a hero and used his much ballyhooed supervirility to "prove" all sorts of unlikely things about homosexuality.

During Whitman's lifetime and long before he was widely accepted as our "national poet," an intensely infatuated cult formed about him. One of these reverent followers, Dr. R. M. Bucke, spoke so extravagantly of his idol to Sir William Osier, classing him "with our Savior, Buddha and Mahomet," that the great physician entertained doubts as to Dr. Bucke's sanity. Bett, in his interesting work, *The Infirmities of Genius*, notes that this admirer "urged people in England to travel to America for the sole purpose of gazing at the poet's ear, 'the most magnificent ear ever modelled and fixed on the head of a man.'" (14)

After listening to several of the cult talk about Whitman, Osier reported:

Though a hero worshipper, it was a new experience in my life to hear an elderly man—looking a venerable seer—with absolute abandonment tell how *Leaves of Grass* had meant for him spiritual enlightenment, a new power in life, new joys in a new existence on a plane higher than he had ever hoped to reach. All of this with the accompanying physical exaltation expressed by dilated pupils and intensity of utterance that were embarrassing to uninitiated friends. This incident illustrates the type of influence exercised by Whitman on his disciples—a cult of a type such as no other literary man of our generation has been the object. (15)

Gide's argument in *Corydon* seems to take for granted that if one agrees that Whitman was a homosexual he must, as a corollary, admit homosexuality to be completely normal. Of the poet he says:

". . . Whitman was in perfect health. He was, properly speaking, the most perfect example presented in literature of the natural man. . . ."
"But Whitman was a homosexual."
"Therefore homosexuality is normal. Splendid!" (16)

At Whitman's death the ardent disciple, John Addington Symonds, thus expressed himself:

He is the circumambient air, in which float shadowy shapes, rise mirage
towers and palmgroves. He is the globe itself; all seas, lands, forests, cli-
mates, storms, snows, sunshines, rains of universal earth. . . . He comes to
us as lover, consoler, physician, nurse; most tender, fatherly. . . . (17)

From Whitman's letters to a young Washington streetcar conductor which are among those later edited and published by ardent Whitman followers, Bett quotes these excerpts:

"Dear boy and comrade," "Take care of yourself, dear Pete, we will soon
be together again," "my darling boy," "Dear Pete, dear son. . . . Good
night, my darling son—here is a kiss for you, dear boy. . . ." "I pass my
time alone, and yet not lonesome at all (often think of you, Pete, and put
my arm around you and hug you up close, and give you a good bus—Often)" (18)

Whether or not Whitman's work justifies his great renown, or
whether, as some claim, his homosexuality gave him superior insight into the principles of democracy, it is difficult to see how
even his most intoxicated followers can fail to admit the banal and
puerile fraudulence of such an outburst as:

It is I, you women, I make my way,
I am stern, acrid, large, undissuadable, but I love you,
I do not hurt you any more than is necessary for you,
I pour the stuff to start sons and daughters for these States,
I press with slow rude muscles,
I brace myself effectually, I listen to no entreaties,
I dare not withdraw till I deposit what has so long
        accumulated within me. (19)

It is not my purpose to offer a judgment on Whitman's art as a
poet. I say only that his opinions and personal reactions cannot be
well understood without full knowledge of what he is talking
about. Whitman often announced himself as a "fine brute," "the
most masculine of beings," "one of the roughs, large, proud, affectionate, eating, drinking and breeding." (13) Though poets in general are not popular as idols for the small boy, such a figure as
Whitman says he is might attract some favorable attention.

Untermeyer, who deserves credit for his frankness, writes thus:

It requires little psychology to analyze what is so obviously an overcom-
pensation. In these anonymous tributes to himself, Whitman revealed far
more than he intended. None but a blinded devotee can fail to suspect a
softness beneath the bluster; a psychic impotence poorly shielded by all
the talk about fine brutishness, drinking and breeding, flinging his arms
right and left, "drawing men and women to his close embrace, loving the
clasp of their hands," and "the touch of their necks and breasts." The poet
protests his maleness too vociferously. . . .

The split was actually a gulf. Whitman's preoccupation with the details of clothes—he was as fastidious about the way a workman's shirt should be worn as he once was about the set of a high hat—his role as nurse during the Civil War, his pathetic insistence that he was the father of six children, none of which ever appeared, and his avoidance of women make it clear that this "fine brute," this "most masculine of beings," was really an invert. Whitman's brother told Traubel that "Walt never fell in love. . . . He did not seem to affect the girls," and even Edward Carpenter concluded "there can be no doubt that his intimacies with men were much more numerous than with women." Not the least of his inconsistencies is Whitman's delusion that an "adhesive" love, the love of "comrades," was the basis on which a broader democracy would be built. (20)

An example similar in some respects can be furnished by Proust. It is true that Proust is not a legend throughout the world symbolizing earthy virility, but he is generally accepted as a great novelist who will be studied perhaps for centuries. His concepts and evaluations of sexual love, long regarded among the highly educated as those of a genius, have recently been discussed in books by Mauriac (21) and Maurois. (22) In *Remembrance of Things Past* (23) Proust devoted countless pages to laborious and minute analysis of his erotic relations with the fictional mistress, Albertine. Seldom will a reader find elsewhere such a dismal outlook on human relations, such a subtle and sustained wail about the frailties of woman. Distrusts and jealousies not only thrive but are cultivated in an elaborate sophistication of personal detachment. The endless fretting and agonizing is manipulated and remanipulated with a sickly relish. While carping on the illusory nature of love, Proust propounds a philosophy that desire can be kept alive only through the pain and humiliation of knowing that one's partner is unfaithful and is outraging the union by sexual relations with others. All this becomes less mysterious when we learn that the Albertine of the novel was, in actual life, a man, probably Proust's chauffeur. (24)

Though Oscar Wilde is no longer a very popular author, every child sooner or later hears those famous lines about how "each man kills the thing he loves." (25) Despite the wide knowledge that prevails concerning Wilde's sexual predilections, few stop to realize the kind of "love" he is describing. He is, in an important sense, I think, accurate in his estimate of homosexual liaisons. But is one justified in applying his conclusions about these affairs to another and a very different matter?

Towne apparently is less concerned with the open presentation of homosexuality in art than with the subtle or disguised distortion of fundamental orientations and human values often found in the production of inverts. Is it possible that these insidious appraisals of life sometimes bewilder and mislead the immature?

Cynical contempt for "love," often expressed by sexually deviated writers, may be mistaken by the unpretentious reader for a revelation about normal biologic relations; furthermore, as a revelation by some genius whose esoteric insight into life it might seem to him either impudent or absurd to challenge.

The reader familiar with Oscar Wilde's personal life realizes that the opinions he expresses are those of a homosexual and reflect the disillusionment of homosexual relationships. The adolescent, however, may mistake them for profound evaluations of normal love by one whose rare intellect enables him to see beyond conventional superficialities.

Towne is to be congratulated for emphasizing this significant point. He must realize that his courage in dealing with such a subject is likely to bring censure. I think his article deserves attention. Let us return to his discussion:

One is treading on dangerous ground. Because a fashionable, eagerly-awaited ballet is written by one recognized homosexual, scored by another, choreographed by a third and designed by still a fourth, can we conclude that it will be a "homosexual ballet"? (By which I mean, a work reflecting, consciously or otherwise, images, ideas or situations that could be said to be either homosexually characteristic or motivated by those specific maladjustments which cause homosexuality.) Freud says quite clearly that homosexuality is psychogenic; and, in another context, that art and neurosis are intimately connected. Relying on this, it might be safe to assume that at least some of the content of this ballet would reflect the sexual attitudes of its creators. . . .

In other words, symbolic or actual love between men would be idealized, women would probably come off badly as sexual objects, and the dominant visual images of decor and choreography would be of a homosexual nature. But is this bad? . . .

Most intellectuals today would look askance if one chanced to say "Yes, in one sense this is bad." Their look would imply that one was a kind of sexual antisemite. The sexual proclivities of the artist have only casual bearing on his work, they would reply; and as this ballet has no specific reference to homosexuality, the fact that it was created by four homosexuals is really beside the point. . . .

But this is no answer, and again we must repeat: Is a ballet (or book or magazine or movie) whose content may be said to be homosexual, bad for that reason? If clearly labeled as such, the non-homosexual can have no objection to it except that his own sexual preferences limit the interest the work can have for him. But the fact that more and more of the highly touted, new novels by "bright young men," and more and more movies and plays, mask the homosexual nature of their content under a mock, non-homosexual surface, simply depriving the content of a name, changes the implications of the question. (26)

Such art may be immediately appealing to dilettantes, esthetic and intellectual poseurs, affected and shallow "high-brows." (27) These works seem to attract particularly other sexually disordered and frustrated people who are numerous enough even in rather small communities where they often constitute cults or groups sometimes regarded, with mixed feelings, as intelligentsia.

It is indeed difficult to establish reliable evidence for or against such a contention, but I have been impressed by the apparent unity, among the more intelligent and aggressive homosexuals whom I have observed clinically, in seeking an aloof position from which to scoff at the novel, play, poem, or cinema production that portrays human relations, particularly relations between man and woman, as meaningful, or that regards the natural goals of life as worth while. A decade or two ago, the terms "sentimental," "bourgeois," and "philistine," were mechanically invoked to dispose of such evaluations or their reflection in any form of communication. More recently, "subliterate" has served as an epithet to damn, among other things, the expression of normal biologic attitudes. The play or novel that does not reflect deviated reactions may also be criticized as not "serious." I do not mean to argue that these terms have no good referents; I argue only against the glib misuse of them.

The homosexual attitude usually reflects more than an estimate of abnormal relations between men. Nearly always, in addition, woman must be derided; perhaps not as the obscenity pictured by Swift and others, but more often as an absurdity. Towne has something to say about this that, I believe, deserves attention:

For example, a movie (*Once More, My Darling*) whose heroine is paraded through five reels in shorts, a tee-shirt with "Killer" written across the front, and hair grotesquely gathered into a baseball cap, and whose hero is an aspiring actor living with his dominant mother, who acts love scenes, while dressed in kilts, to a burly prop-man because the actress for whom his impassioned lines were meant did not make rehearsal, and who is finally captured by the predatory "Killer" in the tee-shirt when she hits him over the head with a slot-machine: A movie of this sort is seen by millions of non-homosexuals who might have done one of two things if the picture had been clearly labeled a homosexual comedy: (a) stayed from it entirely, or (b) written off the overt anti-feminism as mere special pleading. As it is, they have been exposed to a biased idea without knowing it. Like the German people between the wars, they have been propagandized by the subtle juxtaposition of images or situations which might have little effect if seen separately, but which add up, when taken together, to a typical homosexual case against women. (28)

This rejection of woman and this derision of her and of her natural role in love-making is an almost invariable characteristic of homosexual orientation. For the sacred mother, for the desexualized woman, respect may be granted. Gide's attitude toward his wife is illustrative. (29) But woman in the flesh is seen as vile, or as something trivial, provoking only contempt. Some observers believe these reactions, so often expressed verbally, may be embodied even in the dance. Let us quote Anatole Broyard, another contributor to *Neurotica*:

The Afro-Cuban rumba was conceived as a choreographed mock coitus; in its evolution, to Mambo, the mockery became the dominant dement. The rumba was a very literal sexual image: it was danced with the pelves pressed together, to a pulsing, regular rhythm. . . .

In Mambo, the sexual image which was the root of rumba has been torn apart. The male is now involved in an adventure of abstract rapine, while the female remains in the catatonic throes of her abandoned intercourse. Discontinuity being the chief characteristic of Mambo, the instinct of male sexual aggression is turned loose at large in an ambiguous cosmic quest. . . .

. . . although the female has lost her sexual function and now has a most unexciting role, she has actually suffered no loss of status. It is as though not she but intercourse itself were rejected, the male being subsequently condemned to a dervish and masturbatory progress through the world, and the female reduced to an uninteresting stabilizing adjunct and point of departure.

The symbolic act was described by a recent writer as "the dancing of an attitude." Conversely, "the dancing of an attitude" may be described as a symbolic act. So seen, Mambo is the Dance of Life's last step in the transition from instinct to alienation. (30)

Let us return to Towne's article. Perhaps he does exaggerate the influence of homosexuals in art, yet he deserves attention. It impresses me as remarkable that what he discusses has been virtually ignored by psychiatric writers. He continues:

But isn't this view frankly alarmist? Perhaps so, until one looks closer. The magazine *Flair*, for instance, would be harmless if it were aimed at homosexuals, and filled the same place in their erotic fancies that *Beauty Parade*, *Wink* and other fetish magazines do in those of non-homosexuals. But the fact of the matter is that *Flair* is aimed—need one say like a double barrelled shotgun—at woman. Disguised rather shallowly as a new kind of fashion magazine, it is actually directed at the victims of the message of ridicule that fills its pages. (Genet is featured in the April 1950 issue, Jean Cocteau in issue #1.) When one sees women in the subways or on the streets—girls who are perhaps secretaries, models, housewives, or students, who wish to keep up with things in the world of fashion and the arts—clutching a copy of *Flair* in which one knows there are minute drawings of the dissection of a woman's breast, countless pictures of women in men's clothes brandishing whips, a card game the aim of which is to pierce the Queen of Hearts with a dagger, and articles which chronicle the peregrinations of the new homosexual intelligentsia, one wonders at the craft of this underground pressure group which has somehow succeeded in getting its victims to eagerly pay fifty cents for the dose of poison that may maim them for life.

The truth is this: if one wants to be in the know as far as poetry, fiction, the theatre, magazines and movies go these days—woman or no woman—one has got to expose oneself to art which is homosexual in nature. But this raises the question: How much exposure does it take before infection, mild or otherwise, sets in? Can women continually see members of their sex destroyed, mocked, isolated and humiliated; pictured as shrews, whores, idiots and mantraps, and retain any self-confidence or sense of personal worth? And can non-homosexual men swallow the same amount without eventually coming to think that their wives, sweethearts, sisters and mothers have something of the "menacing, aggressive Poles" about them? To say "no," is to conclude that art has no effect whatsoever on the people who give their attention to it. We know this is not true, and if propaganda can bring whole nations to war, why should the sexes be immune? (31)

It is appropriate here, I think, to remark once again on Towne's courage. If he is correct or even approximately correct in his estimate of these influences, it is easy to see that he is likely to damage his career as a man of letters. That he is himself entirely aware of this danger is made plain by these additional quotations:

It would not be erring in the direction of prophecy to clearly state that homosexuality, far from merely receiving sympathetic cultural attention, is actually becoming a cultural force. If this only implied that the increased number of homosexuals were simply being given a kind of proportional representation in the arts, the non-homosexual might say, "Let them have a voice!" But the disquieting implications of Miss Clarke's treatment of Genet seem to indicate that something far more serious is happening. Is it proper critical procedure for the non-homosexual to ignore the fact that, though Genet may be one "of the most gifted prose writers of this generation," he is also its most articulate homosexual? In Genet's case, is it possible to ignore that fact and still do him justice? Certainly Miss Clarke's inability to deal head-on with the specific content of Genet's work is an example of the most serious effect on non-homosexuals of the new aura surrounding homosexuality, from wherever it has come. And this brings up delicate questions. . . .

How are critical criteria influenced by this mass of overt or masked homosexual literature? Miss Clarke's participation in this new Gentlemen's Agreement is one indication. There are many more. When New Directions republished five novels by Ronald Firbank, a powder-and-puff Genet of an earlier period, the books were reviewed in several national newspapers by recognized homosexuals. Conceivably this choice of reviewers could have been justified with the argument that only a homosexual could assess Firbank in terms of an intimate knowledge of his material: it takes one to understand one. None of these reviews, however, discussed Firbank's novels as homosexual fantasies. The uninformed reader merely learned that they were "interesting," "special," "sensitive," and "amusing." The question that comes immediately to mind is this: Has the non-homosexual the right to conclude that these reviewers were somewhat biased in Firbank's favor, and that their failure to mention the underlying nature of his work constituted what amounts to a conspiracy to lure non-homosexuals into the reading room, if not the boudoir? . . .

Belvedere, and other homosexuals-who-are-not-homosexuals, resemble a kind of fifth column who sell dissension by refusing to name the cause for which they do so. Our altered attitude toward homosexuality, whether fostered by homosexuals or the result of an enlightened tolerance toward them, has allowed us to listen to Belvedere (and even see him as a folk-image); but this has brought about a new kind of Gentlemen's Agreement, by which the minority seeks to impose its views of life and love upon the majority. The reluctance on the part of creators, critics and informed audiences to utter the "nasty word," or the implication that it has no bearing if they do, is the cause; and a gradual effeminization of artistic and sexual values, the foreseeable result. (32)

Towne is discussing, I believe, a most important matter. If it is true that some of the very greatest poets and philosophers and artists were sexually disordered, and the evidence for this seems strong, there is little doubt that some deviated geniuses are able to express profound matters in human experience without reflecting primarily the distortions and abnormal evaluations so common in their disorder. In current literature, nevertheless, and in well-known works from the past, many examples demonstrate the dispirited, perversely cynical, and one might say *life-hating*, reactions and judgments that I believe are typical of the brilliant and aggressive homosexual.

The features I refer to, in homosexual literature or teaching, are not usually met in an open argument for abnormal sexual practice, such as that found in Gide's *Corydon*. A generalized mockery and rejection of basic life values is reflected without direct pleading, sometimes subtly and sometimes jejunely but thoroughly in disguise. Oscar Wilde's *Picture of Dorian Gray* is a fair illustration. Many even better examples might be cited except for the obligation not to suggest that any particular person who has not himself publicly announced it is thus disordered.

The reliability of judgments on artistic and esthetic worth is difficult to test. Highly specialized experts not only disagree, but often one condemns as utter vulgarity or banal nonsense what the other insists is sublime. Some confident judgments made by leaders in super-highbrow circles suggest that mere unintelligibility itself may and often does attract praise. It is quite understandable that persons who find ordinary or actual life intrinsically boring or disgusting might welcome nearly anything that makes nonsense, finding in it an unspoken but satiric comment on an existence which displeases them. Mere gibberish is itself a kind of negation and may, indeed, enlist the sympathies of those burning to express negation.

Some may be driven to embrace nonentity or vacuum by the very fact that nonentity and vacuum are at least an opposite to positive human values. A rejection of what is natural, less sweeping than that exhibited by Des Esseintes in *Against the Grain* (33) could, it seems to me, do much to explain such tastes. I myself have encountered in actual men and women so strong a repugnance for any affirmation of life, for the simplest of enjoyments, that it is easy for me to understand how even a jumble of words and syllables, a random confusion of lines or paint splotches signifying nothing, might actually be welcomed by them as delightful.

Not all such persons are homosexual; yet I believe that all of them have distorted sexuality of some sort—a disability in love.

Along with truly creative artists, homosexual or non-homosexual, who express themselves in new ways that are not yet comprehensible to many people, there are, possibly, a good many unhappy cynics who busy themselves making nihilistic and lunatic art.

Just a few years ago, the fallibility of expert judgment in drawing a distinction between the truly valuable and what is less so was stupendously illustrated. The incident was widely reported in news magazines, and is, I think, worth recounting here. The editors of a very advanced literary journal called attention to what they took to be a poem or a prose-poem, and pronounced it an astonishingly significant and original work of art. Their discovery was critically praised, subtly analyzed and hailed as perhaps too splendid for popular understanding, but in very truth, superb for advanced and discerning spirits.

Soon afterward, the authors of this esoteric gem provided the explanation of their inspiration and of their creative technique. To have a little fun, they had decided to make as much nonsense as possible. They wondered if anyone would react seriously to their hoax. Making random selections, they took words and phrases from income-tax forms, bills of lading, a Sears, Roebuck catalogue, laundry lists, an almanac, and other miscellaneous forms of printed matter. These they scrambled together impartially into a hash of meaningless gibberish, which they typed out in blank verse form, and submitted for publication.

Like Towne, I propose that the persistent influence of homosexual attitudes and reactions, aside from overt physical seduction or frank praise of abnormal acts, may cause perplexity and serious conflict in the immature over an area of experience far broader than that ordinarily regarded as sexual. The sexually disordered person usually feels and evaluates the basic aims and issues of human life differently from the normal person, and pathologically. Whatever the sincerity of his intentions or his technical brilliance in expressing himself, whether in teaching or otherwise, he often promotes pathologic concepts which, to the immature, may be disturbing and perhaps tragically harmful.

SOURCES

1. L. F. Tolstoy, "The Kreutzer Sonata," in *World Classics* (London: Oxford University Press, 1940).

2. E. J. Simmons, *Leo Tolstoy* (Boston: Little, Brown & Co., 1946), pp. 430–40.

3. *Ibid.*, p. 443.

4. Alfred Towne, "The Sexual Gentleman's Agreement," *Neurotica*, VI (Spring 1950), 23–28.

5. D. W. Cory, *The Homosexual in America* (New York: Greenberg, Publisher, 1951).

6. Anomaly, *The Invert* (London: Baillière, Tindall & Cox, 1948).

7. Gore Vidal, *The City and the Pillar* (New York: E. P. Dutton & Co., 1948).

8. Fritz Peters, *Finistère* (New York: Farrar, Straus & Cudahy, Inc., 1950).

9. André Gide, *Corydon* (New York: Farrar, Straus & Cudahy, Inc., 1950).

10. Plato, "The Symposium," *Dialogues of Plato*, trans. by B. Jowett (London: Oxford University Press, 1892), Vol. I, pp. 541–94.

11. Plato, "Phaedrus," *ibid.*, pp. 431–89.

12. Louis Untermeyer, *Modern American and Modern British Poetry* (New York: Harcourt, Brace & Co., 1950), pp. 33–40.

13. *Ibid.*, p. 35.

14. W. R. Bett, *The Infirmities of Genius* (New York: Philosophical Library, 1952), pp. 45–56.

15. *Ibid.*, p. 52.

16. From *Corydon*, p. 7. Copyright 1950 by André Gide. Published by Farrar, Straus & Cudahy, Inc.

17. Bett, *op. cit.*, p. 56.

18. *Ibid.*, p. 50.

19. "A Woman Waits for Me," from *Leaves of Grass*; quoted in Bett, *op. cit.*, p. 48.

20. Untermeyer, *op. cit.*, pp. 35, 38–39.

21. F. Mauriac, *Proust's Way* (New York: Philosophical Library, 1950).

22. A. Maurois, *Seven Faces of Love* (New York: Didier Publishing Co., 1944).

23. Marcel Proust, *Remembrance of Things Past* (New York: Random House, Inc., 1932).

24. Harry Levin, introduction to *Letters of Marcel Proust*, ed. and trans. by Mina Curtiss (New York: Random House, Inc., 1949).

25. Oscar Wilde, "The Ballad of Reading Gaol," in *A Treasury of Great Poems*, ed. by Louis Untermeyer (New York: Simon & Schuster, Inc., 1942).

26. Towne, *op. cit.*

27. H. G. Greenspan and J. D. Campbell, "The Homosexual as a Personality Type," *American Journal of Psychiatry*, CI (March 1945), 682–89.

28. Towne, *op. cit.*

29. André Gide, *The Secret Drama of My Life* (Paris: Boar's Head Books, 1951).

30. Anatole Broyard, "Mambo," *Neurotica*, VI (Spring 1950), 29-30.

31. Towne, *op. cit.*

32. *Ibid.*

33. J. K. Huysmans, *Against the Grain* (New York: Hartsdale House, 1931).

Chapter 21
PIED PIPERS OF PATHOLOGY

It might be worthwhile to ask ourselves again: What is a genius? "A man endowed with transcendent ability" is, with other definitions, listed in many dictionaries. Is it reasonable to believe that the recognized genius will conduct his life with more than average or ordinary wisdom? Some argue that his creative productions should be judged entirely apart from his personal career. It has often been maintained that his music, his books, his sculpture, or his painting embody the essence of a profound wisdom, of an indisputable greatness, even though he has failed to manifest these qualities in relations with his wife, his children, his friends, or with the community.

Do the paintings of Pablo Picasso prove him to be a human being of uncommon discernment, of spectacularly great worth, despite his flourishing allegiance to the uninspiring tyrannies of world communism? Edgar Allan Poe's life is reported as one dominated by irresponsibility, drunkenness, and failure. Do his stories and poems, despite this, contain such wisdom and beauty as to prove him immensely superior to well-adjusted ordinary citizens of his time?

Few lyric poets of the last century have been awarded more appreciative recognition than Paul Verlaine. Great admiration for his work has been expressed by critics throughout Europe and America. Young people in our universities today are likely to gain the impression of him as a spirit of superb sensitivity whose esthetic judgment immeasurably eclipses any reaction that they are likely to encounter among their socially well-adjusted fellows. The recorded story of Verlaine's career, his indolence, parasitism, distasteful folly, and sometimes incomprehensibly sordid antics might evoke doubts about this man's transcendent status in some

commonplace observers. His lofty reputation in the world of letters notwithstanding, let us ask: Was he a man of authentic personal superiority? (1, 2, 3) His unprovoked assaults—apparently
with truly murderous intent—on Lepelletier, a dear friend, on his
choice homosexual associate, the poet Arthur Rimbaud, and even
on his own mother, may be explained by some students of his life
as a result of extraordinary passions that are common in great creative artists. Could it be possible that perversity, callousness and a
deficiency of ordinary human responses might have played an important part in such deeds and in the habitual misconduct of his
life? One commentator has expressed the opinion that "probably
the greatest misfortune ever to befall Paul Verlaine in his tragedy-
riddled career was the fact that he was sentenced to only two
years in jail—instead of life imprisonment—for the attempted
murder of Arthur Rimbaud." (2) This commentator believes that
the two years in prison were the least ignominious and unhappy
in his adult life, the most nearly normal ones he ever knew.

It is not likely that many will deny that the sculptor or dramatist
who is a pathetic fellow, as measured by the ordinary standards of
society, sometimes produces works regarded as eternally valuable
to civilization. Surely from some personalities maimed or soiled
by sexual perversion, crime, cruelty, affectation, cowardice, or
psychosis, there have emerged artistic and literary productions
that eventually won the gratitude and admiration of generations.
Despite emotional handicaps and intellectual distortions such
artists have expressed their rare and beautiful talents in work em-
bodying values that unquestionably enrich the world.

If this is true, should we not say that the greatness of their work
must derive from a real superiority rather than directly from the
weakness or illness that was also part of these men? The man
whose legs are paralyzed may develop herculean strength of arm.
One who fails egregiously and regularly in every business he attempts, may be an excellent pianist or violinist. One who has committed grave crimes may in remorse achieve unusual recognition
of evil and thus sincerely inspire others to virtue. Psychotics,
sometimes, despite delusions and hallucinations, do possess and
successfully exercise real talents.

This does not, however, justify the assumption that great technical virtuosity in some art, when used to express pathologic or
criminal points of view, necessarily transmutes that which is expressed into wisdom. Though we may properly acclaim the arms
of the man with crippled legs as strong, we would be foolish indeed to trust our fortunes to his chances of success in a footrace.
Though a patient with schizophrenia may brilliantly solve problems in higher mathematics, far beyond our capacity, this does not
make us assume he is correct when he tells us that he hears the

voice of Cleopatra through the umbilicus of a dead man buried in Yucatan.

Let us distinguish between those who, despite depravity or psychiatric illness, utilize real wisdom and insight to enlighten or awaken posterity through their art or philosophy, from others who in their work reflect chiefly the judgments of serious disorder. Is it not possible that some may achieve, at one time or another, each of these effects in turn?

The artist's personal life has often been identified with unconventional behavior and Bohemian indulgences, which moralists condemn as sensuous or licentious. In defense of the creative genius it has been said that his stronger and more vital passions naturally defy bourgeois restrictions, that because of his high esthetic mission he must be exempted from the ethical standards of behavior that properly apply to lesser men. (4) Deeds that in a commonplace fellow might be classified as irresponsible, or even as criminal, are regarded by some spokesmen as nullified, perhaps even as ennobled, by the poet's or composer's extraordinary spiritual accomplishments and fulfilments.

Another traditional belief is that the man of genius is often ignored or, because of a scarcely comprehensible blindness and stupidity in his fellows, sometimes condemned by them with egregious injustice. Few legends are more familiar than that which depicts the misunderstood artist scorned in his time but recognized by succeeding generations who at last become enlightened and realize that he was correct in his vision despite the neglect or censure of the social group in which he lived. Even if the musician's, poet's, or sculptor's known conduct does not justify specific admiration or lend itself readily to hero worship, many will insist that a rare personal magnificence emerges to us through his symphonies, his poetry, his statuary.

Thomas Mann, in an estimate of Dostoevsky, reveals a viewpoint that differs considerably from the ones just mentioned. He speaks of the idolized Russian novelist as an imposing figure among "the great sinners and the damned, the sufferers of holy disease." (5) He is unequivocal in proclaiming his belief that Dostoevsky showed major psychiatric disorder and also very serious inner criminal tendencies. He writes: ". . . I am filled with awe, with a profound, mystic, silence-enjoining awe, in the presence of the religious greatness of the damned, in the presence of genius of disease and the disease of genius, of the type of the afflicted and the possessed, in whom saint and criminal are one." The great German man of letters seems to entertain no doubt that Dostoevsky was himself obsessed with impulses toward, or fantasies of, abnormal brutality such as the treacherous rape of a little girl which he dwelt upon in *Stravrogin's Confession*. Mann tells us: "Apparently this infamous crime constantly occupied the author's moral imagination."

Mann apparently regards Dostoevsky as great not despite disease but chiefly because of it and through it. What Mann attributes to "the criminal depths of the author's own conscience" is acclaimed as the precious core of his worth, not as an infirmity redeemed somehow by art. He identifies disease and genius, saying:

... the disease bears fruits that are more important and more beneficial to life and its development than any medically approved normality. The truth is that life has never been able to do without the morbid, that probably no adage is more inane than the one which says that "only disease can come from the diseased." Life is not prudish, and it is probably safe to say that life prefers creative, genius-bestowing disease a thousand times over to prosaic health; prefers disease, surmounting obstacles proudly on horseback, boldly leaping from peak to peak, to lounging, pedestrian healthfulness. Life is not finical and never thinks of making a moral distinction between health and infirmity. It seizes the bold product of disease, consumes and digests it, and as soon as it is assimilated, it is health. An entire horde, a generation of open-minded, healthy lads pounces upon the work of diseased genius, genialized by disease, admires it and praises it, raises it to the skies, perpetuates it, transmutes it, and bequeathes it to civilization, which does not live on the home-baked bread of health alone. They all swear by the name of the great invalid, thanks to whose madness they no longer need to be mad. Their healthfulness feeds upon his madness and in them he will become healthy.

In other words, certain attainments of the soul and the intellect are impossible without disease, without insanity, without spiritual crime, and the great invalids and crucified victims, sacrificed to humanity and its advancement, to the broadening of its feeling and knowledge—in short, to its more sublime health. . . .

They force us to re-evaluate the concepts of "disease" and "health," the relation of sickness and life; they teach us to be cautious in our approach to the idea of "disease," for we are too prone always to give it a biological minus sign. (6)

Mario Praz, in his well-known study of de Sade's influence in literature, *The Romantic Agony*, writes thus of a group of French decadents:

[They] found or thought they found in the novels of Dostoievsky a sadism which had become more mystical and more subtle, no longer limited to the grossness of physical torture but penetrating like a worm-hole into all moral phenomena . . . they found also a thirst for the impossible, and impotence elevated to the height of a mystical ecstasy. . . . In Sade and in the sadists of the "frenetique" type of Romanticism, it is the integrity of the body which is assaulted and destroyed, whereas in Dostoievsky one has the feeling . . . of the "intimacy of the soul brutally and insolently violated." (7)

Praz offers overwhelming evidence to support his contention that the work of many literary figures, generally regarded as among the most eminent of their period, is rooted in profoundly pathologic reactions and that the perverse and morbid qualities of this work have won veneration from many disciples and been accepted as esoteric wisdom or beauty. He repeatedly illustrates in the writings of Gautier, Baudelaire, Flaubert, Swinburne, Huysmans, Verlaine, and many others, persistent and strong influences of the Marquis de Sade. In contrast to Thomas Mann, Praz expresses no admiration for these unusual tastes and their reflections in art.

He is apparently unable to share Mann's faith that there is in such disease a mystical value superior to the value of health. He does not find in perverse reactions anything that leads him to claim that they redeem subsequent generations and save them from madness. The large group of creative men studied by Praz demonstrate in their literary work an imperious attraction toward gross algolagnia and toward many concomitants and nuances of this perversion. In their poems, plays and other writings, appallingly corrupt and subtle depravities of impulse and choice are repeatedly expressed. Some of the viewpoints and tastes embodied in these works of art are likely to impress the reader as being not only antisocial and unnatural but as thoroughly deserving to be called by such a term as antibiologic. The impulses of sexual inversion become rococo, sometimes even burgeoning into weird lust and quasi-ecstatic rapture over such monstrous and pathetic imaginary figures as the hermaphrodite of Greek mythology. (8, 9)

Persistent gestures of veneration are accorded to nearly all qualities detestable to the sane. Through peculiar esthetic sensibilities, putrefaction, pain, disgrace, and torture are fondly welcomed and cordially treated. A positive relish seems to emanate from the contemplation and artistic portrayal of disfigurement, death, ennui, and profanation. All these negative, uninviting, or deplorable aspects of human experience are sometimes speciously identified as glory or love and greeted as precious inspirations. In these impressive literary works Praz illustrates the decadence through which woman is almost uniformly perceived as a foul murderess, an implacable and vampirish foe. Man is regularly presented as a sexually inadequate and frightened weakling whose only furtive hope is to escape her. A few of the group seem to have definite and positive inclinations toward necrophilia or coprophilia, sometimes in the more indirect or sublimated forms of these predilections. Delight seems to arise not merely in response to experiences and things naturally shameful and disgusting, but sometimes even for shame and disgust as abstract symbols of a perverse ideal.

Do these artistic productions truly represent the reactions to experience and the personal judgments of the authors quoted and discussed by Praz? If the statements of these authors accurately reflect their allegiances and tastes, can one who reads them carefully refrain from wondering why they are acclaimed as spiritually elect mentors to whom we should look for inspiration and guidance?

Let us grant that Baudelaire and Swinburne have, each in his own way, achieved a genuine excellence of idiom, of rhythm, and of other specific features of poetic expression. If this is an effective and perhaps a unique form of art, should we examine its substance? Should we concern ourselves with the argument it advances or the judgments it embodies or implies? Perhaps poetry or other forms of art can be evaluated by a canon of pure esthetics, without regard to its substance. But I wonder about the validity and worth of such judgments. If the work presents reactions to experience, and appraisals of experience, that are obviously perverse or psychotic, must we insist that this is irrelevant? If the critic of art can fully disown his status as a human being when he contemplates poetry, painting, and sculpture, perhaps he can honestly say that this is irrelevant. To most of us these abstruse attempts to separate art and personal experience, to judge art without consideration of the motives from which it has arisen or the effects it attempts to achieve, are likely to appear hypocritical or, at least, speciously unenticing. If the true and unbiased position from which one can give judgments on art excludes the participation in all feelings that are fundamental to happiness and normal human relations, then one might say that it is only the form and never the substance that deserves attention.

Let us go back to Baudelaire. Reports of his career indicate that he displayed various forms of self-conscious affectation. It is difficult to deny that he was a wastrel, that he showed little evidence of normal passions, or of capacity for real friendship. It is reported that he dyed his hair, often in a harsh shade of green, and, sometimes accompanied by a live lobster which he led on a leash of pale blue ribbon, walked out on the boulevards of Paris to be observed in his proud eccentricity. His biographers report that he lived at times with an ignorant mulatto girl in an atmosphere of disgust and vexation. His unusual liaison with her is said to have been an attachment more "cerebral than sensuous." (10) Some who have studied his life bring out many points to support their conviction that he must have been sexually impotent. His flaunted disdain for what is ordinarily regarded as morality was apparently less intense than his repulsion when offered the opportunity for sexual relations with beautiful and intelligent women for whom he had expressed what they construed as desire or love. (10, 11)

If what is known of Baudelaire's career fails to evoke the admiration justly due genius, can we find in his work evidence of superior understanding, superlative esthetic taste or other qualities that reflect a transcendent spirit? If his poetry reveals wisdom or beauty of surpassing worth there is perhaps good reason to maintain that we should in estimating him ignore the uninspiring features of his life and accept with reverence his teaching or his inspiration.

Mario Praz in *The Romantic Agony* exhibits in Baudelaire's work many examples of that "inversion of values which is the basis of sadism, vice [representing] the positive active element, virtue the negative and passive. Virtue exists only as a restraint to be broken." This poetry, he says, has given "a psychological turn to the refinements of perversity." In it he repeatedly demonstrates an "inexhaustible need to be occupied with macabre and obscene subjects. . . ." The poet's positive response, his genuine affinity with this material, is difficult to deny. In Baudelaire's work the fraudulent or counterfeit seems to be regularly chosen and esteemed above what is real and natural. The sexual mate repeatedly appears as a figure of obscenity. Derision replaces love as the desirable basis for a sexual relation. Again and again we find ignominy accepted as an agreeable substitute for beauty or triumph. Ennui is embraced with quasi-fervor and cherished morbidly as a mark of superiority. Praz vividly illustrates in examples from Baudelaire's writings an unappeasable taste for defilement, for ingenious abortions and butcheries of natural human response. His works abound in positive responses to nearly every reversal of instinctive choice. What would ordinarily be shunned as damnation is actively pursued, even by such means as attempting to achieve genuine religious faith in order to make more meaningful the horror and treachery of actively desecrating it. (12)

Like Huysmans, he appears to be specifically attracted to such negative rites as those celebrated in the Black Mass. (13, 14) Admiration has often been expressed for his claim that he sought to "extract beauty out of evil." (15) Does this extract become good or delightful, however rapturously Baudelaire may welcome it, however lyrically he may rename it? Few of this poet's statements are more revealing and more typical than his well-known pronouncement: "Woman is natural, that is to say abominable." (16) During his life a court came to the decision that *Les Fleurs du Mal* should be recognized as "an outrage upon morals and decency." (17) Today this work is cherished as a rare and precious item in the cultural depositories of civilization. The author is often referred to in such terms as "a soul of . . . profound spirituality . . . a mind of such heightened sensibility." (17) Of him it has also been said that "through his sufferings he came to understand the sufferings of mankind." (18) Is it true that his poetry reveals this understanding, this spirituality? Has the negative judgment of the court expressed during his lifetime now been satisfactorily proved to be absurdly in error?

Algernon Charles Swinburne is often accepted by the immature as a particularly lusty spokesman for sensuous joys and physical passion. "I have loved overmuch. . . ." this poet proclaims. In college, or perhaps in high school, the responsive boy who encounters the sumptuous rhythms of his verse, the efflorescence of his imagery, the cumulative richness of his alliteration, can scarcely fail to conceive of Swinburne as a particularly virile figure, a daring singer whose vigorous song of mating defies Puritan asceticism, sweeps away all petty conventions and artificialities. It is not difficult to see how the unsophisticated youth finds in the ardor of this poetry something he can identify with his own hot and natural desires in the stir and confusion of a first love.

These lush images, these resonantly ringing lines, do indeed convey an intensity that seems to match an amorous youth's wildest aspirations, to embody the very vigor of his own aroused and still unfulfilled physical yearnings. Young men and women who find no interest in most poetry, regarding it vaguely as something bookish or effeminate, may be suddenly fired by lines from "Dolores" and enthusiastically identify themselves with what they presume is the subject and the attitude and the spirit of this untamed and defiant author. He seems to speak out in great eloquence and power against the restraints that fret and deny, to sing sublimely of the very joys and enticements that others fear to endorse—with unabashed delight.

Society insists that the young man and woman must defer consummation of the intense desires that urge them and sometimes seem almost to consume them. Here, they are likely to think, is one who knows how they feel when they read:

By the ravenous teeth that have smitten
Through the kisses that blossom and bud,
By the lips intertwisted and bitten
Till the foam has a savour of blood,
By the pulse as it rises and falters,
By the hands as they slacken and strain,
I adjure thee respond from thine altars,
Our Lady of Pain. (19)

Many young readers will assume that this refers to what their own natural impulses yearn for with such vigor. Let us assume that they respect the principles which at the time deny them so much. In their vivid anticipation they picture the still unattained fulfilments as breath-taking, hot-blooded, and extreme. Here is a voice that seems to express their longings wholeheartedly and without evasion. Such a term as "Our Lady of Pain" is not likely to give them pause. The heart is said to ache and surely there is suffering in the restraint and denial they know so well. Love and sorrow are often joined in speech. Now Swinburne depicts a female image:

> As of old when the world's heart was lighter,
> Through thy garments the grace of thee glows,
> The white wealth of thy body made whiter
> By the blushes of amorous blows,
> And seamed with sharp lips and fierce fingers,
> And branded by kisses that bruise;
> When all shall be gone that now lingers,
> Ah, what shall we lose? (19)

Many readers have impulsively assumed that the poet is expressing a sexual ardor. What if a lip should sustain an abrasion in this love-making, or signs of an incidental bruise remain? In the wholehearted vigor of happy consummation, who would care? The thoughtful person, still unaware of Swinburne's real theme, may wonder for a moment about this comment:

> Fruits fail and love dies and time ranges;
> Thou art fed with perpetual breath,
> And alive after infinite changes,
> And fresh from the kisses of death;
> Of languors rekindled and rallied,
> Of barren delights and unclean,
> Things monstrous and fruitless, a pallid
> And poisonous queen. (19)

But the bewildered youth will probably say to himself that a poet's speech is not as exact as mathematical equations. He does not speak in the cool and precise terms of an accountant. If the youth reads on, his perplexity will probably vanish under the impact of such a stimulus as this:

> Thou wert fair in the fearless old fashion,
> And thy limbs are as melodies yet,
> And move to the music of passion
> With lithe and lascivious regret. (19)

Some readers have still believed that Swinburne is referring to familiar passions and normal biologic aims after they read:

> I could hurt thee—but pain would delight thee;
> Or caress thee—but love would repel;
> And the lovers whose lips would excite thee
> Are serpents in hell. (19)

Everyone knows that lovers can never say precisely what they feel. Inexact words, wildly inappropriate metaphors, are often seized in genuine passion and purblindly used in the hope of conveying a meaning that eludes speech. This is what many readers are likely to decide that Swinburne has done.

But if we soberly consider the facts, and acquaint ourselves with Swinburne's life and his more explicitly expressed preferences, we come to realize it is extremely unlikely that he "loved overmuch." Could we say, with honesty or reasonable accuracy, that he ever loved at all? From what is recorded, one is not justified in believing that he had normal relations with any woman. (20) His lack of interest in such matters was so conspicuous that his fellow poet and close friend Rossetti discussed his plight with a vivid, enterprising and sexually adventurous woman, currently regarded as the epitome of carnal appeal. Rossetti is reported to have wagered ten pounds with this playful and agreeable lady on the proposition that she would not be able to arouse even a simple erotic interest in Algernon Charles Swinburne. After doing her best to engage his attention, the hearty and honest girl confessed her failure and returned to Rossetti his ten pounds. (21) Avoiding all natural relations with women, Swinburne drank alcoholic beverages so disastrously and proved himself so inept in conducting his financial and ordinary affairs that he was obliged to turn over most responsibilities to his bachelor friend and protector, the solicitor Watts-Dunton. During most of Swinburne's adult life this semi-guardian conducted his affairs. (22)

Mario Praz presents evidence that makes it difficult not to believe that Swinburne had a specific taste for flagellation. There is reason to believe that habitually he pursued the ignominies and bizarre sensations offered in "queer houses" where opportunities were offered to receive or inflict substantial physical pain as a weird substitute for sexual fulfilment. The records make it plain that Swinburne, from his early years, read with avidity and hero worship the works of the Marquis de Sade. The poet's writings emphatically convey to all who read them carefully his acceptance of brutality and perverse humiliation as the essence of what he conceives to be love and sexual satisfaction. Nothing in his literary work or in what is reported of his life indicates that he ever achieved awareness of even the simplest feeling that an ordinary man has toward a woman. (22, 23)

In Swinburne's poetry Mario Praz repeatedly illustrates the influence of an unmitigated algolagnia that sometimes becomes brutally cannibalistic. Malignant perversion is pervasive and the entire universe is perceived in distortion and interpreted in terms of scorn and derogation. Swinburne tells us of "The mute melancholy lust of heaven." Praz is convinced that in this image "heaven merely reflects the mute melancholy lust of the poet himself." (24)

In some depictions of what he apparently conceives of as sexual love Swinburne becomes enthusiastic and explicit:

> I would my love could kill thee; I am satiated
> With seeing thee live, and fain would have thee dead.
> I would earth had thy body as fruit to eat,
> And no mouth but some serpent's found thee sweet.
> I would find grievous ways to have thee slain,
> Intense device, and superflux of pain;
> Vex thee with amorous agonies, and shake
> Life at thy lips, and leave it there to ache;
> Strain out thy soul with pangs too soft to kill,
> Intolerable interludes, and infinite ill;
> Relapse and reluctation of the breath,
> Dumb tunes and shuddering semitones of death. . . .
>
> Ah, that my lips were tuneless lips, but pressed
> To the bruised blossom of thy scourged white breast!
> Ah, that my mouth for Muses' milk were fed
>
> On the sweet blood thy sweet small wounds had bled!
>
> That with my tongue I felt them, and could taste
> The faint flakes from thy bosom to the waist!
> That I could drink thy veins as wine, and eat
> Thy breasts like honey! that from face to feet
> Thy body were abolished and consumed,
> And in my flesh thy very flesh entombed!
>   . . . O, that I
> Durst crush thee out of life with love, and die,
> Die of thy pain and my delight, and be
> Mixed with thy blood and molten into thee!
> Would I not plague thee dying overmuch?
> Would I not hurt thee perfectly? Not touch
> Thy pores of sense with torture, and make bright
> Thine eyes with bloodlike tears and grievous light?
> Strike pang from pang as note is struck from note,
> Catch the sob's middle music in thy throat,
> Take thy limbs living, and new-mould with these
> A lyre of many faultless agonies? (19)

Perhaps both Swinburne and Baudelaire exhibit in their poetry creative brilliance so original and extraordinary as to deserve classification as geniuses. If Praz is correct, or even partly correct, it would hardly be sane to insist that the judgments conveyed or implied about human experience, the basic tastes and reactions, should be admired as excelling the judgments and tastes of the ordinary untalented member of the community. It is difficult to deny that the writings of both poets often suggest a truly perverse orientation, an outraging of the deepest axioms of human response. What we sometimes encounter in this poetry might be justifiably regarded as an expression in art of impulses not unlike those that have been memorably illustrated in conduct by Gilles de Rais, Jack the Ripper, and more recently by Neville George Clevely Heath. (25, 26, 27) Is it possible to regard such inclinations and choices as anything other than literary manifestations of disease and of disease that is unprepossessing and malignant?

The author of *The Romantic Agony* repeatedly demonstrates the strong influence of earlier devotees to a perverse and pathologic esthetic canon on artists and men of letters with similar basic tastes who emerge in subsequent periods. Baudelaire and Gautier both appear to have accepted the Marquis de Sade as a valid prophet and a mentor. These apostles of a decadent gospel seem in turn to have exerted a major influence on J. K. Huysmans, Swinburne, Oscar Wilde, Walter Pater, Barbey Aurevilly, Gabriele D'Annunzio, Octave Mirabeau, and on many others. (23)

The work of a good many creative artists who are accorded a very high rank in their field seems to show no less clearly than the recorded events of their lives many features not ordinarily regarded as compatible with accepted standards of greatness and wisdom. If the core of this work is indeed compounded of pathology and negation, how are we to account for its continuing prestige, for the opinion of some experts that it is a product of rare inspiration and enlightenment? A confident explanation for this is probably beyond the scope of this book. Let us briefly consider a few points that may be relevant. Arnold Bennett in his little essay, "Why a Classic Is a Classic," argues that only a numerically negligible minority of people, even among the well educated, care enough about literature to keep alive the greatest works. It is his opinion that no writer, even if universally renowned, is really popular in the sense that his books continue to be read by many. He says:

In the face of this one may ask: Why does the great and universal fame of classical authors continue? The answer is that the fame of classical authors is entirely independent of the majority. Do you suppose that if the fame of Shakespeare depended on the man in the street it would survive a fortnight? The fame of classical authors is originally made, and it is maintained, by a passionate few. Even when a first-class author has enjoyed immense success during his lifetime, the majority have never appreciated him so sincerely as they have appreciated second-rate men. He has always been reinforced by the ardor of the passionate few. And in the case of an author who has emerged into glory after his death, the happy sequel has been due solely to the obstinate perseverance of the few. . . .

And it is by the passionate few that the renown of genius is kept alive from one generation to another. These few are always at work. They are always rediscovering genius. Their curiosity and enthusiasm are exhaustless, so that there is little chance of genius being ignored. . . .

. . . Do you suppose they could prove to the man in the street that Shakespeare was a great artist? The said man would not even understand the terms they employed. But when he is told ten thousand times, and generation after generation, that Shakespeare was a great artist, the said man believes—not by reason, but by faith. And he, too, repeats that Shakespeare was a great artist. . . . (28)

If the interest of this passionate few mentioned by Arnold Bennett persists over centuries and keeps alive great books ignored by the majority, is there not also another minority, the small but articulate group in every generation, of cynical and emotionally deviated cultists, who just as persistently welcome what is pathologic?

If it is true that some who are generally regarded as geniuses of literature and art are, in an important sense, dedicated advocates for pathologic causes, is it to be wondered at if they continue to win disciples in each new generation? Baudelaire and Swinburne apparently found in the perverse standards of the Marquis de Sade inspiration for a morbid creed of estheticism which they fervidly embraced. August Strindberg, who is still widely regarded as one of the foremost men of letters ever produced by the Scandinavian countries, expressed schizoid misogyny throughout his numerous works. It is scarcely surprising then to note that he fervently acclaims as a genius Otto Weininger, the unhappy Viennese youth who perhaps even more bitterly denounced woman in his book *Sex and Character* a number of months before committing suicide. (29) Art arising from pathologic and perverse viewpoints seems to have immediate and specific appeal to men and women suffering from similar emotional illness. Those who find the normal goals of human life unacceptable or distasteful are likely to greet with enthusiasm poetry or philosophy that reflects an appraisal similar to their own. If they find the ordinary premises of life hateful they are likely to hail as truth and beauty expressions of rejection by another. Perhaps it is not surprising that such reactions and tastes appear as achievements of exquisite discernment, as a precious wisdom available only to the elect, to coteries of sexually distorted and often brilliant intellectuals who in each generation are drawn together through veneration for the morbid.

Helen Lawrenson in a magazine article, "The Cool Cat Era," gives an interesting discussion of some *avant garde* Greenwich Village groups. In some members of this "young futility set" she portrays an emotional vitiation and peculiar effeteness that is indeed remarkable. Intellectual and esthetic distinction is among these people apparently measured by the degree of disinterest and boredom that can be achieved:

They don't dance; they don't flirt; their laughter is a mechanized device infrequently used; and their conversation is of a genre that is utterly forgettable. . . .

. . . For the great, outstanding quality about this cool-cat generation is its overpowering inertia. Everything is simply too much effort and what's the use, anyway? Down through the ages, the one never-changing mark of youth has been its enthusiasm. This is probably the first generation in history that hasn't got any. That is what strikes you most forcibly when you see its members in the slightly dank bars where they cluster like fungi. You look at them and listen to them—all young and bright enough, with handsome men and pretty girls—and suddenly you realize the incredible, the shocking, the obvious fact: *they aren't having any fun!* Sex, liquor, dope, perversion—they try it all, and it's all so much spinach. This is not youth on a spree, or the classic wild oats of the younger generation. . . .

. . . Their attitude toward sex is possibly the strangest in the history of youth. By and large, they think it's a lot of bother. In the bars they inhabit, you almost never see a young man panting over a pretty girl, oblivious to all else, straining every nerve to convince her that she's the most beautiful creature he ever saw and that he's madly, rapturously in love with her. That is for squares. What you may see is an attitude of "Well, sex is a bore. Life is a bore. I don't really feel anything but you're here and I'm here and we can't think of anything else to do, so let's give it a try."

Most of the time, they don't even make that much of an effort at courtship. When you hear an apparently healthy young man in his early twenties say, with a faintly nauseated look, "I had sex last Thursday," in exactly the same tone as if he had said, "I ate some cottage cheese and it didn't agree with me," you begin to realize that something has certainly gone haywire. . . .

Things have come to a pretty pass when young girls are so bored with men that they prefer dope. But even the "please pass the heroin" set finds its own routine anything but sheer pleasure. They spend a lot of time screaming, or retching endlessly, until they manage to kill themselves one way or another, and they're cool forever. . . .

. . . These are the archetypes of the "cool cats," that new cult of youngsters whose attitude toward life, toward love, toward themselves is one of frantic apathy. There are probably more of them in the Village than anywhere else, because the Village has always been the unofficial headquarters for rebellious youth. What makes this group different from all its predecessors is that the chief thing it seems to be rebelling against is life itself. . . .

. . . "It's ugly, Carter, it's all so terrible and useless."

"What is?"

"Everything. Life." (30)

Is it remarkable that among people such as this, disdainfully withdrawn from the usual interests of life in behalf of art, pseudo-art or Bohemian emancipation, apologists for life perversion and pathologic values find devotees in each succeeding generation? It may be true as Arnold Bennett says that great books are sustained through the centuries by those he designates as "the passionate few." Are not other works of art sometimes kept in high repute by another and different minority to whom normal reactions are alien and in whom ordinary passions are feeble?

J. Donald Adams, writing in *The New York Times*, offers pertinent comment:

Who, and what, is an intellectual? The word is one of the fuzziest in current use. It resists definition, and is bandied about with an appalling breadth of latitude. I shall offer two: one with tongue slightly in cheek; the other a more serious effort. First, a person of any one of the several sexes whose thinking is both muddied and muddled; second, a person who places great faith in, and derives his values from, man's rational capacity, at the same time underestimating his intuitive promptings, and the urges of what, for lack of a better term, we refer to as the human heart.

Having thus attempted to define him, let us examine some of his more obvious characteristics. First of all, the intellectual seems frequently incapable of clear exposition of his thoughts. His words are too often shrouded in mist—a mist that they rarely penetrate. He is, in addition, likely to be a literary snob.

Irresistibly, he is attracted by the esoteric and obscure. Whatever he can readily understand he views with condescension and, frequently, with contempt. (31)

Though relatively few in number, these dispirited and unhappy persons appear to play a considerable part in establishing what are accepted among influential cults as the highest esthetic standards of the day. If such intellectuals admit the worth of an author who in general speaks the ordinary language of mankind and reflects reasonably human reactions, it is likely to be some negative aspect of his work which they find acceptable. Adams continues his interesting discussion:

He regards the heart as an organ far inferior to the mind, and one properly restricted to its literal function of pumping blood throughout the body, though why he should recognize even this simple capacity I find it difficult to imagine, because he gives little indication of its reality in his own physical and mental composition. What is pumped through his own veins is hard to determine; some viscid and colorless substance, perhaps, considerably cooler than his body temperature. . . .

. . . Melville, of course, the intellectual admits to the somewhat circumscribed circle of his admiration, because Melville was held in thrall by a profoundly pessimistic view of man's experience. Complete disillusion is part of the intellectual's credo. It seems difficult for him to grasp that one may have the tragic sense of life without surrendering to despair. Melville was too, at times, incoherent, and that makes an enormous appeal to the intellectual's sensibilities. Melville's frequently windy rhetoric which would ordinarily be offensive to the intellectual, is pardoned by him because of its despairing content. That he retired defeated, like Rimbaud, is also a point in his favor. The intellectual dotes on frustration, and he will smell it out even in places where it never existed, or, if it did, was compensated for by an underlying zest for life. . . .

. . . The mazes, too often leading nowhere in particular, upon which James lavished his skill and his undeniably subtle insights, were made expressly for the intellectual's delectation. He delights in intricate parlor games. Indeed, has not his high priest, T. S. Eliot, spoken of poetry as merely a superior form of amusement? (31)

Is it sensible of us to concern ourselves with a small minority of unhappy people who draw together in a pale pessimism and claim to find in boredom and negation something too precious for the ordinary man? Are they too few to constitute an important influence? In his article "The Cult of Unintelligibility," Burman brings out points that bear upon these questions:

In politics most Americans are brave as lions; in literary opinions we are timid as mice. . . .

One of the tragedies in the artistic development of America today is that so many individuals do not say what they think but what they think they should think. . . .

. . . This contradiction between our approach to literature and politics arises from the fact that culturally we are still very young; because we are so young we are insecure.

It is this basic insecurity which has given rise to the cult of the obscure and the unintelligible, which like some mysterious and malignant disease has infected so much of our literature. Most men and women recognized that the meaningless phrases spread on the printed page were counterfeit —pretentious sound and fury. But the fashion of the moment was to pronounce these absurdities works of genius. So they kept silent. . . .

Literature is life in all its variety, its beauty, its ugliness, its sorrow, its laughter. The disciples of the obscure accept no such definition. They permit no grace, no rich humanity; they allow only the shallowness and artificiality of Gertrude Stein and the later James Joyce, at once the revealers of their faith and the gods they worship.

The cause lies not in the method. It lies in the lack of talent among the practitioners. When weaklings follow in the wake of nonsense, folly must be multiplied many fold. . . .

Novels that can be distinguished only with difficulty from the scribblings of unfortunates in mental institutions are not calculated to send readers racing from their television sets to a bookstore. I have put down here some writings of individuals affected by a brain injury or mental disease together with sentences from the works of Gertrude Stein and the later James Joyce. It may be interesting for the reader to try to decide which is which:

1. "Have just been to supper. Did not knowing what the woodchuck sent me here. How when the blue blue blue on the said anyone can do it that tires. Such is the presidential candidate."

2. "My dear dear dear dear dear dear my dear my dear dear."

3. "Five and five over five. Five fifty five. Fifty five and fifty over forty-five. It is very usual to think of a name. Follow me after follow me after follow me."

4. "Than as she is on her behaviorite of quainance bandy, fruting for firstlings and taking her tithe, we may take our review of the two mounds to see nothing of the himples here as at elsewhere, by sixes and sevens."

5. "As we there are where are we there from timtitbot to teetootom to-
talitarian. Tear tea too coo. Whom will comes over. Who to caps ever."

6. "The Lord is my hospital. I shall not want. He marries me green pas-
tors parters. He leadeth me leadeth me leadeth."

7. "Ack, ack, ack. With which clap trap and soddenment, three to a
loaf, our mutual friends the fender and the bottle at the gate seem to be
implicitly in the same bateau so to ringen, bearing also several of the ear-
marks of design."

8. "No history of a family to close with those and close. Never shall he
be alone to be alone to be alone to be alone to be alone to lend a hand and
leave it left and wasted."*

Why link Stein and the later Joyce? Because their methods have been at
base the same, a deliberate confusion of thought which has been worse
than their confusion of language; because their effect on the public mind
has been likewise identical, the creation of the sorry cult where incoher-
ence passes for greatness.

Now let us see what the students at those universities giving courses in
the work of Joyce and Stein would learn if they faithfully followed the examples of their masters. It is fortunate that Miss Stein has left for posterity
a volume of many pages which tells her method in explicit detail so that
her devotees may fall into no error. The book is called *How to Write*. I
quote a typical passage:

"A sentence is proper if they have more than they could. They could.
Without leaving it. A sentence makes not it told but it hold. A hold is
where they put things. Now what is a sentence. A sentence hopes that
you are well and happy. It is very selfish. They hate to be taken away. The
minute you disperse a crowd you have a sentence. There were witnesses
to it even if you did not stop. There there is no paragraph. If it had a different father it would have."

To aid the student and make things clearer the book is divided into sec-
tions with headings such as Regular Regularly in Narrative, Arthur a
Grammar, Formally George a Vocabulary.

How does it come about that in America a large number of seemingly
cultured men and women, including teachers in a few of our foremost
universities, should be fooled so easily by literary charlatans whose writings cannot be readily distinguished from the pathetic scribbling of the
mentally ill? How does it happen that a forgotten work by one of these
authors will be reissued as though the publisher were conferring some
priceless boon on humanity, or an opera by the other is revived with almost religious fanfare, to be attended by devotees as though they were

---

**** 1. From the letter of a patient with schizophrenia (quoted in *The Human
Mind*, by Karl A. Menninger).

2. From the efforts of a man to write a letter who had had a stroke of
apoplexy, involving the writing center of the brain—verbigeration
(quoted in *The Human Mind*, by Karl A. Menninger).

3. *Lucy Church Amiably*, by Gertrude Stein.

4. *Finnegans Wake*, by James Joyce.

5. *Finnegans Wake*, by James Joyce.

6. Another type also due to brain injury, the result of the mental faculties
being unimpaired (quoted in *The Human Mind*, by Karl A. Menninger).

7. *Finnegans Wake*, by James Joyce.

8. Introduction to *Lucy Church Amiably*, by Gertrude Stein.

entering a sacred cathedral? The answer, again, is our insecurity, the fact that culturally we are still in our swaddling clothes. We accept frauds at their own valuation, just as some Hollywood producers believe their own publicity. (32)

It is not likely that the immature will be influenced directly either for better or for worse by the later writings of Joyce or by the relatively unreadable offerings of Miss Stein. It would be interesting to know how many people feel they have actually read *Finnegans Wake*. More interesting still would be an answer to this question: How has anyone who may have turned those 626 pages ever been able to determine how or when he could honestly consider any one of them as read?

The halo of genius may come to rest on the brow of those who offer us a wisdom otherwise beyond our reach. Apparently such a halo is also held by maladjusted minorities over some decadent figures in the literary world whose contributions chiefly reflect inadequate reactions to life that are familiar in psychiatric disorder. These works contain many bizarre and unhappy appraisals of human life, many subtle and soft impeachments of sexual love.

Let us not now attempt a comment on the content, or possible content, of such writings as those discussed so interestingly by Burman. Instead, we might more profitably meditate on the processes through which they become widely accepted as among the most valuable literary achievements of mankind in our century.

SOURCES

1. Mario Praz, *The Romantic Agony* (New York: Oxford University Press, 1951).

2. M. L. Wolf, introduction to Verlaine's *Confessions of a Poet* (New York: Philosophical Library, 1950).

3. Robert Baldick, *The Life of J. K. Huysmans* (Oxford: The Clarendon Press, 1955), pp. 109–10, 119–20.

4. H. M. Hyde, *The Trials of Oscar Wilde* (Edinburgh: William Hodge & Co., Ltd., 1948).

5. Thomas Mann, introduction to *The Short Novels of Dostoevsky* (New York: Dial Press, Inc., 1951).

6. *Ibid.*, pp. xiv-xv.

7. Praz, *op. cit.*, pp. 336–37.

8. Edmund Wilson, *Eight Essays* (Garden City, N.Y.: Doubleday & Co., Inc. 1954), pp. 167–80.

9. James Cleugh, *The Marquis and the Chevalier* (New York: Duell, Sloan & Pearce, Inc., 1951).

10. W. R. Bett, *The Infirmities of Genius* (New York: Philosophical Library, 1952), pp. 103–14.

11. Praz, *op. cit.*, pp. 150–51.

12. *Ibid.*, pp. 106, 147, 151.

13. Jules Michelet, *Satanism and Witchcraft* (New York: Citadel Press, 1946).

14. J. K. Huysmans, *La Bas* (Chicago: John K. Potter, 1935).

15. Praz, *op. cit.*, p. 143.

16. Erwin Straus, *On Obsession* (New York: Journal of Nervous and Mental Disease Monographs, 1948), p. 17.

17. Bett, *op. cit.*, pp. 103–1.

18. *Ibid.*, p. 110.

19. A. C. Swinburne, *Selected Poems of Algernon Charles Swinburne* (New York: Dodd, Mead & Co., 1928).

20. Humphrey Hare, *Swinburne: A Biographical Approach* (London: H. F. and G. Witherby, Ltd., 1949).

21. Praz, *op. cit.*, pp. 217, 236–37.

22. Bett, *op. cit.*, pp. 57–68.

23. Praz, *op. cit.*, pp. 213–44.

24. *Ibid.*, p. 227.

25. Allan Barnard, *The Harlot Killer* (New York: Dodd, Mead & Co., 1953).

26. D. B. Wyndham Lewis, *The Soul of Marshal Gilles de Raiz* (London: Eyre & Spottiswoode, Ltd., 1952).

27. MacDonald Critchley, *The Trial of Neville George Clevely Heath* (London: William Hodge & Co., Ltd., 1951).

28. From "Why a Classic Is a Classic," in *Literary Taste and How to Form It*, by Arnold Bennett. Copyright 1927 by Doubleday & Company, Inc. Quoted by permission of the owners of the copyright and Messrs. Jonathan Cape, Ltd.

29. D. Abrahamsen, *The Mind and Death of a Genius* (New York: Columbia University Press, 1946), pp. 148–49.

30. Helen Lawrenson, "The Cool Cat Era," *Park East* (January 1953), pp. 36–39.

31. J. D. Adams, "Speaking of Books," *The New York Times Book Review* (March 15, 1953), p. 2.

32. B. L. Burman, "The Cult of Unintelligibility," *The Saturday Review* (November 1, 1952), pp. 9–10, 38.

Chapter 22
MISOGYNY AND THE FLESH

We have already noted René Guyon's attack on what he calls "antisexuality." In his book, *The Homosexual in America*, Gory maintains that our society is not really heterosexual but antisexual:

The anti-sexual nature of modern civilization is apparent wherever one turns. In the description of the virgin birth, the term "immaculate conception" is used, thus the inference is made that all conceptions that take place by means of sexual intercourse are not immaculate and therefore unclean. Any humor pertaining to sex is called a "dirty joke." It is "lewd" to fail to conceal the sexual organs, and the strongest epithets in the English language—and in many other languages—are synonymous with having sexual intercourse. . . . The fact is that it is only apparently a heterosexual society. The anti-sexual culture pretends that it is heterosexual, in order to better suppress all sex for pleasure! (1)

Despite what appears to be a confusion here of two separate religious beliefs, one concerning the Virgin Mary and the other concerning the Virgin's mother, something emerges that is obviously true. Surely anyone will grant that a multitude of unpleasant synonyms for "filthy" or "disgusting" are commonly applied to nearly anything that may stimulate sexual desire and to the desire itself. The relation between these expressions of repugnance and basic orientations deserves attention.

Though the woman who especially arouses erotic impulses may be, and probably is, called beautiful, she may, if she publicly exposes more of her charms than is customary, be called indecent. If a girl of surpassing loveliness should come to a college dance totally unclothed, even those most capable of appreciating the excellence of her body would scarcely argue that her behavior was not genuinely distasteful and vulgar. Suppose a newly married couple were to carry out sexual relations at high noon in the display window of a department store on Fifth Avenue. Great curiosity and excitement would no doubt be aroused by such a performance, but even the most liberal-minded commentator could scarcely maintain that it is not a shameful and degrading act.

Let us distinguish clearly between real antisexuality and the normal distaste for perversion or degradation of sexuality. The nude girl at the college dance and the couple who have sexual relations in public are misusing or devaluating their sexuality. They throw away a potentiality or an opportunity for something much more satisfying. The girl's body maintains its excellence, but the young men who have beheld her naked at the dance are not likely to feel that she can give a real or highly prized personal intimacy. The act of the couple demonstrates that their relation has but little meaning, or chiefly a negative meaning that reflects scornful indifference, the impulse to cheapen or mock.

Only irresponsible extremists would deny that the human being in his progress through childhood and adolescence must learn to restrain sexual impulses. It is not always easy to explain to the immature why such restraint is necessary. The happily married man of thirty-five appreciates how regrettable it would be if his wife began to have sexual relations with other men—even though he could not adequately put this appreciation into words, especially words that could convey what he knows about this to his fifteen-year-old child.

It is not so difficult a task for parents to help ordinary children understand the reasons and incentives against lying, stealing, cruelty, or cowardice as it is to explain somehow that love is good, sex is bad, yet sex is love. There must, nevertheless, be some deterrent, some very strong deterrent, already long implanted and developing in the child if he is to be helped adequately to control and direct the tremendously powerful and at first undiscriminating sexual urges that, particularly during adolescence, will press for fulfilment and deeply bewilder him.

It is perhaps not remarkable that parents, teachers, and the morally responsible adult world, have put considerable emphasis in their teaching on what is *bad* about the sexual activities that children and teen-agers would inevitably undertake, if they were not substantially restrained from within. It is scarcely to be denied that a true antisexuality has, over the centuries, been enlisted in support of efforts to control erotic impulses in the immature. These tactics have no doubt been used by many who hoped that much of what was taught would be outgrown or somehow unlearned in time for the child to accept sexuality when he or she becomes mature enough to find it in adult love.

Just telling the boy or girl that genital activity is wrong may not always suffice. So it became the custom to say also that sex is "dirty"; that desire for it and thoughts about it are "filthy." Such terms as "foul play" and "a dirty trick" show diffusion of a literal meaning into other forbidden areas. But in sexual matters, above all others, the chief effort has been to extend a disgust developed first in connection with bladder and bowel training, and to enlist this repugnance to help inhibit what should normally be retained as desire.

Without some reasonably effective restraint during maturation of the simple, impersonal sexual impulses, it is doubtful if human beings could develop so as to acquire the capacity for a relation that is wholeheartedly sexual and profoundly that of love. Distaste or disgust implanted in a person and affecting his emotional reactions is a more constant source of inhibition than fear of external punishments. If one escapes detection, the punishment may be evaded. If the incentive for what is forbidden is sufficient, the punishment may be braved. Without an intrinsic distaste for what is ignoble, it is difficult to understand how man could achieve any virtues that would be real.

But who can fail to see the flagrant and abundant evidence of misallocation of such distaste, of misdirection in the aim of this indispensable reaction of disgust? Within a single week of psychiatric practice I have encountered several examples. Among others is a woman, who, after the first ardent kiss from the man she was to marry, fled to the bathroom, washed out her mouth, and vigorously brushed her teeth and gums. After twenty years of marriage, she still feels that sensuous intimacy is "dirty." Another is a man who, several years ago, during sexual relations with his wife, with enthusiasm took her breast in his mouth, giving her an exquisite delight and a fulfilment that she had not before experienced. Apparently he, too, participated in the pleasure. But later he felt such disgust with himself for what he had done that he has not dared to repeat the act.

Over the centuries there has persisted a tendency to define as "the flesh" all that is trivial, evil, or vile, and to contrast the ambiguous referent of this term with what is accepted as noble or spiritual. Granted that such a contrast of values can be real, let us not overlook the fact that deep and often tragic confusion results from what is included under various concepts of "the flesh."

Few have pointed out so clearly as has Havelock Ellis the relation of this confusion to sexual pathology and human unhappiness. (2) Some concepts of the flesh necessitate that any love involving the body and its voluptuous responses be cursed and degraded. Let us quote Havelock Ellis in one of his memorable illustrations:

Man is nothing else than fetid sperm, a sack of dung, the food of worms. . . . You have never seen a viler dung-hill. Such was the outcome of St. Bernard's cloister *Meditationes Piissimae*. . . .

Sometimes, indeed, these mediaeval monks would admit that the skin possessed a certain superficial beauty, but they only made that admission in order to emphasize the hideousness of the body when deprived of this film of loveliness, and strained all their perverse intellectual acumen, and their ferocious irony, as they eagerly pointed the finger of mockery at every detail of what seemed to them the pitiful figure of man. St. Odo of Cluny—charming saint as he was and a pioneer in his appreciation of the wild beauty of the Alps he had often traversed—was yet an adept in this art of reviling the beauty of the human body. That beauty only lies in the skin, he insists; if we could see beneath the skin women would arouse nothing but nausea. Their adornments are but blood and mucous and bile. If we refuse to touch dung and phlegm even with a fingertip, how can we desire to embrace a sack of dung? The mediaeval monks of the more contemplative order, indeed, often found here a delectable field of meditation, and the Christian world generally was content to accept their opinions in more or less diluted versions, or at all events never made any definite protest against them. (3)

As Ellis points out, this rejection of flesh as filth, this specific disgust for what is sexually appealing, did not originate with Bernard or Odo de Cluny. Centuries before them, Augustine had found the sexual organs shameful, denouncing these parts as loathsome instruments of original sin. Sexual desire or lust impressed him as evil and horrible. This specific excitability, he insisted, renders the genitalia repulsive and worthy only of condemnation. (4) The great theologian expressed profound scorn for man because we are born *"inter faeces et urinam"* (5) His meditations on these questions were apparently protracted; his pronouncements still have influence.

But judgments such as these were not confined to religious ascetics. Men of science have apologized and expressed shame for having to study the generative organs of women. Linnaeus dismissed such a project as "abominable." (5) Havelock Ellis quotes a distinguished French physician, Des Laurens, who referred to "the incredible desire for coitus," and wondered how "that divine animal, full of reason and judgment, we call Man, should be attracted to those obscene parts of women, soiled with filth, which are placed, like a sewer, in the lowest part of the body." (6)

Freud maintains that the eliminative functions should be called sexual and that in all love there are elements derived from anal sensuality. The contrary interpretation of Theodor Reik offers a more plausible explanation for ordinary modesty and for such unhealthy reactions of disgust and shame about sexuality as those just cited. As we all know, children are taught to gain control of their eliminations and to value cleanliness. The first reactions of distaste and abhorrence, Reik argues, are cultivated in connection with the child's toilet training. The child must be given some incentive to avoid soiling himself and his surroundings. Reik says:

... The tabus introduced earlier in order to instill cleanliness and neatness became prototypes for the sexual behavior of men and women. Not only do the persons who were forbidden objects in connection with excretion later on become untouchable as incestuous objects, but the excretory processes themselves also become patterns for sexual activity. Here is the origin of the puritanical view of sex and of the fact that often similar expressions were used for both functions (purity in sex, sex as polluting, as something unclean, "dirty stories"). Chastity has, so to speak, its prototype in tidiness. . . .

The molding influence of toilet-training on the sexual attitude, conditions not only the relationship of persons but also, and more so, the functioning in sex. The inhibitions are carried over to the new sphere in the psychology of impotent men and frigid women who consider sex as something degrading, like urine and faeces, as something to be ashamed of as they were made to be of those other functions in their childhood.

This pattern governs the processes of reticence and freedom, keeping back and letting go, holding out and surrendering in the intimate activities of sex, as it did in elimination. It is, to a great extent, responsible for the split between love and sex which many men experience: where they respect, they cannot function sexually, and where they can enjoy themselves uninhibitedly in sex, they cannot respect their partners. Persons whom they consider as mother and sister substitutes become sexually untouchable because the old excretion-tabu unconsciously conquers the sexual desire and makes these respected persons inappropriate as sex-objects. (7)

Unlike orthodox analysts, Reik does not attribute a primary sexual quality to defecation. He maintains that the shame and loathing acquired about being soiled with excrement becomes attached later to sexuality and reinforces the restraints set up against unrestricted sexual activity.

It appears that this process, like many others that serve a healthy purpose, may proceed to pathologic degrees. Though the ordinary person finds excrement unprepossessing, his rejection of literal filth is moderate in comparison with the extreme repugnance and loathing expressed in denunciations of healthy, erotic flesh, that may be met with. From a confused and exaggerated identification of excretion and sexuality, sometimes truly malignant potentialities emerge. This hybrid concept, like a cellular malignancy, may grow and metastasize in the spirit, invading and destroying the most delightful areas of experience, turning everything to foul disease and corruption. The ordinarily limited negative reactions to excretion seem capable of sometimes uniting with the germinal beginnings of sexuality to shape a pathologic zygote doomed to monstrous deformity and fed with all the irresistible fecundity of cancer.

In addition to such antibiologic misogyny as that just discussed, we also find woman, and necessarily the act of love, cursed on other grounds by Sprenger and Kraemer. Those enthusiastic witch-hunters and authors of the *Malleus Maleficarum* insist that she, in contrast to the male, is by nature a vicious liar, the embodiment of fraud and iniquity:

What else is woman but a foe to friendship, an unescapable punishment, a necessary evil, a natural temptation, a desirable calamity, a domestic danger, a delectable detriment, an evil of nature painted with false colors! (8)

It is strange, indeed, that similar derogatory concepts of woman, when proclaimed in 1903 by Otto Weininger, should have aroused so much excitement. (9) Though this peculiar young intellectual concluded, like Freud, that femininity is a purely passive quality or essence, he was moved further to heap strong abuse upon this inert concept he had devised of woman. Asked by his father how he could "with so little experience pass such a devastating judgment upon women," he answered that it is "a great mistake to believe that experience would yield true understanding." (10)

These appraisals of woman as worthless, of sexual desire as vile, particularly in the female, were already old centuries before Weininger, as a youth of twenty-three, proclaimed them vehemently as a major "discovery." During his short life this young scholar, precocious in book-learning, apparently had no appreciable experience with any girl, either as a sweetheart or friend. There is a record of but a single direct social contact with any representative of the other sex, aside from his mother and his sisters. On a postcard he mentions making the acquaintance of a Miss Meyer. Of this incident Abrahamsen, his biographer, writes:

It is peculiar in that it is the only written proof from his own hand that he ever wanted to meet a girl. It appears that Miss Meyer had often asked to meet him, and that later he actually did meet her. His sister reports, "she spent one hour with him, and she wrote, 'I have been with Jesus Christ.'" (11)

Weininger's philosophical revelation of woman as mere emptiness and bestiality was apparently achieved through another discovery—namely that all men are part woman, and vice versa. Through his own misfortune, namely, of sharing her vile and worthless essence, he felt that he was able to judge her and reveal her to the world.

The published opinions of this brilliant and pathetic youth naturally invited rebuttal. One critic referred to his *Sex and Character* as "an unparalleled crime against humanity." (12) Like others who have offered a philosophy to interpret their own abnormal reactions as profound discoveries, he also was acclaimed as a genius. August Strindberg, generally regarded as Sweden's greatest man of letters and one of the outstanding intellectual figures of his time, wrote in wild enthusiasm, "Here is the man who has solved the most difficult of all problems." (12) Finding in Weininger a confirmation of his own feelings, Strindberg modestly says: "I spelled out the words, but he put them together." To the young man he sent this letter: (13)

Doctor,
   To be able, at last, to see the solution of the problem of woman is a great relief to me. Therefore please accept my reverence and my thanks.
                                                    August Strindberg

Weininger's suicide at the age of twenty-three, a few months after the publication of his *Sex and Character*, called forth further praise from Strindberg. This eminent writer confirms Weininger's discoveries, and offers his admiration in these terms:

The single fact that men have created all culture, spiritual as well as material, shows man's superior position; only the feebleminded would try to contest this statement. . . . According to the latest analysis, female love consists 50 per cent of sexual desire and 50 per cent of hatred . . . we find that when a woman loves a man she hates him, hates him because she is tied to him and feels inferior to him. In her love there is no constant flow, but a continual repolarization, eternal changing in the current, which shows the negative, the passive element in her being, as opposed to the active in man. . . .
   Put in a few words this was the secret that Otto Weininger had the courage to disclose; this was his discovery of the feminine being and nature, which is set down in his virile book *Sex and Character*, and for it he had to pay with his life. . . . I place a wreath on his grave because I honor his memory as that of one of the courageous masculine thinkers. (14)

Note how Strindberg seems to feel that virility is measured by the force of an attack on the female. Why does he, and why does Weininger, find it an urgent necessity to prove man superior to woman? These men of great intellect seem quite unable to grasp the fact that woman is obviously not man's sexual competitor. Each assumes that woman, whether created suddenly by God or evolved through eons of time, is expressly designed to be not herself but a male.

Amazed at the discovery that woman is not the male, these men condemn her as a biologic fraud, a ghastly and detestable blunder of nature. Neither one shows even primitive awareness of what is clear to many dullards long before puberty, that male and female are complementary; that it is madness to curse either for not fulfilling the natural and biologic specifications of the other. These afflicted intellectuals seem wholly unable to grasp what is so plain in nature and in normal feelings. They can only point to woman as a biologic monstrosity. Discovering that insofar as she is genuinely woman she is not a sexually perfect man, they perversely see in the very features that give her status as female only the most revolting deformity.

They are correct in one thing, in finding the specific sexual attributes of woman inconsistent with a normally conceived masculine ideal. Apparently without any healthy inner concept of woman's biologic purpose, without any realistic image of what she normally is to man, they shrilly berate her as worthless. They are astonished that mankind in general cannot see that woman is an absurdity; this seems quite plain to them since they can find no role for her except one in which she is inappropriate. Similarly miscast, let us say in the role of conceiving and bearing a child, the male might also be found absurd. The degree of his shortcomings might then be measured by the degree of his normality as a male.

Weininger projects other imperfections found within himself onto this fictitious woman for whom he has found no place, making her appear, in such eyes as his and Strindberg's, quite revolting. His own effeminacy, and probably some personal homosexual inclinations, he evidently took to be identical with the normal femininity of woman. (15) Despising this insofar as he recognized it, he reads it into actual woman where he can more effectively denounce and revile it. In reality, however, what in the male constitutes effeminacy does not represent what is feminine in woman any more accurately than normal body temperature is represented by a malignant fever.

It is not surprising that such a man as Strindberg embraced Weininger's concepts with desperate enthusiasm and found in them profound comfort for his own pathologic unhappiness and misanthropy. Remarkable only is the fact that this old and antibiologic reaction expressed over so many centuries by afflicted or fanatical spokesmen should, at the beginning of the twentieth century, be hailed as an original discovery. (16)

The concept of a normal and universal bisexuality which appealed so strongly to Weininger had for a number of years been considered by Wilhelm Fliess as his own discovery and as one of great magnitude. Since Weininger was little more than a child, Fliess had been confidentially expounding his ideas about this to Freud. Freud had, in fact, proposed that the two of them collaborate on a book that would adequately present the subject that had long impressed them both. When Weininger's *Sex and Character* appeared, Fliess concluded that Freud had been guilty of revealing his highly cherished but still unpublished discovery to the young Viennese writer. For this he bitterly criticized his former friend and admirer. (17)

Scornful devaluation of the flesh does not always lead to the literal rejection of sensuous aims. Often it appears to contribute to a confusion in which physical satisfactions are defiantly and selfishly pursued without respect or affection for the object, often indeed with contempt or cruelty.

It is interesting to observe how commonly those who take this course are mistakenly looked upon as real and even as superior lovers, as men of extraordinary passion and vitality. It is true that these pseudolovers, inwardly unsatisfied and restless, often need an audience and make a great display of what they do sexually. It is perhaps not remarkable that Lord Byron seems to have enjoyed his reputation as a dangerous despoiler of women and even posed considerably to enhance it. The curious point is that he has been historically accepted as the veritable incarnation of what is most enticingly romantic. Mario Praz offers us this glimpse of Byron as a lover:

Byron puts forward heroic argument in order to extract sensations from marriage. "The great object of life is sensation, to feel that we exist, even though in pain," he had written to his future wife, who, though she might have been forewarned by it, was impelled by love and protective instinct towards her ambitious and rather puerile attempt to reform the poet. The first thing Byron said to her after the wedding ceremony was that it was now too late, that Annabella could have saved him if she had accepted him the first time he had asked for her hand, but that now there was no remedy: something irreparable had happened, Annabella would realize that she had married a devil, because he could only hate her: they were a damned and accursed pair. Even this was not enough. Annabella must be made to believe that the marriage was the result of a pique, of a bet, in which the woman had been treated as a mere object. Had Annabella refused Byron's hand the first time? Byron had plotted with Lady Melbourne to punish her stubbornness. Now he held her in his power, and he would make her feel it. At the moment of going to bed, Byron asked his wife if she intended to sleep in the same bed with him: "I hate sleeping with any woman, but you may if you choose." After all, provided she were young, he went on, one woman was as good as another. . . . In the middle of the night Annabella heard her husband cry out: "Good God, I am surely in Hell!" The fire in the grate shone through the red curtains of the marriage bed. Profiting by his youthful reading of *Zeluco*, John Moore's romance, Byron entertained his wife on the means employed by that monster to get rid of his own child. And he concluded: "I shall strangle ours." Later, when Annabella was suffering the pains of childbirth, Byron told her that he hoped she would perish together with her baby, and when the child was born, the first thing he asked on coming into the room was: "The child was born dead, wasn't it?"

But the most subtle torture, the torture which was to wring the most exquisite cry of anguish from its victim was this: Byron, by every kind of allusion and insinuation, sought to instil into Annabella the suspicion of his incest with Augusta, his "terrible" secret. When Augusta was living under the same roof, Annabella must be given to understand that Medora was Byron's daughter, and must be convinced that Augusta was still having intercourse with him (which was not true). Byron Felt a perverse joy at the simultaneous presence of the two women, with all the amusement of innuendoes and double meanings which it afforded him, and the continual sensation of hanging over the edge of an abyss. Annabella was beside herself with desperation, to the point of feeling herself driven to kill Augusta: the thought of imminent catastrophe filled Byron with exultation:

. . . There was that in my spirit ever
Which shaped out for itself some great reverse. (18)

Even in the celibates cited by Havelock Ellis, one scarcely finds expressed a more thorough rejection of the flesh than in some distinguished homosexuals. John Addington Symonds insisted, as has been noted, that the pederasty he prizes is neither "depravity nor a sensual vice." He made a great point of distinguishing it from "the passion that grovels in the filth of sensual grossness. . . ." (19) Though he also has good things to say about bodily contact between two men, it seems clear that he learned somewhere, and thoroughly, that old lesson about the shames and horrors of the vile flesh—particularly woman's.

André Gide's sharp distinction between anything erotically sensuous or voluptuous and personal love has already been emphasized. He makes it plain that he feels that physically erotic relations would desecrate the devotion for his wife which he regards as of extraordinary quality and intensity. (20, 21) On the other hand he repeatedly insists that with the boys and young men to whom he turned for sexual purposes, he preferred no personal relations at all. His most lascivious feelings seem to have been specifically aroused by waifs, gamins, and other more or less disreputable specimens he found roaming in sordid streets. (22) Some of Gide's statements indicate he was convinced that a similar dismemberment of love is natural and desirable for heterosexual mates:

I say that if a young man falls in love with a girl, and if that love is profound, then there is a good chance of it remaining chaste and not being crossed at once by desire. This is exactly what Victor Hugo understood so clearly, when in *Les Miserables*, he convinces us that Marius would rather have gone with a prostitute, than so much as entertain an impure thought for Cosette; and similarly Fielding, in *Tom Jones*, makes his hero tumble the inn-keeper's daughters all the better, the more he is in love with Sophia. And it is this that Merteuil expressed so well in de Laclos' book, when the young Dancenis falls in love with the young Volange. But I add that, in view of marriage, it would have been better, and less risky to each of them, had their provisional pleasure been of a different kind. (23)

Gide, in fact, even goes so far as to say that heterosexual love causes misogyny, insisting that, as homosexuality diminished in Athens, decadence and effeminacy progressed and that, with these unfortunate developments, men lost their respect for women. In *Corydon* he writes:

. . . we owe our respect for women to homosexuality . . . and just as respect for women accompanies homosexuality so we find that women are less highly honored as soon as they are generally desired. You must see that that is natural. (24)

Those who read Gide's own account of his wife's deep unhappiness and isolation will not be likely to believe that she was ever able to see that this is natural. (25)

Though some inverts undoubtedly maintain respect and affection for female figures whom they scrupulously desexualize, their deep misogyny toward woman in her natural role is usually apparent. Theodor Reik offers this interesting observation:

The aping of feminine modes and manners by the homosexual seems evidence of admiration of women. Is there not a saying that imitation is the sincerest form of flattery? But the fact that such feminine males choose men, not women, as objects seems contradictory, and close observation reveals other contradictory features, which not only destroy the faith in the genuineness of such a supposed devotion, but even exclude it. Whoever has the opportunity to observe the behavior of homosexual men among themselves gets the impression that they do not simply imitate femininity, but travesty it. When you listen to their conversations, as one man speaks to another, you hear clearly in their feminine imitation the sounds of unconscious mockery and hateful sneering.

Here are a few sentences picked up from conversations between homosexual men: "Darling, you are so cute!" "Dearie, what a time we had!" "Let's take our baskets and go to market." "She took her hair down and said. . . ." (told about another man). Homosexual men are called "Belles" or "Bitches." Movements such as removing a resisting lock from the forehead, swaying of the hips, and so on, are not merely imitated; they are ridiculed in the imitation. The imitation of women in fantasies can go to grotesque lengths, like that of a man who calls himself "Auntie Caroline" and imagines himself as a prostitute in long stockings being attacked by a man, or as a coquette girl "who plays them all and belongs to none," and even as an abandoned woman, when his male lover deserts him. A homosexual patient asserts that he cannot feel attracted to women because he is himself one. These pseudo-women unconsciously hate the real ones. One of them said in psychoanalysis: "If there were no women, I would not be a homosexual. For all I care, all women might be drowned except a few who create the need to run away from them to men." What ties homosexual men unconsciously together is their secret hatred of women. It is apparent that similar factors operate in homosexual women. . . . This attempt to caricature reveals a hostility, and we begin to understand that to take the place of a woman in the plays of love and sex has the uncon-

scious meaning, to remove the object and to take for oneself the significance she once had. (26)

The tendency to separate the physically sensuous aspects of sexual love and to condemn them as evil or dirty appears to act as an
impediment to the development of normal erotic orientation. It
seems reasonable to believe that the influence of this true antisexuality may, during maturation, deflect or impoverish natural aims
and impulses, and may play some part in the cause of homosexuality as well as other inadequacies and deviations. This does not,
however, justify explaining, as Cory does, the general distaste for
inversion as a product of an "antisexual culture." Such distaste,
however, like our distaste for the aforementioned married couple
who would choose to have relations in public, like our estimate of
Lord Byron's attitude toward his wife, is a reaction to what we regard as a misuse or travesty of sexuality.

Real antisexuality, the condemnation of physical desire, may
sometimes play a part in restraining people from undesirable acts,
but it is my belief that far more regularly it contributes to pathologic developments.

I believe that any normal man in the United States will agree
that it would be wrong for him to go to bed and have sexual relations with the wife of a respected friend. This belief does not
spring from disgust with the woman's body. Neither she nor her
husband would particularly appreciate loyalty derived from or
dependent on so unflattering a foundation. Further, no ordinary
father has sexual relations with his daughter. He is not restrained
by tastes that cause him to regard her on the whole as a mass of
corruption, her genitalia as the epitome of revolting ugliness. That
husband is indeed unfortunate who can be faithful to his wife only
by cultivating toward the flesh of all other women such reactions
as those expressed by the ascetics and other antisexualists quoted
above. In establishing such reactions to other women, he would
undoubtedly acquire some feelings about his wife also that would
not promote happiness in the marriage.

Though relatively few parents are familiar with the actual utterances of Odo de Cluny or of Otto Weininger, and few teachers or
scoutmasters would support or choose to convey such teachings,
yet in one form or another these very teachings do regularly influence practically all children. Thus a perverse confusion has been
acquired by almost every child before he reaches puberty.

Has any boy or any girl in our civilization grown up without in
some way being taught these basic premises? I very much doubt
it. If the parents themselves are wise enough to avoid thus confusing a child, the chances are that he will learn it from an aunt, a
servant, a schoolteacher, or perhaps from some physician or

clergyman. Many of those who teach him this sad perversion of values do not themselves believe it, or realize what they are doing to the child. They instinctively use an idiom that has, over the centuries, worked into most languages. If the average parent, or the ordinary Y.M.C.A. secretary, tries to impart to a child the true and important knowledge that sexual love is too important to deform or stunt by abuse, and that restraint is necessary during the period of growing up, and when grown, except under specific circumstances, the child nearly always learns to believe that sexual lust is filthy and dishonorable and that you can only love girls and women by keeping even your thoughts about them above your belt and away from their bodies.

No matter what actual words are used or what words avoided, I sincerely believe that this is what every child learns. If he fails to learn it from parents and other figures in authority, he will still learn it from his playmates. They, too, make it clear that the "flesh" is dirty and all pleasures of the "flesh" a foul degradation, whether confined to himself or longed for in conjunction with female flesh. Many of the playmates, however, accept this so-called filth and corruption as too pleasant to forego. Some even revel in the defiance of seeking what has been forbidden in such terms. By word and by example, they show him that what he has been taught to regard as the very foulest things, the most dishonorable practices, are also the most exciting. The nature and quality of all these things of the flesh, more euphemistically named by his elders, are made vivid and clear by his own contemporaries, who constantly use the forbidden verbs for love-making and the forbidden nouns for sexual organs almost interchangeably with four-letter words for excrement. All these terms are continually employed not only for real insult, or in playful affection, but also, along with blasphemy, to express both enthusiasm and chagrin. Sometimes they serve as mere exclamations or to embellish idly a matter-of-fact remark. Meanwhile they designate literally, for the young, the act of making love which is much discussed. So whether he is a "good boy" and minds his parents, or a "bad boy" who goes along with the rest of the fellows, he learns, as few lessons are ever learned, essentially what was expressed by the celebrated men whom Havelock Ellis quotes.

What happens then is that before he can normally love girls, even a little, each boy must unlearn this deeply ingrained lesson. If he cannot unlearn it satisfactorily, he must force himself, by some hypocritical ruse, not to let what he believes direct either his conduct or his feelings in sexual matters. He may choose to be "bad" (his idea of virile) about sex and do things to girls that he believes will degrade them; but he cannot, until he begins to unlearn his earlier lessons, in this way find out how to love them. He may be "good," and even succeed in "keeping his thoughts above his belt" as far as girls are concerned, but if he really succeeds in thus restricting his thoughts, he does so at his peril.

Here let me repeat the words of a wise and liberal physician, who disagreed with a strict and perhaps fanatical counsellor of adolescents on the subjects of dancing and feminine sports attire. The strict counsellor insisted that contact between boy and girl in dancing will arouse sexual desire, and that the sight of a well-built girl moving about the tennis court garbed in a tight T-shirt and shorts may promote lascivious feelings among the boys.

To this the physician replied that he, for his part, believed dancing even the most fervid rumba, watching even the most provocative form twist and spring about in a sports costume that conceals so little will not be harmful for young people who have "the right sort of thoughts."

Who could honestly disagree with either of these contradictory opinions? There can be no question but that feelings or impulses distinctly erotic will be aroused. I am confident that the physician is wise enough to know this. What he no doubt meant to say is that he did not believe the erotic sensations and aspirations thus aroused are wrong or dirty or harmful to any reasonably well-integrated adolescent.

To his own fourteen-year-old son, however, his words would almost surely have conveyed the false information that he believed it permissible to dance with, or to delight in the sight of, a voluptuous girl only if one failed to react normally to these opportunities. Unless the son were precocious in unlearning earlier lessons about "the flesh," he would recognize his own thoughts as *not* being of the right sort, and would feel that they disqualified him from decently participating. The more normal and the more conscientious the boy, the more clearly he would realize that his own reactions did indeed involve "thoughts below the belt" and, furthermore, thoughts about all sorts of matters that the fellows had for years been calling "dirty" and referring to in unprintable words.

SOURCES

1. D. W. Cory, *The Homosexual in America* (New York: Greenberg, Publisher 1951), pp. 232–33.

2. Havelock Ellis, *Studies in the Psychology of Sex* (New York: Random House, Inc., 1936).

3. *Ibid.*, Vol. II, p. 119. Used by permission of Random House, Inc.

4. *Ibid.*, p. 126. Used by permission of Random House, Inc.

5. *Ibid.*, p. 120. Used by permission of Random House, Inc.

6. *Ibid.*, p. 137. Used by permission of Random House, Inc.

7. Theodor Reik, *Psychology of Sexual Relations* (New York: Rinehart & Co., Inc., 1945), p. 27.

8. Gregory Zilboorg, *The Medical Man and the Witch During the Renaissance* (Baltimore: The Johns Hopkins Press, 1935), p. 42.

9. D. Abrahamsen, *The Mind and Death of a Genius* (New York: Columbia University Press, 1946).

10. *Ibid.*, pp. 126–27.

11. *Ibid.*, p. 124.

12. *Ibid.*, p. 4.

13. *Ibid.*, p. 122.

14. *Ibid.*, pp. 148–49.

15. *Ibid.*, pp. 132–33.

16. *Ibid.*, pp. 43–44.

17. Ernest Jones, *The Life and Work of Sigmund Freud* (New York: Basic Books, Inc., 1953), Vol. I, pp. 287–318.

18. Mario Praz, *The Romantic Agony* (New York: Oxford University Press, 1951), pp. 72–73.

19. L. J. Bragman, "The Case of John Addington Symonds," *American Journal of Psychiatry*, CVIII (September 1936), 375–98.

20. André Gide, *The Secret Drama of My Life* (Paris: Boar's Head Books, 1951), pp. 23–25, 28, 62.

21. Harold March, *Gide and the Hound of Heaven* (Philadelphia: University of Pennsylvania Press, 1952), pp. 37–38.

22. *Ibid.*, pp. 133–35.

23. From *Corydon*, p. 149, Copyright 1950 by André Gide. Published by Farrar, Straus & Cudahy, Inc.

24. *Ibid.*, pp. 141–42. Quoted by permission.

25. Gide, *The Secret Drama of My Life*.

26. Reik, *op. cit.*, p. 49.

Chapter 23
THE FOX AND THE GRAPES

In the brief comment on the 1920's with which this book opened, we noted that those acclaimed as passionate rebels against sexual restraint sometimes expressed surprisingly dispirited or tepid reactions to what was generally regarded as the new freedom. Anti-sexuality, though it may emerge in such violent repudiations of the flesh as those cited in the preceding chapter, seems also to manifest itself in ennui, languor, and a curiously vain artificiality. Reversals of normal response are not, of course, confined to the area of sex but sometimes extend broadly over the entire scope of human reactivity. On this generalized reversal of ordinary evaluation, Edith Hamilton in her article on William Faulkner makes important observations:

"I detest nature," Picasso said. He is the spokesman for the art of the age, our age, for the music we are listening to, the pictures we are looking at, the books we are reading. Today the usual and the normal, which is to say the natural, is being discarded. What is called abstract art has taken a foremost place. One of the most recent prizes was given to a sculptor for her figure of an animal shape, not like any animal that ever lived, but a representation of an indeterminate animal vaguely applicable to many kinds of living creatures. The sculptor had turned away from nature to depict an image she had conceived, a form existing only in her mind. When Picasso detests nature he is doing the same thing. He shuts out the detestable world his eyes show him and takes refuge in the inner world of himself where he perceives shapes only dimly connected with things that have actual existence.

Our artists are escaping from reality. This is no new thing, to be sure. In almost all ages there have been artists who escaped. What is new in our age is the direction they are taking. In the past a detestation of nature, a determination not to be dominated by fact, led persistently to the land of heart's desire where everyone and everything was good and true and beautiful. Now it leads to just the opposite, where nothing is good or true or beautiful. Of course one is just as much an escape as the other. It is just as far from reality to shut out all that is agreeable as to shut out all that is disagreeable. Both extremes are equally unreal, and both are equally romantic.

The danger to the romantic, equally present whether he turns his back on ugliness or on loveliness, is sentimentality. It is easily recognized in the first case, but not in the second. There is a general impression that to describe things as dull and drab and unpleasant is realism and farthest removed from the roses and raptures of sentimentality. That is not true. The extremely unpleasant can be extremely sentimental. Sentimentality is always false sentiment. It is such a danger to the romantic artist because he has escaped from the domination of fact and sentimentality is falsehood to fact. When an artist detests nature he has thrown away his best defence against that danger. Nature is not sentimental.

When Edgar Lee Masters describes a baby:
> She was some kind of a crying thing
> One takes in one's arms and all at once
> It slimes your face with its running nose,
> And voids its essence all over you,
> And there you stand smelling to heaven—

he has fallen into one extreme of sentimental unreality as truly as Swinburne has into the other when he writes:
> A baby's eyes—
> Their glance might cast out pain and sin,
> Their speech make dumb and wise,
> By mute glad god-head felt within
> A baby's eyes.

Neither Masters nor Swinburne, of course, were in the least concerned with what a baby is really like. They had escaped from that limitation. Perhaps each in his own way was seeking for some other truth than the truth of nature, but all we know is that the result was falsehood for both of them, pure sentimentality, as much in the case of the nasty baby as in the case of the baby with the momentous eyes. (1)

Extreme idealists of one sort may ignore or even reverse the data of perception to create needed illusions of the ethereal Mrs. Mary Baker Eddy, as Reginald Reynolds so effectively put it:

> ... having decided that matter was an illusion (which did not prevent her from amassing a very material fortune as a reward in this world for her denial of its existence) ... concluded *a fortiori* that dirt, being matter displaced, was the displacement of a fictitious substance, having an entirely fictitious importance. (2)

So, too, extremists of another kind appear unable or unwilling to accept what is directly at hand, if this be delightful. They must turn immediate actuality inside out to find what is revolting. Moralists have seriously tried to talk sweethearts out of kissing by arguments that the human mouth is teeming with bacteria. They are, of course, right about the bacteria. Recently the *Journal of the*

American Medical Association published a letter inquiring about the risks of catching tuberculosis by such contacts as the light-hearted, general exchange of kisses with the ladies that men at a New Year's Eve party usually hope for at the stroke of midnight. The medical authorities replying admitted the possibility of minute risk, but apparently being human, they suggested that this be ignored. (3)

I remember listening in astonishment, many years ago, to a scholar of outstanding scientific learning who, in my presence, counseled another man in behalf of chastity:

"Never forget, my friend," he said with earnest conviction, "that when you kiss a girl, you're just sucking on one end of a tube twenty-four feet long and that the other end is filled with. . . ."

His emphasis on the last word (unprinted here) strongly conveyed repugnance. For all my naiveté, I could not but wonder if it did not also suggest relish, a bitter relish in what he took as proof that behind what appeared to be delectable, there stood a disgusting reality. What moralist would insist on chastity at such a price?

During World War II, *Life* magazine published photographs of a more than ordinarily well-endowed girl clad in black lace lingerie. The provocative attire was referred to in captions as a "Furlough Nightgown." There was little need for accompanying text to make explicit the idea that husbands returning home from long absences in military service might look with enthusiasm upon wives so adorned to receive them.

Letters to the editor expressed a number of reactions. These ranged from the equivalent of hearty cheers to indignant criticism. Some serious commentators felt that such emphasis on physical charm and sheer lingerie suggested a lack of deeper and more important realities in the love of American men for their wives. In addition to these generally understandable reactions there were others that seemed to reflect points of view that deserve consideration here.

Life magazine had often before published photographs of equally voluptuous ladies in equally enticing garments. Some of the protests seemed not primarily against displaying the female body, or against displaying it so delightfully. These seemed to find outrage in the magazine's implying that legally married women possessed such charms and might be pleased to offer them wholeheartedly in love to returning husbands. Apparently the uninhibited expression of erotic passion was regarded by some critics as inappropriate between wedded mates. In several letters to the editor, the situation suggested by the "Furlough Nightgown" pictures was referred to as disgusting. (4) Wives who would wear such garments in welcoming their husbands were compared to prostitutes and the incentives involved termed as fit only for a brothel. It is indeed difficult to say just what may have been the basis for the various judgments expressed, but it would not be remarkable if readers concluded that some commentators believed it particularly regrettable and shameful for vigorous participation in sexual love to occur between man and wife; that such activities, if they must occur at all, should be relegated to the bawdy house. Such a concept becomes still more puzzling when we recall that professional prostitutes are reported to be almost universally frigid in the performance of their tasks.

What is this tempting goal that some earnest people say man should sedulously avoid in sexual relations, even with the one woman he has chosen and who is his legal mate? Is it to be presumed that marital partners should not fully accept each other physically? That they are forbidden to do their utmost to obtain and to give the last full measure of erotic joy to each other? This is, indeed, a curious and unfortunate corollary that logically arises from estimating the "flesh" as despicable.

Such an attitude is well illustrated in a kindly, and, generally speaking, liberal clergyman whose sermons I well remember. He continually warned the men of his congregation against some sort or degree of physical desire which he plainly felt was always and necessarily in opposition to real goodness and to a love that extends beyond sensual contact. He pictured marriage as lawful and beautiful, but he insisted that it could be this way only if the husband somehow held back and refused to accept in full the carnal possibilities of his mate. He did not tell his parishioners just where they should stop, just what they should not do, but he often emphasized his point thus:

And this I say unto you, look not deeply into a woman's eyes. Not into the eyes of *any* woman. Yes, even though she be your sacredly wedded wife, look not too deeply into her eyes or the immortal soul may be tarnished by lust.

In contrast with such a warning in the name of ethics or religion, many cynical caricatures of love-making abound in recent novels. None are perhaps more contemptuous than those presented over and over again by Evelyn Waugh. (5) Aldous Huxley, (6) though milder, also seems often to feel that man and woman cannot even make a tragedy of their love—merely a dull farce. Of him, Reginald Reynolds writes:

Here is the weakness of Mr. Aldous Huxley, if a cowardly Paris may venture a shaft at the heel of Achilles. . . . Mr. Huxley is obsessed with sex to show its ugliness, having a most excremental loathing for what appears to him the grotesque antics of lovers. (7)

In the plays of Noel Coward, (8) erotic relations are sometimes pictured as so stupidly trivial that it is difficult to see why the characters bother to carry them out. Creative writers who have recently achieved the highest critical approval seem particularly to emphasize this viewpoint, and often to express no other.

In my capacity as a practicing psychiatrist I have sometimes wondered why so many of the poets and novelists currently accorded honor by the most influential and sophisticated critics regularly avoid all reference to any real satisfaction in love between man and woman. Of our most celebrated commentators on life, few seem to be aware that woman can give a real even if transient delight. Those who approach these subjects more sympathetically often interest the general public, but few are considered by prevailing critical circles to be real men of letters. Apparently they are set aside automatically as writers who are not "serious."

Many literary men who always write bitterly or dispiritedly about everything concerning erotic relations between man and woman have, curiously enough, gained immense reputations as impetuous foes of Puritanism, as bold, hot-blooded artists who defy prim conventions in order to reveal the true sexual joys and fulfilments of life. This is a paradox that invites consideration.

During the 1920's and 1930's, no idol of the intellectuals could dispute with D. H. Lawrence for supremacy as spokesman of eros. Adulation amounted almost literally to worship, a sort of worship by vague phallic rites involving literary apotheosis not merely into Pan, but more specifically into the demigod Priapus. (9) It is not my wish to deny that Lawrence was a great novelist or a great man. I am concerned here only with what his works show of sexual love. Most of this writing, hailed as a literal as well as a literary aphrodisiac, actually, as any reader can see for himself, seldom shows man and woman as able to have even a little satisfaction with each other. The results of mating, one is led to believe, can result only in tepid boredom, pitiful failure, or in some distinctly anaphrodisiac, lukewarm mixture of such ingredients.

Despite a brave flourish of four-letter words and a good deal of frankness about a couple having intercourse adulterously, even in the banned *Lady Chatterley's Lover*, (10) this "supervirile" protagonist of physical passion will, I believe, leave unbiased readers in agreement with John Middleton Murry, Lawrence's biographer, who wrote:

Let anyone read the story of Bertha Coutts in *Lady Chatterley* as it follows in Mellor's narrative after the story of Miriam and Helen: when he understands its meaning and its implication, when he recognizes the woman to whom it refers, he will be aghast at the intensity of loathing for woman in the sexual relation which Lawrence felt and uttered at the end of his life. (11)

However great an artist and however great a spirit D. H. Lawrence may have been, he was unable to show in his writings even a suggestion of erotic happiness, of normal sex relations. In all his work there is not a glimpse of what is so thoroughly realized by legions of undistinguished people, even by little men whose meager general abilities scarcely enable them to provide a mate with ample bread and meat. The figure of Lawrence, hailed by an intellectual world as the dangerously vivid spokesman for temptations of the flesh, despite its pathos, suggests an old saying to the effect that "Those that can, do; those that can't, teach."

Many have found in art some sort of vicarious or substitutive fulfilment of what their own tragic handicaps denied them in life. I would be among the last to insist that Lawrence's art does not deserve respect. He did not, however, even in art, achieve any realistic or happy expression of what men find in women. The sad impoverishment of his fictional characters is illustrated in the following quotation from *Women in Love*:

> "Did you need Gerald?" she asked one evening.
> "Yes," he said.
> "Aren't I enough for you?" she asked.
> "No," he said. "You are enough for me, as far as a woman is concerned. You are all women to me. But I wanted a man friend, as eternal as you and I are eternal."
> "Why aren't I enough?" she asked. "You are enough for me. I don't want anybody else but you. Why isn't it the same for you?"
> "Having one, I can live all my life without anybody else, any other sheer intimacy. But to make it complete, really happy, I wanted eternal union with a man too: another kind of love," he said.
> "I don't believe it," she said. "It's an obstinacy, a theory, a perversity."
> "Well—" he said.
> "You can't have two kinds of love. Why should you!"
> "It seems as if I can't," he said. "Yet I wanted it."
> "You can't have it, because it is false, impossible," she said.
> "I don't believe that," he answered. (12)

Few men who have practiced psychiatry for years could remain so cruel as to deride D. H. Lawrence because of the crippling handicap of sexual impotence that Murry ascribes to him. Lawrence is continually preoccupied with the theme of sexual love. From the great novelist's own writings, the biographer illustrates how regularly Lawrence evaluates the act of mating as only a bizarre and distasteful sapping of man's vitality, an inevitable destruction of his "intrinsic male" core. (13) Kisses and embraces are described that would be breathtakingly welcome to the ordinary man, but Lawrence through his heroes finds them "corrosive, seething with his destruction, seething like some cruel corrosive salt around the last substance of his being, destroying him in the kiss." The women in Lawrence's writings are portrayed as vampirishly enjoying the outcome of this anything but amorous duel. "And her soul crystallized with triumph, and his soul was dissolved in agony and humiliation. So she held him there, the victim, consumed, annihilated. She had triumphed: he was not any more." (13)

Even complete physical impotence could scarcely make a man of ordinary reactions respond thus to a handsome woman's passionate and wholehearted embrace. Something deeper than mere physical disability is necessary to account for such a reversal of natural taste. It is curious that Lawrence, who regularly depicts erotic relations as more or less of this nature, should regard himself as well endowed to reveal sexual truths to mankind. "To the last," Murry says, "he conceived it as his mission to teach us the way to sexual regeneration, and he claimed to give the world the ultimate truth about sex." (14) It is far more peculiar that in this mission he was acclaimed by so many intellectual critics almost as a messiah. Murry offers additional evidence in Lawrence's account of a more ambitious attempt at love-making by Anton and Ursula, whose kiss was mentioned above:

Then there in the great flare of light, she clinched hold of him, hard, as if suddenly she had the strength of destruction, she fastened her arms round him and lightened him in her grip, whilst her mouth sought his in a hard, rending, ever-increasing kiss, till his body was powerless in her grip, his heart melted in fear from the fierce, beaked, harpy's kiss. The water washed again over their feet, but she took no notice. She seemed unaware, she seemed to be pressing in her beaked mouth till she had the heart of him. Then, at last, she drew away and looked at him—looked at him. He knew what she wanted. He took her by the hand and led her across the foreshore back to the sand-hills. She went silently. He felt as if the ordeal of proof was upon him, for life or death. He led her to a dark hollow.

"No, here," she said, going out to the slope full under the moonshine. She lay motionless, with wide-open eyes looking at the moon. He came direct to her, without preliminaries. She held him pinned down at the chest, awful. The fight, the struggle for consummation was terrible. It lasted till it was agony to his soul, till he succumbed, till he gave way as if dead, and lay with his face buried, partly in her hair, partly in the sand, motionless, as if he would be motionless now for ever, hidden away in the dark, buried, only buried, he only wanted to be buried in the goodly darkness, only that and no more. (15)

This is what the heralded spokesman for sensuality finds in sexual intercourse and what he offers, over and over again, to a rapt generation who look to him for instruction, who apparently hang

on his words for guidance to full carnal expression of love between man and woman. Let us turn to Murry's comment:

This is the end. Anton has failed at the proof. Ursula lies in a cold agony
of un-satisfaction, and he creeps away a broken man.

To discover all that underlies this fearful encounter, we should have to
go to *Lady Chatterley's Lover*, to Mellors' account of his sexual experience
with Bertha Coutts. That is, in the present state of affairs, unquotable. But
in that page and a half the curious will find not only the naked physical
foundation—"the blind beakishness"—of this experience of Ursula and
Anton, but also Lawrence's final account of the sexual experience from
which both the sexual experience of Will and Anna, and of Anton and Ursula is derived. *The Rainbow* is, radically, the history of Lawrence's final
sexual failure. (15)

Is there a man so inhumane as to mock the anguish revealed in
Sons and Lovers, (16) or to make light of that tragic love, however
malignant its fruit, that Lawrence expressed sometime after the
death of his mother? If there be one so inclined, let him read in full
Lawrence's poem about his mother that begins:

My love lies underground
With her face upturned to mine,
And her mouth inclined in the last long kiss
That ended her life with mine. (17)

The biographer, Murry, who, chiefly from Lawrence's own
writings, offers an interpretation of the latter's problems has this
to say about his own study:

If, at the end of the story, they feel that this great and frail and lovely
man, this man of sorrows, this lonely hero, has been judged by one who
was once his friend; then not Lawrence has been judged, but the friend.

This is the story of one of the greatest lovers the world has known: of a
hero of love, of a man whose capacity for love was so great that he was
afraid of it. We little lovers do not know and cannot dream what it is to be
afraid of love as he was. Love grows slowly in us little men, if it grows at
all. But in him it was a devouring flame while yet a boy: a love that consumed his soul, and threatened his very life. It was not love of his mother
only, but love of all men and all women and all things created: a devouring flame of universal love.

This fierce and devouring flame of love would burn him up; it did
burn him up. He was half burned away by it before the great fear took
hold of him: a fear as mighty as the love which caused it. So he strove to
kill his love; he fled away from it, he hid his face from it, he sought oblivion from it: in woman. The more avidly he sought oblivion from this con-
suming flame of love, the less he could find it, the less capable he became
of finding it. And slowly and inevitably, the love turned into hate. Hate,
first and last, of himself, who had feared his love and sought to kill it;
hate, next, of woman to whom he had fled for refuge from the fire that
consumed him, and from whom he could not take the oblivion for which
he hungered; hate, finally, of a world of men which had caused him to
suffer as scarcely any man has suffered before.

Only he can judge Lawrence, who has loved as he loved. There is no such man living: of that I am convinced. I believe that once there was such a man, who loved as Lawrence loved and did not fear as Lawrence feared, or if he did, he conquered his fear. He alone could judge Lawrence; and it was he who spoke the word: "judge not that ye be not judged." (18)

Lawrence's male characters seem regularly to react to the amorous female with disgust and despair, to respond to the opportunity for unrestrained sexual love with angry protest and wailing impotence. There is apparently little or nothing in them that conveys anything accurate about the carnal pleasures of erotic experience.

Other curious and profoundly unnatural reactions are well demonstrated in some currently revered superesthetic or superexotic art forms. Scholarly exegetes (19, 20) have devoted years of their lives to the task of deciphering and revealing the content of what James Joyce wrote in *Ulysses* and *Finnegans Wake*. Poring over this superficially unintelligible word-salad or gibberish, they proclaim a meaning which they offer to the reader in translation. When the *ponies* are used which they have devised to admit the ordinary layman to the sublime thought that is said to be behind these widely acclaimed masterpieces, he naturally hopes to discover something of rare value. But let us turn to what is actually found:

"Nobirdy aviar soar anywing to eagle it," he is told, means "nobody ever saw anything to equal it." (21) This may be a poetic improvement on our ordinary English, though I must confess myself as skeptically unappreciative of it. Assiduous translators and interpreters of this venerated jargon, such as Levin and Tindall, express devout and enthusiastic admiration for the fictional characters whom they acclaim as warm and robustly human. The language used by Tindall at times seems to imply that he regards a few of them as more or less divine.

Leopold Bloom of *Ulysses* has aroused in some scholars an admiration which I must admit I find remarkable. Of this figure as he is presented by Joyce, Tindall writes:

If we take Mrs. Bloom and Stephen and combine them with Mr. Bloom, we compose something like ideal man. Mrs. Bloom is his feminine flesh, Stephen his male intellect and imagination, and Mr. Bloom all that lies between these extremes. That the ideal figure will lie closer to Mr. Bloom than to the others is a tribute to his humanity. (22)

The idealization of Bloom is, indeed, extreme. Tindall says, "God the Father in *Ulysses* is a metaphor for Bloom." (23) His zeal waxing, the same enthusiastic critic insists, ". . . Bloom is not only Odysseus but Jesus-God." (24) This allegedly magnificent specimen of natural manhood is particularly acclaimed in the cuckoldry to which he knowingly and unprotestingly submits. Insofar as anything definite is conveyed by the jargon of *Ulysses*, it appears that Bloom accepts his wife's role in bed with other men not only without indignation but almost in a sort of pride. Much of the reverence expressed by critics seems to center about this attitude. He is lauded as emerging "heroically in the end as one of the greatest representatives of human dignity." In contrast to the imperfect Stephen Dedalus, Bloom is pronounced complete in that he "is son, father, husband, cuckold, and friend." Tindall says: "To Joyce's way of thinking, not even Jesus, with whom Bloom is compared, approaches the humanity of Bloom." (25)

The real triumph of this extravagantly venerated character is said to lie "in his attitude towards Mrs. Bloom." This woman's lavish infidelity is strongly emphasized by admiring commentators. Levin tells us that "the cold statistics of the previous chapter reveal that twenty-five others have shared her favors with Bloom." (26) And Tindall notes that "Mulligan is one of the few in Dublin who have not enjoyed Mrs. Bloom." (27) The husband is described as being content to have her continue relieving rather casual sexual tensions in various residents of the city "for a number of reasons." One of these, according to Tindall, is that "he likes to suffer." (25) But there are others:

He needs her not only for support, but as we have seen, for the contact she provides with other men. . . .

He suffers his wife's admirers because through them he enjoys a kind of relationship with other men. (28)

This hero, proclaimed so vehemently as a godlike ideal, is said to achieve a "final equanimity," reflecting that of his literary creator and arising from

. . . his knowledge that he is part of a great cycle, the series of Molly's lovers. He knows that "he is neither the first nor last nor only nor alone in a series originating in and repeated to infinity." With Ben Pollard and Pisser Burke and Blazes Boylan he belongs to something larger than himself. That cycle is natural he concludes, and however injurious to vanity, inevitable. (29)

This figure, who, we are told, is humanity in heroic mold and virtually the approximation of a demigod, is shown examining with care, and perhaps even with some relish, signs on the sheets of his bed indicating his wife's acts of adultery some hours earlier. These signs, "some flakes" of Plumtree's Potted meat "in the bed upon the imprint of Boylan's form," become a complex symbol. "Potted meat is now Boylan's enjoyment of Mrs. Bloom." The terribly serious and reverent commentator has this to say of Bloom's reaction: "Expanding from context to context, this symbol expresses life, death, love and home." (30) Can such ignominious reactions in a living man be justly glorified and praised in these extravagant terms? Who can explain why they are so evaluated in the fictional Bloom by enthusiastic scholars and intellectuals?

In the male characters of D. H. Lawrence's fiction we have noted a circumscribed repugnance for the ordinarily tempting attributes of a sexually attractive woman. In Joyce's Leopold Bloom students find and seem to praise what might be termed not only an acceptance but a positive talent for cuckoldry that an ordinary person is likely to find extremely unattractive. Like Joyce's prose, the evaluations of life he is said to expound apparently are not designed for the bourgeois or the philistine majority. Perhaps there are select groups possessed of special esthetic sensibilities which enable them to appreciate some recondite charm here that escapes most of us.

Other literary figures of enduring fame have expressed a generalized distaste for human life in all its aspects, a weary lassitude that manifests itself in withdrawal from everything natural into an artificiality that is literally perverse. Sometimes little or no enthusiasm, even for the perverse, prompts or sustains this withdrawal. Even among the chosen artifacts only a tepid boredom can be won. This is, however, preferred as somewhat less obnoxious than all the small and large interests of humanity. The choice is, in a sense, apparently used to insult ordinary feelings. If a man forsakes his bride for the avowed purpose of consorting with paper dolls and furthermore emphasizes his preference by confining his attention to them for the rest of his life, we can scarcely marvel if she detects the insult. More subtle insult, no doubt, might be conveyed if the errant husband proclaimed forever after that even the paper dolls actually bored him and that he just could not be bothered to respond to them actively.

Few examples of this watering down of disgust to ennui, this spread of rejection to all areas of human feeling, can equal that presented in Huymans' novel, *Against the Grain*. In this true masterpiece of pathology, we see Des Esseintes, the hero, after he has withdrawn in lukewarm disdain from nearly all natural activities, take another step:

. . . and a pale smile hovered over his lips when finally his servant brought him a nourishing enema compounded with peptone, and informed his master that he was to repeat the little operation three times every twenty-four hours.

The thing was successfully carried out, and Des Esseintes could not help secretly congratulating himself on the event which was a coping stone, the crowning triumph, in a sort, of the life he had contrived for himself; his predilection for the artificial had now, and that without any initiative on his part, attained its supreme fulfillment. A man could hardly go farther; nourishment thus absorbed was surely the last aberration from the natural that could be committed. . . .

"What a delicious thing," he said to himself, "it would be if one could, once restored to full health, go on with the same simple regime. What a saving of time, what a radical deliverance from the repugnance meat inspires in people who have lost their appetite! What a definite and final release from the lassitude that invariably results from the necessarily limited choice of viands! What a vigorous protest against the degrading sin of gluttony! Last but not least, what a direct insult cast in the face of old Mother Nature whose never varying exigencies would be forever nullified!" (31)

In Des Esseintes we feel pure revulsion against life itself. Though complete, this revulsion is somehow sickened and attenuated into an insipidity that lacks the vigor to become either real hate or wholehearted contempt. In this fictional character, the decadence has so progressed that he is sensed as little more than a gelatinous mass undefined, commenting only in manneristic gestures of negation, by feeble and bloodless poses in artificiality. Too bored even to sustain a sincere disgust or flourish its boredom, the miasmic ghost of vitality left in Des Esseintes can only hint at vague obscenities and derisions. Here we truly see all impulses turned against the grain, a full antibiologic reaction of perversion.

SOURCES

1. Edith Hamilton, "Faulkner: Sorcerer or Slave?" *The Saturday Review* (July 12, 1952).

2. Reginald Reynolds, *Cleanliness and Godliness* (Garden City, N.Y.: Doubleday & Co., Inc., 1946), p. 224.

3. "Queries and Minor Notes: Petting, Kissing and Tuberculosis," *Journal of the American Medical Association*, CXLVII (December 22, 1951), 1719.

4. Letters to the editor, *Life* (March 5, 1945).

5. Evelyn Waugh, *Brideshead Revisited, A Handful of Dust, The Loved One, Vile Bodies* (Boston: Little, Brown & Co.).

6. Aldous Huxley, *After Many a Summer Dies the Swan* (New York: Harper & Bros., 1939) and *Point Counter Point* (New York: Grosset & Dunlap, Inc., 1928).

7. Reynolds, *op. cit.*, p. 236.

8. Noel Coward, *Play Parade* (Garden City, N.Y.: Doubleday & Co., Inc., 1933).

9. F. J. Hoffman and H. T. Moore, *The Achievement of D. H. Lawrence* (Norman: University of Oklahoma Press, 1953).

10. D. H. Lawrence, *Lady Chatterley's Lover*. (Privately Printed.)

11. J. M. Murry, *Son of Woman* (London: Jonathan Cape, Ltd., 1931), p. 27.

12. D. H. Lawrence, *Women in Love* (New York: The Viking Press, Inc., 1920), p. 548.

13. Murry, *op. cit.*, p. 67.

14. *Ibid.*, p. 72.

15. *Ibid.*, pp. 70–71.

16. D. H. Lawrence, *Sons and Lovers* (New York: Modern Library, Inc., 1922).

17. Murry, *op. cit.*, p. 45.

18. *Ibid.*, pp. vii–viii.

19. Harry Levin, *James Joyce* (New York: New Directions, 1941).

20. W. Y. Tindall, *James Joyce* (New York: Charles Scribner's Sons, 1950).

21. Levin, *op. cit.*, p. 189.

22. Tindall, *op. cit.*, p. 38.

23. *Ibid.*, p. 76.

24. *Ibid.*, p. 102.

25. *Ibid.*, p. 35.

26. Levin, *op. cit.*, p. 126.

27. Tindall, *op. cit.*, p. 98.

28. *Ibid.*, pp. 36, 11.

29. *Ibid.*, p. 66.

30. *Ibid.*, p. 115.

31. J. K. Huysmans, *Against the Grain* (New York: Hartsdale House, 1931), p. 325.

Chapter 24
ANTISEXUALITY

No one, to my knowledge, has ever made so clear some deeply important features of the disgust that seems to underlie antisexuality and broader rejections of life as Erwin Straus has done in his book *On Obsession*. (1) This study is primarily concerned with pathological reactions of disgust found in patients with obsessive illness; but what Straus so ably explains and illustrates seems to be no less germane to what immediately concerns us here. "Disgust and delight," he points out, "we experience not as neutral observers. . . . We always experience the world and ourselves." (2) Let us go further with Straus in his discussion:

Although disgust . . . is not a quality which can be measured, located or objectively identified, it is no mere X which evades all determination. Here again the variability may enable us to find the permanent character.

Curls on a head look lovely and attractive, but the same hair found in the soup is disgusting; perhaps we should like to cut one of these curls as a souvenir, but we should be disgusted to collect the hair left in a comb. Saliva spit out is disgusting, an expression of our contempt, but on fresh lips and tongue the saliva is not disgusting. Separation from the integrity of the living organism turns the physiognomy from delight to disgust. This separation indicates a transition from life to death; it signifies decay. Disgust is directed more against decay, the process of decomposition, than against the dead. A skeleton, a mummy, may be frightening, even horrible, but not as disgusting as a cadaver which has just been brought from a river to the morgue. (3)

This discerning observer offers much more that is pertinent to our present problem. Let us follow him once more in his interpretation of these complicated human reactions:

Since life and death, blooming and fading, dwell so closely together in the living organism, and since physiognomies make their appearance only within the direct sensory I-world relation, it will depend also on us

whether we will find the physiognomy of living or of dying. It will depend on our inclination and capacity to unite. For the friends of Rubens
the world bears a different impress than for the followers of Malthus.
Franz Hals painted ragamuffins and hoboes who, in their tatters, look
richer than many of Van Dyck's princes in silk and brocade. . . .

"Still-life" says the English language, "nature morte" the French.
Sometimes indeed our grip is more important than the matter we lay
hand upon. . . .

For a young, healthy boy the plate cannot be full enough. But what di-
etitian does not know that to put a full plate in front of a sick person is a
certain means of frightening away his weak appetite? One has to be equal
to abundance.

If appetite and hunger are lacking, apathy instead of interest character-
izes our attitude towards the viands on the table. . . .

The sick and the weak man is frightened by abundance. He retreats
from the world and withdraws into himself. The healthy and the strong
man is attracted by exuberance. . . .

To the eye, turned back on retreat from beauty, the view is changed.
On a bright day, life is still more a burden to the depressive. Abundance
is not seen any longer as abundant, that is, as the fecund wave flowing
over the too narrow borders. Abundance, as Rubens painted it, is seen as
a shapeless mass, exuberance as obesity, procreation as pollution. In retreat from abundance the autumnal beauty may come in sight, fall in its
sweet melancholy. We feel attracted by waning life, but still by life.
One step downward and the emphasis is shifted from life in decline to
the decline of life: the theme and tune of Baudelaire's work and existence. . . . (4)

Here I think Straus brings us near the very core of perversion,
close to its true and deepest meaning. He points out the deliberate
and morbid preoccupation with decomposition or with some regressive equivalent, in preference to a participation in life. The in-
vitations of ordinary biologic existence are rejected. Mortality in
some of its aspects continues to evoke disgust in the perverted response, but this disgust itself apparently holds a fascination. Regressive aspects, though found repellent, in some respects are accepted with an ambivalent but insistent relish. Little or no recognition is made of positive biologic manifestations and opportunities,
and these bring no welcoming response.

In his discernment Straus has noted also how a positive, life-accepting health can ignore relatively inconsequential items ordinarily repulsive, or even major obstacles of this sort, in pursuit of a
natural goal:

Since the context in which something presents itself frequently decides
whether we will be attracted by it or frightened away, whether we will
see in it the physiognomy of decay or of life, the same matter can express
abundance, the growing life, or decomposition, the passing away. The
sweat of an athlete who has just won the contest will not prevent his girl
friend from embracing him. The perspiration which covers the face of the
sick has quite another effect. The difference is determined by the difference of context to which the parts belong. In the first case, sweat, breath-

lessness, even exhaustion, still carry the expression of strong, healthy life. They express the lavishness of someone who can afford it. Although in the second case a loving soul may overcome all initial sensual aversions, yet in kissing the sick one, as St. Francis kissed the leper, one does not follow a longing for unification. The legend reports that St. Francis first passed the leper. When he had turned his horse back and had approached the outcast, he found the strength to express a charity which reaches beyond disgust, sickness and death. . . .

It may be well . . . to remember that the doctor of old had to taste urine (hence the term *diabetes mellitus*). Laboratory techniques have freed us from this painful duty, but others remain. Every doctor, and still more every nurse, is expected to serve a patient with actions not less disgusting. The question what power enables us to overcome primary sensory tendencies while they continue to work is still unanswered.

The physiognomical ambiguity of disgusting matters has a deep reason. In our talk and our thoughts we oppose life to death, and in opposing one to the other, we separate them, as if they were two different entities. In the living organism, however, life and death are closely interwoven. The skin, in growing, in rejuvenation itself, produces its own waste.

So do all other organs. The more vigorous the vital processes, the more luxuriant the bodily functions, the greater the waste. The biological terms, metabolism, assimilation or dissimilation, aim at these phenomena. But the biological terminology is not appropriate here. A stanza of poetry would do better than a scientific formula. In scientific notions, in abstract formulas, the original physiognomic meaning vanishes. (5)

It is well to bear in mind that these cogent distinctions drawn by Straus are not distinctions between diverse external objects—one naturally acceptable, the other naturally distasteful. Rather, a distinction is drawn between two types of reaction to an integrated biologic process, a process in which growth and decay are not separable elements but more truly aspects of a unitary continuum. One reaction is basically life-accepting. The other is a revulsion so primordial that it might accurately be thought of as antibiologic.

In discussing Jonathan Swift, Straus points out that this man of prodigious intellect, not content with natural powers of perception, takes a magnifying glass the better to observe the imperfections of woman's flesh. So, too, he creates in *Gulliver's Travels* a race of Brobdingnagian giants so that he can be outraged by the monstrous exaggeration of a skin pore, perhaps a mole, an otherwise invisible discoloration, each capillary, every bead of sweat, on female breasts "not less than sixteen feet in circumference." He similarly magnifies smells from the skin of these giantesses and luxuriates in their offensiveness. It is a matter of special concern to him that they, naturally, one might say, pass a large amount of urine: "to the quantity of at least two hogsheads," he almost gloatingly insists. (6)

After returning from these and other experiences, Gulliver is welcomed by his wife. About their meeting, Swift gives us this report:

My wife and family received me with great surprise and joy, because they concluded me certainly dead; but I must freely confess the sight of them filled me only with hatred, disgust, and contempt, and the more by reflecting on the near alliance I had to them. . . . And when I began to consider that by copulation with one of the Yahoo species I had become a parent of more, it struck me with the utmost shame, confusion, and horror. As soon as I entered the house, my wife took me in her arms and kissed me, at which, having not been used to the touch of that odious animal for so many years, I fell in a swoon for almost an hour. (7)

In one of his poems, "Strephon and Chloe," Swift describes a wedding night. Of this, Straus says:

The poem begins with praise of Chloe's charms, only to show by contrast what is hidden in every beauty. Whoever has eyes to see will discover filth as the very nature of everything. (6)

As Freud found need to postulate a philosophical monad, the libido, from which to derive and by which to make identical all the positive interests of mankind, so Swift, too, must have his monad. It is a different monad, to be sure, but the insistence on it is again absolute. Swift cannot rest until he has convinced himself that the ultimate unitary reality behind all our perceptory illusions must be a corruption that disgusts.

Straus' elucidation of repugnance in the erotic experiences of obsessive patients contributes substantially toward an understanding of other problems. Basic and extremely significant features of all true antisexuality emerge and are clarified in these cogent observations:

Whenever sex occurs it appears characteristically distorted, more often obscene and fetishistic than overtly sadistic. Sex is experienced as the impure and indecent, the lewd and unchaste. It is infected with disease and dirt. Dissociated from intimate personal relations, severed from the longing for unification, sex becomes obscene. Through the fetishistic isolation of the genitalia from the whole of the body, sexual functions are experienced as excretions and as decay. (8)

From the writings of Swift, remarkably convincing illustrations are drawn by Straus. These reflect a not-otherwise-visible substratum beneath sexual disorder in general that I believe is not readily described but that is of unique significance. Swift's strange relations to the two young women, Stella and Vanessa, for whom he seemed to feel both desire and a peculiar aloofness amounting to contempt, become more comprehensible in the light of reactions expressed in his verse and prose. The romanticist is said by some, as we have already noted, to endow commonplace or even ugly things with charm and wonder born of the relation between observer and object. Whether we should call such pleasant attributes real is an unanswered philosophical question. There is little reason to doubt that it gives the romanticist delight. Swift uses his uncommon powers in a different kind of romanticism, a reverse of the ordinary process, to discover for himself sources of disgust in what to others is most delectable. Do these feats of perverse idealization bring him pleasure or the opposite? Or does he achieve the paradox of finding a weird fulfilment in disgust itself? Let us, for the present, leave these questions unanswered, and return to Straus:

Jonathan Swift has depicted this reversal of normal reaction and has indulged in more than one description of sex as an execrated power. His biography leaves little doubt that he spoke from personal experience. In a poem, "The Lady's Dressing Room," he tells the story of a young lover, Strephon, who during the absence of his sweetheart steals into her room. There he finds nothing but dirt and stink. The poem gives an "inventory of all the litter as it lay." A few examples of this inventory will suffice:

> And first a dirty smock appear'd
> Beneath the arm-pits well besmear'd. . . .
>
> Now listen while he next produces
> The various combs for various Uses,
> Filled up with Dirt so closely fixt
> No brush could force a way betwixt.
> A Paste of Composition rare,
> Sweat, Dandruff, Powder, Lead and Hair. . . .
>
> But oh! it turn's poor Strephon's Bowels,
> When he beheld and smelt the Towels,
> Begumm'd, besmatter'd, and beslim'd,
> With Dirt, and Sweat, and Ear-Wax grim'd
> The stockings, why shoul'd I expose,
> Stain'd with the Marks of Stinking Toes,
> Of greasy coifs and Pinners reeking
> Which Celia slept at least a Week in?

Finally Strephon turns to "the Chest," Celia's chamber pot. "He lifts the lid." Swift compares Strephon with Epimetheus when Pandora's box is opened:

> A sudden universal Crew
> Of Humane Evils upwards flew;
> He still was comforted to find
> That *Hope* at last remain'd behind. . . .
> But Strephon cautious never meant
> The bottom of the Pan to grope. . .
> Thus finishing his grand Survey,
> Disgusted Strephon stole away
> Repeating in his amorous Fits,
> Oh! Celia, Celia, Celia—!

In the ending stanza Swift gives an epigrammatic summary of the obsessive fascination by dirt and decay:

But vengeance, Goddess never sleeping
Soon punish'd Strephon for his Peeping;
His foul Imagination links
Each Dame he sees with all her Stinks:
And, if unsav'ry Odours fly,
Conceives a Lady standing by:
All Women his Description fits,
And both Idea's jump like Wits:
By vicious Fancy coupled fast,
And still appearing in Contrast. (9)

The items catalogued by Swift are not imaginary. No one can deny the commonplace facts of physiology, that sweating, excretion, the replacement of hair and epithelium, the elimination of debris, do occur in the human body. This occurs in women as well as in men. But why should he become so exercised about it? Why seek out these details to arouse his disgust? Concerning Swift's horror over the bowel function, one commentator has very pertinently remarked to the effect that it would have been the true catastrophe if Celia *didn't!* (10) Havelock Ellis has emphasized the fact that many of these very details of human anatomy and physiology that freeze Odo de Cluny and Dean Swift in nauseous horror may give delight to a lover. In contrast to Odo's reaction to the female body, Ellis quotes Sir Kenelm Digby, who reports some glimpses of a sleeping woman:

. . . and her smock was so twisted about her fair body that all her legs and the best part of her thighs were naked, which lay so one over the other that they made a deep shadow where the never-satisfied eyes wished for the greatest light. A natural ruddiness did shine through the skin, as the sunbeams do through crystal or water, and ascertained him that it was flesh that he gazed upon, which yet he durst not touch for fear of melting it, so like snow it looked. Her belly was covered with her smock, which it raised up with a gentle swelling, and expressed the perfect figure of it through the folds of that discourteous veil . . . and out of . . . darkness did glisten a few drops of sweat like diamond sparks, and a more fragrant odour than the violets or primroses, whose season was nearly passed, to give way to the warmer sun and the longest days. (11)

"They play with the same counters, you observe," says Ellis, "these two, Odo and Digby, with skin, sweat, and so forth, each placing upon them his own values. Idealists both of them, the one idealizes along the line of death, and the other along the line of life which the whole race has followed, and both on their own grounds are irrefutable, the logic of life and the logic of death, alike solidly founded in the very structure of the world, of which man is the measuring-rod." (11)

I realize that I may be rebuked for expressing disrespect for the judgment of those who are my betters. No doubt there is much about all these great figures—Odo, Swift, Lawrence, and Huys-mans—diverse as they are, that commands admiration. I trust, however, that I can express vigorous disagreement with what I take to be delusion even in a genius, without deriding the per-sonal handicap that I believe so plainly accounts for the delusion, and without necessarily passing judgment on his other attain-ments. However we may honor them in other respects, I maintain that they have nothing to teach us about what is normal in sexual love.

Many years after the first publication of *Against the Grain*, in a preface to a new edition, Huysmans wrote that only one person had understood his book:

In all this hurly-burly, a single writer alone saw clear, Barbey d'Aurevilly, who be it said, had no personal acquaintance with me. In an article in the *Constitutionel* . . . which was reprinted in his *Le Roman Contemporain* . . . he wrote: "After such a book it only remains for the author to choose be-tween the muzzle of a pistol or the foot of the cross."

The choice has been made. (12)

Who will not join in respect for this choice, and in a prayerful hope that Huysmans, in his latter years as a retreatant at a Trap-pist monastery and, finally, as an oblate at the Maison Notre-Dame, achieved the religious orientation he sought, and found at last peace and happiness and meaning in this life and in his hopes of the next? (13)

The inability to accept beauty in woman or to love her was not all that there was to Jonathan Swift. If we understand this afflic-tion of his, it may modify our distaste for his peculiar and some-times brutal treatment of Stella and of Vanessa. Some schoolboys may remember Swift best as the literary figure who offered "A Modest Proposal for Preventing the Children of Poor People from being a Burden to their Parents or the Country, by fattening and eating them." His real aim, apparently, was to bring substantial re-lief to the poor. Contemporaries and posterity agree that he was a brilliant man, and a man of imposing dignity. His charity and gen-erosity, though carefully concealed, are said to have been magnifi-cent. After his death a paper was found among the things he had saved. In it was clipped a lock of hair. On the paper were written the words: "Only a woman's hair." Not only his virtues but also his sufferings may lend a touch of awe to our feelings as we con-template the simple epitaph he chose for himself: *Ubi Saeva Indig-natio Ulterius Cor Lacerare Nequit* [Where savage indignation can no longer rend his breast]. (14)

It is sometimes said that this antisexuality, this rejection of physical love, began with Saint Paul. (15) A glorious pagan wor-ship of the body, many have insisted, prevailed in classic Hellas and elsewhere. Even for Greek scholars it is, I think, more than a little difficult to say just what intimate and personal feelings prevailed among these people so long ago. Above all other figures, Plato has been hailed century after century as the most noble spokesman among all the poets and philosophers of Greece. Long ago his name, in conjunction with the word "love," became in many languages a cliche that has not yet been discarded. Plato expressed himself at length on love and sex. What he wrote is well preserved and readily available today in accurate translations. What Plato wrote, and apparently what he felt and thought, bears little resemblance indeed to what nearly everybody has been taught about Platonic love. Practically everyone has heard about this high and noble passion that is supposed to be beyond the reach of most human beings.

Despite all this, I maintain without hesitation that no sane physician who reads what Plato says of love would be likely to let him associate with his own teen-age son, nor would he fail to protest against Plato's being employed as a teacher in the local high school. This will undoubtedly be taken as impudent folly by all except those who actually are aware of what is set down in the "Phaedrus" and the "Symposium." It is not for me to judge whether or not Plato is supreme among philosophers and a great figure among the poets of all time. What I do say is that he appears to be poorly qualified as a teacher of adolescents. Anyone interested in how absurd my opinions about Plato are may in a few hours read these two dialogues and find out for himself. Excerpts are not adequate as illustrations, but a few may be worth while. So let us quote Plato:

Phaedrus: My tale, Socrates, is one of your sort, for love was the theme which occupied us—love after a fashion: Lysias has been writing about a fair youth who was being tempted, but not by a lover; and this was the point: he ingeniously proved that the non-lover should be accepted rather than the lover.

Socrates: O that is noble of him! I wish that he would say the poor man rather than the rich, and the old man rather than the young one;—then he would meet the case of me and of many a man; his words would be quite refreshing, and he would be a public benefactor. (16)

It is clear, of course, that this "love" is between males. Note how argument is now advanced that a man does better to enter such relations with another man who does not even pretend to love him:

Phaedrus: . . . But the non-lover has no such tormenting recollections; he has never neglected his affairs or quarrelled with his relations; he has no troubles to add up or excuse to invent; and being well rid of all these evils why should he not freely do what will gratify the beloved? If you say that the lover is more to be esteemed, because his love is thought to be greater; for he is willing to say and do what is hateful to other men, in order to please his beloved;—that, if true, is only a proof that he will prefer any future love to his present, and will injure his old love at the pleasure of the new. And how, in a matter of such infinite importance, can a man be right in trusting himself to one who is afflicted with a malady which no experienced person would attempt to cure, for the patient himself admits that he is not in his right mind, and acknowledges that he is wrong in his mind, but says that he is unable to control himself? (16)

Thus the argument extends on and on, surfeiting the reader with details. It emphasizes chiefly what any ordinary farm hand would call selfish or material advantages to be gained by the youth in giving himself sexually to a "non-lover" instead of to a "lover." Many points in this supposedly sublime dialogue impress me as embarrassingly petty and as tediously expounded. Nor can I deny that the considerations stressed, if they should determine a female's choice of sexual partners, would make me fear that she had a great deal in common with girls who can be picked up in bars any evening for a few dollars. The wisdom of choosing a nonlover is supported by argument against the behavior of one who loves:

Phaedrus: . . . Wherefore also he debars his beloved from society; he will not have you intimate with the wealthy, lest they should exceed him in wealth, or with men of education, lest they should be his superiors in understanding; and he is equally afraid of anybody's influence who has any other advantage over himself. If he can persuade you to break with them, you are left without a friend in the world; or if, out of a regard to your own interest, you have more sense than to comply with his desire, you will have to quarrel with him. But those who are non-lovers, and whose success in love is the reward of their merit, will not be jealous of the companions of their beloved. (16)

After a great deal more of this, Phaedrus, not overwhelmed with modesty, asks:

Now, Socrates, what do you think? Is not the discourse excellent, more especially in the matter of the language?
Socrates: Yes, quite admirable; the effect on me was ravishing. And this I owe to you, Phaedrus, for I observed you while reading to be in an ecstasy, and thinking that you are more experienced in these matters than I am, I followed your example, and, like you, my divine darling, I became inspired with a phrenzy. (16)

Socrates, it appears, was more appreciative of this than the present writer. Let us now consider the "Symposium," in which sharp distinctions are drawn between a low common love and one that is sublime. This superior love is derived by the philosopher from a heavenly Aphrodite "in whose birth the female had no part." Not only is the girl physically excluded from the young men, but even the goddess who inspires these spiritual raptures of pederasty must have no woman among her immediate ancestors. This appears to me to be going even farther than Odo de Cluny to get away from woman's flesh. In contrast, the low and earthly

Aphrodite, who inspires the love of man for woman, is said to have had the misfortune to be born of a mother.

... The Love who is the offspring of the common Aphrodite is essentially common, and has no discrimination, being such as the meaner sort of men feel, and is apt to be of women as well as of youths, and is of the body rather than of the soul. ...

But the offspring of the heavenly Aphrodite is derived from a mother in whose birth the female has no part,—she is from the male only; this is that love which is of youths, and the goddess being older, there is nothing of wantonness in her. Those who are inspired by this love turn to the male; and delight in him who is the more valiant and intelligent nature; any one may recognize pure enthusiasts in the very character of their attachments. For they love not boys, but intelligent beings whose reason is beginning to be developed, much about the time at which their beards begin to grow. (17)

The argument, as Plato puts it, is so one-sided that an ordinary reader may be inclined to wonder why philosophers should wish to keep on talking about it. Any opposition to this allegedly highest form of love is shown to spring from mercenary interest in the unworthy:

... In Ionia and other places, and generally in countries which are subject to the barbarians, the custom is held to be dishonourable; loves of youths share the evil repute in which philosophy and gymnastics are held, because they are inimical to tyranny; for the interests of rulers require that their subjects should be poor in spirit and that there should be no strong bond of friendship or society among them, which love, above all other motives, is likely to inspire, as our Athenian tyrants learned by experience. (17)

Only barbarians, apparently, could fail to see the superiority of pederasty. Tyrants, for political reasons, may be base enough to deny its beauty. We are then told that "so great is the encouragement which all the world gives a lover" that he may in his raptures over his boy-friend and "in the pursuit of his love," carry out all sorts of antics without censure. "He may pray, and entreat, and supplicate, and swear, and lie on a mat at the door, and endure a slavery worse than that of any slave." We are informed, furthermore, that no friend will admonish him or "charge him with meanness or flattery; [for] . . . the actions of a lover have a grace that ennobles them . . . there is no less of character in them." Would this be our reaction if, let us say, the principal of our local high school should lie past midnight on a mat at the door of a second-class scout to pray and entreat and yell out his supplications? Has the baseborn Aphrodite, tainted by her female mother, so perverted us that we cannot share this sublime judgment?

It is interesting to note also that this swearing and entreating need not be sincere. At any rate, this is what Plato says:

... and, what is strangest of all, he only may swear and forswear himself (so men say), and the gods will forgive his transgression, for there is no such thing as a lover's oath. Such is the entire liberty which gods and men have allowed the lover, according to the custom which prevails in our part of the world. From this point of view a man fairly argues that in Athens to love and to be loved is held to be a very honourable thing. But when parents forbid their sons to talk with their lovers, and place them under a tutor's care, who is appointed to see to these things, and their companions and equals cast in their teeth anything of the sort which they may observe, and their elders refuse to silence the reprovers and do not rebuke them—any one who reflects on all this will, on the contrary, think that we hold these practices to be most disgraceful. (17)

I am fully aware that it is easy to misrepresent anyone by quoting him out of context. Therefore I can but repeat my earlier suggestion that the reader examine the actual dialogues for himself.

I have refrained from quoting statements in these dialogues advising that the soul of the boy be loved by the older man even more than his body, and that the really noble lover, the mature man, should cherish his nubile boy-friend not only at the age when our children go to junior high school, but all through his life. Plato says that, too. Nor shall I comment on possible techniques by which the soul might be so loved in pederasty. As for references to lifelong fidelity, I think that for all these talkative middle-aged Athenians, this was purely a Sunday belief. I have found no reason for disagreement with the author of *The Invert* who wrote:

We learn from the Greeks that they discarded them [the boys] as soon as they began to look like men. . . .

A few quotations [from Paton's translation in *The Greek Anthology*] will show that when boys even began to approach manhood they were accounted undesirable by the Greeks:

"*Flaccus:* Just as he is getting his beard, Lado, the fair youth, cruel to lovers, is in love with a boy. Nemesis is swift. . . .

"*Statyllius Flaccus:* If the Polemo I parted from came back to me in safety, I promised to sacrifice to thee. But now Polemo is saved for himself. It is no longer he who has come to me, Phoebus, and arriving with a beard, he is no longer saved for me. He perhaps prayed himself for his chin to be darkened. . . .

"*Alcaeus:* Your leg, Nicander, is getting hairy, but take care. . . . Then shall you know how rare lovers are. But even now reflect that youth is irrevocable. . . .

"*Phanias:* Thy love, Pamphilus, has but a little time to last. Already thy thigh has hair on it and thy cheeks are downy, and Desire leads thee hence forth to another kind of passion. . . .

"*Strata:* Does not the word itself teach you by the words from which it is truly derived? Everyone is called a lover of boys, not the lover of big boys. Have you any retort to make to that?" (18)

I am not unaware of the fact that Plato finally decided, rather late in life, I think, that the noblest of all human love demands a complete denial of bodily contact. Will Durant, a professional scholar in philosophy, summarizes Plato's views thus:

... Love is the pursuit of beauty, and has three stages, according as it is love of the body, or of the soul, or of truth. Love of the body, between man and woman, is legitimate as a means to generation, which is a kind of immortality; nevertheless this is a rudimentary form of love, unworthy of a philosopher. Physical love between man and man, or woman and woman, is unnatural, and must be suppressed as frustrating reproduction. This can be done by sublimating it in the second or spiritual stage of love; here the older man loves the younger because his comeliness is a symbol and reminder of pure and eternal beauty, and the younger loves the older because his wisdom opens a way to understanding and honor. But the highest love is "the love of the everlasting possession of the Good," that love which seeks the absolute beauty of the perfect and eternal Ideas or forms. This, and not fleshless affection between man and woman, is "Platonic love"—the point at which the poet and the philosopher in Plato merge in the passionate desire for understanding, an almost mystic longing for the Beatific Vision of the law and structure and life and goal of the world. (19)

Since it is not the subject of our concern here, we need not argue about "everlasting possession of the Good," or about the beauty of perfect and eternal Ideas and forms. So far as human love is concerned, it seems clear enough that Plato, like Gide, has come to the conclusion that physical passion of any sort, that the "flesh," in other words, is rather trivial and unworthy at best. He does not cry out wildly that it is foul, like Odo, or luxuriate in a Swiftian magnification of its excretions and physiologic debris. He finds it, however, in any form whatsoever, unworthy of a philosopher.

Abrahamsen, in his illuminating study of Otto Weininger, says of that bitter and precocious embodiment of antisexuality:

Weininger's ascetic tendencies may show an interesting parallel to the attitude of Plato toward sex. Some students of Plato believe he was forced into an ascetic philosophy by his own tendency towards sexual perversion. We may possibly see a similar process in Weininger. (20)

After years of philosophic rhapsody about physical pederasty, which there is no reason to believe was not also his practice, Plato finally speaks out to deny the flesh. For over two thousand years, men have continued talking in awed tones about these supernal evaluations of love. The fact that Plato is evaluating homosexuality, not the love between man and woman, is ignored. Can one assume that a man who has emphasized so vigorously his preference for pederasty will have a profound, or even a real, message for us about the love of man and woman?

SOURCES

1. Erwin Straus, *On Obsession* (New York: Journal of Nervous and Mental Disease Monographs), 1938.

2. *Ibid.*, p. 12.

3. *Ibid.*, p. 13.

4. *Ibid.*, pp. 15–17.

5. *Ibid.*, p. 14.

6. *Ibid.*, p. 43.

7. *Ibid.*, pp. 43–44.

8. *Ibid.*, pp. 40–41.

9. *Ibid.*, pp. 41–42. The quotations from Swift's poem are from *Poems of Jonathan Swift*, Vol. II, and are used here by permission of The Clarendon Press, Oxford.

10. Reginald Reynolds, *Cleanliness and Godliness* (Garden City, N.Y.: Doubleday & Co., Inc., 1936), p. 8.

11. Havelock Ellis, introduction to Huysmans' *Against the Grain* (New York: Hartsdale House, 1931), pp. 45–46.

12. J. K. Huysmans, preface to *Against the Grain*, pp. 72–73.

13. Robert Baldick, *The Life of J. K. Huysmans* (Oxford: The Clarendon Press, 1955).

14. Richard Garnett *et al.*, "Swift," *Encyclopaedia Britannica*, 1949 Edition.

15. W. J. Fielding, *Strange Customs of Courtship and Marriage* (New York: The New Home Library, 1942), pp. 108–10.

16. Plato, "Phaedrus," *Dialogues of Plato*, trans. by B. Jowett, Vol. I, pp. 431–89. By permission of Oxford University Press.

17. Plato, "The Symposium," *ibid.*, pp. 541–94. By permission of Oxford University Press.

18. Anomaly, *The Invert* (London: Baillière, Tindall & Cox, 1948), pp. 249–50. The quotations are from Paton's translations of *The Greek Anthology*.

19. Will Durant, *The Life of Greece* (New York: Simon & Schuster, Inc., 1939), pp. 518–19.

20. D. Abrahamsen, *The Mind and Death of a Genius* (New York: Columbia University Press, 1946), p. 133.

Chapter 25
MEDUSA

Disgust with the human body, or with much or all that ordinarily elicits reactions that are sensually pleasant, appears to be a basic component of antisexuality. The development of hatred or contempt toward the sexually stimulating object is also typical. What we are here concerned with is a pathology of sexual love that is broader than inversion. I have already expressed the conviction that it is to some degree, usually to a serious degree, always part of inversion. It appears to be a causal factor in the abnormal choice of mates; not necessarily the only cause or the primary one, but certainly an important influence. So, too, there is reason to believe that homosexuality, and all other distortions of love and sex, in their turn, play a causal role in this morbid disgust with flesh and sensuous passion.

Obstacles to the sexual goal that is complete and natural, that is most desirable and most satisfying, are many and peculiarly various. Many deferments and restraints are obviously demanded not only by morality and convention but also by common sense. As with all other basic human urges and strivings, the erotic urge is influenced and shaped by physical maturation and by education in its broadest sense, by interpersonal relations, and by the whole of human experience. Physical limitations and differences, inborn or acquired, may become obstacles of varying influence in directing or shaping, deflecting, or distorting erotic aims and all erotic reactions.

Though the erotic drive is generally regarded as among the strongest experienced by mankind it is, apparently, sometimes denied. The celibate may eschew all recognized sensual pleasure because of fear, because he is unaware of desire, because of his religious convictions, or because of a Swiftian disgust. Perhaps several of these and many other factors will be influential at one and the same time in some celibates. It is not unusual, however, for the impulses toward sexual satisfaction, when frustrated in their ordinary course, to seek some sort of expression in an alternative. Often the incomplete or substitutive activity is made to resemble or approximate as nearly as possible the full natural goal. The usual teen-age boy who masturbates is likely to conjure up in imagination a voluptuous girl as his cordial partner in sensuous activities elaborately dwelt upon. When the obstacles to fulfilment are more complex and more profound, an image of the real goal may be lost; curious aims and scarcely conceivable attitudes may develop. Sometimes acts and functions that scarcely resemble or suggest the original are blundered upon as a means of attaining sensuous pleasure. The emotional experiences of the subject and his attitudes toward the object vary through a scale so wide that truly antithetical reactions are included. The hate of a sadist scourging a child may blend with sensations that accompany orgasm. For one of my patients the pain from a lighted cigarette held against his skin by a prostitute produced a response that was for him uniquely satisfying and lascivious.

The object or partner sought in erotic aims that are seriously distorted may vary through an astonishing range of substitutes for the natural choice. Sometimes the substituted object is paradoxical or grotesquely inappropriate. Or there may not be a personal or even a distinct object at all. Only when screened from normal stimuli by pathologic developments is man likely to respond specifically to those that are abnormal. When natural responsiveness has been blocked by severe disability, sometimes only very odd stimuli will evoke erotic reactions by means that are incomprehensible to the ordinary person.

From my practice I recall one young man who was regularly aroused by the colors about the altar and the vestments worn by priests conducting Mass. Filling his vision with these images, he enjoyed strong sensuous feelings, mixed with deep shame, that produced penile erection and sometimes ejaculation. The priests themselves did not stimulate him at all, nor did similar colors under different circumstances. He had found no other source of comparable sensations. Another young man's passion was aroused only by watching boxers in action. He too experienced erection and, particularly when the opponents really began to slug it out, often ejaculated as well.

When one considers the inevitable and tormenting delays in attaining sexual fulfilment that every person must endure, the many disappointments and disillusionments, the immeasurably vast difference between simple physiologic orgasm, as in nocturnal emission, and the profound complexities of love between mature mates, it is easy to grant that obstacles and distorting influences in the course of a person's development are beyond enumeration.

Whatever part inborn physical characteristics and potentialities may play, they, like the influences of personal experience, cannot direct male toward male sexually, unless this particular man has developed in such a way that he loses his normal erotic awareness of woman. Though some homosexuals are able to complete heterosexual physical intercourse, none are able to react to woman in a normal or adequate manner. Men have been known to complete sexual acts with calves and geese, but the relation is usually masturbatory. With the immense diversity of examples available to demonstrate other distortions of sexuality, we have no need of assuming a natural and universally present component of the libido that preferentially reacts toward the same sex. Bergler, it seems to me, is only emphasizing what is obvious when he reports that his psychoanalytic studies show that the homosexual is "a frightened fugitive from misconceptions he unconsciously builds around women." (1)

The fetishist who chooses to fondle lingerie instead of the girl who might be wearing it, seems at least to be aiming in the general direction of the chosen object. He may caress nylon stockings, high-heeled shoes, lace panties, and brassieres until he has an ejaculation. It seems clear that if he were not somehow blinded or emotionally blocked he would be able to see and feel that it is really the girl he needs. What blocks or distorts his functioning? It is not my task here to attempt an answer. Surely there is more reason to suspect a limitation or deflection than to assume a normal component of the libido naturally directed toward such objects as women's garters, nightgowns, kid gloves, and so on, in preference to the female who wears them.

The man who gets lascivious sensations from setting a barn on fire or from beating a horse at once impresses us as being complexly misdirected. We may say in such instances, if we like, that destructive drives (hate) have invaded and contaminated the sensually erotic responses. One could scarcely argue that such reactions as affection or admiration enter here at all. Most children think at first when they see farmyard animals having sexual relations that the rooster is fighting the hen and that she is being not only hurt but humiliated. All, or nearly all, have already learned the lesson that the flesh (in a sexual sense) is considered low and loathsome. They have heard about boys "laying" girls, and about grown women being "ruined" by men. Most of what the ordinary little boy first learns about sex indicates that it is an act of male overcoming female, or of his prevailing upon her by guile to establish his dominance, and debase her for his pleasure. It is no great mystery that, in this confusion, hate and contempt are sometimes shunted over into channels which are normally designed for erotic gratification and for devotion.

It is said that hell hath no fury like a woman scorned. And men scorned sexually also resent it. In love relations hurt may be administered in diverse ways. When the erotic aim is blocked, chagrin is certain, and vexation may evolve into both wrath and despair. The jilted suitor may decide that the once-desired sweetheart who spurned him is, after all, no good. In time he may convince himself that most or all women are shallow, vain, and generally inferior members of the race; that *la donna e mobile*—and is not to be taken seriously. Only men, he may now tell himself, can truly understand each other and only they are able to value fundamental things correctly.

From his experience of several decades in psychoanalytic work, Reik concludes that, early in life, the homosexual has been hurt through his attachment to a woman and that, feeling hopelessly rejected by the female, he becomes motivated by vengeful feelings to compete with women for the erotic attention of other men. Of this reaction he writes:

> . . . we would say that the homosexual man once had a great admiration for women, was envious and jealous of them. The original attraction their charms held for him was transformed to revulsion. In other words, he was on the way to love them but he did not achieve this aim, or if he did, hostility was the eventual result. . . .
>
> . . . The motive behind this behavior is revealed by the person's efforts to appear as not jealous and at the same time to make others jealous. There is only one explanation: there exists a deep-rooted unconscious resentment against women, in homosexual men. We can guess its origin. It lies in a previous love-disappointment, perhaps in childhood, which was accompanied by passionate jealousy. What was felt before in one's own person is now provoked in the other person. The boy was once abandoned for a man, and now he abandons the woman for a man, not only turning the tables on her, not only inflicting the hurt he once experienced, but in bitter, unconscious mockery inflicting it by the same means. It is as if he would say to the woman, his original love-object, his mother or sister: "You preferred a man to me, now I prefer a man to you. I have taken your place, and I shall be loved by such a man." His behavior shows, then, that he takes the man away from her, as a woman would lure a man away from a rival. (2)

Reik further expresses the belief that the need to avoid rivalry with other males plays an important part in turning the boy's erotic interest from its natural object, as seen in the following quotation from *Psychology of Sexual Relations*:

Homosexual tendencies develop only after the boy steps aside for another boy, avoids competition and gives the other the middle of the road. . . .

There is no doubt that homosexuality means also acceptance of failure and defeat and an effort to make the best of them. (3)

A report by G. V. Hamilton on the behavior of monkeys offers many points indicating that the homosexual role is adopted as a ruse or a placative measure by the weaker animal who feels threatened by an overwhelming competitor. By assuming the position of the female in the sexual act, he surrenders his place as a rival and avoids combat with a dominant bullying figure. Hamilton says:

Any male, mature or immature, was likely to assume the female position for copulation when attacked by a more powerful fellow of either sex if escape by flight was impossible. . . .

After the monkeys had fought their way through to some sort of tribal integration, the big fellow was admitted to the alley. All of them fled at his approach excepting the largest of the females. One recently weaned little male darted into an empty cage and crouched in a corner on the floor. The giant followed, leering at him as if about to attack. The little fellow squealed in terror and looked about for an avenue of escape. Finding none, he assumed the female position of copulation. His enemy now displayed only friendliness and mild sexual excitement, but the youngster ducked between his legs and escaped. . . .

. . . A monkey dashing to a ferocious attack upon a fellow would promptly cease to manifest hostility if the intended victim assumed the female position. . . .

Mature males would sometimes lure weaker males to them by assuming the female position, only to spring at the intended victim as soon as the homosexual bait brought the latter close enough to make escape impossible. Such behavior lacked all appearance of sexual motivation on the part of the luring male, who would move to attack before sexual contact occurred. . . .

No uncastrated sexually mature male was ever observed to assume the female position unless there was a defensive need of doing so, or an obvious intention of luring a timid enemy to non-sexual combat. (4)

Men separated from women, in prisons and during wars, apparently sometimes fall back on masturbation by themselves or with each other. Under such circumstances, there is no reason to believe that in most instances romantic love affairs, or even caricatures of such affairs, accompany whatever substitutive physical acts they may carry out. It is not the instinct-heretofore-inhibited-in-its-aim that now becomes conscious of the aim, but rather the familiar example of man looking for and accepting an imitation of what is unavailable in reality.

Condemnation of the flesh, I believe, may serve as a strong pathologic influence in confusing the child about his natural love-object and in distorting the development of normal erotic attitudes. It also confuses him in his development of normal and appropriate aims or forms of behavior by which to achieve sexual satisfaction. This concept of flesh as shameful, whether it emerges in moral warnings or in the obscene language of sexually unre- strained playmates, is most often applied to the flesh of the fe- male. Girls also hear a good deal about being "ruined" by sexual impulses which are pronounced indecent. Through various influ- ences restraints are developed to check and control the natural im- pulses toward indiscriminate sexual adventure between boy and girl.

Male friends, on the other hand, at age fourteen or at age forty, are not ordinarily restrained from erotic acts with each other be- cause they find each other physically disgusting, nor by moral scruples that resist a spontaneous impulse. They simply do not find anything particularly interesting, in the erotic sense, about the other's body. Absurdity, not the overcoming of a temptation, ex- plains why they keep caressing hands off each other. Interpreta- tions of sex as filthy or vile, if heeded by the child, tend to block the development of his natural sex aims. If taken literally, they may serve to promote the development of pathologic attitudes to- ward the normal object. The man, deflected from a normal goal, who resorts to feminine lingerie for sexual satisfaction has only his own role and feelings to consider. The mental defective or the teen-ager who, in the barn, indulges in sexual intimacies with a heifer is not likely to enter into personal or profoundly emotional relations with his partner. Perhaps the animal experiences some annoyance, but he continues treating her as before, and she is likely to react to him as if nothing had happened.

On the other hand, a homosexual who tries to get another man interested in being kissed upsets a natural human relationship. As I have mentioned earlier, the more real and valuable, the more de- voted and affectionate a friendship, the more outlandish and in- compatible would be any attempt on the part of one friend to mis- take the other for a sexual partner.

Ferenczi, very unrealistically I think, presumed that a coolness between men, a lack of warmth in friendship, has resulted from too great a repression of "homosexual libido." (5) He seemed also to feel that more expression of "anal eroticism" would promote happier and more cordial fraternal relations. It is difficult for me to imagine anything less likely to foster congeniality, intimacy, re- spect, affection, or any of the other attractions found in each other among Rotarians, medical students, fraternity brothers, real broth- ers, or politicians at a barbecue, than to have homoerotic attitudes or activities emerge. My guess is that the next worse remedy would be a little "anal eroticism." Whether in the direct form of excitement about playing with feces or in the sublimated traits listed by Freud as excessive obstinacy, orderliness and parsimony, anal expressions are seldom socially enticing. How would these two components serve as seasoning at a psychiatric meeting?

One of the strongest aversions that ordinary people have to homosexuality lies in the very fact that it is essentially an unhappy travesty of friendship. The artificial position that each of two normal friends would be called upon to assume transforms any concept of what is understood as friendship into a curious and uninviting farce. The dearer a friendship, the less one wishes to destroy it. Few means of destruction are less inviting than those of farce.

In this respect the homosexual misses the mark even more widely than does the fetishist about whom we have already spoken. It is true that the homosexual does turn toward flesh and blood, even to another person. But he turns to an object who has feelings and ideas of his own. Unlike the boy and the heifer, and also unlike the sailor and the prostitute, he enters into an area of relationship that is normally warm and personal. Understanding, intimacy, and affection are natural in friendship between man and man. What the invert attempts to bring into this relation is incompatible with friendship as it is known to others. When a mature deviate insinuates sexual aims into a role ostensibly similar to that of a protecting father-figure toward an immature boy, the perversion of parental feeling is indeed obvious. Could there be a more unhappy, or a more malignant, travesty on the normal role of a father toward his son?

In contrast to the situation between a boy and a girl who are "just friends," there is no soil in normal male friendship in which to plant (sensuously) erotic seed. The basic attitudes of ordinary friendship must first be destroyed or twisted out of recognition, before these alien relations can enter. Just as any effort to introduce sexual aspirations turns friendship into caricature, so, too, all efforts to attempt such an inappropriate mating can yield only caricatures of heterosexual love. Enough examples of these have been cited. I have not seen happy or adequate emotional results from any of them, whether they be judged as examples of friendship or of mating. Embitterment accumulates as disappointments are repeated. Whether because his homosexuality has primarily made woman's body unattractive to him erotically, or whether because early lessons about the "foulness of the flesh" have turned him from her and influenced his deviation to man, what we find is a vicious circle: woman is distasteful; sex and love lead only to disillusionment; behind all that glitters is only vileness. Thus the invert inevitably becomes antisexual—not simply antiheterosexual, but more broadly antisexual. He may, like Gide in *Corydon*, praise pederasty in his books, but we have noted Gide's real and privately recorded estimates of physical passion. Though Gide may have found sensual pleasure with his Arab lads and French gamins, he comes to regard it in retrospect as sour and trivial, often even as horrible.

The "wolf" or "Don Juan" who tries to have sexual relations with as many women as he can is likely to reveal himself also as antisexual in some important respects. Somewhat like the invert, he cannot really function as an adequate lover or wholehearted sexual partner, nor can he find anyone whom he genuinely accepts as a mate. So he accumulates disappointments and grows ever more bitter in his convictions that love is a fraud and that sex is eventually a bitter frustration. The great promiscuity of inverts is not a contradiction, but rather a confirmation of the antisexuality that, I believe, is universal among them.

The erotic practices of Gide and the erotic preferences of Plato do not appeal to the majority of mankind. Those with natural reactions find such attitudes and acts, whatever else, artificial to the point of absurdity, often sufficiently uninviting to arouse repugnance. To this natural rejection of perversion as a counterfeit of love is added the homosexual's own rejection of what he thinks is sexual love and what he calls by that name. Having had to reject woman's flesh and woman's love, he is inevitably disillusioned with whatever imitation he may choose, with whatever functional approximations he devises to mimic the acts and feelings of love. He expresses his disappointment or his disgust in terms that do not specify sexual pathology as the referent, but stand as accusations against the eros he has never known.

This appraisal, as well as the normal person's rejection of perversion and the gross misuse of sexuality, seems to work insidiously into the implications of language by which children are unintentionally taught so much about the vileness of the flesh. Both these reactions, I think, contribute to a confusion that must be misleading to the child. Together with other influences they make him feel that God says the only admiration or love man can decently feel for women must be kept wholly free from any wish to touch, wholly free from sensuous desire for her body which, insofar as it is desired, becomes unclean. This concealed and involuntary teaching, however, is not successful in driving many to life-long celibacy, nor does it always adequately restrain teen-agers from inopportune sexual adventures.

Most human beings are driven by their physical desires to embrace this flesh, however ignoble it is said to be. Many, I think, particularly among the wanton and promiscuous, are never able to be wholehearted or even to find love in what, despite their personal rejection, they embrace to obtain a simpler, incomplete, and self-centered gratification, or pseudo-fulfilment. These, too, are likely to report that physical passion is degrading, but they nevertheless seek it with profane women while more or less ascetically enshrining a wife as the pure Madonna whom they touch sexually, but only with pallid emotions bleached of the strongest yearnings, and of any genuine intimacy in what is erotic.

There are many patterns—all, I believe, influenced by antisexuality—in which man and woman are caught and diverted from full acceptance of each other as mates, from joining without finicky reservations in what they were born to share. One of these patterns is illustrated by the advice a father offers his daughter in a play by Maxwell Anderson which is quoted in *The Bankruptcy of Marriage*, by V. F. Calverton:

Marriage is no love-affair, my dear. It's little old last year's love-affair. It's a house and bills and dishpans and family quarrels. That is the way the system beats you. They bait the wedding with a romance and they hang a three hundred-pound landlord around your neck and drown you in grocery bills. If I'd talked to you that night I'd have said—if you're in love with him, why, have your affair, sow a few wild oats. Why the devil should the boys have a monopoly on wild oats? Fall in love—have your affair—and when it's over—get out! (6)

Antisexuality plays its part in this cynical rejection of love as something that could never amount to more than a caprice or a passing whim. As resolutely as the celibate rejects physical contact with woman, the father just quoted renounces all possibility of real and personal and satisfying erotic union between man and woman.

In a vicious cycle of great complexity, antisexuality promotes pathologic compromises and perversions of eros, which in turn promote antisexual attitudes and behavior. This furnishes evidence to support additional antisexual reactions and arguments.

Thus, it seems to me, the point is clear enough. If we are going to examine relations between man and woman, we are not likely to discover and prove much about our subject by quoting what philosophers and poets have found to be true of pederasty, or of algolagnia in its diverse forms and degrees. It is my belief that antisexuality, whether manifested in the cool withdrawal of Plato from what he has found to be an unworthy triviality, or in the nauseous preoccupations of Dean Swift, is a reaction to sexual pathology, not to biologically normal love. By this I do not mean that Swift was a homosexual. Not all sexual disorder takes this particular form.

How much of Swift's unattractive and malignant misevaluation of human life was learned from his environment? Let us wonder about his entire environment; not only the influence of his parents, of the children he played with, the sermons he heard, and so on, but also of his reading which, in so scholarly a clergyman, surely included Plato and might well have included works by the holy father of Cluny himself. In this unhappy man, one might surmise that innumerable influences may have served to warp or contaminate ordinary, healthy biologic responses.

It has already been pointed out that every child today, and no doubt in Swift's day as well, receives ample training in what for brevity we may call the school of Odo. Most of them are fortunate, however, and learn that this is not the only viewpoint from which man can look upon woman.

Those who do not learn this, if they express their sexuality at all, must express it pathologically. The picture, not originally conceived by Odo but faithfully rendered in his words, is indeed a Gorgon's head that can turn to stone an inquisitive Eros still infantile and unprepared for such a vision.

Among the environmental influences that may deflect the growing child toward homosexuality or toward any other perversion, few if any seem to me more real than a long and careful scrutiny of this malignant countenance. Those who never break away to seek and to find and to see the female in aspects more natural and more realistic but who continue in the conviction that this Gorgon is, indeed, woman, will, if they are articulate, continue to present her portrait in various disguises—but always in one medium. The only medium to which they can turn is that of disgust derived, as Straus explains, from reactions appropriate only to filth and putrefaction. Whether in novels, poems, or in psychological treatises, each artist's portrait will serve its purpose in the perverse edification of another generation.

This is the essence of antisexuality. Uncorrupted human feelings could never have created this concept or image from naturally biologic sexual experience. All whose emotional handicaps limit their experiences to pathologic relations can report only on the fruits of such pathologic relations, Even the most honest observer, the most stupendous artist, will paint in the medium he possesses—not our earthly eros, but its tragic caricature.

SOURCES

1. Edmund Bergler, "The Myth of a New National Disease," *The Psychiatric Quarterly*, XXII (January 1948), 66–88.

2. From *Psychology of Sexual Relations*, pp. 52–53. Copyright, 1945, by Theodor Reik. Reprinted by permission of Rinehart & Co., Inc., New York, publishers.

3. *Ibid.*, p. 55.

4. G. V. Hamilton and C. Legman, *On the Cause of Homosexuality* (New York: Breaking Point, n.d.), pp. 6–7.

5. Sandor Ferenczi, *Sex in Psychoanalysis*, trans. by Ernest Jones (New York: Basic Books, Inc., 1950), pp. 314–17.

6. V. F. Calverton, *The Bankruptcy of Marriage* (New York: The Macaulay Co., 1928), pp. 83–84.

Chapter 26
THE LOVE THAT DARE NOT SPEAK ITS NAME

Despite Guyon's objections to the word "perversion," it has its necessary place in our language. (1) Let us seek the true and deeper meaning of this term in what the acts so designated express, in what the object or imitation of an object signifies for the alleged lover. At present, science offers little to help us in this respect—hardly more, perhaps, than to teach us that we can report only opinions.

Consider first, the frustration of an exhibitionist reported in the psychiatric literature not so long ago. This man's chosen sexual practice, his substitute for a love relation, was to hang about in places where he might encounter a solitary woman. When he displayed his penis, the startled beholder usually screamed and fled. In such instances, he nearly always gained satisfaction by ejaculating. One evening a cool and somewhat brazen woman upset his plans. Confronted with his erect organ, the intended victim, quite undisturbed, looked it over in deliberate appraisal. Instead of the anticipated scream, an unflattering comment was what she quietly offered:

"So what! That don't look like anything much to me!" The man's genital excitement vanished like a puff of smoke. This time he, not the victim, fled.

The incompleteness of a relation such as merely showing oneself in this way could hardly be accepted by the ordinary man as a reasonable equivalent for sexual relations. The real perversion, however, lies in the exhibitionist's basic aim and attitude. He does not want to please a partner; he wants to frighten a victim. He is isolating himself from her, not joining her. Plainly, such feelings are a perversion of natural aim.

Let us consider another reaction. This particular man's desire for sexual relations with a woman were very definite and urgent. Probably no one could describe adequately the complex negative feelings which for years prevented him from responding to the desire. He said he felt it would be wrong, but he seemed to have no clear or adequate convictions on this point. To me it seemed plain that his conflict was not merely between passion and ethics. Though some ordinary inhibiting influences no doubt pushed against what stimulated him, it seemed to me that in his desire itself there was a true element of revulsion. When, at last, he proceeded to carry out sexual relations he not only refrained from kissing the girl but, despite a perineal intimacy, kept his head at a considerable distance from hers by seizing her shoulders and holding her at arms' length. Here we see a true reflection of what I regard as perversion of natural emotional reactions.

It is a sad confusion indeed when disgust must serve as handmaiden to desire. Sometimes the demanded proximity of these two affects is even more intimate; it is as if desire can be encountered only when welded to disgust by inseparable bonds.

There are other caricatures, less gross but scarcely less surprising. An old saying, still well known, conveys attitudes that are illustrative in this connection. Lord Chesterfield, I think, in a letter to his son, deserves credit for the authentic version. This is not at the moment available to me, so I paraphrase: *The position is ridiculous; what pleasures attained are trivial and transitory; on the whole it's hardly worth the effort.* Frank revulsion is not openly expressed here. But beneath this world-weary tone of blasé sophistication even the most naive can discern reactions that are far from natural.

Bergler's report on his study of homosexual behavior is enlightening. Of the homosexual he says:

. . . He wards off this attachment with pseudo-aggressive means, by rejecting the woman. Hence his compensatory aggression towards the mother (projected on the homosexual partner) results in the repetitive tendency to discard the partner after using him as a sexual object exclusively. Nowhere is the impersonal part of the human relationship so predominant as in homosexuals, as visible in the fact that some of them have masturbatory activities in a comfort station without either knowing or looking at their "partners." (2)

Even Leonardo da Vinci, despite his astounding originality and genius, expressed his revulsion:

The act of coitus and the members that serve it are so hideous that, if it were not for the beauty of faces and craftsmen's ornamentation and the liberation of the spirit, the human species would lose its humanity. (3)

Though Leonardo is classed by Freud as a homosexual, and was officially charged with sodomy, some of his biographers seem to believe that the evidence does not indicate his indulgence in such practices. (4) Though his objective achievements as artist and scientist have astonished the world, everything indicates that his personal erotic experience was meager and miserably unrewarding. In his reaction to coitus we cannot ignore what is perverse. In other ways also he reveals unfortunate responses to what is basic. He may not be entirely incorrect in claiming that some men "deserve to be called nothing else than passages for food, augmenters of filth, and fillers of privies," (5) but surely it is not a natural reaction when he congratulates his half-brother, who has happily announced the birth of a son, on "having provided yourself with an active enemy whose one desire will be for the freedom which cannot be his until you are dead." (6)

Another example of perversity of normal feelings is offered by a financially successful man of uncommon intellect whom I know to be peculiarly unhappy. Even while observing every small rule of external politeness, he is able to convey an almost sickening disdain for his attractive wife, both to her and to others. Over many years he has missed few opportunities to make her feel unworthy and rejected. He has learned to express his derogation of women in general in subtle ways, and to focus this personal attitude specifically on his wife. Apparently he has identified woman and love with triviality, rather than with literal corruption. Marveling at his incapacity for enthusiasm about these matters, some of his friends once, half-seriously, agreed about him that in sexual relations with his wife, rather than to reach orgasm, he might prefer to achieve such boredom at the crucial moment that he could yawn in her face at her silly goings-on. Though this otherwise able and ethical citizen shows no inclination toward any physically unusual sexual acts and is, apparently, not technically unfaithful to his wife, his inner reactions and evaluations unquestionably reflect what is deeply pathologic.

In contrast, there is the superficial behavior of a dignified and rather distinguished lawyer. Ordinarily courteous and considerate, he habitually abuses his wife in private, sometimes even before their children, in terms that cannot be printed. Real anger and contempt are in his voice as he calls her a bitch and a slut and worse names that are almost incredibly monstrous. At times, too vexed with her to speak, his only reply is to spit vehemently and repeatedly on the wall each time she addresses him. I think he has affection of a sort for his wife and finds her, in many respects, an attractive sexual partner. It is obvious, however, that something very different from love is deeply integrated into his erotic responses.

Another husband treated his wife with ordinary politeness and consideration most of the time, reserving abuse for those periods during which he was actually engaged in sexual relations with her. Then he taunted her with obscene insults, comparing even her most private anatomical features unfavorably and in foul terms with those of cheap prostitutes whom he would, in these truly inopportune moments, tell her he had freely patronized. This man showed no inclination to leave his wife. Apparently he valued her as a sexual partner not for the ordinarily desired aims and feelings, but as a particularly satisfying object of his contempt. Only insofar as he could portray his wife's body as vile and could experience disgust for it, could he, it seems, find sensual passion that was acceptable to him.

Most of us are familiar with the self-designated sophisticate who finds a specific appeal not merely in crafty attempts to intrude himself into the sexual relations of married couples by seducing somebody's wife, but who even tells himself that his warm relations with the husband are thus enhanced. Most of these pseudo-lovers appear to have strong homosexual inclinations, of course, but whether this is true or not, the perversity of normal feelings is here once more obvious.

Only recently an emotionally confused husband discussed with me his reactions to such a situation. Finding his wife *flagrante delicto* with one whom he had regarded as his most admired friend, he was further appalled by their efforts to persuade him that he and the other man, now having even more in common than before, should be even more devoted. Older and more worldly, the other man declared that the husband should be sufficiently civilized and emancipated to see that both could love the woman and thereby become more congenial. It should be regarded, the ostensible friend insisted, as something beautiful for them to share. Though almost bereft of his wits by shock, the husband still retained sufficient natural orientation to realize the absurdity of such an argument.

A pertinent example is furnished by a successful business man long tormented with jealousy. For a year or more, each time he had sexual relations with his wife, he harassed her with accusations and kept insisting that she tell him every amorous act that she had experienced with others since she was born. Having a strictly limited supply of actual indiscretions on which to draw, she was soon forced to invent fictitious seductions. To all this he reacted with pain and horror, genuine I believe, but nevertheless he insisted on more detail and seemed plainly to be stimulated sexually by what so hurt and shamed him.

After months of persuasion, he finally prevailed upon his wife to let him bring another man to their hotel room. Returning with some gigolo or pimp, to whom he paid fifty dollars, he insisted that his wife begin intercourse in his presence with the hired helper. In anger and humiliation, she finally complied. After permitting this man to proceed for a while, he interrupted the performance he had demanded and, taking over himself, completed the act that the other had begun. This unhappy man's basic motivations appeared to be more complex than that of a peeping tom, or of a man dominated merely by unrecognized but specific homosexual urges. This is no place to attempt a full explanation for such behavior, but I am sure that the tormenting introduction of shameful distaste and of vengeful hate toward his wife, and their identification with elements that ordinarily enter attractive constellations of affect, constitute a notable perversion of erotic aim and response.

Maurice Spandrell, as he is presented by Aldous Huxley in *Point Counter Point*, (7) sedulously pursues women and often seduces girls who are naive and who welcome what they accept as love. Spandrell's real purpose is to present love to them as a degrading humiliation, and he is usually clever enough to do this. This book ably conveys the actual sexual relish that finds its true satisfaction in turning love wrong side out. Spandrell could not have satisfied himself similarly by other types of vengeful cruelty to these women. The goal, for him, could only be reached by vengeance upon them in sexuality, by mutilating with fetishistic discrimination the warm and sensuous responses they offered. Similar examples are common in every psychiatric practice.

Many of these reversals of natural response, these perversions of erotic acts into outlandish and malign aims, suggest features of the Black Mass and the Witches' Sabbath. (8) Along with peculiarly vicious essays in blasphemy, ingenious methods of mocking sexuality are said to have prevailed in such rites. It would not be surprising if mockery and desecration were reserved for chastity in these ceremonies. The real point is that simple lust itself is also outraged, mocked, and mercilessly gutted of its ordinary sensory rewards. (9)

The accepted virtues of love are violated, to be sure. Michelet notes that, according to some reports, these violations are extreme:

Incest would seem to have been publicly, indiscriminately and ostentatiously indulged in, by way of reproducing the old satanic conditions needed to originate the Sorceress—that is to say the mother's impregnation by her own son. (10)

Michelet expresses doubt about this point but tells us that the use of sexual acts to hurt another, to foul with indignity the deepest human feelings, was not overlooked. Let us again quote:

They would entice to the festival some ill-advised married man, whom they proceeded to intoxicate with their deadly brews . . . till he was *spellbound* and lost all power of motion and speech, but not the use of his eyes. His wife *also* spellbound, but in a different way, with erotic beverages and reduced to a deplorable state of self-abandonment, would then be shown him naked and unashamed, patiently enduring the caresses of another before the indignant eyes of her natural protector, who could not stir a finger to help her. . . .

His manifest despair, his unavailing efforts to speak, his violent struggles to move his torpid limbs, his dumb rage, his rolling eyes, all provided the spectators with a cruel pleasure. . . . (10)

As in all outraging of eros, as in all real perversion, a truly antisexual basis emerges in the Witches' Sabbath. "Loveless love," says Michelet, "was the dominant note; the festival was expressly and avowedly a celebration of female sterility." (11) He continues:

This mournful reserve, this fear of mutual love, must have rendered the "sabbath" a cold wearisome function had not the expert mistresses of the ceremonies, who managed the entertainment, exaggerated the burlesque element, and diverted the spectators with many a ludicrous interlude. (12)

Not only is love absent, but pains are taken to snatch away brutally from hopeful participants all anticipated sensory fulfilment. The act, according to Michelet, is cut short

. . . by another travesty, a Lavabo, a cold purification (to chill and sterilize), which she received not without grimaces expressive of shuddering and mortal chill, the whole forming a broad farce. . . . (12)

The man who promiscuously woos women only to lose interest in them soon after possessing them is a familiar specimen. I have seen others who seemed quite sure that their love was serious, who chilled even at the lady's early manifestations of warmth and acceptance. In them, infatuation regularly turned to distaste even before consummation, despite retention of physical potency otherwise expressed. One man of this sort was not inclined to turn away from the girl who had become no longer desirable to him, but seemed to wring a kind of satisfaction out of his distaste and disillusion during protracted periods of quarreling and vexation. Though he continued to go through the motions of kissing and caressing the girl whose affection he had won and would not directly deny that he loved her, he expatiated on the inevitable unhappiness of loving, dwelling upon dreary pictures of anguish and boredom as its fruit. He alleged such unhappiness to be the natural condition of all lovers, and insisted also that frustration and this alone accompanied all love from its very inception. Once he was accepted, he habitually derided the folly and fickleness of women and found innumerable faults in the particular woman he had chosen, faults which he carpingly threw up at her in a din of protest. Though apparently enthusiastic in his quest before being cared for, impulses apparently more intense made him persist in the travesty of normal courtship that seemed to satisfy him with miseries, for himself and for his partner.

On one occasion, after having asked a woman to marry him, with the understanding that it would bring chiefly sorrow and absurdity, he further discouraged her by predicting that he might be unfaithful to her with chambermaids on the honeymoon. Actually he had been technically faithful during months of unhappy relations with her. He was never a promiscuous person and would probably not have fulfilled his gloomy prophecy. Had he done so, the infidelities would have been provoked less by charms of the new partner than by some curious need within him to demonstrate the farcical unreality of any real happiness in love. This belief he did not dare to question.

In expressing disagreement with Freud's assumption that perversions are merely a more open expression of what is universally present in sexual desire but in varying degrees repressed, Theodor Reik concludes:

A careful and unprejudiced re-examination of the problem leads to a surprising question: are sexual perversions only sexual in their origin and nature? The answer is surprising too: they never are. We admit that Freud's theory is founded on excellent observations, but they are used as a springboard for diving into the dark. I believe that in all perversions, not sex, but the ego-drives are dominant. I admit that the original impulse is of a sexual nature, but it has met external or psychical hindrances on its way to its gratification and has had to yield its place for a shorter or longer time to the other drives, which alone can help to reach this original goal. . . . (13)

The gratification derived from sadistic activity is to a great extent the satisfaction of aggressiveness. The psychoanalysts may now argue that it is precisely this aggressiveness which belongs to the very nature of sexuality, because without it the resistance of the object of sexual impulses cannot be broken. Such an argument, however, would be as meaningful as if one were to say that aggressiveness is inherent in hunger. Hunger in itself is not aggressive. It can become aggressive if gratification is denied, from outside, but nothing in its nature points to any such immanent quality. . . . (14)

But if this view is correct, the whole libido theory of Freud breaks down: the child does not appear as polymorph-perverse, sexuality has not the components of sadism, masochism, of peeping and showing off. The perversions are exaggerated manifestations of the old ego-drives now directed to a sexual object. . . . (15)

. . . when the reaching of the sexual aim is inhibited, the person resorts to violence and cruelty to attain satisfaction. Later on, sexual gratification becomes so blended with the other that violent or cruel fantasies or actions arouse sexual desire. . . . (16)

The genius of Freud as a psychologist will in the days to come be more and more recognized and admired. His libido system, however, will, I am afraid, have the sad destiny which Herbert Spencer once bemoaned in speaking of "a beautiful theory that was murdered by a gang of brutal facts." . . . (17)

. . . the psychological research into the perversions is a study of violence and degradation, of fear and defiance rather than of sex. I know, of course, that the view expressed here is only a provisional hypothesis accounting roughly for the facts known to us, but I hope it accounts more satisfactorily for them than the outdated analytical theory, the shortcomings of which are obvious. We have a final question: what is the relation of the perversions to love? I am of the opinion that perversions are aberrations of the impulses of aggressiveness and domination directed towards a sexual object. Their character is a blending of a large proportion of ego-drives with a minor quantity of sex-urge. (17)

When acts and sensations distinctly sexual are diverted from the normal purposes of love they sometimes fall into the company of, or work with, impulses so bizarre as to be scarcely recognizable as human. The erotic practices of a young husband about whose problems I was consulted are illustrative of fundamental points:

This prominent and intelligent man, though somewhat indifferent, customarily treated his wife with respect and politeness. Apparently he felt, most of the time, a measure of personal affection for the attractive woman he had married. Ordinary intercourse was practiced usually and both partners enjoyed physiologic satisfaction.

At intervals of five or six weeks the husband insisted upon carrying out a different and rather remarkable procedure. The routine varied little. Forcing his wife to take a servile role and to address him as "sir," and in every conceivable way to humiliate herself, he got her to cooperate with him in choosing instruments for her flagellation. Agreement being reached on a hairbrush, he would then send her out to cut a stick from the limb of a nearby tree. The two together picked what dress she would wear for the beginning of the ceremonies planned.

He himself meanwhile discarded his own clothes, put on the wife's girdle, her stockings and sometimes other lingerie. Not being able to get his feet into her shoes, he had bought himself a pair of high-heeled evening slippers which fitted and which he wore. Before the actual beating began, and also during its progress, he insisted that she prostrate herself in various indignities, that she grovel while describing herself in obscene terms, calling herself a dirty slut, and so forth. Kissing his feet while he expressed loathing and made gestures of contempt and derision, she tried to cooperate despite her extreme distaste.

Often he tied her to a chair while she was completely dressed and beat her until she bled and screamed. Later, tearing off her clothes, he continued the blows using now the hairbrush, now the rough stick she had cut for him. Sometimes her wounds and bruises remained visible for a week or more.

During the course of his endeavors he usually dragged her into the bathroom and, handling her with unnecessary roughness, administered an enema. A weird figure to behold, clad in the woman's girdle, the lingerie, silk stockings and high-heeled slippers, he worked himself into a sweat, reviling and abusing his wife in the vilest language as he struck her. After exhausting whatever sensations he sought in these procedures, he sometimes, but not regularly had intercourse with her *per anum*.

In many frank efforts at pornography, as in the case just cited, a basic perversion, in the sense described above by Reik, is grossly demonstrated. That classic work in this field, *The Memoirs of Fanny Hill*, (18) often seems to emphasize racking pains in the readily obliging women partners even at the expense of dwelling less fully on their voluptuous reactions. Though some of these enthusiastic details may be given to convey exaggerated ideas of the powerfulness of the male organ, it is difficult to overlook a certain relish for almost rending asunder the female genitalia.

Illegal moving pictures, sometimes shown in college fraternity houses or before other stag groups, display vividly lascivious details of sexual activity. Nearly always, however, the creators of this art are not content to let remain enjoyable what it would seem natural to portray as attractive. In some of these pictures printed captions are added in which the man disparages the sexual features of his partner, or implies boredom. In one film of this sort, after many exploits by an enterprising girl whose performance covers almost the entire range of an inexperienced boy's yearnings in fantasy, the male partner withdraws just before orgasm and, pushing the girl away, laughs scornfully in her face.

The Erotic Professor, (19) a more modern book of pornography than *Fanny Hill*, almost abandons real sensuality in its preference for disgust and indignity. The sensuality cannot of course be entirely ignored. Without it as a base, the chosen perversions of human reactions could not be created. It is, however, little more than a necessary means to a far different end. This work presents the spectacle of a scholarly husband who is constrained to witness his good-looking wife being ravished time after time by a couple of men. The author is apparently more excited about the horror and disgust and rage of the professor than about the lubricity afforded by the woman to those who have intercourse with her repeatedly, adopting one technique after another. There is a peculiarly perverse preoccupation with all repugnant aspects of each situation in which the lascivious reactions themselves would ordinarily demand chief attention.

It is not sufficient, however, to present disgust and humiliation side by side with this lasciviousness, or even to show so plain a preference for the former; the author cannot be satisfied until he transmutes each into the other. The professor is made finally to enjoy the shame itself, to relish his own disgust sexually, and to embrace horror as delight.

Is it not possible that those who seek to protect the young from pornographic stimuli, worthy as their efforts may be, have overlooked the most objectionable features of most pornography? The dangers of an adolescent becoming unduly excited by what is genuinely sexual and normally attractive impress me as small in comparison with the dangers of his being shown sex chiefly in the guise of perversion.

When sensuous impulses become integrated with hate, disgust, or contempt, instead of with positive feelings, we see the beginning of a deeply pathologic process. Here we have not only a perversion of eroticism but a perversion also of other important human capacities which become enlisted in the unnatural cause. In what is truly perversion, one finds regularly this paradoxical and unhappy mismating of incompatible biologic reactions. I do not maintain that hate and contempt have no normal role in life. Most or perhaps all of the feelings that are grossly abnormal as part of a sexual attitude and a sexual response have roles that are natural elsewhere in human experience. Who would say it is perversion for a father to feel rage against a criminal who without provocation murders his child? If the father would not use the utmost violence to defend the child against such an attacker one cannot avoid suspecting in him a malignant distortion of basic feelings as deeply rooted as those of sex. The contempt that he would evoke in many is a natural reaction and not to be identified with the disgust and contempt that abnormal people find and welcome in their distorted erotic sensibilities. A positive admiration for the father who refused to defend his child could exist only through profoundly disordered reactions.

It seems highly probable that Neville G. C. Heath (20) and the Marshal Gilles de Rais (21) expressed unmitigated cruelty in their mutilations and murders. One might, if one chooses, call such callousness and brutality, of itself, perverse as well as evil. Let us, however, reserve this term for a more specific purpose. Let us use it to indicate the fact that in these instances prolonged and elaborate torture and gross butchery were apparently employed as a means to achieve libidinous feelings and satisfactions. Here, in all its unpleasant clarity, we have an unmistakable example of the reversal of aim, the outraging not only of another human being but also of nature itself, in the misuse of impulses adapted to achieve a goal so different. The fierce destructiveness of Neville Heath or of Gilles de Rais, if exerted by a man in combat for his life, or for his country, loses at once the perverse quality it possesses when we see it mingled with and affording satisfaction to impulses biologically designed for an erotic aim.

Let us also look briefly at the other side of sadomasochism. The alliance of voluptuous sensations with physical pain or ignominy to oneself is perhaps even more incomprehensible to many than what we have been considering. It is difficult to conceive of one deliberately seeking such pain, or any sort of real distress, for its own sensory rewards. On the other hand, it is plain that man must learn to endure hardship, to accept suffering, in order to strive for the normal goals of life. Even the exhaustion of an athlete in the quarter-mile race as he comes off the last turn and commits all his ebbing strength to the full and final effort for victory is likely to cause physical distress of more than minor degree. In football and in boxing, it is customary to accept jolts, blows, and bruises that inflict appreciable pain and sometimes serious injury. The quarter-miler who can wring out the last of his resources, the football player or boxer who willingly accepts unpleasant and perhaps even dangerous impact, in order to continue, unflinching and wholehearted, on his mission, often feels in the ability to proceed a fulfilment that might correctly be called joy. The captive soldier who can undergo hardship and perhaps even torture, but, despite this, loyally withhold information that might damage his country must experience a rare and genuine satisfaction rooted in the healthiest core of human purpose. Surely it is conceivable that one might even achieve ecstasy in carrying out an act that is heroic. And to be genuinely heroic, such an act must be one carried out at the cost of great fear or anguish.

It is obvious that the acceptance of pain has its normal place, and that courage to sustain it is a quality almost universally sought and admired. The willingness to undergo disgrace and humiliation also has its rightful place in the normal patterns of life. Cordelia's course of action at the beginning of *King Lear*, whether or not we deem it wise, is not likely to suggest anything perverse.

Stories of espionage and of counterintelligence agencies abound in examples of men who are willing to be regarded as traitors by those who have respected them in order to serve their country on important missions.

Sacher-Masoch regularly pursued women whom he could persuade to inflict pain upon him while he groveled at their feet attempting to enact with emotion the abject role of a mistreated slave. (22) He also insisted that his wives engage in sexual affairs with other men. His desire for this was so strong that he gladly paid the expense for such affairs. Apparently he found an inimitable satisfaction in disguising himself as a servant so he could play a menial role at their meetings, act as a go-between for them, and thus relish to its last dregs the dishonor he chose to bring upon himself. De Sade also, despite his predominant taste for administering pain and ignominy to those he regarded as sexual objects, also showed on occasion predilections for similar self-abasement. (22, 23)

It is reported that on a pleasure trip to Marseilles he posed as a servant to his valet and, in what he regarded as a sexual adventure, poisoned some prostitutes and had himself flagellated. He also gathered a few disreputable spectators to observe the valet carry out the relations of sodomy upon him. (24, 25) These deeds, of course, were only mild, extremely sublimated expressions of De Sade's actual doctrine. The compassion that most people are likely to feel for this strange man's psychiatric disorder will scarcely enable them to understand why many poets, scholars, and other renowned literary figures have hailed him as "the Divine Marquis," "one of the glories of France," and so on, and continue to extol his teachings as an almost unparalleled prophetic enlightenment. (26) In our own time the prominent intellectual, Guillaume Apollinaire, has enthusiastically called him "the freest spirit that has ever existed" and predicted that, having been unjustly neglected in the nineteenth century, his message might well dominate the twentieth. (26, 27)

André Gide portrays Michel, the homosexual hero of his celebrated work *The Immoralist*, as taking a curious delight, apparently in some way lascivious, in joining the poachers who were pillaging his lands and in helping them damage his own estates. It is made clear that he is sexually attracted to some of these men, perhaps to all. He also finds what he apparently regards as sexual love for a small Arab boy specifically aroused by the fact that this boy is dishonest and steals from him. (28) In minor forms such paradoxical reactions appear to play some part when homosexuals choose to dress in the clothes of women, whom they reject, in order to please others who also reject women. In these attitudes and tastes the perversion of many human impulses, other than sexual desire, is obvious and arresting.

In contrast to such exploits of perverse degradation, there is, to be sure, a true and natural role for humility, and for self-efface-ment, in human life. The examples just mentioned seem to have little or nothing in common with the attitude of a person who de-clines wealth and distinction, or in other ways sacrifices himself, in order to serve inconspicuously in a high cause. Obtuse, indeed, would be the observer who would find difficulty in distinguishing the humility of such a man as Albert Schweitzer from what we have just discussed. It is not necessary to possess unusual reli-gious vision to realize that the motives which led St. Francis of As-sisi to turn back and kiss the leper are not to be identified with those which seem to seek what is disgusting or ignominious for its own sake, or as an integral part of sensual pleasure. Even self-abasement seems to have, in profound remorse, a natural place that is very unlike its role in the exploits of Sacher-Masoch and De Sade. In algolagnia we usually encounter not only a perversion of sensuous feeling but, along with this, a perversion of humility, of courageous action, or of pride from its normal role into inappro-priate channels where it becomes bizarrely distasteful and malig-nantly pathologic.

This indeed, is the essence of "the love that dare not speak its name." When the erotic drive is deflected to an unnatural object we do not find it uniting with, or developing into, any satisfactory love that is real. In homosexuality, fetishism, incest, coprophilia, necrophilia, and in all the other activities and attitudes that Guyon urges us to accept as equally valuable variations of sexual love be-tween man and woman, we will discover, under various kinds and degrees of disguise, the literal and unhappy perversion of ba-sic biologic impulses that is already obvious in sado-masochism. There is good reason for this alleged love not to dare speak its name.

SOURCES

1. René Guyon, *The Ethics of Sexual Acts* (New York: Alfred A. Knopf, Inc., 1948).

2. Edmund Bergler, "The Myth of a New National Disease," *The Psychi-atric Quarterly*, XXII (January 1948), 66–88.

3. Antonia Vallentin, *Leonardo da Vinci* (New York: The Viking Press, Inc., 1952), p. 39.

4. *Ibid.*, pp. 30–39.

5. *Ibid.*, p. 116.

6. *Ibid.*, p. 344.

7. Aldous Huxley, *Point Counter Point* (New York: Harper & Bros., 1927).

8. Jules Michelet, *Satanism and Witchcraft* (New York: Citadel Press, 1946).

9. *Ibid.*, pp. 100, 106–7, 160–62.

10. *Ibid.*, p. 162.

11. *Ibid.*, p. 160.

12. *Ibid.*, p. 161.

13. From *Psychology of Sexual Relations*, p. 37. Copyright, 1945, by Theodor Reik. Reprinted by permission of Rinehart & Co., Inc., New York, publishers.

14. *Ibid.*, p. 38.

15. *Ibid.*, p. 39.

16. *Ibid.*, pp. 40–41.

17. *Ibid.*, p. 43.

18. Frank Cleland, *The Memoirs of Fanny Hill* (privately printed, 1889).

19. Give Murray, *The Erotic Professor* (privately printed, 1933).

20. McDonald Critchley, *The Trial of Neville George Clevely Heath* (London: William Hodge & Co., Ltd., 1951).

21. D. B. Wyndham Lewis, *The Soul of Marshal Gilles de Rais* (London: Eyre & Spottiswoode, 1952).

22. James Cleugh, *The Marquis and the Chevalier* (New York: Duell, Sloan & Pearce, Inc., 1951).

23. Simone de Beauvoir, *The Marquis de Sade* (New York: Grove Press, 1953).

24. *Ibid.*, pp. 34–39.

25. Cleugh, *op. cit.*, pp. 75–79.

26. Geoffrey Gorer, *The Life and Ideas of the Marquis de Sade* (London: Peter Owen, Ltd., 1953), pp. 15–17.

27. Edmund Wilson, *Eight Essays* (Garden City, N.Y.: Doubleday & Co., Inc., 1954), pp. 167–80.

28. André Gide, *The Immoralist*, trans. by Dorothy Bussy (New York: Alfred A. Knopf, Inc., 1930).

Chapter 27
EROS

At some length we have considered caricatures of love—cruel transmutations of eros by disease and deformity into what is no longer eros, sometimes into that which is actually a hideous opposite. The opinion has been offered that when the homosexual speaks of love, we must often translate this term before we can identify his subject. An attempt has been made to describe some of these negative reactions which deserve to be distinguished from love. It is, I think, of immense importance to recognize that sexually disordered geniuses have often written into their works undeserved and confusing impeachments of human love.

So far as we know, our fellow mammals do not often suffer from serious distortions of their sexual behavior. Despite a few reports of confusion produced experimentally, (1) or occasionally occurring under extraordinary circumstances, dogs and cats, like chickens and ducks, seem to know what they are about and seldom pursue unnatural paths to biologic frustration. Why then should man sometimes become so profoundly disoriented that he mistakes another man for his mate? What could account for any man's conceiving of woman's flesh as unclean and abhorrent? What prompts the human being to sacrifice his opportunities for a gratification and fulfilment uniquely ecstatic, by mistaking the profoundly cooperative and congenial process of mating for a treacherous duel, a deadly contest between derisive and merciless foes? Surely the vigor and spirit in man must have suffered a profound attrition if he can find in the natural and luxurious excitements of sexual love little more than a trivial antic. It has been said that "the thalamus outdid itself in devising pleasures to go with the conjugating act itself." (2) Is it not strange and sad that we should sometimes so falter in our course that we can greet such blessings only with anemic and supercilious gestures of mockery?

These pathologic and malignant manifestations are not uncommon in our species, though they are apparently rare in the mammals and other vertebrates we see about us. It is worth noting that among horses, dogs, fowls, and fish, the sensuous rewards of a sexual act are at best brief and relatively small. Even where the impulse is strong and excitement intense, as with dogs, after a moment of localized pleasure, the participants look disappointed and forlorn. No animal that I know behaves toward its mate as if motivated by even a faint approximation of the voluptuousness that a couple of relatively innocent teen-agers can attain petting in a parked automobile. Even if the teen-agers remain fully clothed and refrain from genital contact, their sensuous resources compare with those of the mating dogs as ten symphony orchestras compare with the brief squeak of a toy whistle. In all creation we find only the human male and female abundantly and exquisitely equipped to give each other such complex, prolonged, and intense physical delight. We must remember, however, that it takes virtuosity to conduct ten symphony orchestras and that from them could emerge perverse and hideous cacophonies quite beyond the range of any toy whistle. They could, indeed, be used to butcher music beyond anything possible even with a steam siren.

I do not mean to imply that our fellow mammals lack capacity for affection and devotion. Do we not humbly respect the dog who fights to death against odds for the child he loves? And also the dog who, sensing sorrow in his master, comes to lay his head silently on the human knee? If this behavior can be lightly dismissed by calling it mere conditioned reflex, then I fear all human behavior might be similarly debunked. The dog's strongest feelings, however, his major commitments, seem isolated from his brief and relatively rare sexual pleasures. There seems to be little sense of sharing, no important intimacy, even when the male and female dog are anatomically united. Unlike the distorted or retarded human being, the dog, it may be noted, does not attack or deride his mate. Nor does the dog show reactions that indicate that he finds canine flesh vile or disgusting. For every species except mankind, nevertheless, sensuously erotic relations seem impersonal; they seem to be a relatively small part of the animal's interests and excitements.

Man and woman, on the other hand, live in constant awareness of sexual stimuli. A girl's lips, breasts, hands, legs, every inch of her skin, every glance of her eyes, can excite in the male erotic reactions that echo and reverberate into sensual patterns of desire and delight, too vast and complex for description. A gust of wind blows, lifting a dress six inches, and even this little glimpse may provoke in some man fifty feet away lusts and yearnings that run and ripple, accumulate and elaborate, into endless creations of impulse, hope, and fantasy. It is curious indeed that men have so often misused their unique gift of speech to call sexual desire "bestial" or "animal." All our biologic fellows seem, in comparison with *homo sapiens*, to be relatively free of sensual preoccupations. Man is obviously playing for bigger stakes in even the simplest and most casual erotic exploits. Complex and ambitious tasks or projects nearly always offer specific and manifold possibilities of failure. He who climbs a sand pile runs little or nothing of the risks undertaken by one who sets out to scale Mount Everest.

Man's erotic distinction is not limited merely to his persistent, complex, and infinitely more voluptuous sensual potentialities. He has also the challenge and the opportunity of sharing all this with another—all this and far more. Only man, it appears, can join fully with his mate in what becomes a recognized common and simultaneous participation in joy as vigorous and ravishing as it is unique.

As human sensuality, in contrast to that of other forms of life, is spread or extended far beyond the genital focus, so too his potentialities and his needs in mating are otherwise inclusive. Man seeks an intimacy with woman far beyond all bodily contact. He wants and needs to give her satisfactions throughout the whole content of human experience. All intimacies, all interests, and sometimes even hardships, can take on qualities that are erotic and peculiarly delightful.

To try for such complex and vast goals, man must stake what he most values and must proceed on no simple or clearly charted course. Perhaps it should not surprise us, after all, to find only in man perversion, tragic paradox, and confusions that are scarcely sane, as the price of failure in so ambitious a biologic endeavor.

Let us at this point recall what Straus has said about biologic realities. (3) Very cogently he calls our attention to the fact that waste and excretion are part of growth and of life itself. He does not minimize disintegration or the detailed facts of mortality. In pointing out the pathologic preoccupations of some with exclusively regressive aspects of human life, he makes clear the positive aspects which they ignore. Only in pathologic illusion can one insist on a division which falsely separates this actuality into segments, one abstractly ideal, the other unrealistically perverse. Neither separate segment nor aspect will be found a biologic reality. There are illusions which lead to denial of all that is uncomfortable or disturbing. Another illusion is that of Swift. If eros is genu-

ine, however, I think the full biologic facts are accepted, in pride
and in reverence.

Theodor Reik believes that Freud's interpretation of love as
merely sublimated or "washed out" sexual urge "leads to disastrous confusion and unsound conclusions." Love, he maintains, is
derived from other sources and only recently in man's history has
participated in sexual aims and feelings:

Between love and sex there are differences of such a decisive nature that it
is very unlikely they could be, as psychoanalysts assert, of the same origin
and character. These differences are best realized when both phenomena
are contrasted in their purest form. Here are a few examples: sex is a biological urge, a product of chemistry within the organism; love is an emotional craving, the creation of individual imagination. In sex there is a
drive to get rid of an organic tension; in love there is a need to escape
from the feeling of one's own inadequacy. In the first there is a quest for
physical satisfaction; in the second there is a pursuit of happiness. One
concerns the choice of a body; the other, the choice of a personality. Sex
has a general meaning; love or romance was unknown for thousands of
years to men and is unknown to millions of people even now. Sex is indiscriminate; love is directed to a certain person. The one relaxes muscles;
the other opens the floodgates of personality. Also the sexually satisfied
individual can feel love-starved. The sex-drive is extinguished in an act;
there is a tension, a spasm, and a release. The ultimate act of pleasure cannot later be remembered, just as the taste of a particular food cannot be
vividly recalled. No such ultimate indifference to the object is to be observed in the phenomenon of love. Every word and every gesture of your
sweetheart is deliciously remembered. Sex is dramatic; love is lyric. The
object of sex is desired only during the short time of excitement and appears undesirable otherwise; the beloved person is the object of continued
tenderness. (4)

These statements are indeed plausible. No matter from what
sources love may be shown to arise, no explanations convey much
of its nature as a subjective experience. With this Reik seems to
agree:

The story of individual romance has been told and sung a hundred thousand times, in a hundred thousand poems, novels, and plays. It has not
been told by psychology. It so happens that the only science which should
have been able to describe and explain the phenomenon became inarticu-
late before it. Can it not be put in scientific language? Is there something
in the subject which eludes research? Whatever the causes may be, the
psychological story of love has remained untold.

The great poets have recognized that love is a psychological problem.
Bassanio hears this song when he has to choose between the three caskets:

Tell me, where is fancy bred,
Or in the heart or in the head?

To solve the problem, however, is not the task of the poet. What he
presents is not a solution but an allusion. He does not explain; he hints at

an explanation. He does not solve a riddle but indicates its solution in the form of a charade. Like the Greek oracle, he conceals what is implied in mysterious and meaningful images. The meaning is there, but it does not present itself and is audible only for ears able to hear what remains unsaid. (5)

Reik seems to be entirely correct in distinguishing between a crude, relatively simple and impersonal sexual drive and the many needs, desires, goals, and satisfactions we find in affectionate interpersonal relations. These may, as he maintains, derive from nonsexual ego-drives, from needs to attain an ego-ideal. Surely such a concept is more plausible and useful than any interpretation we can arrive at through sweeping redefinitions of *libido*, which, as Reik says, have "now made the word unserviceable." (6) Can we not also agree when he states:

. . . No progress has been made in the analysis of love since Freud declared that it is nothing but aim-inhibited sex. When you consider that this concept is almost forty years old you will admit that the domain of psychoanalytical research is a slow sort of country. Psychoanalysts could speak like the Queen to Alice: "Now, here, you see, it takes all the running you can do to keep in the same place." (7)

Is it possible to arrive at an adequate appreciation of sexual love by conceiving of it as a mere combination of various elements that can be named and recognized elsewhere in isolation? Let us grant that in sexual love there may be sensuous passion plus reverence, plus a longing for and attainment of the ego-ideal, plus devotion, plus shared interests, plus adoration, plus friendship, plus compassion, plus understanding, plus mystery, plus innumerable other items of human experience. What does such an additive description convey? Very little, I fear, that would reveal, even to one quite familiar with all the elements, much that is accurate about the nature of the integrate.

Does not sexual love emerge in subjective experience as something more and something different from what we define by saying "sex plus love?" If we assume that its origin lies in a fusion of two such things must we not also admit that from this, as from the union of ovum and spermatozoon, there may emerge what cannot sensibly be reduced in description or even in imagination to identity with the original parts? Even if we insist on libido, or any other metaphysical monad, as a solitary source of origin, must we not grant ensuing miracles of growth, transformation, evolution, differentiation, and fruition that would constitute a parthenogenesis?

Attempts to break down this entity of experience which perhaps we may be permitted to call sexual love or eros will not serve our present purpose. Do we not require first a more adequate under-

standing and realization of what man encounters of it directly in his personal experience?

In approaching such a subject, great difficulties oppose all efforts to formulate our concepts. Referring to some of the terms often used for this purpose, Walter de la Mare says, "Like poor frames to good pictures, fake and flashy books for children, and namby-pamby hymns, they cheapen the invaluable." (8) This, perhaps, has some relation to another of his observations:

How then of the word Love? If it has been used with any seriousness, response to it in company is unlikely to be encouraging. It will share the mental recoil and uneasiness that may follow the mention of God, or sin, or soul, or death. Mishaps of this kind should be avoided. We have been guilty of that little social disaster—an error in taste. We have trespassed not on the forbidden perhaps, but on the dangerous. At such moments, as at family prayers, or when listening to music, we forbear even to glance at one another's faces. We become self-conscious, though of which self we may fail to enquire. The snail within draws in his horns. The echoes of the challenge die away; the drawbridge is up; the citadel is ranged for defense. (9)

What, then, is eros? It is no surprise to find that one lacks the means to state what no mortal has yet satisfactorily conveyed by words to another. Who would not be proud indeed to find himself blessed with articulateness so magic? Human utterance may, at some instant, impart some fragment of definition to another. Though preserved intact the words are not likely to reflect indefinitely, or even once again, what is not essentially in words but deeper in the idiom of experience. It is more often the silent turning of a head, level eyes that remain tearless in sorrow, or the clasp of a hand, that may catch and reflect in an unnamed and inexact perception what fragments of this any of us has ever communicated to another. Each person may find, in a poem or in a prayer, some symbol that, not quite articulately but validly, evokes a little of what he has felt in loving. To another that symbol may convey nothing genuine; or perhaps even the very opposite of what it enabled the first to sense. Seldom if ever can we pin down in actual statement anything significant about what we feel in this experience. The life, the meaning that we find is not stated but implied. The statement, be it a beatitude, an ungrammatical phrase, or a line from Keats, draws something else—the meaning —from within us. Like an evanescent nimbus it may surround what is articulate but it always evades the grasp of utterance. In such matters, what is said or written does not define what it may cause us to feel. The statement comes into a clear central field of macular vision. All that is important lies in far peripheral areas, indistinct, blurred, on the borders of consciousness. Nothing can be quoted from any source that will disclose an aspect of eros that one has not first met in experience, directly and personally. Eros is not without speech, but for this speech there is no audible translation.

It has been said that there are no words for the emotions. We have words without number, to be sure; but unlike those with objectively perceptual referents they are unreliably protean and inadequate for their purpose. The cumbersome neologisms and flabby abstractions of popular psychiatric jargon seem to be less useful for such a purpose than almost any other language.

Korzybski has made much of the point that nothing satisfactory can be spoken about so simple a sensation as what we feel when we are pinched. Each of us can reproduce this sensation at will and thereby achieve in direct perception what language only hints at in pale abstraction. Eros cannot be so simply approached by nonverbal detours. For the idiom of this experience there are no reliable or adequate symbols.

Words have been used for this purpose since man first devised speech. But no combination of them, whether found in Holy Writ, devised by Shakespeare, Dante, or Aeschylus, or wrung fresh from human lips at this very hour, is likely to convey much that is the same, or much about eros, to the inner ear of another. This man may find among the cherished utterances of history a facsimile that for him represents something of his own experience. If he offers it to another as valid coin of communication it is possible that it may be rejected as counterfeit. Even the phrase of an illiterate girl may offer someone else the specific symbol which for him and for him alone refers to what is as real as it is unutterable.

Let us note another opinion expressed by Walter de la Mare:

. . . Can any sensitive experience of life have failed to teach that love, however fallible, to whatsoever it has been given, from whomsoever it has been received, bitter though its afflictions may have been, and lamentable its defects and mistakes, was that life's transcendent blessing? Unloved, unloving, we should have escaped its suffering, and be less apprehensive of our last farewell. But without it, what would have remained? (10)

Few words have been so badly beaten out of shape as the word "love." Misuse and too much use have left it where it may imply anything and is even more likely to represent nothing clearly or adequately. What does *hell* mean? To different persons it can be cold as hell, hot as hell, fast as hell, slow as hell. Similarly, God is love—make-love—get her out and hang some loving on her—pitch woo—lay the neighbor's wife—sexual intercourse—f . . . ing —foul insult—cheat and swindle—performing marital duties—Platonic love of eternal Ideas and forms—patriotism—devotion of father and son-sentimentality—sissified overdependence of an adolescent on his mother, and so on, and so on. It is plain that the word may "mean" any one of a number of things and that in this almost infinite versatility it can indicate nothing very specifically, or accurately, or consistently.

Mere reiteration has through the centuries made unreliable all words in our dictionaries that designate serious human feelings. This influence has, perhaps, dealt more harshly still with well-known utterances by the great poets. What makes a cliché can also make of the truest statement a mere sieve incapable of holding import—or capable only of retaining debris and trivialities. Repeated use, scarcely less than misuse, can devaluate any verbal expression somewhat as progressive inflation would obviously devaluate dollars, and did, after World War I, so drastically devaluate German marks. There is no combination of words ever made that cannot be offered in counterfeit. Any insipid fraud may quote the Bard, also the Bible. This, it has been said, is a favorite practice of Satan.

What has been set down in words quite distinctly often evolves into an opposite. Fluids delectable as a precious wine often break down into vinegar. Have not deleterious potations, even lethal poisons, often been distilled by time from sparkling truth? Let us but think for a moment of all the massacres and wholesale executions that have been carried out in God's name.

No definition, no exposition or analysis of sexual love that would be instructive to the reader can be offered here. All attempts at direct description would surely obscure or devitalize more than they would reveal. Even if the present writer possessed within himself a knowledge of this subject more extensive, more accurate, and more profound than any heretofore attained by man, there would still be no medium available for its explicit communication.

SOURCES

1. C. S. Ford and F. A. Beach, *Patterns of Sexual Behavior* (New York: Paul B. Hoeber, Inc., 1952).

2. A. J. Woods, "Courtship and Marriage," *Psychiatry and the War*, ed. by Frank J. Sladen (Springfield, Ill.: C. C. Thomas, 1943), p. 193.

3. Erwin Straus, *On Obsession* (New York: Journal of Nervous and Mental Disease Monographs, 1948).

4. From *Psychology of Sexual Relations*, pp. 17–18. Copyright, 1945, by Theodor Reik. Reprinted by permission of Rinehart & Co., Inc., New York, publishers.

5. *Ibid.*, p. 87.

6. *Ibid.*, p. 32.

7. *Ibid.*, p. 83.

8. Walter de la Mare, *Love* (New York: William Morrow & Co., Inc., 1946), p. 10. Quoted by permission of the Society of Authors as the literary representative of the estate of the late Walter de la Mare.

9. *Ibid.*, p. 4. Quoted by permission of the Society of Authors as the literary representative of the estate of the late Walter de la Mare.

10. *Ibid.*, p. 126. Quoted by permission of the Society of Authors as the literary representative of the estate of the late Walter de la Mare.

Chapter 28
THE UNDEFINED

A small, solitary hound may investigate the tracks of some huge and formidable beast that has passed. He may sniff the air and perhaps discern something indirectly of the mysterious and unseen invader. If he wanders about the woods he may come upon a slain ox, discover a bit of fur caught in a broken branch, note that the bark has been torn from a huge pine tree, as if by claws. Such signs may enable him to formulate gradually something about the size, power, disposition, habits, and other characteristics of what he has not yet encountered, without venturing an immediate approach to the object of his interest. He may by chance find a cave where the great beast has slept, infer from tracks that it has swum a river. Among the first items acquired by our hound may be a strong suspicion that it will not serve his purpose to risk an actual view of the other, and that it would be fatal to attempt extension of his knowledge by direct bodily contact.

Similarly, let us here merely note signs and traces, possible sources of inference, rather than hazard immediate encounter in words with our subject. Any valid understanding or adequate evaluation of it must of course come for each of us from within. But if we follow the cautious hound's tactics we may happen upon some blurred footprint, some obscure scratch upon a sapling, perhaps the ghostly remnant of an odor capable of stimulating our capacities for an unspoken, inner formulation. Not with any aim or pretense of offering instruction but with the hope of provoking more or less by chance subjective reactions for each to shape as he may within himself, let us wander a little farther, and virtually at random.

Would it not be unwise for us to ignore even relatively simple aspects of the erotic? Lord Chesterfield, as we have noted, judged

the position ridiculous, the sensual rewards so trivial as scarcely
to merit the exertion. Has even this aspect of our subject ever been
reliably described? A less effete report than the nobleman's was
offered by an unlettered adolescent who compared the localized
sensations to what one would imagine might be felt if a covey of
unanticipated quail suddenly rose in the unfathomed depths of
his body and flew right out of the perineum. Only those actually
once startled and breathless on blundering into a large covey of
quail can understand the peculiar and permeating vividness of
this explosive and sky-encompassing commotion. I know no pertinent statement to quote on the intensity or quality of awareness
when realization is shared by two who love, and who, through
such a common medium of sensation, join in final intimacy.

Genuine erotic feelings may filter through literally implausible
evaluations of the beloved. The wildest and most extravagant—or
the simplest or the silliest—words may be seized upon in efforts to
convey what truly cannot be spoken. Even the most banal language, even sounds that are not words at all, may as a private and
personal idiom mean for two people what would never be suggested to someone else.

Walter de la Mare has emphasized this point:

As for "literature," the tenderest, and most revealing of love letters may
be wholly innocent of it. The most tragic also. Misspelt, reckless of grammar, they have sprung, like the Fountain of the Muses or blood from an
artery, from the very heart, without the least care or thought except for
the loved one. Helter-skelter, i's undotted, stops wanting, paper tear-
stained, p's and q's incontinently *un*-minded, they pelt along; and, oddly
enough are often not only unusually condensed, but wildly original. Are
they any the less human, true, tender, and consoling for that? Love may
revel in humour, delight in wit, adore the fantastic, welcome the rash, forgive the solemn and the high-faluting; but it will instantly stiffen at the in-
formative, jib at preachments, and abhor the superior. (1)

When Shakespeare, the greatest of poets, wrote: "My mistress'
eyes are nothing like the sun," he did not say that they were therefore less radiant to him or less marvelous. I wonder if he did not
mean that even he could not say what her eyes really were like for
him?

The plainest woman, the most mediocre man can be thought of
or spoken of with no insincerity in terms that to an outsider would
be judged as vulgar and unconvincing exaggeration if applied to
the sea-born Aphrodite, or to Hector of the glancing helm. So eros
has been called blind. But falsely! Foolishly! We must remember
what Straus has emphasized about the varying reactions to perception before we smugly conclude that eros offers only an illu-

sion. To Swift and Odo de Cluny even the most obvious beauty of any woman is illusion.

For all we know, Dirce may have been what men today would call unattractive. Despite this and despite our realization that there is no such river as the one mentioned, can we not, in this, catch at least a syllable or a sigh from what is nonverbal and quite unspeakable:

> Stand close around ye Stygian set
> With Dirce in one boat conveyed
> Or Charon seeing may forget
> That he is old and she a shade. (2)

Nothing I may quote can contribute more toward a definition than a small bit of stained and broken glass fallen more or less at random might do if it should by accident catch a better than dubious reflection, and thus transmit some imperfect and indirect visual fragment of what cannot be brought into actual perception.

In untold thousands, schoolboys still bravely comment. Scribbling on the secluded walls of latrines, and often on fences and sidewalks, they register the affirmation: *P. . . . is good*. These simple words may serve a wish to shock, a need to revolt from various niceties. Whether or not the schoolboy writes from personal experience, he seems to hit upon a statement that is accurate. It surely seems that Dean Swift and the holy father of Cluny might profitably, on this subject, have sat at the boy's feet. Influenced to a degree, it seems, by what restricts the fetishist, he abstracts or detaches a part from the female. He is perhaps still afraid to admit an interest in the whole of her flesh. But so far as his statement goes, it is, I think, unchallengeable.

Suppose we turn to a statement somewhat more amplified. Some may react to the words I am about to quote chiefly by calling them a bad attempt at poetry and by experiencing esthetic disdain. Whether poetry or not, and whatever the author may have intended, these lines are likely to convey concepts about flesh considerably less restricted than what the lad writes on the fence:

> I love you as men love the strength of cities;
> You are darkness and rivers of darkness under the stars;
> None so gazed on Troy—oh, a thousand pities
> That marked Troy down for terrible calendars!
> There have been sailors and merchants and long-eyed dreamers
> Hollow, cadaverous, bearded, who left all ease
> For the wild beauty of a ship with streamers
> And the sweet madness of Asiatic seas.
> Surely, these burning men who have desired
> The throat of Stamboul or the buoyant hips

Of young untamable, Tartar-sinewed ships—
Surely they drank deep and their hearts grew tired
For the cool tusk of the moon, a woman cool. . . .
You are my ship with streamers, my Stamboul. (3)

Though less direct than the schoolboy's primitive and somewhat wistful affirmation, this imagery and rhythm may suggest an
unambiguous eagerness for the whole woman. Despite such
words as "cool" and "tired" there is much that indicates the specific wish for a love-object who is ardent and anything but lack-
adaisical. The boy's endorsement is confined to that which might
even be reached through a wide crack in the fence and without
other contact or relation with an unknown partner. The lines of
verse seem to ask for a much more wholehearted and truly sensuous sort of getting together.

Putting aside for the moment most of what might be suggested
by such terms as "devotion" or "adoration," it is surprising to find
how little language is available to convey reliably an unstinted
sensuous approval, a physical acceptance and admiration that is
truly wholehearted. We have noted that the old stark words for
love-making and for bodily parts most sensitive in this act have
been contaminated by scorn and hate and disgust until they are
more likely to reflect insult than honest passion.

It is indeed dangerous to use these words freely for what they
once meant. It seems likely that misconceptions of "the flesh" and
of its part in love had much to do with the contamination of certain words and with their banishment from all serious use except
that of obscene insult. I suspect, too, that these strong old words
may have carried with them, when they were driven underground, some of the vigor and lustiness of sexual love. Despite the
newer implications of hate and disdain, some of this absorbed
erotic vitality seems to remain in these vivid expressions, buried
under outer layers of antithesis. In casting off entirely these so-
called dirty words, in order to avoid the negative reactions that
they now paradoxically imply, is there a possibility that the respectful lover may, with them, sacrifice in his feelings and in his
physical acts something of that clean, vigorous, and far from unflattering gusto that he might otherwise offer and enjoy?

Lockridge seems to feel that the exile of these words may preserve in them values quickly worn out of generally acceptable
terms. Those wise enough to use and understand this proscribed
language correctly, he believes, may find in it a rare articulateness.
He writes:

The prudery which has forbidden certain words in print and public
speech for so long, has made of these the perfect and precise language of

the night that men want and expect of their women. Try as they will, many women misunderstand completely the reason underlying the half-shamed request of men that they "talk dirty" in love. Women of more breeding than brains often imagine that a man is trying to "drag them down" thereby, or "make them no better than prostitutes," or other absurd misconstructions. . . . The truth is that the average man who teaches his mistress or wife a few erotic words she never knew before—or says she never knew before—is attempting to create a private language between them with which the transports of love can be expressed with emotion as well as with clarity. The efforts of certain well-meaning libertarians and semanticists to repeal the laws and curtail the power of censors to object to words (instead of things) will, if successful, force the average Occidental male to fall back on the throat gutturals and tongue trills of India. (4)

Years after he has first scribbled his immemorial observation on the latrine wall, our growing boy, in considerable dismay despite his outer callous air, is likely to venture some direct compliment to a girl. The form of such a compliment may vary much, the import seldom at all. This import and a typical degree of originality shine clearly in the not-quite heroic couplet:

> Roses are red and violets are blue,
> Sugar is sweet and so are you.

A generally mobilized desire is implied in this sort of approval. Little or nothing about the speaker's personal fealty is brought up. Is it not likely, however, that in risking such a sentiment he offers something of himself? Jack and Butch and the rest of the gang might, indeed, find him rather silly in these feelings of his, well recognized as tender and, perhaps, suggesting effeminacy to them. When one of the gang wants to register approval of a girl whose bodily endowments are notably appealing, he avoids estheticism and sentimentality by manfully admitting that "she's built like a brick s . . thouse." Studs Lonigan in Farrell's fine novel (5) was, in most respects, a truly courageous boy. He freely enjoyed fornication and accepted as natural and virile the young male's behavior in "laying" or "jumping" any female who might succumb. But he seems never to have found it possible with any girl to take the small initial step toward genuine love that is ventured by the lad who risks his feelings in the banal little rhyme quoted above. Apparently he lacked the impulse, or perhaps the courage, to do so.

Just what is offered, if one genuinely offers himself? If eros, insofar as eros is genuine, demands a commitment, then what is committed and how? This subjective transaction, however real, does not find its way into language. Perhaps it is too complex, perhaps too simple to obtain embodiment in conscious thought.

There are many phrases about the "offering of one's heart," about "his entrusting to her his honor," and so on, but all these have sounded in our ears so long and so tritely that their metaphor has been bleached almost beyond discernment.

A good deal about this might be conveyed to some people by Sydney Carton in Dickens' *A Tale of Two Cities*. What he says about the grounds for his decision to accept, with no hope of defense, the fury and scorn of the mobs and the guillotine, meant very little to most of my college classmates who took their literary interests seriously. Dickens was too well recognized as a vulgar and dated sentimentalist, they felt, to deserve serious attention in anything he might offer. Ronald Colman, in the role of Carton in the old motion picture, said very little in comparison with what is written in the novel. In this laconic abridgment it is possible to find something more articulate; in his silence, what is most articulate of all.

Whether or not one is moved by Sydney Carton's words or by what can be surmised of his feelings, these remain only imperfect and abstract representations of the commitment he embraces. Even his act can do no more than reflect something of what is within him and quite beyond the reach of his words; of all words, and of all sounds. Doubtless, many will find little if anything about eros revealed by this particular symbol. Others, receiving no direct illustration, may still understand what G. K. Chesterton meant in speaking of the spirit that conceived Sydney Carton as "a naked flame of mere natural genius" that, despite the lack of culture and other advantages, was sometimes capable of "revealing a light that never was on sea or land, if only in the long fantastic shadows that it threw from common things." (6) For a few, something about Sydney Carton might serve as a glass fragment that catches at least a small reflection of what is as real as it is inexpressible.

Small and ordinary people, like the great, insofar as they achieve what is fully erotic, appear to give or commit what is central and vital, the core of self, to the loved one and to the union. In so doing, however commonplace this or that person may appear to the sophisticated observer, he accepts a unique peril, freely chooses a risk of loss, of anguish and shame, not otherwise encountered in life.

> Now here is love—and it is yours to wreathe
> The circumstance with smiles more light than petals—
> Love, a quick sword no pretty words can sheathe.
> A shining blade of haughty, tempered metals.
> Now here is love—and if you can, deny
> That it is sharp to hold, and swift and bright;

> Say you can blunt the sure edge with a lie,
> The edge of fire, the naked line of light!
> Roses and kissing lips of lovers turn
> From less and lesser sweetness into dust;
> But love a glittering weapon, still can burn
> Keen and aware beneath the creeping rust.
> Now here is love, precise and proud and hard:
> Say if you will love shall not leave you scarred. (7)

What is the woman saying who wrote that? Or trying to say? It is unlikely that any two readers will agree on an answer. Whatever she herself had in mind, her sonnet seems to reflect indirectly some components of nameless danger dared by one who loves. It is a danger she appears willing and glad to accept.

Othello, blind with anguish, decides that he must "Put out the light, and then put out the light." Thinking of Desdemona dead, of that uniquely precious light once quenched, he hesitates and tells himself: "I know not where is that Promethean heat / That can thy light relume." A little later he makes his last request of memory:

> Soft you; a word or two before you go. . . .
> No more of that.—I pray you in your letters,
> When you shall these unlucky deeds relate,
> Speak of me as I am; nothing extenuate,
> Nor set down ought in malice; then must you speak
> Of one, that loved not wisely, but too well;
> Of one, not easily jealous, but, being wrought,
> Perplex'd in the extreme; of one. . . .
> And say, besides, that in Aleppo once . . . (8)

It is strange to hear sometimes that Othello's weakness was jealousy and to realize one is hearing that he was particularly subject to some blind greed akin to what men sometimes feel in abnormal intensity for material possessions. It is stranger far to encounter psychologic explanations of Othello's behavior in which dynamic principles are used to simplify this far-from-simple Moor and demonstrate him as a latent homosexual. With a glibness that is truly dynamic the complexities and depths of human feeling are by-passed and it is proclaimed that Othello, unconsciously but actually, wanted perverse relations with his friend Cassio. Othello's outraged love for Desdemona, apparently regarded as superficial, is ignored in the haste of some learned interpreters to offer us a "scientific" explanation of the tragedy. (9)

It is astonishing to find that from psychiatric theory a dogma could be conjured to hide from any reader the nature of this doom, to make invisible what, through his commitment to Desdemona, Othello had exposed to those stratagems of Iago that were "more fell than anguish, hunger, or the sea." There is today no scientific knowledge that confutes the reality of this commitment or that compromises Cassio's last simple comment on the self-slain Moor: "For he was great of heart."

If the awful articulateness of Shakespeare reveals to some so little of love and of mortal hurt in Othello, who dare speak of such matters with confidence of being understood? I am quite willing to leave to Shakespeare his task of revealing Othello's experience of eros and the nature of his relations with Desdemona.

Can we find in Othello some further clue? Or in the feelings of Thomas Hardy's *Jude the Obscure*? Or in a letter written by John Keats to Fanny Brawne? The key that may open a lock for one person here might for another open the door to a different room. Or it might fit no lock at all.

As the singularly untalkative character, Axel Heyst, with that utterly female and matchless incarnation called Lena (and Alma), contemplate true horror backed by a triply threatening annihilation, does anything emerge except in irony to explain Joseph Conrad's title, *Victory*? (10) I believe it does, but who can be sure?

Both Heyst and Lena have been impregnably walled off from true human intimacies. Even Conrad, as if in awe of a great deformity sustained in dignity and silence, respects their reticence. Though they differ in most characteristics, one feels that Heyst and Lena are the same in that neither can or will lay down a last and only defense of emotional isolation. Behind this inner barricade the little that life has left for each of them contains no possibility of happiness. But there remains this modest area of lonely dignity that each will defend forever. This man and this woman, in unlike sorrow and defeat, have learned in severe schools to trust no hope, even for a moment. Heyst, perhaps more truly than any other man, might have said:

> I to my perils
>   Of cheat and charmer
>   Came clad in armour
>   By stars benign;
> Hope lies to mortals
>   And most believe her,
>   But man's deceiver
>   Was never mine.
> The thoughts of others
>   Were light and fleeting,
>   Of lovers' meeting
>   Or luck or fame;

> Mine were of trouble
> And mine were steady,
> So I was ready
> When trouble came. (11)

Those unfamiliar with Leo Kanner's study of the parents of autistic children cannot adequately realize what Heyst's father must have done to him. (12) The cold mutilation of his spirit has presumably been fatal, but not with the mercy of physical extinction. It is his fortune to breathe and act, but without a nucleus of life. A stir of warmth, a reaching out toward hope, the most tentative offer of self would, after this central crippling, be less like some totally beaten fighter, insensible and helpless, struggling from the floor, than like Alcestis rising from the shades.

As Heyst and Lena turn at last toward each other, some rare quality in their impulse seems to keep even Conrad, their creator, at a respectful distance. We do not violate their privacy. Involuntarily our eyes close rather than stare at this inexpressible resurrection. But somehow we grasp its nature as one can only feel what is within oneself. No criminal or imbecile had so little chance for love as Heyst. And we slowly come to know that in him the murdered capacities for this were unique.

In the rockiest and most devastated soil, the most hopelessly barren matrix, stirs a belated germination—perhaps not of the greatest oak, or the tallest pine—but of a Spartan plant with one brief bud, to no earthly avail, but like no other since the first electron moved. Held remote from the inner experience of Heyst and Lena, those who read may find within themselves, from what is not said, a realization that speech can never construct.

Conrad does not call attention to the never-quite-visible image, the inexplicit echo that seems to haunt a silence, as that story ends. This mute hieroglyph does indeed evade full perception. It can transmit no didactic statement. Can it otherwise inform us of matters it is not quite possible to discuss? To my mind, this unspoken comment is the real subject of the book. If I surmise correctly, that silence fills with the realization of a love, late-born and doomed, but absolute. Who would attempt to translate its significance? Since Conrad at the end of that story chose to say no more, it is only fitting that I do likewise.

In just a few lines, Edna St. Vincent Millay suggests a great deal about human experience that cannot be expounded in strictly rational terms:

And, reaching up my hand to try,
I screamed to feel it touch the sky.
I screamed, and—lo!—Infinity
Came down and settled over me;
Forced back my scream into my chest,
Bent back my arm upon my breast,
And, pressing of the Undefined
The definition on my mind,
Held up before my eyes a glass
Through which my shrinking sight did pass
Until it seemed I must behold
Immensity made manifold;
Whispered to me a word whose sound
Deafened the air for worlds around,
And brought unmuffled to my ears
The gossiping of friendly spheres,
The creaking of the tented sky,
The ticking of Eternity. . . .
And as I looked a quickening gust
Of wind blew up to me and thrust
Into my face a miracle
Of orchard-breath, and with the smell,—
I know now how such things can be!—
I breathed my soul back into me. (13)

Note that the poet does not explain how this "pressing of the Undefined" set a "definition" on her mind. Nor does she directly tell us the definition. I, for one, am grateful that she did not try. Because she said no more, each one of us is perhaps more likely within himself to reach some understanding of it.

An incident reported by the newspapers not so long ago deserves our consideration here: A middle-aged author, financially successful and in excellent health, received from his wife's physician the report of a routine examination which he forbore to give her directly. She had not the least idea that cancer had been discovered and that furthermore its stealthy dissemination had already made unlikely any chance for survival even through mutilating and repeated surgical procedures. These two people had no children. Apparently the man never conveyed to his wife the report of her doom. Quietly he took pains to see that, on going to sleep that night, she would not awaken. So, too, he joined her, ending his own life without the security from anguish he had fully won for her. There was no note left to explain or justify what he had done.

It is true that this conduct violates the strongest of our laws. It also contradicts the basic teaching of our churches. Every physician knows that often the patient who has a hopeless disease will yet choose to live with this knowledge and to endure constant and increasing pain. Many have tasks which they feel it is crucially necessary for them to perform. There are many reasons that could be advanced to show how this husband may have been wrong, even tragically wrong, in his decision. No physician could advise a human being to take the step he took. And yet I wonder if there is any person so presumptuous that he can condemn this man for what he did? He sought no advice in the decision he made and so quietly executed. He left no word to tell us of his feelings.

The little schoolyard rhyme about roses and violets, and equally naive paraphrases of its sentiment, have often served a groping child to indicate a tentative commitment to another. Let us not then hold it in scorn. Even the small boy's scribbled words on the latrine I am pleased to accept as eternally valid. Is it not more worthy of respect than the cynical impeachments of love made by many whom we have called geniuses? Guyon cites the poet Lamartine as a man who slept alternately with five or six women while composing verse about the romance and tragedy of love that "brought tears to many sensitive eyes." (14) Oscar Wilde's acceptance of ecclesiastical rites on his deathbed, according to one of his biographers, was "like all his gestures perfectly sincere at the moment it was made." (15) It is my conviction that no true erotic commitment can be known in human experience from which that dimension of reality that we call time is strictly deleted. Passions and other feelings may be brief and nevertheless vivid. But nothing that lacks the strength to sustain itself beyond the moment should, even by fools, be confused with sexual love.

In contrast, let us turn finally to a few lines, not written by a professional man of letters, but by a physician who spent most of his years and his finest effort in laboratories. Perhaps they may evoke in some reader inexplicit reflections of what seems to have eluded all the renowned observers who composed the caricatures we have examined:

> Never a dirge of roses for that the summer is done,
>   for that the year's gate closes quenching the flood of the sun,
>   now that a bank of snows is that where the roses shone.
>
> Fear not for anguish any lurking below thy throat;
> Love will not waver when he steppeth to Charon's boat;
>   pain is a silver penny bringing a golden groat.
> Love in sere seed-fields sieving braves the thorned things ungloved;
> . . . .
>   loving is more than living, more than to be beloved. (16)

SOURCES

1. Walter de la Mare, *Love* (New York: William Morrow & Co., Inc., 1946), p. 102. Quoted by permission of the Society of Authors as the literary representative of the estate of the late Walter de la Mare.

2. Walter Savage Landor, "Dirce," in *British Poets of the Nineteenth Century*, ed. by Curtis H. Page (New York: Benjamin H. Sanborn & Co., 1922), p. 437.

3. Joseph Auslander, "Stamboul," from *Sunrise Trumpets* (New York: Harper & Bros., 1924). Copyright 1924 by Harper & Bros.

4. Norman Lockridge, *The Sexual Conduct of Men and Women* (New York: Hogarth House, 1948), pp. 228–29.

5. James T. Farrell, *Studs Lonigan* (New York: The Modern Library, 1938).

6. G. K. Chesterton, "Charles Dickens," *Encyclopaedia Britannica*, 1949 Edition.

7. Marjorie Meeker, "Now Here is Love," in *Modern American Poetry*, ed. by Louis Untermeyer (New York: Harcourt, Brace & Co., 1925), p. 555.

8. *Othello*, V, ii.

9. W. Stekel, *Sadism and Masochism* (New York: Horace Liveright, 1929), pp. 262–63.

10. Joseph Conrad, *Victory* (Garden City, N.Y.: Doubleday & Co., Inc., 1915).

11. From *The Collected Poems of A. E. Housman*, pp. 15–16. Copyright 1940, by Henry Holt & Co., Inc. By permission of the publishers.

12. Leo Kanner, "Problems of Nosology and Psychodynamics of Early Infantile Autism," *The American Journal of Orthopsychiatry*, XIX (July 1949), 416–26.

13. From *Renascence and Other Poems* (New York: Harper & Bros.). Copyright 1912, 1940, by Edna St. Vincent Millay.

14. René Guyon, *The Ethics of Sexual Acts* (New York: Alfred A. Knopf, Inc., 1948), p. 181.

15. Hesketh Pearson, *Oscar Wilde: His Life and Wit* (New York: Harper & Bros., 1946), p. 332.

16. C. S. Sherrington, *The Assaying of Brahantius* (London: Oxford University Press, 1925), p. 43.

INDEX

Printed in Poland
by Amazon Fulfillment
Poland Sp. z o.o., Wrocław

13315288R00186